*Our Own Words*

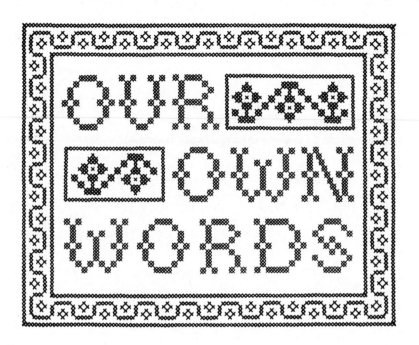

*Mary Helen Dohan*

*"If we had a complete history of all the words
which America has preserved, invented, or modified,
we should possess the most revealing history
conceivable of the American people."*
—Robert L. Ramsay, *A Mark Twain Lexicon*

*Alfred A. Knopf    New York    1976*

THIS IS A BORZOI BOOK
PUBLISHED BY ALFRED A. KNOPF, INC.

Library of Congress Cataloging in Publication Data

Dohan, Mary Helen.    Our own words.

Bibliography: p.
1. English language in the United States—History.
2. Americanisms. I. Title.
PE2809.D6    427'.9'73    73-17432
ISBN 0-394-48209-3

*Manufactured in the United States of America*

Published April 23, 1974
Reprinted Twice
Fourth Printing, September 1976

*To My Family, With Love*

# Contents

◆◆◆◆◆◆

Introduction
by Alistair Cooke, ix

Foreword, xiii

*I. New Words for a New Nation*, 3

*II. "A Glorious Artifact,"* 13

*III. Birth of a Language*, 35

*IV. Splendid Words, Angry Words*, 62

*V. Lost Words and Echoes*, 83

*VI. A Native Medley*, 113

*VII. New Accents, New Frontier*, 137

*VIII. City Voices*, 166

*IX. Tall Talk and Go-aheadity*, 196

*X. Lickety-split the Language*, 226

*XI. T.R. to TV*, 256

*XII. A Legacy of Words*, 292

Suggested Readings, 311

Indexes follow page 315

# Introduction
## by Alistair Cooke

❖❖❖❖❖

Just forty years ago, having arrived at Harvard as a graduate student intending to study theater direction, I was surprised to find myself registering for a course in "the history of the English language in America" under the American Henry Higgins, the late, great Professor Miles L. Hanley, and subsequently to be sitting at the feet of Edward Sapir, Leonard Bloomfield, and A. Lloyd James. On a first automobile tour of the United States, I had come on something much more dramatic than the Broadway offerings: namely, the language of the people I was living with, and the exciting hints from old-timers along the way of how the language got that way. Simply, I was making the discovery, which every Englishman has been making for most of the past three hundred and fifty years, that the languages of the old and the new country vary in infinite and fascinating ways. They are always flowing together and leaving deposits on each other's territory, which the recipients at first resent, then accept, and then stoutly claim as their own alluvial property.

For well over a hundred years, the tidal current has been running from America to Britain. After the Second World War, however, the British enjoyed a stimulating social revolution in which the working classes asserted a wholly new sense of *amour propre* and thus powerfully affected—in dress, manners, accent, and slang—the customs of the people who had always been known as their "betters." The result has been a dramatic modification of English educated speech and a lively feedback of British slang into American. Today, in any mixed group of British and American young, it is often difficult to guess at a first hearing who is English gone American and who is American succumbing to the indestructible patois of the Cockney.

However, since the arrival of the cheap jet charter, and the subsequent migrations of students, rustling like cockroaches across several continents, American English has become the universal *lingua franca* to a degree not even guessed at by its foreign practitioners. The British television crews with which I recently conducted a three-year safari across the United States were calmly concerned about preserving the chastity of their native tongue, but they were blissfully unaware that they had been ravished in their cradles; for more than half the slang and much of the idiom they used was American in origin. They routinely employed phrases, nouns, adjectives that in my young days I had noted as alien oddities and that had eventually been allowed into England, if not at the point of a sword, at least at the shiver of a nostril.

But every British generation believes it is the first to recognize the threatened invasion of an Americanism. Until the Second World War, certainly, every new British arrival was another Francis Moore, the 1735 emigrant to Georgia who was appalled to discover that the bank of the Savannah River was something which "they in barbarous English call a *bluff*." I well recall the deathly pallor that overcame an old Londoner when he heard the abdicating Edward VIII announce that he was "at long last able to say a few words of my own" over "the *radio*"! Today the attitude of tolerating the barbarians has all but vanished from English society. Americanisms are often chic or amusing, and more often still assumed to be native sprouts from the egalitarian Welfare State.

Yet in both countries, the general knowledge of how language comes about, and how it grows, is not part of general education. In neither country are children taught anything about the origins of their language, or how and why it changes from one era to another. Similarly, the vast majority of people never learn phonetics but are expected to deduce the musical structure of the spoken tongue from principles of "grammar." Bloomfield has a withering comment on this tradition: "Like much else that masquerades as common sense, it is in fact highly sophisticated." I imagine that ninety-nine scholars in a hundred, asked to name the most common vowel sound in English, would pick a written letter, though the answer is the upside-down "e" known to the International Phonetic Alphabet: the unaccented syllable that runs through all forms of English (except, possibly, the Indian) like a musical beat— as in the first syllable of "abbreviate," "observer," "attend," the last syllable of "custom," "sofa," and in all pronunciations of the indefinite article (only United States Senators say "eh man" instead of "a man").

What the phoneticians have done haltingly to notate the spoken language, Miss Dohan has done triumphantly to anatomize for us the living organism of our vocabulary, tracing it back to its Germanic and Latin origins and forward to the last grunts of the hippies and the current contortions of Federal Prose (or what may soon become known as Watergab). She is up on the latest junkie slang, not as a conscientious note-taker but as the psychologist of an emotional turmoil peculiar to our time. She knows how, and why, immigrant names were amended or disguised. She can trace the movements of settlers through the nomenclature of farming. She has done an extended job, worthy of Empson or Robert Graves, on the "mental atmosphere" that introduces new words and changes the meanings of old ones. I could go on and on. I can only say that I know of no other work that performs such a deep and invaluable probe of the primitive body of the language while maintaining the liveliest awareness of the spoken and written language of our own day. We don't, and shouldn't, expect to find the racy virtues of Eric Partridge in old Sapir, or Mencken's wryness lightening the majestic scholarship of Jespersen. But Miss Dohan seems to have it all, and have it all together.

A.C.
New York,
October 1973

# Foreword

Long ago, when I read for the first time Logan Pearsall Smith's *The English Language*, I was already in love with words. His use of them as lanterns to the past offered enchanting glimpses of historical vistas waiting to be explored and a sense of the marvelous continuity of our speech. Since Smith's day, other lanterns have been lighted, many of them American. Mencken's *American Language*, the *Dictionary of American English on Historical Principles* and Mathews's later *Dictionary of Americanisms*, the *Linguistic Atlas of the United States and Canada*, the works of Krapp and Kurath and Baugh and other lovers of words have provided new light for journeying into history. Led on by it, I have ventured—with an amateur's temerity but with trepidation too—to explore the American language and the past from which it came.

Especially helpful as a guide to the faraway past has been the section on Indo-European roots in the *American Heritage Dictionary* (1969), with the accompanying articles by Calvert Watkins, which motivated deeper exploration than I had originally planned. Not just helpful but indispensable have been the directional signs posted by Harold Strauss, of Knopf, whenever I showed signs of straying. Without his unflagging interest and encouragement, my journey might never have been made.

I am grateful indeed to Mario Pei, who has himself lighted so many linguistic lanterns, for graciously reviewing my book in manuscript and snatching me back from the brink of some philological pitfalls. And to Mary Lyell, who has typed so valiantly, I am grateful too.

*Our Own Words*

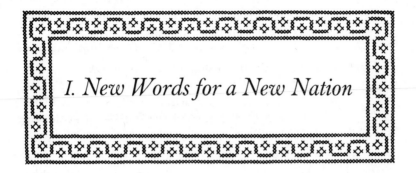

# I. New Words for a New Nation

When the story of our times is told, the teller of the tale will use words that until recently did not exist—*astronaut* and *laser, urbanologist* and *sexism, psychedelic* and *smog*. He may even (knowing that language mirrors a culture as speech does the soul) tell his story by presenting the background of those words. For the vocabulary of each generation reflects its historical climate and—unconsciously created—reveals as no mere history can the spirit of a time.

It has been so always, especially in the rich and varied language that is our heritage. Words we speak that are older than history describe our ancient lineage. Words that have become part of our language over the years record our history. And words that we ourselves create portray ourselves.

"The new circumstances under which we are placed," wrote Thomas Jefferson in 1813, "call for new words, new phrases, and for the transfer of old words to new objects."[1] At the time he wrote, one of the principal circumstances of American life was war with England, a second and decisive war that convinced the world—and the American people themselves—that the new republic was here to stay.

For a while, its survival had been in doubt. The first flush of Revolutionary victory was followed by a period of turmoil and dissension in which controversy reigned and anarchy threatened, when the shaky new republic seemed headed for

1. In a letter from Monticello to John Waldo, August 16, 1813.

collapse and the establishment of serenity at home and credit abroad appeared impossible. Disaster waited in the wings, and history had yet to write the drama's end. A new nation, politically untried, culturally dependent on the mother country, torn by internal conflict, and disillusioned by the gap between promise and reality, had still to find its own identity; and there were those who wondered if the brave Revolution might have been, after all, a mistake. In New England, the Federalists were plotting secession; in Philadelphia, radical forces swirled around Jefferson; in New York, Alexander Hamilton and all his monarchial tribe decried the dangers of democracy. There was in the land the beginning of a troubling conflict between inherited tradition and native self-expression, between nostalgia and progressivism, between idealism and pragmatism, dream and fact, a conflict reflected in acrimonious wrangling over such seemingly peripheral issues as language and literature.[2] Like the political and ideological disputes it paralleled, the cultural conflict, too, would be resolved only in the wake of a second war for independence, one foretold by Benjamin Franklin when the ink on the Treaty of Paris was hardly dry.

Conceivably there might have been no second war, no Jacksonian democracy, history might have been different, had the British accepted the loss of the colonies with better grace. Heady as was victory, however bright independence, "every habit of thought and of business, every natural prejudice," as Henry Cabot Lodge would write, "still bound the Americans to England."[3] Hostility from Britain was expected, economic and diplomatic problems recognized as inevitable, even the great issues of impressment and border quarrels thought

---

2. The troubles of the new republic have been studied exhaustively by historians, among them Beard, Adams, Schlesinger, and others (see Suggested Readings). The elements of the cultural conflict are ably illustrated in contemporary document and art in Charles Sanford, ed.: *Quest for America—1810–1824* (New York: New York University Press; 1964).
3. *The Story of the Revolution* (New York: Charles Scribner's Sons; 1898), vol. 2, p. 561.

amenable to negotiation; but supercilious scorn, uncomfortably recognized in the days of dependence, became intolerable with victory. As Americans saw their conciliatory overtures rejected, their diplomats flouted, their speech and manners continually derided even by British visitors who had been hospitably received, resentment flared. A people more secure might have shrugged off the ridicule and met the attacks head on; but national self-confidence, already shaken by criticism on the home front from both Anglophiles and honest critics, was not yet matured. Its maturing was hardly hastened by a barrage of attacks on American culture, or the lack of it.

The great war of words about "American" words and inextricably about American literature had begun long before. In 1735, an adventurer and writer named Francis Moore, who had spent some time in the new colony of Georgia as a storekeeper, made what is probably the first public criticism of the American vocabulary. Describing the city of Savannah, he wrote: "It is about a mile and a quarter in circumference; it stands upon the flat of a hill, the bank of the river (which they in barbarous English call a *bluff*) is steep."[4] The term "barbarous" was to be echoed continually in later criticisms; apparently Moore and his descendants were no more impressed by the superiority of the word *bluff* to *bank* as a precise metaphor than by the picturesque quality of other American coinage like *eggplant* and *foothill* and *eel grass,* all suggesting the direction in which the upstart vocabulary was heading.

By 1754, so many "barbarisms" were arriving in England from America that one English author suggested the need for a glossary; and in 1756, a displeased Samuel Johnson, reviewing an American work, proclaimed: "This treatise is written with such elegance as the subject admits, tho' not without some mixture of the American dialect, a tract [trace] of corruption to which every language widely diffused must al-

4. *A Voyage to Georgia, Begun in the Year 1735* (London, 1744), vol. 1, p. 24.

ways be exposed."[5] Little was done about producing the glossary or eliminating the "corruption" until twenty-five years later; and then the effort was made by an impeccably patriotic American, Dr. John Witherspoon (to the later bafflement of H. L. Mencken, who equated criticism of the language with an attack on the flag). Witherspoon was a Scot who had come to the colonies as president of the College of New Jersey (later Princeton) and who served in both the Constitutional Convention of New Jersey and the Continental Congress. In 1781, he wrote, for the *Pennsylvania Journal and Weekly Advertiser,* a series of papers designed to present "some observations upon the present state of the English language in America, and to attempt a collection of some of the chief improprieties."[6] These "improprieties" he called *Americanisms* (his coinage), equating them with *Scotticisms* and defining the term as "ways of speaking peculiar to this country." His collection included such then characteristic national idiom as *mad* in the sense of angry; *fellow-countryman,* "an evident tautology"; and *clever* in reference to conduct. Impartially, however, he pointed out "vulgarisms" in Britain and America alike, and even found fault with the sacrosanct Dr. Johnson. Generally open-minded toward the principle of linguistic development, he noted: "Time and accident must determine what turn affairs will take . . . whether we shall continue to consider the language of Great Britain as the pattern upon which we are to form ours; or whether, in this new empire, some center of learning and politeness will not be found, which shall obtain influence and prescribe the rules of speech and writing to every other part."

Witherspoon's interest in the "purity and perfection" of English was shared by many on both sides of the Atlantic in the eighteenth century; and by the time he wrote, it was generally recognized that—like it or not—Americans would

5. *The Literary Magazine* (September–October 1756).

6. The papers appeared in series in May of 1781 under the heading of *The Druid* and are reprinted in Mitford M. Mathews, ed.: *The Beginnings of American English* (Chicago: University of Chicago Press; 1931).

have much to do with the course the language would take. Some thoughtful Americans saw in this inevitable development an opportunity for cultural influence to reinforce political influence; and in 1780, in a letter to the president of Congress, John Adams suggested that inasmuch as England had never done so, the government of the United States should set up an academy, like those of France, Spain, and Italy, for "refining, improving, and ascertaining the English language."[7] (*Ascertain* at this time meant to set rather than to find out.) With English, according to Adams, "destined to be in the next and succeeding centuries more generally the language of the world than Latin was in the last or French is in the present age," the establishment of the academy would not only bring honor to the Congress, but would also have a favorable effect on the unity of the states. It was clearly not in his mind nor in that of any other advocate of an academy, however, that the language of America should differ from that of England.

It was in Noah Webster's! Controversial, outspoken, and crotchety, this man who more than any other single individual affected the course of the English language in America saw language as a vital force subject to no man's governance. As a student lawyer and backwoods schoolteacher after the Revolution, he wrote, under the grandiloquent name of *A Grammatical Institute of the English Language,* a set of three books—grammar, reader, and speller—that were the first books of their kind published in this country. For more than a century after his time, American children would learn their spelling Noah Webster's way, be taught to pronounce Noah Webster's way, and absorb with their lessons a generous dose of Websterian morals. In 1789, he published the *Dissertations on the English Language,* in which he bluntly proposed that America develop a literary and linguistic standard separate from that of England. "As an independent nation," he wrote, "our honor requires us to have a system of our own, in lan-

7. From Amsterdam, September 5, 1780. Reprinted in full in Mathews: *Beginnings.*

guage as well as government." Then boldly he placed himself
out on a limb by predicting that in time to come the language of North America would be "as different from the future language of England as the modern Dutch, Danish and
Swedish are from the German, or from one another."[8]

The *Dissertations* was dedicated to Benjamin Franklin,
who was a strong advocate of spelling reform; but Franklin's
response to the compliment was lukewarm. Spelling reform
was one thing, those new words quite another! Like most
educated Americans, Franklin considered English—meaning
British—usage the only proper vocabulary guide for Americans; his attitude is made clear in an astonishingly humble
apology he wrote, while in England, to John Hume, who had
objected to Franklin's use of certain "Americanisms." "The
*pejorate* and *colonize*," he wrote, "since they are not in common use here, I give up as bad."[9] But if Franklin's response
to Webster's ideas was lukewarm, the reaction of many
others was thoroughly heated. Both the man and his ideas were
attacked. "A pedantic grammarian," "a toad in the service of
sans-culottism," "critick and coxcomb-general of the United
States" were a few of the epithets hurled at Webster; the
coinage he encouraged, it was said, would produce "manifest
corruption" and "intolerable barbarisms." A writer in the
*New England Palladium* lamented that Americans might as
well go ahead and "adopt, at once, the language of the
aborigines."[1] All in all, according to Lodge, Webster was
"snubbed, laughed at, and abused. He was regarded as little
better than a madman to dare to set himself up against John-

8. The quotations are from the opening essay of the *Dissertations*
(Boston; 1789), portions of which are reprinted in H. L. Mencken:
*The American Language,* 4th ed. (New York: Alfred A. Knopf; 1936),
and *Supplement I* (New York: Alfred A. Knopf; 1945).

9. *Writings,* ed. Albert H. Smyth (New York: The Macmillan Company;
1907), vol. 4, pp. 83–4.

1. Pertinent quotations are taken from the account of the controversy
given in Mencken: *American Language.*

son and his successors."² But he did have some support. Dr. Benjamin Rush, in a plan for a federal university, had suggested similar ideas even earlier; and Thomas Jefferson, although he could not abide Webster, was in accord with his ideas to the point of predicting, in a letter to John Waldo (dated August 13, 1816), that "an American dialect will be formed."

Jefferson could hardly have *not* been in accord; when his own *Notes on the State of Virginia* had appeared, in 1787, the comments of British reviewers, especially upon his vocabulary, had been scathing. "Freely, good sir," cried the *European Magazine and London Review,* "will we forgive all your attacks, impotent as they are illiberal, upon our *national character*; but for the future spare—O spare, we beseech you, our mother-tongue!" By the 1800's, English journals were maintaining that the American vocabulary had departed so far from what it should be that to redeem it was more or less hopeless; and the language used in American literature— such literature as there was and what there was of it—aroused harsh criticism. In 1808, the *British Critic* offered little hope for improvement; "the common speech of the United States," it said, "has departed very considerably from the standard adopted in England." Other reviews attacked "that torrent of barbarous phraseology" consisting of words "as utterly foreign as if they had been adopted from the Hebrew or Chinese." "Uncouth," "affectations and corruptions of phrase," "uncultured minds," "perversion of good words"— such were the comments of British critics in the first decade of the nineteenth century. And in 1812, Robert Southey wrote to Walter Savage Landor about the low quality of the American character in general. "See what it is," he complained, "to have a nation to take its place among civilized states before it has either gentlemen or scholars!"

Most American authors, sharing the national inferiority

2. "Colonialism in America."

complex, tried in this period between the wars to conform to British standards. A favorable review from an English journal was the imprimatur of excellence; self-consciously, even Washington Irving and James Fenimore Cooper, just beginning their work, catered to English taste. In every aspect save the political, the new republic was colonial in spirit, looking to the mother country for guidance and example. Painfully aware of their undeniable cultural deficiencies, the American people chafed under the British scoldings and tried to conform—until they could take it no longer. *So* much became at last *too* much; accumulated political grievances, added to swelling resentment against incessant hostility and disdain, exploded at last into war. When that war was over, an exuberant people, caught up in the euphoria of victory and the excitement of a great migration, began kicking over any lingering traces of colonialism, including the King's English.

As they crossed the Alleghenies in their lumbering Pittsburgh wagons, leaving axles and baggage and lives along the way, or floated down the Ohio into the continent's heartland, westering Americans had little concern for language except that it should work. If *hornswoggle* and *grit* and *absquatulate* made sense in Missouri, who gave a hoot that an Englishman would not understand? Gathering with their wagons at Independence and at Council Grove, hearing the shouts of drivers, the lowing of oxen, and the tattooing echo of hoofbeats over the plains, they jeered at high-falutin talk that made a man sound like a *slooney with the peedoodles*—one of their more eloquent expressions for a nervous nincompoop. Let lickspittles who liked it stay home—in Boston, maybe.

Back East there was culture, British culture, and a proper English tongue. The speech of proper Bostonians was still properly British; English manners and English diction were still the prevailing mode. The Brahmins of Boston continued to join their British counterparts in deploring the "corruptions and barbarities" of the "Yankey dialect"; but there was no more unanimity in the chorus. And on the literary front, American material and American vernacular were pushing their way into what had been closed territory. In 1820, writing in the *Edinburgh Review*, Sydney Smith could ask with some validity: "In the four quarters of the globe, who reads an American book? or goes to an American play?" But in that same year, Washington Irving's *Sketch Book*, which would gain tremendous popularity abroad, was published; and in the year following, James Fenimore Cooper's second novel, *The Spy*, with an American setting and American characters, launched him on his long and successful career. Bryant's *Thanatopsis* had been published in 1817 (apparently Smith was unaware or unimpressed); and in only a few years Hawthorne and Poe and Longfellow would emerge to command the attention of the literary world. The American scene became the inspiration for writers once too timid to brave the derision of English critics, and without apology they began using the everyday language they heard.

Scholarly support appeared too. America's first critical quarterly, *The American Review of History and Politics*, had been established in 1811 and was followed by *The North American Review* in 1815. Now satire and criticism, which had been a British monopoly, began to cut both ways. English reviewers assailed American "barbarisms"; American critics scoffed in return at British "vulgarisms." The verbal battles raged back and forth among disputants eminent and obscure (Cooper and Irving entered the lists briefly); and serious treatises like Robert Walsh, Jr.'s *An Appeal from the Judgments of Great Britain Respecting the United States of America* joined satirical works like J. K. Paulding's *The Diverting History of John Bull and Brother Jonathan* and *John Bull in America, or The New Munchausen* to quell some of the British fire. By 1824, when *The North American Review* warned that continued abuse would "turn into bitterness the last drops of good-will toward England that exist in the United States," the tone of British criticism was becoming less strident.

It hardly mattered. The American vocabulary had been going its own way for some time, and it would continue to do so. Language, as Noah Webster remarked, has a way of absorbing words and expressions as it will, "in spite of all the exertions of all the writers in the world."[3] The new American words would take their place in the great deposit that is the treasure and the testament of the English-speaking people, a heritage that was ancient when history began and that is being constantly renewed. We use today words whose roots we share with Iranian and Welshman, Greek and Slav, because long millennia ago our ancestors traveled together; and these words are evidence of that ancient bond. We use words that tell of meetings not remembered; just as in some remote island of Oceania we may glimpse occasionally the hawk nose of an ancient Phoenician and speculate on early voyages, so in a modern word we may hear the echo of an ancient tongue not ours and know that somewhere, somehow, our ancestors met a man whose tongue it was. We use words that are ours because some medieval knights went riding toward the East and returned with gifts of rich cloth and jewels for their wives and brought, too, the names for them. We use words bequeathed to us by brave and often illiterate pioneers who found a world new to Englishmen and named the things within it. And we use words that we ourselves have made because the language had no words for what we wished to say —and thereby leave *our* record for posterity.

3. Reported by a British visitor, Captain Basil Hall, in his *Travels in North America in the Years 1827–28* (Edinburgh and London; 1829). His conversation with Noah Webster is reprinted in part in Mencken: *American Language*.

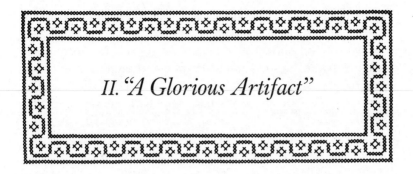

## II. "A Glorious Artifact"

The Englishmen who settled America in the seventeenth century, and who were to give it its dominant character and its speech, brought with them a language deep-rooted in the past. Theirs was basically a Germanic tongue, come to Britain with the invading Teutons a thousand years before and ancient even then. Its oldest words told of a still earlier era, reaching far back into the remote and unrecorded past, when the ancestors of many nations spoke a common language and traveled a common path.

That the languages of Englishman and Persian, Irishman and Greek should be kin seemed wildly fantastic two hundred years ago, when the discovery of Sanskrit by Western scholars toppled theories held for centuries. The Tower of Babel had stood firm until then, with each language supposedly having its separate laws; and historical perspective still struggled to be born.[1] During the Middle Ages, medieval ways and thought and even dress had been attributed to the Greeks and Romans; and the notion of an *anachronism,* as something out of harmony with its time, had yet to emerge. Only in the eighteenth century did the idea of progressive human culture develop; and not until the nineteenth, when the word *prehistoric* was coined to express a startling new concept, did

1. The recentness of historical perspective is interestingly discussed in Logan Pearsall Smith: *The English Language* (New York: Henry Holt and Co.; 1911), pp. 227 ff.

revelation of the earth's antiquity—and man's—make possible the full unfolding of the past.

Even in the sixteenth century, however, the vocabulary was hinting at the slow gestation of new thought. As the Reformation turned men's thoughts to an earlier age and the Revival of Learning acquainted them with classical civilization, the word *primitive,* used by the reformers with reference to the early Church, suggested that past might differ from present by more than its place in time. The idea, extending to the secular area, found concrete expression in the words *ancient* and *modern,* first recorded in 1585; and in the course of the seventeenth century, *antiquated* and *old-fashioned* and *out of date* appeared. *Epoch, century,* and *decade,* also new, provided convenient pegs on which to hang history.

Most histories that were written were still mere chronicles (had not Aristotle said, in the *Poetics,* that history has no plot?) and were concerned principally with recent events in England. Local antiquities were collected, but coins and art objects and ancient inscriptions brought back from Greece or Italy by travelers were valued for their aesthetic interest only; no one thought of dating them. The idea that artifacts have historical value had not occurred even to historians.[2] In the language field, a few scholars were noting some curious relationships. It was evident that French, Spanish, and Italian were decadent forms of Latin and that English, Dutch, and German were somehow linked, as were Hebrew and Arabic— but why should neighboring Welsh and English differ so? Hardly remembered was a report by a sixteenth-century Italian traveler, Filippo Sassetti, of strange similarities between some Sanskrit words and their Italian equivalents; and a suggestion by Marcus Boxhorn, a Dutchman, that all European languages might have a common ancestor (which he named Scythian) had made little impression. In contemporary thinking, language had no more to do with history, or history with language, than did a Grecian urn.

2. As late as the eighteenth century, artifacts were popularly thought to be the tools of dwarfs and witches and were usually left alone.

In 1687, the *Principia* was published, science rode the times, and the Age of "Enlightenment" began. Because order, exemplified in the classics, was the measure of all things, it seemed clear that language, like everything else, must have an ideal form, which should be not only determined but also imposed. That the language might have a mind of its own, or that events and not scholars might shape it, was hardly conceivable in that neat Augustan age.

Italy and France had purged their languages of corruption by means of academies; and John Dryden, like John Adams later, urged that his country do the same. Declaring that "our language is in a manner barbarous," Dryden wished that "we might all write with the same certainty of words, and purity of phrase, to which the Italian first arrived, and after them the French." Others echoed his thoughts; ". . . we write by guess," wrote Thomas Stackhouse, "more than any stated rule, and form every man his diction." A deplorable situation indeed; and the contemporary arbiters of the language, Swift and Addison, Pope and Defoe, began flexing their muscles, all agreeing on the need for an authority that "should preside with a sort of judicature over the learning of the age, and have liberty to correct and censure the exorbitance of writers." Swift, in a typically modest *Proposal*,[3] declared that such an authority should have the power of "ascertaining and fixing our language for ever."

Some scholars, albeit less illustrious ones, did not agree. An anonymous critic, apparently not hardy enough to challenge the high priests openly, thought that the edicts of the French Academy, instead of making the language better, "have spoiled it"; and John Oldmixon, writing in the same year Swift's *Proposal* appeared, suggested that scholars "may as well set up a Society to find out the *Grand Elixir,* the *Perpetual Motion,* the *Longitude,* and other such Discoveries, as to fix our Language beyond their own Times. . . ." When, in 1755, these humbler men were joined by that eminent dictator

3. *A Proposal for Correcting, Improving, and Ascertaining the English Tongue* (1712).

Samuel Johnson, who rumbled in the preface to his *Diction-ary* that the establishment of an academy would be inimical to the "spirit of English liberty," supporters of the idea might as well have given up the ghost, so nearly mortal was the blow to it. Men were discovering that language, like so many other aspects of human behavior, simply refused to fit into a mathematical equation. What, then, was its nature? What made it what it was?

Such questions were being asked about many things by mid-century. Scientific rationalism, by whose light great scientific advances had been made and new philosophies created, left still dark many areas of speculation. Somehow, Hume's "constant and universal principles of human nature" did not adequately explain man in his infinite variety. Exploration of new-discovered lands was introducing an awareness of exotic customs and beliefs, of inexplicable practices and mysterious happenings. New words entering the language, *totem* from America, Tongan *taboo, nirvana* from far-off India, expressed concepts new to Western thought; and it became apparent that there were more things in heaven and earth than were dreamed of in the rationalist philosophy. Scientists were even suggesting, disturbingly, that the world was more than six thousand years old, that fossils and earth strata told the story of a creation incredibly prolonged.[4] And even as past and present were being pushed beyond their comfortable boundaries, historians jumped in to help push. Giambattista Vico's revelation that the Homeric Greeks were not only primitive, myth-bound, and barbaric but also spoke in a different way from the Greeks of a millennium later suggested that the "unchanging" classical languages had kept their "ideal" form only because they were dead. With the contention of Johann Hamann and his disciple Johann Von Herder that in the language of a people its soul is revealed, the

4. That, in fact, the earth showed "no vestige of a beginning, no prospect of an end," the (then) startling conclusion of James Hutton, the Scottish geologist largely responsible for initiating modern geologic principles.

stage was set for the dramatic revelation of Sanskrit as the key to our linguistic past.

Penetration into India was making possible the study by European scholars of ancient Indic literature, including the sacred texts of the Vedas. Around 400 B.C., these texts had been grammatically analyzed by the Hindu scholar Pānini; and as European scholars studied his techniques and applied them to the study of other languages, they made some startling discoveries. In 1767, the Jesuit Gaston Laurent Coeurdoushad sent a memoir from India to the Institut de France on the similarities of Sanskrit to Latin and Greek, concluding that only a common ancestor could explain them; and, in 1786, Sir William Jones, an English jurist and Orientalist of renown, announced to the Asiatick Society in Calcutta his theory that Sanskrit and Latin and Greek had a common source, perhaps no longer existing, a source from which Celtic and Germanic might also have descended. The announcement shook the scholarly world.

There had already been, as has been seen, speculation about language relationships—Noah Webster was one who noted, at about this time, the resemblances between Greek and Latin and Teutonic languages—but never before had the idea of a common ancestor had documentary support. Now, as the connection of European languages with Sanskrit became unquestionably evident, scholars went racing off in all directions; and the questions flew. The implications were enormous. *Was* there an original home from which all nations came? (In Asia, then, and the Bible was right!) Had there been indeed a Golden Age when all men spoke one language and the whole world was at peace? What had caused diversity? Where did the Chinese language fit into the picture? Slavic? American Indian —so far impossible to fit into known language patterns? How could anybody *know*?

How anybody knows—as much, at least, as we can be reasonably convinced we do know—is a fascinating story in itself. Given the observable premise that certain languages present similarities among themselves so numerous and so precise that they cannot be dismissed as fortuitous, the student of comparative linguistics assumes some historical relationship among the languages involved. Coincidence of form alone means little; the phonetic identity of English *leap* and German *lieb*, for example, has no significance—the number of phonemes (phonetic elements) in human speech is limited.[5] However, when form and meaning coincide, when we find English *good, better,* and *best* corresponding to German *gut, besser,* and *best,* or such cognates as English *brother,* Dutch *broeder,* German *Bruder,* Irish *brathair,* Old Slavic *bratŭ,* Sanskrit *bhrātar,* Greek *phratēr,* and Latin *frāter,* it is impossible to dismiss the similarities as happenstance; and we must suppose that they have some historical explanation. Two explanations are possible: the word or inflectional pattern has been borrowed by way of some historical contact between the speakers, or there is a genetic relationship between or among the languages.

Borrowing is suggested if certain tests are met: if the similar words occur in a specialized field, for example, like our musical terms from Italy, *cello* and *piano* and *opera*; or if the similarities are so close in form that none of the changes natural to a genetic life span are indicated. Borrowing is indicated also if the similarities fit (or, for a reverse finding, do not fit) historical plausibility or if they violate the long-term developmental trend of the language. If, however, none of these situations exists, a consistent pattern of correspondence strongly suggests a genetic link, especially if the oldest known forms of the languages show even closer correspondence. When the identical word *horn* appears in Old Norse, Old Frisian, Old Saxon, and Old High German, and its cognate *haurn* in Old Gothic, it is impossible not to suspect a genetic link; when, to add to the evidence, the word *horna* is

5. The number of phonemes in historical languages seems to range somewhere between fifteen and ninety, according to Morton Bloomfield and Leonard Newmark: *A Linguistic Introduction to the Study of English* (New York: Alfred A. Knopf, Inc.; 1963), pp. 104–5.

discovered in runic letters on a golden horn unearthed in Denmark, the scholar "infers" with assurance the existence of a proto-word, or "formula," determined by specific linguistic factors found in the descendant languages, in this case the proto-Germanic word *hornan.*[6] It is from the oldest forms that can be determined historically, or "attested," that comparative linguists infer such ancient words; and although a particular proto-word may or may not be the actual word that was spoken, it has been shown that remarkably precise results can be obtained by such reconstruction. The postulated proto-Germanic word *kuningaz,* "king," appeared in ancient Finnish documents long after its reconstruction by scholars, with evidence to show that it was borrowed from Germanic tribes before the word assumed its later and diverse forms.

To establish a family relationship between such dissimilar languages as Latin and English appears on the surface difficult. Surely there is little resemblance between English *foot* and Latin *pes,* between English *knee* and Latin *genu.* The links between these languages and among others in the Indo-European family, however, were made clear with the discovery of what came to be called Grimm's Law (after Jacob Grimm, who was not only a maker of enchantment but a great scholar as well), a set of regularly occurring consonant shifts that took place during the time in which the various descendant languages diverged from the parent tongue. In proto-Germanic, the early Indo-European *p,* *t,* and *k* became *ph,* *th,* and *kh* (later English *f,* *th,* and *h),* while Italic, from which Latin eventually came, retained the original Indo-European sounds. Other changes taking place with systematic regularity and determined by means of the new science of comparative linguistics explained changes in vowel sounds, as well as some apparent exceptions to Grimm's Law. In the first decades of the nineteenth century, therefore,

---

6. According to regular linguistic convention, an asterisk is placed before a reconstructed form (one that is not attested in documents).

as scholars pursued the evidence, it became clear that certain root words, like *gena-[7] for the notion of begetting, *sen- for old, *tu- for the second person, were carried in some form in all of the languages classified as Indo-European. Inflectional relationships confirmed the findings, and there was no conclusion possible except that at some time there had existed an earlier language from which all of these languages descended.

The study of this language—or family of dialects—has continued since those pioneer days. Aided by the findings of archaeology, it has introduced to us linguistic relatives we did not know we had. Ancient tablets unearthed in 1907 at the site of the Hittite capital at Boghazkoi, in Asia Minor, indicated that Hittite, too, was Indo-European, perhaps the first of the family to leave; and, more recently, fragmentary texts discovered in central Asia added to the group another tongue, Tocharian. Because the language's characteristics link it with Western rather than Eastern relatives, the finding suggests that a Balkan people may have moved eastward not quite three thousand years ago. Thus—as those early scholars did not suspect—are language and history linked.

The initial supposition that a homogeneity of language establishes a homogeneity of race or other genetic links among its speakers has long been abandoned. Language is transmitted by too many agents—conquest, migration, trade, assimilation—for conclusions about such relationships to be drawn; but as evidence of cultural continuity it binds together those who share it. In a world of constant change, where few of us can trace our genealogies back more than a century or two, where the merging of peoples of many races is more and more occurring, our most far-reaching and all-embracing heritage is the language we speak. Not only is it the expression of the accumulated culture into which we are born or which we

7. Indo-European and Germanic roots, unless otherwise noted, have been taken from the listings in the *American Heritage Dictionary*. The hyphen following a word indicates that the form is the basic root of derivative formations in the descendant languages.

have made our own; it also reflects the contemporary influences that, for better or worse, shape our individual lives and our national direction. To know how our own words have come to be, therefore, is to know much about ourselves.

The search for that early time and distant place in which our oldest words were made takes us on a long and shadowy trail, through history and beyond, where only the words themselves can light the way. The path abounds in mirages and false turns and tempting cul-de-sacs; but somehow, at the end of it, we reach a place where we can see in the distance the culture from which ours came, the culture that was the first stage we can be sure of in the long journey that led from that remote past toward our own land and this day. It has been said that a reconstructed proto-language is "a glorious artifact, one which is far more precious than anything an archaeologist can ever hope to unearth."[8] From such an artifact, buried in our speech, we can learn of the lives our linguistic forebears led and of the thoughts that they expressed.

From the evidence of language, we surmise that the Indo-Europeans lived the nomadic life of neolithic man somewhere in central Europe, sometime before the third millennium B.C. The presence in the language of such words as *snow* and *beech* and *bee* (*sneigwh-* and *bhāgo-* and *bhei-* in the proto-tongue) eliminates as a possible homeland any area where these things were not known and so would not have been named—the Asian regions, for instance, that have been proposed for it. The absence of a common word for sea suggests an inland location; *mori-*, whence came Germanic *mari-* and so Old English *mere* (and our *mermaid*), referred evidently to small bodies of water on which *boats* (*nāu-*, the ultimate source of *navy* and other such *nautical* words) were rowed. The region most favored by scholars lies between Lithuania and the steppes of southern Russia, a theory strengthened by the fact that of all the Indo-European languages Lithuanian is closest to the parent tongue—a Lithuan-

8. Calvert Watkins: "The Indo-European Origin of English," the *American Heritage Dictionary*, p. xx.

ian peasant, it is said, can understand simple phrases in Sanskrit. Moreover, Lithuania stands close to the line from which the eastward and westward migrations of the original tribes seem to have taken place.

Wherever their original home, these speakers of Indo-European lived for a considerable period in close proximity, related in language and in their way of life, culturally if not ethnically kin. And we know from the evidence of history that before 2000 B.C. they had scattered, to become over the centuries Indian and Persian, Slav and Roman, Greek and Teuton and Celt. Eventually they would diverge in appearance and culture and custom and come to forget whatever kinship they had known; but the essential character of the words they had shared would linger in each language as a common heritage, forging an ancestral bond between modern Englishman and Hindu, Frenchman and Kurd and Greek.

As one would expect, from this primitive Indo-European vocabulary we inherit the words (and, changed in form as most of them are, we know from such evidence as has been cited that they are the same words) for basic things, for *man* and *woman,* for *head* and *nose* and *tooth* (\**dent-* we could hardly mistake), for *mother* and *brother* and *son* and even *brother-in-law.* The numbers up to ten were named; \**dwō* and \**trei-* are not far from our *two* and *three.* The personal pronouns, which have been called the "Devonian rocks" of Indo-European, are unlike any other paradigms in the language and show the same disparity as does modern English between subjective and objective cases. We may not easily recognize our *I,* which came to us through Old English *ic,* in \**eg* (although, of course, *ego* leaps out); but \**me-* belongs to us today, and \**tu-,* \**we-,* and \**yu-* seem comfortably familiar. There was no pronoun for the third person—surely ground for some anthropological treatise. In two verbs expressing existence, \**es-* and \**bheu-,* we see easily the Latin *esse,* which is akin to our own *is,* and our indispensable verb *to be.* Other enduring words, the sources of our *door* and *hearth* and *eat* and *cook* and *grain,* tell us that human concerns have been always much the same, that personal relationships, food, and shelter were paramount then as now.

The shelters constructed were wooden or wicker huts— windowless huts, we think, for we have no early word for window—with roofs of thatch. And these ancestors of ours were troubled, alas, with bedbugs and other unpleasant pests; *knid-* and *lus-* have changed little over the years. Perhaps for that reason among others they preferred a life outdoors! Surely their lives were spent closer to nature than ours; their speech was filled with words for such things as snow and stars and trees and the rising and setting of the sun. They knew the wolf, whose name carried a taboo, as did the bear's; they talked of the beaver, the hare, and the mouse, and of most of the domestic animals familiar to us today. From the names of these domestic animals, the goat and the cow, and from the development of the word *peku-* (from which comes *pecuniary*) from a term for wealth to one for cattle, we know that they lived a pastoral existence in which stock was both the source and the measure of good fortune. Rudimentary agriculture was practiced, however; two root words for grinding are attested, and the probable base of a term for *hand mill* is found throughout the Indo-European-speaking world. The arts of spinning and weaving, the use of copper and perhaps bronze, the taming of horses—these and other activities are preserved like flies in amber in the ancient words. And the call of home, or return to a familiar place, was expressed in the proto-word *nes-*, from which our word *nostalgia* comes.

Other words tell of notions of government, of sovereignty, of honor and friendship and law that must have evolved over many centuries. Some of the words, like *reg-*, from which came both Indian *rajah* and Latin *rex,* are still easily recognizable in their descendants. Religious faith played a great part in the lives of the people; the word *deiw-os*, whose root was one with the root for day, identified deity with the bright sky, with the coming of light; and from the same root came the lovely phrase *dyeu-pater,* "God the Father," still ours today. To preach, to prophesy, to praise aloud—all were concepts known and expressed. As we echo in our daily speech the voices of an ancient people, using words that first were theirs, past is linked to present by a continuing chain, and all humankind seems kin.

But the people scattered. Perhaps the food supply grew scarce; perhaps, with the recession of the ice sheets, wider vistas emerged, and the same primal urge that sent Columbus toward far horizons and sends us toward distant stars impelled them to move on. Whatever the cause, the tribes diverged, some to the west and the sun-bathed south, some to the east, some northward. The first great split took place when the tribes that would in time speak the Indic and Iranian languages moved eastward into Asia (unless, as now seems possible, the Anatolian-speaking group, which includes the Hittite, preceded them). Those remaining stayed long enough together—over uncounted centuries—to develop new words in common before they too separated. This we know because of words that belong to all or nearly all of the West Aryan, or "European," languages but not at all to the Indic-Iranian group, whose speakers had gone their own way. Even some very basic words are different; *sem-, the root for *one* in Sanskrit and related languages, remains with us in such words as *simultaneous* and *same,* but our *one* comes from a completely different root, *oino-, which appears in Celtic and Latin as well.

From other words exclusively European, the proto-words for the elm and the hazel, the throstle and finch, we learn that the remaining group moved onward also, from relatively treeless steppes and pasture lands into a country of forests; and a marked increase in agricultural terms suggests that agriculture was replacing the grazing of stock as a primary pursuit. Inevitably, as agriculture demands, more permanent settlement was made; and fortifications on nearby hills carried on the Indo-European habit of choosing high areas for defense. From the old word *bhergh-, which meant "high," all of the Europeans would eventually make words of their own, giving us such later forms as *borough* and *iceberg.* Settlement brought closer tribal ties; the important sociological term *teutā-*, which meant "tribe," emerged; we will meet it again as *Teutonic* and as *Deutsch* and *Dutch*. And from a new word for fish, *peisk-,* and one for salt, *sal-,* we guess that some of the tribes reached the sea, whereon in later years their descendants would sail into history.

But still another group of words, a group of enormous significance, was entering the European vocabulary—those relating to the wheel. The metaphorical nature of these words —for they are not primary vocables, the otherwise meaningless phonemes of the initial period of word-making—tells us that they are newcomers to the language and, inferentially, the expression of concepts new to those who spoke them. The word for axle meant simply a pivotlike juncture; that for the nave, or hub, of the wheel meant navel; and the word *wheel* itself was made from a verb used principally to express the notion of herding or watching over stock in the sense of "revolving" or "going around" it. Archaeology confirms this finding of our lexicon; the distribution of the wheel in Europe is believed to date from the end of the third millennium B.C., when the Indo-Europeans would have long been separated into the two great original groups.

Surely life in Europe was drastically changed! Now the people of the tribes could travel in ox-drawn carts over the rutted roads, covering distances not possible before. Trade among the tribes became more practicable; building was made simpler as materials were brought by wagon from a distance. European man was on wheels, and Western civilization was on its way to the Los Angeles freeway.

Some time later (we are still in prehistory), these tribes, too, separated, not all at once but over many centuries. The ancestors of the Slavs and Teutons moved slowly northward into central Europe, those of the Greeks toward the Mediterranean; and the tribes that would at last be Celt and Roman drifted along the course of the Danube toward Italy and Gaul. From linguistic evidence, we surmise that the ancestors of Celt and Latin traveled for a while together, and those of

Slav and Teuton; for the Celtic language seems more nearly related to Latin than Latin to Greek, and Slavic and Teutonic share certain elements. But it is the Teutons we choose to follow now, the speakers of primitive Germanic, as they make their way deep into the forests of northern Europe. It is their words we watch for along our trail, with a quickening sense of familiarity; for it is they who carry our language in their own.

From the words now entering the vocabulary—those proto-Germanic words that have been reconstructed from the oldest written forms of High and Low German, Norse and Dutch, Danish, Swedish, Gothic, Frisian, and English—we see that the way chosen by our linguistic ancestors was rough and hazardous, the land harsh. In a setting curiously prophetic of the migrations of American descendants generations hence, they pushed forward as if in slow-motion preview against obstacles of climate and terrain, of danger from unfamiliar animals, of the terror of the unknown. New and revealing words appear, for *hail* and *sleet* and *marsh* and *moor* and even *prickly shrubs*. The word for storm, *sturmaz,* was made from the old Indo-European form *twer-,* which meant "whirlwind"; for the storms the Teutons met had a new and frightening quality. Deadly peril lurked in the trackless German forests; and a new word for *fear*—which would mean until the time of the Norman Conquest, as Old English *fær,* a dreadful or terrible event—entered the language, its source identical with that of an expression for pressing forward, so surely did danger accompany the act of moving on.[9] Because the basic lesson of survival was to follow a track (*laistjan*), from that idea was made the word for learning, *laizō,* source of the Old English *lār,* lore, and *liznōn,* from which comes the Old English *leornian,* to learn. And until modern times, the word *weary* implied an exhausting journey or a going astray, after the fate of travelers in those days.

In so menacing a world, it was essential to placate new and

9. The full range of the comparative material relating to this root, *per-,* as to others, can be found in Julius Pokorny: *Indogermanisches Etymologisches Wörterbuch* (Bern and München: J. Band; 1959).

powerful gods, rulers of woods and streams and earth. Spirits were everywhere; *ghosts* frightened the wanderer, and *nixes* guarded the streams. Sometimes their mischief could be warded off by enchanters who knew magic words, by the *wizards* (*\*wikk-*); sometimes they could be appeased only by human sacrifice, and the dread word *\*blōthisōjan,* which meant "to hallow with blood," and from which comes *bless,* was uttered before rude altars in deep woods. The people told one another tales of strange and fearsome things, the story-tellers chanted of them before the fires at night, and myths were born, to grow into the fairy tales of a later day.

But even in their *angst* (the word came from these days),[1] the Germanic peoples were building a stable society and establishing themselves firmly in northern Europe. Words indicating civil organization appeared in the vocabulary; the words for *king* and *earl* and the equivalent of *count,* as well as a term for the common man, *\*kārlāz,* which would become old English *ceorl* and eventually *churl,* told of well-developed social classes. The word *\*burgs* had been made from *\*bhergh-,* and meant already a kind of civic community; a new word for house had appeared. These and other comfortable terms, like those we have inherited as *stove* and *loaf* and *broth* and *brew* and *thread for weaving,* evoke a picture of cheery domesticity. A new art had become known, too, a tremendous art; the word *bōkō,* from the ancient *\*bhāgo-,* meant not only "beech" but also a beech staff for carving runes on;[2] and *wrītān* meant "to tear" or "to scratch," as in cutting runes on wood. The rudiments of writing had been learned.

All was not peace and harmony, however. Some of the tribes

1. As *\*augh-os-ti,* from *\*augh-,* which meant "tight" or "painfully constricted."

2. The *Oxford English Dictionary* does not agree with the *American Heritage Dictionary* on the finality of this etymology. However, evidence for it is strong and is supported by Smith: *English Language,* p. 140; by Mario Pei: *The Story of the English Language* (New York: Simon and Schuster, Clarion Edition; 1968), p. 294; and by other notable etymologists.

warred among themselves as well as traded; the neighboring Celts were not always on friendly terms. A new word for "weapon," *wēpnām*, entered the language, but the weapons were primitive; even though iron had come to Europe by the fifth century B.C., when the Germanic tribes had already established themselves in the lands where Caesar would find them, they used it little. Four hundred years later their principal weapon would still be a wooden lance or spear with a point hardened in the fire or perhaps tipped with a short, narrow iron point; and they had no armor. To the Teutons as to the Celts (they shared the word), iron was *isarno-*, the "holy metal," from the same root, *eis-*, that gave to the Greeks *hieros*, "filled with the divine"; for the first iron came probably from meteorites, the great rocks that fell from the heavens. The sinister and magical character of blacksmiths in German legend is perhaps reminiscent of the awe with which the art of forging was regarded.

However primitive their weapons, in the first millennium B.C. the Teutons were feared. Seagoing people by then, they sailed their ships to fishing grounds in cold northern waters or to distant coasts for pillaging; in Britain, across the North Sea, whither many of the Celtic tribes had migrated by the seventh century B.C. or before, they were known with dread. Words entering the vocabulary during this period tell of voyaging, words like *ship* and *steer* and *strand* and *island* and *whale*. The sea had become their element.

Still they lived in relative isolation. Few travelers had made their way northward to report on them, although Pytheas, the Greek geographer, claimed to have visited them in the fourth century B.C. and included their lands in his geography. At the end of the second century B.C., they invaded southern Gaul and northern Italy, where they were annihilated by the Roman general Marius (leaving a reputation for valor behind them); but even today there is little documentary evidence to tell us of this period of Teutonic history, nor have many artifacts been found. It is principally through these words we know are theirs that we can surmise their way of life. As we

listen to the words—vivid and far more numerous than those
we have been able to identify from earlier times—we are
struck by the sound of them. They have not the smooth flow
of the Latin tongue, nor do they sound like Greek. In their
accent, their texture, their actual pronunciation, they carry
a faint, murmuring suggestion of our own speech, like the
first rustle of a coming wind; the Teutonic words for mother
(*mōthar-*), daughter (*dohtēr*), folk (*folkam*), and other old
and homey words sound almost like our own. Those faraway
voices are speaking the language that will, after separating
into three great branches, produce through one of them the
division of the German language from which our tongue will
come. And much of its vocabulary, altered but clearly recognizable, will travel to Jamestown and to Plymouth with the
colonists.

During the many centuries that these Teutonic, or Germanic, tribes were making their way into northern Europe,
their long-forgotten cousins in the South were becoming nations. In the more hospitable Mediterranean area, the migrating peoples had come into contact with the older civilizations
of Egypt and the East; and in the course of generations they
themselves had established the classical civilizations that
would illumine the history of mankind with enduring bril-
liance. Now, after uncounted centuries of separation and
shortly before the Christian era, it was these distant relatives
who brought the Germanic peoples into recorded history,
giving to the story we have been tracing tenuously through
words a supplement and a check.

The first systematic description of the "barbarian" tribes
of the North, the "Germani," was Julius Caesar's, in mid-first
century B.C.; and in A.D. 98 the great historian Tacitus published his *Germania*, "concerning the geography, the manners
and customs, and the tribes of Germany." To both Caesar
and Tacitus, the Germani were barbarians—and indeed, in
Roman eyes and ours, they were; but recorded history has its
limitations. As we have followed our trail of words deep into
the past, we have learned what Caesar and Tacitus could not

know—how far these people had come from more primitive days, what perils they had faced, and what lessons they had learned. It had been easier for their relatives in the South. From the words the Germani made we know their fears and pleasures and something of their dreams. And perhaps, in the light of what the words have told us about them and the challenges they met, we can see why, as they traveled in their lurching oxcarts along the rutted paths or sailed their ships across the cold North Sea, they were moving into history with a force that Caesar and Tacitus could not have guessed.

History interacts with its actors, and the coming of the Romans left its mark on the northern tribes. By the time of Julius Caesar, in the first century B.C., the Teutons, who had earlier inhabited southern Sweden, the Danish peninsula, and northern Germany, were established west of the Rhine and had reached the Danube. In furious battle they resisted the Roman advances; armed only with their thrusting spears or lances and protected only by wooden or wicker shields (the "holy metal" had still not been much utilized), they fought Rome's superior weaponry by rushing the legionnaires in open spaces, then retreating to the woods they knew so well. Caesar succeeded in incorporating into the frontiers of the Roman Empire those tribes that had settled west of the Rhine, but he could not conquer the fierce and independent tribes to the east. Nevertheless, as the Roman presence continued over the centuries, as far-flung outposts of the empire became centers of Roman civilization, with roads and fortresses, stone-built houses, and even marble palaces, new concepts as well as new commodities were introduced and spilled over into neighboring lands. Germanic mercenaries entered the Roman armies; slaves were taken back to Rome. By the fourth century, several million of the Germani were living within the empire; and on its northern frontier, those who lived along the Moselle and the Rhine could glimpse the grandeur that was Rome. New words in their speech reflected it.

One wonders how, Latinized as our language is, we can

know which of our Latin words were adopted in this earlier, or Continental, period rather than in later times in Britain. No Germanic literature is extant from that time, no written history; we must depend for our evidence solely on the words themselves. One clue is the appearance of a word in several of the Teutonic dialects other than Old English; *copper* (*copor*),[3] for example, appears in no fewer than six of the Continental Teutonic languages, and with great frequency, so that we can safely assign it to the period before the tribes departed for Britain. Phonetic forms offer even more conclusive evidence; changes in the sounds of words can often be dated quite closely, and the presence or absence of these changes in a borrowed word constitutes an important test of age. Because we know that in Vulgar Latin the short *i* changed to *e* before A.D. 400, Old English *disc* (from Latin *discus*) had to be borrowed in the earlier time, while *wine* (from Latin *vinum*) entered the Germanic vocabulary before the Latin *v* lost its *w* sound. By way of similar changes, Latin *cāseus* progressed through *\*caesi* and *\*cēasi* to Old English *cīese*, our *cheese*. Historical context, too, can tell us much; the pervasive military and commercial character of the early borrowings contrasts with the predominantly religious character of words borrowed in the later, missionary period.

In all, the Teutons brought some fifty Latin words to Britain from the Continent. *Camp*, which then meant "battle," from Latin *campus*; *pīl*, for a pointed stick or javelin, from *pīlum*; *draca*, from *dracō*, which described the dragon banners of the Roman legions: all play a martial tune. So, too, does *mīl*, a unit of measure, from Latin *mīlia*, based on the thousand steps stepped off by the legionnaires. New words of trade, *pound* and *inch* (*pund* and *ince*, from Latin *pondō* and *uncia*), the verb for "to trade" (*mangian*, from Latin *mango*, "dealer," along with derivatives like *mangere*, "monger," and *mangung-hūs*, "trading house"), tell of busy merchants from

3. The common Germanic was *kupar* (unattested), from Late Latin *cuprum*. Borrowings listed herein are given in their attested Old English form.

Rome and the Levant who walked their loaded mules along the paved roads of the provinces. For centuries, traders had traveled the overland route through Asia Minor and Persia, bringing back spices and ivory and precious stones for the markets of southern Europe; now they were quick to exploit the new and fertile market opened by the military. To the unsophisticated "barbarians" they brought exotic things like musk and beryl and camphor, all recorded in the language. *Pipor*, "pepper" (from Latin *piper* and, by way of Greek *peperi*, all the way from Sanskrit *pippalī*, which meant "berry"), and other condiments entered the Teutonic cook pots and the vocabulary.

Roman building arts were a revelation in a land where the people had lived in rude huts and underground excavations. From the Romans the Teutons learned to build with mortar, adding *chalk* and *tile* to their lexicon; they said *street* and *wall* (*straet* and *weall*) almost as we do now, the best they could manage with Latin *strata* and *vallum*. Words for pillow and carpet and spoon and kettle suggest a marked increase in domestic refinements that fitted ill in wooden huts and perhaps gave incentive to the new art of building. Interesting foods were introduced—cheese and cherries, and mustard, pears, and plums.

It is noteworthy that nearly all of the vocabulary additions were words for material things, for objects and instruments and technical processes. The rich store of Latin words, principally derived from the Greek, that expressed abstract concepts or ideas remained largely untapped; and although many of the tribes in the occupied areas adopted Christianity, the language the Saxons brought to England bore little imprint of it, perhaps because the invading tribes were not among those affected by the new beliefs. The few religious terms adopted, such as *angel* and *devil* and *church*, came directly from the Greek, perhaps through tribal mercenaries serving in the eastern provinces, and had probably nothing but superstitious connotations. Churches were regarded only as tempting objects of pillage. There is little evidence in the language of the softening effect that Roman ways were having on the Celts in Britain. The hardy Teutons remained fiercely independent, and—despite the long years of Roman influence—their language and their culture remained relatively "pure."

But even imperial Rome could not endure forever. By the fifth century the empire was in deep trouble, torn by dissension at home and revolt abroad; and the legions were withdrawn from the far-flung provinces. To the Celts in Britain, who for four hundred years had been living under Roman occupation, the withdrawal had a devastating effect. By now comfortably adjusted to a life of dependency, used to the protection of Roman military might that guarded the coast against the raids of piratical Saxons, lulled into a sense of security by the Roman wall that barred from their land the fierce blue-painted Picts and the Scots of the north, they found themselves suddenly vulnerable—and afraid. According to the venerable historian Bede, who wrote more than two centuries later (and who, as an Anglo-Saxon, may have been prejudiced), the Celts were not only weak but cowardly as well. In desperation, Wyrtgoern, King of Kent, decided to try playing one enemy against the other; to the most formidable of them, the fierce Saxons, he offered an alliance giving to them the island of Thanet in return for their aid against the Picts and the Scots. Brilliant strategy indeed! The Saxon response was so wildly enthusiastic that not only did the Saxons themselves come; so, too, over a period of years, did related Teutonic tribes from Germany and Denmark and from outlying islands—Angles and Jutes and Frisians. The wolves had been called to save the sheep.

By the sixth century, these boisterous "allies" had indeed repelled the Picts and the Scots. They had also driven their Celtic hosts into hiding and destroyed nearly all vestiges of Roman civilization, including the language. On the island of Britain, which was now effectively theirs, they imposed their government, their customs, and the Teutonic tongue that was to remain supreme in their adopted land. The speech patterns of that tongue would change during succeeding centuries, evolving toward simplicity; its vocabulary would come to contain as many borrowed words as native—and be enriched thereby; it would be called English. And in a day generations hence, when English-speaking men would explore the moon and the words of English-speaking leaders would echo in every land, it would be the language that over three hundred million people would claim as theirs and that three hundred million more would use or understand in some degree. It would also have a wider geographical range than any other tongue and would be recognized as the dominant language of that later world.[4]

And its words would tell the story of a people.

4. Lincoln Barnett: *The Treasure of Our Tongue* (New York: Alfred A. Knopf; 1965).

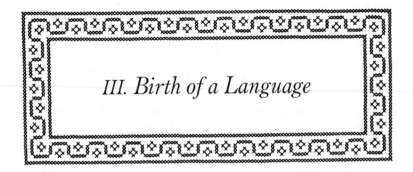

# III. Birth of a Language

The Anglo-Saxon language, or "Old English," was far from the speech that Captain John Smith and his party would bring to Jamestown a millennium later. Foreign and incomprehensible as it appears to us now, however, we can see within it our own language developing. If we read *no* for the *nā* of Old English, *stone* for *stān*, *bone* for *bān*, *home* for *hām*, we discover a consistent vowel change that is like a key thread in a knot—an example of the kind of clue that makes the study of comparative linguistics possible. *Hlāf* does not look like *loaf*, *sāwol* like *soul*, *cēosan* like *choose*, or *hēafod* like *head*; but they are our own words, the changes due to systematic and traceable phonetic processes. And altered as they and others like them may be, it is these old native words that are the building blocks of our language, or—more aptly—the work horses. They are used most frequently; they are needed and repeated over and over by educated and uneducated alike, especially in everyday communication. (The scholar asks no differently for beer.) Words such as *man, woman, come, speak, live, eat* are words we cannot do without; and the concepts they express, with all their semantic associations, lie deep in our cultural consciousness. In any given prose passage, written or spoken, well over half the words used will be Anglo-Saxon, despite their being outnumbered overwhelmingly in the dictionary.

"Anglo-Saxon" and "Old English"—are the terms interchangeable? Did the language of the Teutons who invaded Britain change suddenly from what it had been? At what point was English a new language, our Teutonic ancestors a new people? When did Britain become England? Our oldest English literature dates from the eighth century, most of it from two or three centuries later; and the invasions began in the fifth. How, historically and linguistically, do we bridge the gap?

Historically, the bridge we build has shaky foundations. The earliest account of the arrival of the Teutons comes from a sixth-century British (Celtic) ecclesiast, Saint Gildas, whose *Destruction and Conquest of Britain* is the first authority for the British appeal for help sent to the Roman general Aetius sometime between 446 and 453, as well as for the invitation from an unnamed British king to Saxon mercenaries to enter Britain as allies. Saint Gildas, more moralist than Celt (one who obviously held no truck with the notion that editorial opinion should be separate from reporting), considered it only fitting that his fellow Celts should be "slaughtered in heaps" or forced into emigration, so reprehensible had been the behavior of some of their kings and priests.[1]

Mention of the invaders appears, too, in Continental writings—the Byzantine historian Procopius identifies them as Angles and Frisians—but our principal source for the history of fifth- and sixth-century England is the Venerable Bede's *Ecclesiastical History of the English People,* completed at the monastery of Jarrow in 731. Bede's *History*, carefully drawn from "ancient documents, or from the tradition of the elders, or from my own knowledge," was further tested by submission of the preliminary draft to Ceolwulf, King of Northumbria; in that age, courts were the chief repositories of national tradition. Supplementing Bede's account and giving further evidence of the Anglo-Saxon presence, according to the *Encyclopaedia Britannica,*[2] is the archaeological testimony of arti-

1. *Encyclopaedia Britannica,* "Gildas."
2. Ibid., "English History."

facts found in ancient burial grounds in England, where the Saxon funeral custom of cremation was practiced, and "English place names of an archaic type."

*Place* names indeed! In the whole Old English vocabulary from which ours came we can travel backward in time to the Britain that was. We may not by means of ordinary words establish such specific dates as 449, 597, 865, 1066; but we can discover in those words the flow of history, feel the impact of Christianity and the horrors of war, watch the mingling of peoples and the development of social philosophies, know the aspirations of a people, the effect of conquest. . . .

We establish the form and antiquity of Old English words as we do of earlier forms of Germanic—by means of hypothesis, by comparison with known cognates in related languages, by noting the presence or absence of phonetic changes known to have taken place at certain times, and by study of descendants. In the case of Old English, hypothesis is sometimes confirmed by the appearance of a word in the earliest literature, although such inclusion can rule a word only in, not out. (Many Old English words are forever lost.) But how do we know when all of these words together became "Old English," elements of a new and identifiable language?

There is actually no point at which we can say a dialect becomes a separate language; it is possible that the West German dialect which was to become Old English was already changing before the migration began. However, given the nature of language, we *can* be sure that Primitive Old English of the fifth century differed enormously from Late Old English of the eleventh,[3] even though, lacking significant documentary evidence, we must postulate its character on the basis of what is known.

---

3. The "blank" period of Old English is usually divided into the *primitive*, from about 400 to 500, including the period just before and just after the invasions, and the *prehistoric*, running from about 500 to 700. *Early* Old English begins in 700, *Late* Old English in 900. See Morton Bloomfield and Leonard Newmark: *A Linguistic Introduction to the Study of English* (New York: Alfred A. Knopf; 1963), pp. 136–7.

The speech of all the invading tribes—a grouping of Angles, Saxons, Jutes, and almost surely Frisians—was West Germanic; but within it dialectal differences existed. Over the years of migration, and following settlement in separate regions of Britain, these differences were magnified; and the earliest documents make it evident that soon after settlement four major dialects had developed. Of these dialects, we have extensive literary remains only in West Saxon; but fragmentary remains of the others are preserved in ancient runic inscriptions, in early charters, in brief fragments of verse, and in Biblical glosses. Personal names and place names from them appear also in contemporary Latin documents; and descendant dialects offer further testimony to the characteristics of these early language forms, which were regionally distinct. Northumbrian was spoken north of the Humber, Mercian between the Humber and the Thames—both stemmed from Anglian; West Saxon, coming from the earlier Saxon, was the speech of southwestern England; and Kentish, a Jutish dialect, was spoken in the southeastern corner of Britain. Vestigial dialectal differences remain in these same regions today; and although in America our greater mobility has brought about greater uniformity of language, the traces of difference that came with early settlers from the differing speech areas of Britain are still with us—the strong *r* pronunciation that the Scotch-Irish brought to Pennsylvania and the Midwest, the broad *a* of New England that settlers from East Anglia brought across the sea.[4] Such differences have a long ancestry; they are the progeny of those that began in England fifteen hundred years ago.

No one is quite sure why our language came to be called *English* rather than, say, *Saxon*. Early Latin writers, following Celtic example, called the Teutons in England *Angli-Saxones*, to distinguish them from the Continental Saxons, and

4. The broad *a* came to be considered a rusticism in both England and America, and was restored to respectable status only in the late eighteenth century.

their land *Saxonia.* The terms *Angli* and *Anglia* came into use soon after, possibly because the Angles in Northumbria had gained initial supremacy among the "kingdoms" established by various tribal chieftains (each of whom claimed descent from one of the ancient gods of the Germanic race, usually Woden). In 601, Pope Gregory referred to Aethelbert, King of Kent, as *Rex Anglorum;* and by 1000 the name of the country had become *Englaland,* to develop into *Ingland* during the Middle English period, and then into *England* as we know it. From the beginning, however, writers in the vernacular had called their language *English,* so that the name of the language has a longer lineage than does the name of the country in which it grew.

That language was enormously flexible. A present-day dictionary of Old English contains some thirty thousand words, and we can assume that the entire vocabulary comprised well under one hundred thousand;[5] but with the Germanic gift for compounding, for forming derivative words, and for combining roots and suffixes and prefixes, each word could be put to many uses. Linguistic ingenuity is apparent in such combinations as *læcecræft* ("leechcraft," or medicine) and *eardstapa* ("earth stepper," or wanderer), in *gimm-whyrta* ("gem worker," or jeweler) and *frumweorc* ("beginning work," or foundation). Some fifty words were formed with the simple prefix *wiþ-* ("against," "away"), among them *wiþcēosan,* "reject" (*cēosan* meant "choose"), *wiþsprecan,* "contradict" (*sprecan* meant "speak"), and *wiþstendan,* "withstand"; of them, only *withstand* survives, although two new verbs, *withdraw* and *withhold,* were formed on the same model in Middle English times. Combinations using such suffixes and prefixes as *-hād* and *-dōm* and *be-* and *ofer-* (the last occurs in more than a hundred verbs) resulted in useful words like *cyningdōm* ("kingdom"), *cildhād* ("childhood"), and *oferfēran* ("go over" or "traverse").

5. Mario Pei: *The Story of the English Language* (New York: Simon and Schuster, Clarion Edition; 1968), p. 91.

Perhaps it is this wealth of native resources, combined with a lack of interest in anything the Celts had to offer, that explains the paucity of Celtic borrowings in the language: few Celtic words, save for a number of place names, entered the Old English vocabulary. Teutonic speech was little more affected by that of the Celts whom the Teutons dispossessed than it was by the remnants of Roman civilization in Britain, and for more than a century it retained its almost exclusively Germanic character.

The social system, developed over many centuries, was by the time of the invasions firmly established, its base the *ceorl*, the free peasant, and the *thegn*, a freeman of higher status, who was granted land in return for military service. The word *eorl* was in use also, in the sense of a leading warrior or *thegn*, but without its post-Danish connotation of nobility or command. *Æþeling* meant one of noble or princely rank.

The semantic development of all of these words is interesting, but that of *ceorl* is a social history in miniature. From its earliest appearance as the West German *kerl*, from Old Teutonic *\*karlaz*, which meant simply "man" in the social or legal sense correlative to "wife"; through its usage during the early Old English period as *ceorl*, when ceorldom was an honorable estate and implied land ownership and certain civic and military obligations; to the *churl* and *churlish* of a later era, it tells of ascendancy and decline. In the days we are considering, the ceorl cultivated his *hīgid*, or "hide," the family land, in the full security of *folc riht* ("folk right"), knowing his *hecg* ("hedge") was inviolate, protected by public law. However, as a *twīhynde* man, he himself was legally less valuable than the thegn, a *twelfhynde* man, for whose death an assailant owed a *wergild* ("man payment") of twelve hundred shillings instead of the two hundred due for the death of a ceorl.

Other words, too, tell of an ordered society: *tūngerēfa* ("town reeve" or "bailiff"); *scīr rēfa* ("shire reeve," sheriff); *burgware* ("citizens" or "burghers"); *ealdormǫn* ("alderman"). But this ordered society was not easily or quickly attained. Even as settlement went on and the Teutons took possession of the land, Celtic resistance continued. The *Anglo-Saxon Chronicle* reports that at Andredesceaster or Pevensey a deadly struggle occurred in which all the British forces were exterminated, and we know that a Celtic king still held Lincoln in the sixth century; Elmet and the "Chiltern Hundreds" were long held by the Celts. (Evidently Bede *was* a little biased!) As one would expect, therefore, the roar and din of battle resound in the contemporary vocabulary, in such words as *harry, lay waste, battle, plundering, sword* (*guþ-wine,* or "war-friend"), and *captive,* all evoking the stereotype of the fierce and predatory Saxon. But from other words, homey words, we gain a different impression: *bearn,* a second word for "child," is one full of the warmth and informality of family life, as is its descendant, Scottish *bairn;* in *ymbesittend* ("one who sits [dwells] round about another"), an informal word for neighbor, we hear the hum of friendly conversation more clearly than in the colder word *neahgebur* ("near dweller"), which we have kept.

Another sound, too, travels the centuries, carried from the great, barnlike *medu-heall,* the "mead-hall," where the thanes gathered with their lord between battles, where the *scop* recited tales of valor and sang of joy and sorrow, where the warriors boasted of their deeds, and jests and challenges whipped back and forth. It is "the clear sound of the harp, the song of the gleeman," that echoes in such words as *glīwstæf* ("glee"), *hleahtor* ("laughter"), and *bēor-þegu* ("beer drinking"), in *sǫngcrǽft* ("the art of song") and *sęledrēam* ("hall joy"). The roof beams must have shaken during those noisy gatherings, with their *gebēorscipe* ("banqueting") and *breahtm* ("revelry") and *þryþ-word* ("mighty word," "excellent discourse") and *gilp-cwide* ("yelp-speech," or boasting). And yet no word so strikes the keynote of Anglo-Saxon philosophy, tells so clearly what thinking has come of that long journey through the forests from far away and long ago, as *Wyrd* ("fate"). We hear it over and over in the early poetry, the still pagan poetry; we hear it from the *Ruined City,* wherein, as to all glorious things, Wyrd has brought decay; we hear it in the sad lines "Alas the bright ale-cup, alas the brave warrior" of *The Wanderer;* in Beowulf's lament that Wyrd "hath o'erwhelmed our Weagmunding line, / Swept my kinsmen swift to their doom, / Earls in their prime."[6] But like a deep, splendid accompaniment, there sounds beneath the mournful note an exultant Yes to life. In all the words of action, in the vigor of the language, we hear the words of Beowulf: "Wyrd oft saveth a man not doomed, if he dauntless prove."[7] To be dauntless was the challenge; and if the word *dōm* meant "doom," it meant "glory," too.

Into this land and this primitive, pagan society there came in the sixth century a new force and a new tongue—and the language and the culture of the Anglo-Saxon would not be the same again. This great historical force began with a walk taken one morning in the market place in Rome by a young priest named Gregory; it climaxed in the arrival in Britain of forty missionaries sent by Pope Gregory the Great, who remembered the fair-haired young men he had seen for sale in the Roman slave market and his pity and distress that so fair a people "should be void of inward grace."[8]

Christian missionaries from Ireland had already made some contact with the Teutonic tribes in Britain; but this mission, led by Augustine, was aided especially by the prior Christianity of the Frankish princess Bertha, who was queen consort to Aethelbert, King of Kent. Aid must have been sorely needed; for the task of the missionaries was a monumental one—not merely to substitute one ritual for another, but to change the philosophy of a nation, to instill in a barbaric

6. *Beowulf,* ll. 2814–16.

7. *Beowulf,* ll. 572–3.

8. Pope Gregory's experience was first reported by Bede in his *Ecclesiastical History* as current tradition, and the story has been generally accepted. Albert C. Baugh: *A History of the English Language* (New York: Appleton Century Crofts, Inc.; 1957).

people ideals of humility and patience and charity utterly contrary to the exaltation of aggressiveness, independence, and revenge that had been for centuries the foundation of their culture. Both history and language testify to the success of the mission; within a hundred years after the landing of Augustine, all England was permanently Christian.

The effect on the vocabulary was enormous. A Germanic language had now to express concepts and describe objects completely outside of prior experience, and the Latin of the missionaries was dissimilar to it and in many respects phonetically antagonistic to Germanic speech patterns. Nevertheless, with a flexibility that would become more characteristic of English than of any other language, many Latin or Graeco-Latin words were adopted with little or no change, others were translated into Teutonic equivalents, and, with occasional stubbornness, some were rejected and old words converted in their stead to become vehicles for new concepts. Little changed was Latin *altāre*, (Old English *altar*), which had in pagan Rome meant "material for burning sacrificial offerings." Latin *candēla* (Old English *candel*) was accepted at once; a word of ancient pedigree, it came, like Sanskrit *candanah* ("sandalwood burned as incense"), from the Indo-European root *\*kand-*, which meant "to shine." These and other words gave to the Teutons many terms touched with subtle nuances acquired over the centuries from ancient rites and foreshadowing religions; *Sabbath* (Old English *sabat*) came all the way from Hebrew *shabbāth* (from *shābhath*, "to rest"), which had become Greek *sabbaton* and finally Latin *sabbatum*. *Temple* (Old English *tempel*) came from Latin *templum*, which meant originally the space marked for observation by an augur; and *abbot* (Old English *abbod*) came through Latin *abbās* from Late Greek *abbās*, a derivative of Aramaic *abbā*, "father."

Some words, however, simply did not click. Instead of *patriarch*, the Anglo-Saxons said *hēahfæder* ("high father"); and for the clergy in general they used the engaging phrase *æt gāstlice folc* ("the spiritual folk"). *Scripture* found an exact equivalent in *gewritu* ("what is written"), and *ēvangelium* in *god-spell* ("good tidings"). *Sin* and *hell* and *love* and *God* and *heaven* remained what they had been, the words we have today, modified in meaning to conform to the new faith. *Cross* (Latin *crux*) was refused, Old English *rōd* taking its place; only later, when the Irish missionaries carried the gospel to the Danes in the north, was the word *cross* taken into the English language.

The missionaries brought to the Anglo-Saxons, long isolated from the main currents of European cultural history, not only the message of Christianity and its terminology; they brought also some glimmerings of the light of classical civilization. By the end of the sixth century, much of that light had been extinguished in Europe, and the twilight of the Dark Ages had settled upon the Continent; but the reflection still gleamed in the thought and the language of these Roman missionaries. Along with the *god-spell* came secular concepts and awareness of a world hitherto undreamed of. From the Bible came the names of exotic creatures and plants, *camel* and *palm* and *cedar* and *hyssop*, the last a very ancient Semitic word akin to Hebrew *'ezobh*. New plants sprouted in English earth, new foods appeared on English tables; *beet* and *lentil, millet* and *pear* and *radish* entered the language. New domestic refinements were added to those acquired earlier on the Continent; words like *cap* and *sock* and *mat* and *fan* and *fiddle* suggest that the hardy seafarers were softening a bit.

Most significantly, words of learning were entering the vocabulary, words promising the rich development of English scholarship that, a century later, would make of England the intellectual leader of an otherwise darkened Western world. Caedmon wrote in the seventh century, Cynewulf in the eighth; the towering figure of Bede bridges the two centuries. In them we see the social and intellectual advances made by a people who not long before had been a straggling group of migrating barbarian tribes. "The very mind of Cynewulf," says James Dow McCallum, "not to take into account the advance of his style, is a product of a refined and cultured community."[9] And at the dawn of the ninth century, as Lincoln Barnett points out,[1] England stood at the forefront of Western civilization, its monastery schools internationally renowned, the great works of Bede and Aldhelm received avidly in Europe. A generation later, Charlemagne would call upon Alcuin of York to direct his palace school and promote the Frankish renaissance. It was during this early period of achievement that such words as *school* and *master, philosophe* (replaced later by *philosopher*), *verse, meter, gloss,* and other Latin terms of learning entered the vocabulary. Many of them would be lost during the devastation that was to come, to be replaced later by borrowings from the French; but by the ninth century, the Old English vocabulary had become a rich and varied one.

From a ninth-century litany rises the doleful cry: "From the fury of the Northmen, good Lord deliver us!" It came from the hearts of terror-filled dwellers along Britain's northern coasts, where for two hundred years, beginning at the end of the eighth century, a series of Viking raids brought desolation and death. The raiders, all called Danes in English history and their coming the Danish invasion, began their attacks with the pillaging of monasteries and villages and the transporting of slaves and booty in their dreaded beaked ships. Eventually the small plundering bands became large armies; and in 865 the "Great Army," in a fleet of three hundred and fifty ships, initiated the large-scale invasions that soon shattered the kingdoms of Mercia, East Anglia, and Northumbria and made of a large part of eastern England a Danish colony. The territory the Danes finally controlled, decided upon by treaty after a long-drawn-out war against the armies of the great West Saxon ruler Alfred, became known as the *Danelaw*; there Danish law and speech—but the Christian religion —prevailed. (The adoption of Christianity had been part of

9. James Dow McCallum, ed.: *The Beginnings to 1500* (New York: Charles Scribner's Sons; 1929), p. xvi.
1. *The Treasure of Our Tongue* (New York: Alfred A. Knopf; 1965), p. 109.

the treaty bargain.) The land was fair and green; and more and more of the dreaded invaders brought their families to settle upon it, gradually becoming less "furious," calmer, more English. The English already there had forgotten that their forefathers, too, were invaders in their time.

Two hundred years of turbulence not only left their mark upon the English countryside and on the harried citizens; in shaking the English social system, destroying the monasteries that were the centers of learning, and introducing a new people into the land, they also drastically affected the language. The adoption of new words, the loss of old ones, semantic changes—all reflect a new order of English life. *Ceorl*, which had earlier signified the free peasant, who was a keystone of the Anglo-Saxon social structure, who transacted his own business without the intervention of any lord, who served in the *fyrd*, the local militia, was undergoing—had undergone—severe semantic change. Forced by insecurity during the years of terror to seek the protection of a powerful thane, the ceorl had bartered his freedom for security; in return for bound service, he was given seed corn and stock and protection and was on his way to becoming what in Norman England would be called a *villein*, neither quite slave nor fully free. That this social decline took place during the troubled centuries is evident in the contrast between the Laws of Ine in the late seventh century, which portray a community of free peasants, and the tenth-century codes, wherein lordship is a fundamental assumption. As *churl*, in the Middle English period, the honorable Old English word would become a pejorative.

Neither was *thegn* the proud word it had been, signifying the favored follower of a lord; under the pressure of the Danish invasions, military service had been centralized and the rank of thegnhood diluted and divided, so that the thegn's rank depended upon that of his lord. It held no longer the old Teutonic connotation of a strong personal relationship in which loyalty played an essential part. Old English *eorl*, which in *Beowulf* seems almost a democratic term, now was influenced by Scandinavian *jarl* and came to mean a powerful nobleman or royal governor. Under cover of all the disturbance, feudalism had crept quietly into England.

The looting and destruction of the monasteries had had a devastating effect on the language. Not only were manuscripts destroyed and scholarship halted, but also the language itself was no longer cared for; and many of the fine words of the earlier Latin period were lost to the living vocabulary. Their very absence told a story of disruption and decay. Late in the ninth century, under Alfred, however, learning was revived for a time; and many great works were translated from the Latin, among them Bede's *History*, Orosius's *History of the World,* and Boethius's *Consolations of Philosophy.* The *Anglo-Saxon Chronicle*, a historical record that would be continued by anonymous authors until 1154, was seriously begun. The work started under and by Alfred was eventually interrupted by war; but late in the tenth century, under the Benedictines, a second revival of learning, along with a renewed dedication to religion, took place. During this period, a second group of Latin words, most of them scholarly and including many plant and animal names, entered the vocabulary: *cloister* and *creed*, for example, *apostle, accent, idol, scorpion, cucumber, periwinkle,* and *history* (for a series of lessons from Scripture). Few of them made their way at the time into the spoken language, which was being influenced by a far more powerful force than ivory-towered scholars could exert—everyday contact with the Danes.

It is characteristic of linguistic exchange that the earliest borrowings are nouns.[2] Names of new commodities, new processes, new concepts are the first to be taken into a language, and only with close contact and prolonged communication do other parts of speech become useful and even necessary. Accordingly, the first Scandinavian words appearing in Old English were nouns, reflecting the initially hostile relations between the two peoples: *barda* ("beaked ship"), for the

2. Baugh: *History*, p. 120.

high-powered, menacing Viking vessels; *rān* ("robbery," "rapine"); *scegþmann* ("pirate"). Only later, when the Danes had established their settlements and contact had become routine, were verbs and adjectives, pronouns and connective words adopted, along with countless additional nouns that in many cases are even now indistinguishable in origin from the English. For the two languages were similar; and not only were the English people learning a great deal of Danish, the Danes were learning also the language of their adopted land. In the consequent mingling, in which English triumphed, the Scandinavian element became inseparable from its host.

Most impressive of the nouns borrowed, perhaps, is the great word *law* (Old English *lagu*), which came from *lög* ("that which is laid down")—a word destined to play an important role in English and American history. *Hūstings* came from Old Norse *husthīng* ("house assembly"), a derivative of the old Germanic *hūs*, which we have met before; and from the same root came the legal term *husband* (Old English *hūsbanda*), for the "dweller" (Old Norse *bōndi*) in a "house."

Such words show the influence of Danish legal and administrative systems on English thought; but the extent of social and economic mingling is more evident in such everyday words as *calf* and *skin* and *sky* and *fellow* and *scrap* and *steak*, and in those little words that were adopted because they made communication simpler. The Danish pronouns *þa, þāra,* and *þōem* were less easily confused with the Old English singular forms *hē* ("he"), *hiere* ("her"), and *him* ("him") than were Old English *hīe, hiera,* and *him*; and so the Danish forms gradually supplanted the native. Other borrowed elements were prepositions and conjunctions, like *both, though,* and *until,* and countless verbs and adjectives—*crawl, die, screech, take, flat, ill, low, odd, sly, weak.* Phonetically the words share a harsh, no-nonsense quality; they had none of the gentling effect that Latin was having on the sound of English.

Besides the words of ordinary speech, some fourteen hundred place names, particularly in the northern and eastern regions of England where the Danes settled, tell us today of their permanence in the land. The suffix *-by*, which meant "farm" or "town," appears in more than six hundred of them, in such names as *Derby* and *Rugby* and *Whitby*. *Thorp* meant "village," *thwaite* "an isolated piece of land," *toft* "a piece of ground"—all of them are found in English place names. Danish surnames, too, became common, with the suffix *-son* replacing Old English patronymic *-ng* (as in *Browning*); *Johnson* and *Stevenson* and other such names that fill our telephone book came to England with the Danes.

All of the changes, nevertheless, were within the Teutonic family, and the language retained its Teutonic character. Had another invasion not taken place in the eleventh century, an invasion that would change the course of the language, alter its pronunciation and content, and transform the character of its vocabulary, we would today be speaking a language much like modern Dutch (although—who knows?—were it not for that next infusion of pirate blood, the English might have been less daring, less adventurous, less stubborn; the French or the Spanish might have dominated America and theirs would be the language of this land).

Again, incredibly, the invaders were Teutonic, closely related to both the Anglo-Saxons and the Danes; but they had come a long way from their Scandinavian origins. For one hundred and fifty years they had been settled in the French province of Normandy, where their Viking forefathers had landed with fire and sword in the time of terror. Enterprising and adaptive, they soon made the French culture their own, adding to it their characteristic vigor and aggressiveness. Over the years they adopted Christianity and the French language, built magnificent cathedrals, and produced a superbly organized legal system that embraced important features of Frankish—basically Roman—law. The dialect they spoke (classical French had not emerged) was one descended from the Vulgar Latin of the Roman provinces; and because it was, English would become half sister to the Romance languages, happy product of the marriage of hardy Anglo-Saxon stock and the more advanced Latin culture.

Relations between Normandy and England had been close even before the memorable year 1066, and there were many French favorites at court; but the triumph of William of Normandy at the Battle of Hastings gave to the Normans domination over English life for centuries to come. On the field at Hastings and in subsequent campaigns, the English nobility was practically wiped out; for generations after the Conquest, the important positions at court, the great estates, and official posts were in Norman hands. Merchants and craftsmen from Normandy came to settle in English villages and the burgeoning towns; Norman clergy held controlling positions in the church. Inevitably French became the language of the ruling class, and so it would remain for more than two hundred years.

The effect on the English language was incalculable. Left as it was to the peasantry, who made of it what they would, English became a medley of regional dialects. Inflections that had been retained even under Danish influence were further abandoned, reducing English from what had been a highly inflected language to an extremely analytic one, in which multiple concepts once expressed by single lengthy words combining roots with inflectional affixes were broken down into their separate parts. Simplification is a process that proceeds naturally in any language (primitive speech is extremely complex; in some Eskimo languages, a "noun" can have more than one thousand forms, each with its own precise meaning);[3] and it is probable that we would have a less complicated language than did our forefathers in any case. However, the Norman influence, added to the Danish, accelerated the process enormously. The rapidity of simplification is evident even in a single literary work: between the end of the eleventh century and the middle of the twelfth, the *Peterborough Chronicle* shows the loss of both noun and adjective inflections. Declensions and conjugations were

3. Mario Pei: *The Story of Language,* rev. ed. (Philadelphia and New York: J. B. Lippincott Company; 1965), p. 124.

simplified if not dropped, and grammatical gender was abandoned.

Inevitably much of the Old English vocabulary was lost; and as the lives of Englishmen became more and more entangled in Norman rule, Norman law, and Norman customs, French words entered the language and English tongues did what they could with the strange foreign sound of them. The first words, relatively few, were of the kind that a lower class would learn to know through contact with clergy and officialdom, through awareness of a new noble class, and in encounters with the law. *Prince* and *nobleman* replaced Old English *æþeling*; the verb *to judge* replaced Old English *dēmam* (we keep the native form, if not the legal meaning, in *deem*); *crime* drove out *firen*. Whether *justice* is a better word than *gerihte* ("righting") is moot; the former is now so loaded with historical weight that we can imagine no satisfactory equivalent.

How many English words were actually lost we cannot know; we do know that during this early and bitter period of Anglo-Norman contact about nine hundred Norman words appeared in the English vocabulary. Ecclesiastical terms like *chaplain, procession, incense,* and *relic* pertain especially to external manifestations of religion and suggest the promptness with which the newly established clergy began shepherding their English flocks into the new-built abbeys and cathedrals. *Tower* and *castle, palace, manor, arch, baron* and *noble* and *dame* reflect the new look of the landscape as well as the presence of a new nobility (Old English *cyning,* as *king,* and *cwēn,* as *queen,* survived); and in *minstrel* and *juggler* there stirs a faint echo of the music and laughter that may have helped to warm the great, drafty castle halls. *Prison* and *robber* and *culprit* and *treason* suggest English contact, often painful, with Norman justice; and in one word of the period, now obsolete, we see the climate of the era epitomized: *murdrum* was the heavy fine imposed upon a whole community for the death of a Norman, any murdered man being presumed Norman unless four freemen of the community could give "proof of Englishry." (Then, obviously, the murder didn't matter.) The legal phrase *hu-e-cri* came of these days too; all men were compelled by law to join with "horn and voice" in the hunt for the murderer, whose guilt was considered theirs as well. "Hue and cry" statutes remained on English books until 1827.

But the bitterness passed, as bitterness does; and by 1177 an English jurist could write: ". . . the two nations have become so mixed that it is scarcely possible today, speaking of free men, to tell who is English, who of Norman race."[4] Race, perhaps—class, hardly. The Anglo-Norman aristocracy was closely linked to France by family and property ties; and because the French language was regarded throughout Europe with the highest respect and English as slightly boorish, French maintained its supremacy. Only gradually, as political developments separated the interests of the upper classes from those of their counterparts on the Continent, did English gain equal status.

King John lost his sovereignty over Normandy to the French Crown shortly after 1200; and the increasingly common practice of dividing family estates by giving English holdings to one heir and Norman to another began breaking down the ties of the nobility to France. Descendants of Norman families came to think of themselves as Englishmen; their children often spoke no French. In 1258, in protest against the French-oriented policies of Henry III, the English barons demanded certain reforms, presenting them to the king in the Provisions of Oxford (Magna Carta, for all its fine clauses, had not been very well implemented). When their demands were ignored, the barons imprisoned the king and assumed temporary rule. The struggle united in common cause the nobility and the growing middle class, and ensuing pride in being English brought pride in speaking it. By the end of the century, even the heads of monasteries were com-

4. *Dialogus de Scaccario* (1177), in William Stubbs: *Select Charters and Other Illustrations of English Constitutional History*, 4th ed. (London: Clarendon Press; 1881), p. 168.

plaining that their English-speaking novices "had no French."

Testimony to a new Anglo-Norman relationship is evident in the number of words, as well as the kind, that now entered the vocabulary. The enormous increase is explainable only by the way a foreign-speaking people would use English, choosing familiar words in their own language rather than groping for the English equivalents. French borrowings like *curtain* and *cushion* and *counterpane, quilt* and *lamp* tell of shared refinements in homes that by now boasted *parlors* and *pantries*. Such words as *sculpture, story,* and *literature* show artistic concern; and *treatise, compilation,* and other words of learning indicate that English once again had scholarly status. *Cape* and *petticoat, lace* and *button, tassel* and *plume, satin* and *sable* and *ermine* tell of courtly elegance; *dance* and *revel* and *theater, tournament, falcon, joust,* and *pavilion* suggest court gaiety and the romance of medieval times (but not the squalor; the old Anglo-Saxon words did well enough for that). Additional religious terms, too, *contrition* and *grace* and *penitence,* words less superficial than the earlier ones, emphasize more than the merely ceremonial aspects of the faith, an "internalizing" aspect of the Norman influence that, as Owen Barfield suggests,[5] had a marked psychological effect on the rugged Anglo-Saxon character. "Gentle" words, many of them originally religious terms, came to be used in reference to human relationships; *pity, mercy, devotion, patience* became secular virtues, indicating a growing tenderness that became evident in thirteenth- and fourteenth-century poetry. Even rollicking Chaucer, whose poetry blended a wealth of French borrowings into English with the ease of genius, shows in "The Monk's Tale" a sentimental spirit new to the Teutonic ethos. The mingling of Anglo-Saxon ruggedness with Latin emotionalism, like that of Anglo-Saxon and Romance vocabulary, seems to have resulted happily, in this case in a deeper humanity.

The semantic development of two words during the

5. *History in English Words* (London: Methuen and Co., Ltd.; 1926), pp. 114–16.

thirteenth century is of special interest to us, for between them they tell the story of the beginnings of representative government. *Parliament* is a thirteenth-century word, and so is *burgess*. The first, a simple word from French *parlement,* or "talking," acquired its great historical significance because, by the end of the century, a new voice was being heard among the old—the people's voice. *Burgess* is visibly a descendant of old Germanic *\*bergs-* but—unlike *borough*—came into Middle English indirectly, after travels through Latin (which, reversing the usual direction, had made *burgus* from the Germanic root) and through the later Anglo-Norman *burgeis.* Over the years, the word had come to mean a citizen with full municipal rights; during the thirteenth century it came to mean even more. The growing resentment of the people— barons and commoners alike—toward royal tax policies, com- bined with the Crown's equally growing need for revenue, induced the king to call in for occasional consultation with his select council of nobility and clergy both knights of the shires and representative burgesses of the towns—*especially* burgesses of the towns, where the money was. It was in these meetings, which came almost casually to be called *parlia- ments*, that the voice of the "commons" was heard for the first time and the principle of "no taxation without represen- tation" was conceived. By the end of the century, Edward I was demanding that both knights and burgesses come as authorized delegates from those who sent them, so that citizens might be legally bound to pay the sums agreed to. (Evidently there had been some reneging.) The love of money may indeed be the root of all evil, but it is also the root of representative government.

Other languages, too, Latin and Dutch and Flemish and Arabic, were making contributions to the vocabulary, through trade and scholarly exchange and the tales of travelers, many of the words acquiring a French accent in their coming. *Diamond* (Middle English *diamaunt*) came through French from Latin *diamus; azure* (Old French *azur*) was taken from

Old Spanish *azul,* which itself had come through Arabic *allāzaward,* "lapis lazuli," from ancient Persian.

It was from Arabic that some of the most important borrowings of the period were taken, often through Latin translation; for although Latin continued its role as the language of learning, it was the Arabs, in Spain and in the East, who were keeping the torch of learning alight for a still benighted Europe. The Arabs had preserved, in Syriac versions, the works of Aristotle and much of the astronomical and medical learning of ancient Greece; their own achievements in mathematics and science were the greatest since the Hellenistic period, and it was upon translations from Arabic texts by European scholars during the twelfth and thirteenth centuries that Renaissance science would be based. In such words as *algebra* and *algorism, zenith, nadir, cipher, zero,* the tremendous intellectual impact of Arabic thought is evident. *Cipher* and *zero,* both expressing a concept that completely revolutionized mathematical thinking, came from the same Arabic source, *sifr,* the first through Latin *cifra* and French *cifre,* the second deviously by way of Latin *zephirium,* Italian *zero,* and French *zéro.*

Many words relating to law and medicine, theology and literature came from the Latin: *legal* and *lucrative* and *notary* and *submit, tincture* and *limbo* and *tract.* From the Low Countries came words indicating the increasing trade with Flanders and Holland and northern Germany as well as the influx of Flemish weavers and mercenary soldiers into England, words like *nap* (of cloth), *deck, bowsprit, dock, guilder,* and *freight.* The vocabulary was reflecting the growing importance of trade to an island kingdom.

The sum of all of these words, together with the expanding native vocabulary, gives us an idea of the atmosphere in which the medieval Englishman lived and in which medieval history —of which modern history comes—was made. It is difficult for us, in our post-Columbian, post-Apollo 11, post-Freudian age, to inhabit imaginatively the atmosphere of a world thought to be the geographical center of the universe, subject to constant supernatural intervention, where plants and jewels had magical properties and witches consorted with Satan, where man was a poor and fallen creature in a doomed world that would never change. We would find it oppressive in "the small box of the medieval universe";[6] and yet, as Logan Pearsall Smith suggests, we might find, too, that we had gained therein a dignity and consequence which, in the light of modern knowledge of our place in the universe, we no longer seem to have. In our contempocentricity, which magnifies the achievements of our time, we may find it salutary to contemplate that in a world so contained great and enduring concepts of laws were conceived and representative government begun, vital and distinguished universities were founded and soaring cathedrals built, seeds of theological revolution were planted and the tools of philosophical speculation shaped. It was a small world, even a petty one—but magnificent. A paradox . . .

In the vocabulary we discover the forces that made it so. The series of Crusades begun in the eleventh century brought to Western consciousness the reality of the distant Orient; in their wake, Eastern products and ideas came flowing across the Continent and into England, and knights returning from their pilgrimages brought exciting and exotic things and the names of them, rich cloths and jewels and foods. They talked of lutes and caravans and of the "hashish eaters," the *assassins* (Arabic *ḥashshāshin*), who were sent forth by the Old Man of the Mountain to kill the Christian leaders. They gave up their heavy armor for robes of silk and cotton, in imitation of the Arabs, and brought to their ladies gifts of a rich material called *damask*, from Damascus, and of a rich, brilliantly colored cloth called *scarlet*. The later crusaders told tales they had heard on their way of a faraway land of many people where jade idols sat inscrutably in golden temples and kings on golden thrones. (But everyone knew

6. Logan Pearsall Smith: *The English Language* (New York: Henry Holt and Company; 1912), p. 232.

that Marco Polo was a great liar!) At the ports, more and more ships entered, bringing from foreign lands the products with strange names for which the Crusades had created a demand. The medieval box seemed a little larger than before.

Medical practice had advanced somewhat from the folk medicine of an earlier day; words such as *ointment* and *medicine, anatomy, artery, pore,* and *vein* entered the vocabulary from the Latin with approximately their present meanings, as did *pleurisy, asthma,* and *gout.* Treatment, however, was still based on the old Greek theory of "humors"— blood, phlegm, yellow bile, and black bile—which were thought to be the causes of disease or even of strange behavior. *Gout,* in fact (Middle English *goute*), came through French from Latin *gutta,* "drop," in the belief that the disease was caused by drops of morbid humors. Today we still say *good-humored* and *bad-humored* and use the words *phlegmatic, choleric, melancholy,* and *sanguine,* which originally signified a predominance of one of the four humors. The arteries were thought of as air ducts containing their own fluids, or *spirits;* and *influence* (from Latin *influere,* "to flow in") meant the flowing into men of an ethereal fluid that affected their characters and destinies. In *disaster* and *ill-starred* we echo the astrological orientation of the times; and *lunatic* comes of the belief that mental health is affected by changes of the moon—a theory being given new and scientific study in our own Aquarian Age.

Many words mirror the strange and terrifying notions that filled the medieval imagination, some of them to survive and be carried into the New World. The *specter* and *demon* of the Middle Ages would grin from Cotton Mather's account of the witch trials at Salem; Governor Winthrop's report of rumors of the *monstrous* births that were presumed to prove Mrs. Anne Hutchinson's sinister connections would use the word *monstrous* in its full medieval sense of unnatural, animal-like, evilly ominous, the word coming from Latin *mōnstrum,* from *monēre,* "to warn." To a generation hearing for the first time of such impossible creatures as the *hip-*

*popotamus* and the *crocodile* (which wept while it devoured
its victims), the idea of a *griffin*, which had an eagle's wings
and a lion's body, or of a *basilisk*, which was hatched by a
serpent from a cock's egg and whose glance was fatal, seemed
not incredible. In such a world, it was essential to ward off
evil by supernatural means; so one sought possession of
precious substances like *coral*, to guard against enchantment,
and *chalcedony*, for protection against ghosts and drowning,
or of *sapphire*, to be given the gift of prophecy. With the
devil slavering after one's soul and as real as the man next
door, it was hardly surprising that *demon* and *goblin* should
enter the language, to join the dark *fiend* that was already
there, or that *alchemists*, muttering their incantations over
mysterious *philters* as they sought to turn base metals into
gold, should be held in superstitious awe.

But amidst the superstition were gleams of light that
would, in following centuries, turn full flood. The alchemists,
misdirected as were their efforts, were providing the ground
for scientific study; the word *test* itself comes from Latin
*testa*, "earthen vessel," the name that the alchemists gave,
despite its original earthy meaning, to the metal vessels in
which they made their alloys. Words of art and learning were
coming into the language through French or directly from
Latin, the French words of course coming ultimately from
the Latin. Words like *music, art* itself, *tragedy, poet,* and
*prose*, coming from the French, suggest cultural interests at
least among the upper classes; and direct Latin borrowings
like *prosody, intellect, script, history*, and *metaphysics*, added
to words of science and speculation entering through Arabic
translations, suggest that the stuffy medieval air had some
zesty intellectual currents.

Medieval prosperity reached its climax in the thirteenth
century. By the fourteenth, the manorial pattern of society
was changing, and the social and economic disintegration that
accompanies the breakthrough of a new social system was in
progress. The century was historically one of distress for
England, but, in paradoxical consequence, of tremendous ad-

vance for the English language. The dreary and debilitating Hundred Years' War with France, beginning in 1337 and continuing intermittently until 1453, placed an intolerable burden of taxation on the middle class, focusing resentment toward all things French, including the language. Peasant discontent, which would culminate in 1381 in the Peasants' Revolt, was growing rapidly, with increasing hostility toward the French-speaking upper classes. And then, in mid-century, momentum came from a cruel source; the terrible scourge of the Black Death (in 1349, at least one-third of England's population died in the space of a few months) created a scarcity of labor that gave economic power to the poor and promoted a tremendous rise in the numbers and power of the middle class. Skilled craftsmen as well as common laborers were in desperate demand; so were government administrators, clergy, teachers—no profession was untouched. Inevitably, men not qualified filled the empty places; and because the less well educated spoke only English, business and commerce had to be conducted in that language. The East Midland dialect of London, where the action was, became the accepted standard, although the regional dialects that came of the original Old English divisions endured, and do today.

In the universities, where Latin had been the common language of scholars, the metaphysical discussions that were the passion of the Middle Ages began to be carried on in English; and profound philosophical terms were introduced into the vocabulary. Not only in the universities and monasteries, but also in English villages, where university-trained preachers acquainted their listeners with some of the great abstractions and distinctions of Aristotelian thought, such words and phrases as *ideal* and *intuition, matter* and *form* and *free will* were heard. Wyclif's popular writings and Scriptural translations introduced perhaps a thousand new words into English; and among scholars, such words as *accident* and *absolute, cause* and *essence* and *existence* had their meaning honed in argument, to become the foundation stones of our own philosophical vocabulary. Some would filter into the popular consciousness, to undergo capricious semantic change over the years. *Premises,* a term of logic (Middle English *premisse,* from Latin *praemissus,* past participle of *praemittere,* "to send ahead"), was introduced into legal documents for "the aforesaid"; eventually it came to be used in deeds of equity to mean "the aforesaid houses, lands, or tenements," and by the eighteenth century its origin had been long forgotten—*premises* meant simply real property, that is, land and the buildings upon it.

It was through law, in fact, that much of the philosophical vocabulary—such words as *substance, majority, minority,* and *essence*—was transferred to the language of the people; for it was the lawyer, mediating in civil affairs between scholar and common man, who introduced into the vernacular words useful to both.[7] We use many of the old learned terms casually today; caught on the "horns" of a dilemma, we think little of the challenging *argumentum cornutum* over which scholars agonized. *Quiddity* ("whatness") is a scholastic word, and probably *quandary* also. Certainly the great words like *substance* and *reality* and *identity* and *existence* had not then, nor have they yet, acquired their ultimate meanings; but from the beginning they bore within them the sparks to strike fire in men's minds. If we can imagine the restriction that the lack of these words, and therefore of the concepts they express, would impose on our thinking, we can perhaps appreciate the tremendous contributions of medieval scholarship to our culture. Much of the speculation of the Scholastics, in England as in all of Europe, came to be, by our standards, trivial and irrelevant; but it was through such speculation that the English intellect was trained in abstract thinking and given the verbal tools for intellectual adventure—adventure from which new and daring political philosophies and cultural advances would emerge. Even the most farseeing must stand on the shoulders of the past.

Comparatively, the fifteenth century was a dull, almost list-

7. Smith: *English Language,* p. 187.

less one for the English language. Save for the addition of some Latin "aureate" words—stylistic, artificial, and usually ephemeral borrowings like *diurne, palestral*, and *tenebrous*—plus a number of commercial and maritime terms from the Low Countries which continued to enter unobtrusively, the vocabulary had little notable increase. Curiously, sports made numerous contributions, in terms that we use figuratively today: *to bowl over*, from the game of bowls; *crestfallen*, from the cockpit; *worry*, as dogs do game, from hunting. Their proliferation, in contrast to the paucity of more weighty contributions, suggests an escapism quite expectable after the turbulent events of the preceding century. Then, in 1476, William Caxton introduced the printing press into England, and the language sprang into life. For the first time, books were within the reach of the people; and the demand for them—by 1500, in response to popular demand, twenty-five thousand books had been printed—indicates widespread literacy and enormous eagerness for knowledge (or perhaps, in those simple pre-TV days, sheer delight in reading). The middle class, by now a major element in the political spectrum, was demanding and getting at least a modicum of education for its children, so that at the close of the Middle Ages the number of grammar schools proportionate to population was greater than it would be during Victorian times.[8] England was in readiness for reading the startling news, so soon to come from Spain, of an Italian mariner's Atlantic voyage that allegedly had brought him to the Orient.

For the language, the fifteenth century was largely a time of waiting. As though ready now, expectant, it seemed to be gathering strength for the great challenge of the next century, for expressing the vast explosion of thought and activity that would culminate in the Elizabethan era, that glorious time when Shakespeare would write, when Drake would sail, and when men of many nations would seek riches and adventure in a new-discovered land across the sea.

8. *Encyclopaedia Britannica*, "History of Education."

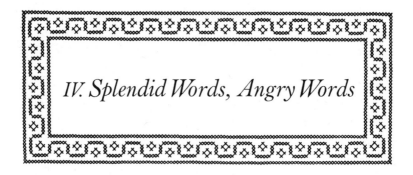

# IV. Splendid Words, Angry Words

*Scalp* meant the top of one's head; it was a noun. The first terrified settler who used it as a verb surely did not think of himself as a maker of language; he was simply naming what no Englishman had ever had to name before—and giving to the vocabulary a word that would drip with bloody history.

Years after the first English settlers came to America, bringing without thought of it their linguistic heritage, James Russell Lowell would quell critics of American speech by saying that "our ancestors, unhappily, could bring over no English better than Shakespeare's," and in so doing would further a popular and continuing illusion. We could say just as informatively that the speech of Churchill's contemporaries was no better than his own. Despite a generous proportion of cultured men among the early settlers, most of the immigrants were humble men, unlettered; and their speech was dialectal and unschooled. Certainly others than Massinger's "condemned wretches . . . strumpets and bawds" and Jonson's "cheating bankrupts" made their way even to Virginia[1] (one

1. A. L. Rowse: *The Elizabethans and America* (London: Macmillan and Co., Ltd.; 1959) points out that many of the English who came early to America had strong ties with intellectual circles in their homeland; see especially the chapter "America in Elizabethan Literature, Science and the Arts," pp. 188 ff. Louis B. Wright: *The Cultural Life of the American Colonies, 1607–1763* (New York: Harper & Bros.; 1957) shows colonial culture as not only existent but even thriving.

thinks of George Sandys, there twenty years, translating the *Metamorphoses* on the banks of the James); but it was hardly the Sandyses and Carrolls, the Winthrops and Saltonstalls who invented such words as *hogwallow* and *kink*, *hoptoad* and *no account* or thought of phrases like *stirring one's stumps* and *happy as a clam* and *noodle-head*. It was, rather, the group that moved John Pory to lament, in 1619, that "in these five months of my continuance here [in Virginia] there have come at one time or another eleven sails of ships into this river, but fraighted more with ignorance than with any other marchansize."[2] Mencken points out that as early as 1628 there was in the area of Boston harbor a whole class of "blackguard roisterers," a motley crew of sailors and artisans and miscellaneous drifters with small reverence for verbal niceties.

The appointed leaders could legislate land rights and, to some extent, overt behavior; the language was beyond their control. Moreover, there were never enough qualified men to perform the necessary administrative and clerical tasks (how like fourteenth-century England!); and as the unfit tried valiantly to serve, they filled early colonial records with evidence of their linguistic struggles. In these records we find numerous misused words, neologisms, and phonetic spellings remarkable even in that relatively freewheeling orthographic age, spellings like *kow ceeper* and *piticler*, *pharme* and *elc*, *engiane* and *injun*. It is unlikely that men so unabashed in meeting *that* challenge would let the mere lack of a word baffle them when new ones were there for the coining. These early Americans may not have known Shakespeare—he would not be accepted at Harvard for a hundred years—but they did have something of his flair.

Had the whole of his vocabulary been theirs, however, it would not have been adequate for this strange new land. Back in England the scenery was easily described; everyone understood such terms as *hill* and *heath*, *meadow* and *moor*. But there were simply no words in the language for these

2. Quoted in H. L. Mencken: *The American Language*, 4th ed. (New York: Alfred A. Knopf; 1936), p. 114.

unending forests, for the vagaries of unpredictable streams, for the land's capricious ways of meeting the sea. And the weather! Just to say *frost* or *snow* told little of the strength of New England cold; *storm* had long lost the force it held in the Germanic forests and gave no hint of the fury spawned in tropic seas. There was a Noah's Ark of animals, too, with no names except the unpronounceable Indian ones, and unfamiliar trees and flowers and new kinds of food, and the startling habits—and habiliments—of the natives. America needed a vocabulary of its own; and these people fresh from the Elizabethan Age, bearing already in their language a rich and diverse heritage, began unaware the task of its creation.

It was the unawareness that would give to the American vocabulary its special quality. The early settlers left England at a time when the language was in full flower, free of inhibition and bold of invention, when *multitudinous* seas could *incarnadine* and men be *stranger'd* with an oath, when friends could be *happied* and enemies *maliced* and new, brash words like *bump* and *bustle* win acceptance in the best literary circles.

An international trend toward the use of the vernacular even in learned writings had coincided with the drift from the Continent of the great humanistic concepts of the Renaissance; and as men of little Latin and less Greek heard of startling ideas in politics and art and education and—most stirringly—religion, they demanded that books about them be written in words that they could read. Since the introduction of the printing press into England in 1476, the reproduction of popular works had given to the people, increasingly literate, a taste for the written word and to the language greater standardization; booksellers, scenting a new market, goaded the scholars to action. "Though, sir," as one told Thomas Drant, "your book [in Latin] be wise and full of learning, yet peradventure it will not be so saleable."[3] The

3. This quotation, and those from Elyot following and from the *Discourse of Warre,* appear in Albert C. Baugh: *A History of the English Language* (New York: Appleton Century Crofts, Inc.; 1957), chap. 8, "The Renaissance," pp. 241–306.

scholars responded with translations of the classics, of the works of Homer and Thucydides, of Plutarch and Cicero, and then of Saint Augustine and of Martin Luther too. Going on to write works of their own, they justified in elaborate apologia to their peers their condescension to popular taste.

After all, wrote Thomas Elyot defensively, "the grekes wrate in greke, the Romans in latine, Avicenna and the other in Arabike, which were their own proper and maternall tongues"—which was all very well; but what did one do when there were no words for what he wished to say? How, for instance, could a writer express succinctly the "manner of governaunce" that "was called in Greke *democratia*, in Latin *popularis potentia*, in Englisshe 'the rule of the comminaltie,' " the last a roundabout phrase indeed? Elyot chose the Greek form and made the English word *democracy*. Or how could technical terms, military and scientific and the like, be expressed in a tongue that had had little occasion to express them? The author of *The Discourse of Warre* stated simply: "I knowe no other names than are given by strangers, because there are fewe or none at all in our language." And how could a scholar to whom a Greek or Latin term conveyed delicate nuances and associations fit all of them into an English word not large enough to carry them? *Ripeness* simply did not mean all that *maturity* did, as Elyot pointed out. Therefore he was "constrained to usurpe a latine worde [which] ones brought in custome, shall be facile to understande . . . reservying the wordes *ripe* and *redy* to frute and other thinges."

Not all words, though, were "facile to understande," even in context; and the earnest innovators patiently explained them. *Circumspection* "signifieth as moche as beholdyne on every parte"; "*industrie* . . . is a qualitie procedyng of witte and experience, by the whiche a man perceyveth quickly, inventeth fresshly, and counsayleth spedily." Not *our* meaning of *industry* (although the term was used also in the sense of diligence); and the difference suggests a caveat for all of us who study words: they do not necessarily mean in one era what they do in another. A change in meaning sometimes offers greater insight into the attitudes of an era than does the appearance of a new word; *influence* and *disaster*, for example, hold none of their astrological meaning now, and *subjective*, today an internalizing word, once meant "existing in itself." Often the learned authors used a self-interpreting synonym to illuminate their meaning, pairing *difficile* with *hard, animate* with *give courage, excerped* with *gathered out of*; later one member of the pair might be discarded as superfluous or, more frequently, the two diverged in meaning, as had other native words and their borrowed synonyms over the years, to provide one of the great excellences of our language—the fine shades of meaning made possible by the presence of such synonyms as *education* and *learning, confidence* and *trust, exhaust* and *tire*.

Even in the sixteenth century, the controversy between purist and innovator had begun; and words like *antique, confidence, contemplate, capacity,* and *native* were derided as "far-fetched," "outlandish," and "fantasticall"—"inkhorn" terms, they were called. The *native* vocabulary, however (what word serves better?), could not contain the great clusters of ideas pouring from the Continent; and other languages were called in to help carry the load. Greek and Latin did the heavy work, Greek usually coming by way of Latin and occasionally French. The Latin vocabulary itself was recruited almost in mass, great and significant words like *jurisprudence, education,* and *scientific* joining simply useful ones like *horrid* and *vast* and *exert* and *irritate*. From Greek through Latin came the expression of many important concepts: *atmosphere, dogma, system, antithesis, climax,* and *crisis,* the last appearing first in connection with disease, then in an astronomical sense, and finally with its present meaning. And from Greek directly, as the renewed study of it led scholars to bypass an intermediary, came *acme* and *catastrophe, lexicon, criterion, tonic,* and other words of equal usefulness. Joining the newcomers, to make the linguistic invasion even more impressive, were the numerous suffixes and prefixes so indispensable today, *-ism* and *-ist* and *-ize* and *anti-* and *de-* and *re-* and *sub-* and *contra-* and all the others that supplement native forms like *-dom* and *-had* (which became *-hood*) and *fore-* and *with-* and *-ness* to help give to the language its great flexibility.

Some of the Latin words made a detour through France, and it is not always easy to identify those that did. The same wholesale enrichment was going on there as in England, and many words were introduced into both countries simultaneously. However, there are clues. *Fact*, we know, represents the Latin *factum* and not French *fait*; for *fait* was already present in the language as *feat*. *Instruct* and *subtract*, if they had come through French, would have entered English as *instroy* (like *destroy*) and *subtray* (like *betray*), rather than in the forms dictated by Latin *instructus* and *subtractus*. *Confisk*, coming from French *confisquer*, competed for a while with *confiscate*, derived from Latin *confiscatus*, but was finally displaced—an illustration of the determination of the genius of the language that one of a pair must go if there is really no shade of difference. *Cohibit*, in like manner, lost out to *inhibit* and *prohibit*, *emacerate* to *emaciate*. Some words had made the trip once before. Chaucer used *declination* and *artificial* in an astronomical sense; sixteenth-century writers borrowed them anew, to be used as we use them today. *Abject* had come over earlier in the sense of cast off or rejected; it came the second time as miserable—a reasonable sequence.

The many French borrowings of the period, *bizarre* and *bombast*, *comrade*, *detail*, *entrance*, *duel*, *vogue* (originally Italian), and *mustache*, suggest increasing travel and trade between France and England in the sixteenth and seventeenth centuries and the influence of French customs and ways on the less polished English. *Genteel*, a new formation from *gentil*, from which *gentle* had been derived long before, referred to dress and manners and behavior rather than to persons; and along with the numerous derivatives of *gentleman—gentlemanlike*, *gentlemanliness*, and even *gentlewo-*

*manlike*—suggests an increasing esteem for elegance and propriety, which was destined to exert marked restraints on the language. English manners and speech, in fact, were acquiring a Continental gloss; as the wealthy traveled through Europe admiring classical architecture and the art of the Renaissance, they gathered up not only art objects and fashions but also verbal souvenirs of their travels. An annoyed Roger Ascham, weary of hearing such un-English terms as *violin* and *stanza* and *grotto* and *trill* and *capricio* (the common form of *caprice* until after the Restoration), as well as Gallicized Italian words like *vogue* and *cavalcade* and *charlatan* and *gazette*, complained in *The Schoolmaster* of all those "Italianated Englishmen" returning from abroad. The Italian influence extended even to the American wilderness; Stefano Guazzo's *Civil Conversations*, a guide to manners, crossed the sea in William Brewster's baggage, introducing Italian expressions and turns of phrase along with etiquette.

So upset were some purists by all the borrowing that they began substituting native equivalents even for foreign words long accepted. They wrote *mooned* for *lunatic, hundreder* for *centurion*. They purged Scripture of alien elements to make *resurrection gainrising* and *parable byword. Foresayer*, they decided (quite rightly), was more honestly English than *prophet*. Poets were particularly fond of old words. *Astound* had been forgotten; so had *doom* and *blameful* and *natheless*, good words all, or so some poet thought. The more venturesome among them, Spenser especially, coined new words congenial in form to the old—*delve* and *squall* and *elfin* and *blatant* and *wrizzled* (wrinkled and shriveled)—and adapted old words or formed derivatives from them to produce such coinage as *baneful* and *briny* and *hapless* and *drear*. Spenser made a slight error in reviving *derring-do*—it had been a verbal phrase in Chaucer's day, but he made it a noun; it is difficult today to imagine it as anything else. And although some of the purists found such "Chaucerisms" objectionable and criticized the poets for trying to revive so foolishly an "old rustick language," surely none of us would do away with products of the back-to-English movement like *glee* and *glance* and *birthright, grovel* and *shady* and *belt.*

At least for a time, the fuming of the critics was in vain; some of them absent-mindedly used the words themselves. Thomas Nash berated Gabriel Harvey for his obscurities and found himself convicted of—among other remarkable phrases —*sillogistrie, disputative finicallitie,* and *infringement to destitute the inditement.* Scholar and Everyman alike found the minting of new terms too much fun to give up, and the coining was still going merrily on as New World colonists set out to cross the sea. Elizabethan Englishmen all, they would bring with them a way with words destined to set permanently the pattern of American word-making, a way that in a new and spacious world would be given undreamed-of stimulus and freedom to expand. Had the first settlers left England earlier or later, had they learned their speechways and their attitudes, linguistic and otherwise, in a different time, our language—like our nation—would be a different thing. But they came of that marvelous era in which the English vocabulary gained some twelve thousand words from over fifty languages and developed unparalleled richness and flexibility, in which the number of words alone tells of the enormous activity going on in every field of human experience, in which the variety of sources indicates the freer intercourse among nations, the expansion of trade, the increase in learning, and the extension of empire that marked the period. The content of the words and their scope show clearly the spirit of the age, a tumultuous and questing spirit which inevitably had to affect all men not insulated from their time and so, forever, the American experience and the way in which Americans would tell of it.

Logan Pearsall Smith, in *The English Language,* comments on the "mental atmosphere" of each epoch that makes certain thoughts, and therefore their expression, current and possible, others impossible.[4] The word *skepticism* appearing

4. (New York: Henry Holt and Company; 1912), p. 215.

in a medieval manuscript would brand it a forgery; *self-conscious* had to await the introspection of modern times. It is this mental atmosphere that gives meaning and pattern to historical events, to the wars and revolutions and crusades and reforms that mark a period; and without awareness of what that atmosphere contains, we grope blindly for an understanding of the whole.

In the mental atmosphere of that tremendous sixteenth century, a new and startling idea, the idea of *progress*, was emerging and changing the meaning of terms already in the language. Never earlier do we find with their present meaning words that express a concept of progressive forward change (even the Reformation reveals in its own name a medieval orientation, the ideal of a return to some primitive and uncorrupted state)—words such as *advancement*; *progress* as verb and noun, with its derivatives *progressive* and *progression*; *improve*; *improvement*. Until that time (and how incredible to us here, now), there were no words—in any language—for the notion of continuous improvement as we understand it. Only during the sixteenth century did the word *advancement*, which had been used variously since the thirteenth century with such meanings as forwarding in motion or promotion in rank, come to be used for "the helping forward of anything in process, toward completion or perfection . . . furtherance, promotion, improvement," the first recorded instance of its use occurring in More's *Utopia* in 1551.[5] The noun *progress* had been used earlier for a procession or a journey, for "forward motion"; but not until Elizabethan times did it acquire the sense of growth or development (*development* itself was waiting in the wings). As a verb, *progress* became common in England by 1590 and was used by both Bacon and Shakespeare; it soon disappeared, however, until its reintroduction from America in the nineteenth century. *Improve*, which meant in earlier centuries to

5. *Oxford English Dictionary.* Unless otherwise noted, definitions, datings, and illustrative quotations for words appearing initially in England are taken throughout from the *OED*.

enclose or cultivate wasteland and "to invest," or even "to re-
prove," was acquiring the meaning of "to make better"; *improvement* (its meaning of betterment only gradually sep-
arable from the sense of beneficial cultivation) was established
in its modern sense by the time the seventeenth century began.

To Smith, this concept of progress is "perhaps, the most
essential difference between our view of the world and that of
the Greeks and Romans." Only when the great force of the
Renaissance had opened that small box of the medieval universe, in which life was static and human destiny prescribed,
did the daring, almost frightening idea that life was open-
ended enter Western minds, to offer a vista both of freedom
and of terrifying individual responsibility—*individual*, too,
having acquired a new and even awesome significance.

The term *individual* (from *individuum*, an indivisible par-
ticle or atom) was originally introduced by medieval theo-
logians in reference to the Trinity; philosophers used it to
mean simply "a member of a species." In the late sixteenth
century, however, first as adjective and then as noun, it came
to refer to human beings as separate and unique; Bacon
used it in such a sense in *The Advancement of Learning*. "As
touching the manners of learned men," he wrote, "it is a
thing personall and individuall."[6] The concept of "I," of
"myself," like the concept of historical development, is relatively new in the history of human thought; emerging as
it did in conjunction with the idea of progress and with
Protestant emphasis on the individual's role as hearer and
interpreter of the Word, it had a tremendous effect on the
thinking of Englishmen in many areas, not least in that of
language. If an individual had a right to interpret the Word
of God, it was only reasonable, surely, that he had the
authority to change the words of men. Religious and political
independence may have been more important concepts historically; but linguistic independence, traveling with them, was
part of the pattern, too.

6. *Works*, ed. J. Spedding, R. L. Ellis, and D. D. Heath, 14 vols. (London: Longman & Co.; 1857–74), vol. I, chap. 3, ¶4.

That *dissent* should enter the language concomitantly with *individual* and *progress* seems inevitable. Tindale used *dissent* in his sixteenth-century religious writings in the verbal and literal sense of "to feel apart." By century's end, both the verb and the noun, which had followed soon after, were applied to the seething religious differences of the time; and because religious dissension paralleled disputes between Parliament and the Crown, both were politicalized. Projected into action by Puritans, who bypassed constitutional precedent to initiate Parliamentary legislation, the developing concept was the opening wedge of a force that would eventually crack the royal power. And almost side by side with *dissent*, in ominous portent, the word *revolt* worked its way into the vocabulary. First used as a verb by Elyot in 1548, it embraced by 1560 the idea that unwilling subjects will rise against their rulers;[7] and the derivatives *revolter, revolting*, and *revolted*, following quickly, illustrated Smith's dictum that one of the best tests of the importance of a word in a given period is the number of compounds and derivatives formed from it.[8] By 1600, *revolution*, which had been an astronomical term in the fourteenth century and in the fifteenth meant also a "turning over in one's mind" or "a great change," had come to mean complete overthrow of the established government or the forcible substitution of a new one. Here, surely, is a classic example of the correlation between the developing vocabulary of a people and the mental atmosphere in which their history unfolds; for in sixteenth-century England, religious and political movements, like the companion words *dissent* and *revolt*, traveled together.

The new philosophy was reflected in an enormous increase in political terms telling of the broadening base of politics. *Politician; political; politics* itself; *legislator; citizenship; franchise*, in the sense of full citizenship; *parliamentary; public*, meaning public-spirited—all entered the vocabulary

7. "Al men . . . bycause they served against their wylles . . . do revolte." Sleidanus: *Commentaries*, trans. Daws.

8. Smith: *English Language*, p. 217.

during this era, to suggest a tremendous advance in public awareness of civic processes. We must beware, however, of interpreting words in the light of our own mental atmosphere; although the middle class was becoming politically active, it would be long before the idea would grow that all men—even those, as Winthrop wrote, of "the inferior class"—should participate in government (and another three hundred years before women would follow *them*). The successful merchant class was the only one gaining power and influence, its voice remarkably amplified by its wealth, which the Crown was most eager to share. *Burgher* had originally meant merely the resident of a *burg*, or fortified town, and later—as *burgess* would continue to mean—a voting citizen; now it identified a member of the growing urban middle class, whose emergence was to change the history of the Western world. (In later years, its relatives, *bourgeois* and *bourgeoisie,* would help to stock the dialectal arsenal of Karl Marx.) As exchange with other countries made available such visible symbols of affluence as *Turkey carpets* and *brocades* and—effete invention—*stockings,* the "rich Bergers"[9] were more and more set apart from the *populace,* a word only recently borrowed from Italian *popolaccio* and used in the derogatory sense of "mob" or "rabble," especially by prosperous citizens disturbed by a sullen undertone increasingly audible under the busy hum of trade.

A growing commercial vocabulary told of economic developments responsible for this greater division between classes. Until mid-century, the English language included few such terms; *commerce* itself is not recorded until 1587, the old word *merchandising* (from Old French *marcheandise*) serving very well for the local trading that was the business of most English merchants. Save for the trade, principally in wool, of the Merchant Adventurers and the Merchant Staplers, international commerce was left to the Lombards, the Jews, and the Hanseatic League. But as new trading

9. "Your Argosies . . . like Signiors and rich Bergers on the flood." Shakespeare: *The Merchant of Venice,* act 1, sc. 1, line 10.

routes opened distant markets early in the sixteenth century, the prospect of extensive international trade (and the desperate need for it—Spain's enormous wealth from Aztec and Inca mines was shaking the economy of Europe) set merchants and monarchs to dreaming. *Joint stock companies,* after the Dutch model, were given royal charters for exploration of the New World; and the language used in the charters would be echoed in American political developments. Often referred to as *bodies politic* or *nations,* these *corporations* were delegated to make laws, to compel obedience, and to impose taxes in whatever *plantations,* or "colonies,"[1] they should establish in their assigned territories. When one considers that the voting stockholders were called *freemen,* it becomes clear why Charles Beard could say, in *The Rise of American Civilization,* that every essential element found in later American state government was present in the chartered corporation.

*Capital* and *contract,* already in the language as legal and diplomatic terms, became specifically commercial; and *incorporation* was extended to the document creating or legalizing a company, one such as the leaders of the Massachusetts Bay Colony would make the basis of their government. The term *monopoly,* coined by Sir Thomas More, had acquired over the years a pejorative connotation because of royal favoritism; but since the developing struggle for the world market demanded regulation, it regained status and its derivatives proliferated. *Monopolist, monopolitan, monopolize, monopolizer* entered the vocabulary within the space of a few years. Even more illustrative of the spirit of the times was the new word *venture,* used as verb and noun. Applied initially to

1. *Plantation* meant, until late in the seventeenth century, quite literally "a planting." Hooker wrote of "the plantation of a Commonwealth" in 1586, Bacon of "the plantation of the faith" in 1605. At the time of American colonization, the word meant "a settlement in a new or conquered country," as in Hobbes: *Leviathan* (1655): "Those we call plantations, or colonies." *Planter* followed the same pattern, and in the early seventeenth century meant "colonist."

cargo sent abroad (*adventurer* once meant simply merchant), it soon acquired the sense of risk and daring, a not surprising development in the era of Hawkins and Raleigh and Drake, when men muttered the new Spanish word *imbargo* and defied its prohibitions to smuggle pearls and slaves and other *contraband* into and out of West Indian ports. *Contraband* was thought of primarily in relation to Spain; but the term came from Italian *contrabbando*, combining Latin *contra-* with a word of venerable etymology, *bannus, bannum*, "decree," ultimately traceable through Germanic to Indo-European *bhā-*, "to speak." *Contraband* was less a catchword after 1587, when the Armada was gloriously defeated and the seaways to America became English lanes. Then, as merchants embarked on new *ventures* and *commerce* flourished, a mania for trading infected even the stay-at-homes, so that "the very air was charged with schemes for growing rich";[2] and the English language set out, along with the ambitious and resourceful men who spoke it, to meet the challenge of a new environment.

What was the climate in which such terms as *individual* and *progress, venture* and *dissent* expressed the spirit of the times?

In the language itself, the climate is easily discerned, a climate of excitement and turmoil. There is poetry in the words now introduced. Like Wyatt's "Andalusian merchant that returns Laden with cochineal and china dishes," travelers and traders came from far places with evocative new terms. Far-voyaging Dutchmen coming from Malaya, Flemish traders bringing from Mediterranean ports exotic products of Persia and Cathay, English adventurers importing hides and sugar and ginger and pearls from the "Western Inde"—all brought new words, new excitement. Through the Spanish and Portuguese came strange words from West Indian languages, from Arawak and Taino—*cannibal* and *hammock* and *canoe* and *barbecue* and *maize*, as well as words they themselves made, *alligator* and *pickanninny*, the latter coming from the West In-

2. Charles and Mary Beard: *The Rise of American Civilization* (New York: The Macmillan Company; 1930); p. 42.

dian pronunciation of *pequenino.* The lovely *breeze,* from *briza,* for the northeast trade winds, was picked up by John Hawkins and his crew along the Spanish Main. Old World words came too: Malayan *bamboo* and *gong* and *cockatoo,* the last from Dutch; *catamaran* and *calico* from India; *harem* from Arabia, and *monsoon,* too, after a journey through Portuguese and Dutch. Spanish accounts of explorations in America told of lands where exotic plants were to be found: *sassafras,* said to be a notable remedy for syphilis, a disease reportedly brought back from America by Columbus's crew; *tobacco,* a plant smoked by the natives and said to cure a variety of ills; the *potato,* not only a marvelous aphrodisiac but tasty besides.

*Discovery* was a new word, a clarion word. Hakluyt used it in 1553 in his *Voyages,* telling of a "voyage intended for the discovery of Cathay and divers other regions." The verb *discover,* which had earlier meant simply to reveal or uncover, became a word that conjured visions, as did the new *discoverer*—Hakluyt's again. Seas never before known, islands undreamed of, a different earth—all had entered the awareness of mankind within the century and created an insatiable demand for books of travel and of speculation. Maps were drawn on the basis of what was known or simply guessed; the Flemish geographer Mercator published a collection of maps that had as a frontispiece a picture of Atlas, and men thereafter called all such collections *atlases.* There was new interest in history, evident not only in the popularity of historical literature but in derivative words like *historical* and *historiographer.* And if not all could read the new books, they could at least pack the pit of the Globe theater and hear Tamburlaine and Henry V speak their glorious lines.

But not all was romance. Other new words tell of the intellectual and religious ferment spilling over into England from the Continent. Before mid-century, Copernicus had upset the foundations of the old, stationary world that was the center of the universe; by its end, Kepler, Tycho Brahe, and Galileo were doing their disturbing work, impudently studying the heavens. The word *universe* referred to a new kind of cosmos, one of immutable order unaffected by magic or divine interference. The word *order* itself, a Middle English borrowing from French, which had meant earlier a monastic group or the heavenly hierarchy or even some kind of fixed arrangement, was now important enough to generate derivatives; *orderliness* and *orderly* appeared, and—the antithesis that testifies to the force of an idea—*disorder*. The pervasiveness of the concept augured the development of the rationalist philosophy that would culminate in the Enlightenment.

Modern science drew its first weak breaths, expressed in words like *analyze* and *investigate* and *distinguish,* in *observation* used in a genuinely scientific sense (*scientific,* as has been noted, was itself new), and in words like *tenacity* and *texture* and *temperature* to describe the properties of matter. Francis Bacon, introducing his inductive method of analysis, tried unsuccessfully to alter the meaning of *axiom* from "a self-evident proposition" to "a proposition established by means of experimental deduction";[3] *experiment* entered the language, with *experimental, experimentally,* and *experimenter* soon joining it.

*Cosmographer* was used as early as 1549, at first synonymously with *geographer* and then in the sense of one who studies earth and the heavens too; *cosmographical* and *cosmographer* were in use before 1600. The bewildering extension of their world made many people uneasy. The idea of unchanging cosmic order was in some ways comforting; but in an unfamiliar, suddenly wall-less universe, what was the meaning of the old familiar words—*up, down, space, the heavens, sky? Earth* itself? What did the new word *atmosphere* mean? Evidently Aristotle had not known everything after all; neither had Saint Thomas. *Dubious, skeptic, skeptical* entered the vocabulary.

Because greater precision of knowledge demanded and brought greater precision of language, the wealth of new

3. Owen Barfield: *History in English Words* (London: Methuen and Co., Ltd.; 1926), p. 134.

words often put the reader at a disadvantage. Sir Thomas
More had recognized the need for explanation of his vocabulary innovations and used the word *define* in relation to words
as early as 1532. Fifty years later, Richard Mulcaster was suggesting the compilation of a *dictionary* of English words
(*dictionary* had referred earlier only to glossaries used in the
study of Latin). Not until 1604, however, did Robert
Cawdrey's *The Table Alphabeticall of Hard Words,* containing some three thousand terms, appear; and the idea that
the entire vocabulary should be so presented would not develop until the next century.

Eagerness for information brought into use another word,
*encyclopaedia.* Elyot introduced it in 1531; "the circle of
doctrine," he wrote, "is in one worde of greke Encyclopedia."
From then on, many book titles contained the word, though
in limited application; and in the early 1600's, the first en-
cyclopaedias as we know them were published. By then, even
Elyot might have been surprised (although—maybe not) by
how much the "circle of doctrine" embraced and by the
extent of the vocabulary to which he had added so much;
certainly the new *freak, chirrup, flout,* and *squall* were not his
style. Other words were, though, especially literary terms.
Most of these came from Greek or Latin, often through
French; and words like *lyric, epic, blank verse,* and *essay*
suggest that the form of literature, as well as its content, had
become interesting. Serious criticism began, based for the
most part on Aristotle's *Poetics*; and *critic,* which had earlier
been used, like *critical,* in relation to disease, became a noun
and took on new meaning. For one pronouncing judgment,
the word appeared first in 1588; and by 1606 its literary context had become paramount. "Take heed of criticks," wrote
Thomas Dekker in 1606; "they bite, like fish, at anything,
especially at bookes." Sir Philip Sydney's *Apologie for Poesie*
and works by other authors struck the first light critical blows;
from then on, poets and playwrights and writers of histories
and etymologies would have to take their lumps.

Nowhere, however, was the critical and questioning spirit

of the time shown more clearly than in the vocabulary of theology. Martin Luther had nailed his theses to the doors at Wittenburg in 1517; since that time, swirling currents of doctrinal dispute had generated a multiplicity of new terms. From 1529, when the formal *Protestatio* was handed in by the German dissenters following the Diet of Spires and the word *Protestant* came to England, group labels alone made up a précis of contemporary religious history. *Separatist, Puritan, Presbyterian, Romanist, Lutheran*—each had its doctrine, each its grievance, each its goal. (*Protestant* itself was not used as a sectarian designation until its adoption by the *Protestant* Episcopal church in America in the nineteenth century.) *Scripture*, subject of acrimony, spawned an extraordinary number of derivatives; *Scriptural, Scriptureless, Scripturian,* and *Scripturing* were in the vocabulary before the end of the sixteenth century, and *Scripturely* appeared soon after. *Dogma*, meaning a system of belief, came to the language through Latin, from Greek *dokein*, "to think," as did *dogmatist*, for "a propounder of new doctrine," and the adjective *dogmatical*. By the turn of the century, so abrasive and ubiquitous had the subject of dogma become that two pejorative derivatives joined them, *dogmatize* and *dogmatism*.

The religious orientation of the times was reflected in innumerable other words. *Evangelical* and *sincere* were much used by Protestants in referring to their doctrine; *godly* and *godliness* were popular, too, and *godless,* for the doctrines of others. *Piety* was gradually differentiated from *pity,* with which it had been synonymous, and acquired a religious sense; *ethics* came to be used for "a system of morals"; and *religion* itself, which had formerly applied to conduct or to the practice of external observances, took on a modern, subjective meaning as a system of belief or opinion. The greater subjectivity shown by this semantic change carried over into other aspects of life and reflected the further development of that "internalization" which had begun during the late Middle Ages. *Self* became for the first time a compounding element; Shakespeare used *self-love* and *self-neglecting* in

*Henry V*;[4] other *self-* words, like *self-regard, self-liking, self-assurance,* entered the language. (Surely Freud stirred in the shadows ahead!) *Duty* acquired the abstract connotation of obligation to oneself, an idea implicit even in the new meaning of *gentleman.*

If the proliferation of religious and moral terms does not sufficiently limn the period, it is given vivid portrayal in the words used by religious people for abusing other religious people. Anger looses the tongues of men in wondrous ways; and in the diatribes exchanged between Catholic and Protestant, between *Church-and-King* man and *Puritan,* pious writers and preachers outdid themselves in name-calling. We can hear the thunderous tones of the times in such new words as *pernicious* and *bigotry, factious* and *malignant* and *libertine,* the last originally meaning "freedman" but now given an invidious meaning. *Dunce* was a scornful parody of the once revered name of Duns Scotus, the Scholastic philosopher; *duncely* and *duncery* came from it. *Reprobate* was a Calvinist term for rejected and therefore damned souls, that is, all those not of the Calvinist persuasion. *Papish* and *monkish, Romish, bigoted, monkery* and *popery* and *popeling,* like the eloquent and popular *whore of Babylon,* carried the self-righteous wrath of churchly men. *Puritan* was at first a term of reproach and was resented, although *Puritanism* was used seriously as early as 1573 for the system of reforms proposed; *Puritanic, Puritanical,* and *Puritanize* were all meant to insult, as they still are. *Atheism,* defined as "utter godlessness," was introduced, and *atheist* and *atheistical* soon followed; evidently, however, Christian was too busy fighting Christian to have much energy left for fighting the common enemy.

In all of these words we can feel with greater impact than in mere historical statements the hatreds and antagonisms that accompanied the religious confrontations of that day; we can better understand how inevitably the bitter conflicts carried on in the name of God were transported to the new

4. "Self-love, my liege, is not so vile a sin as self-neglecting." Act 2, sc. 3, line 11.

land which was in theory a haven from them. And we see that not only did the old words *witch, witchmark, witchcraft,* and related words remain ominously prominent in the contemporary vocabulary, but new derivatives, *witchery* and *witched* and *witchmonger* (one who deals with witches) and *witch-knot,* joined them, as did the dread *witch-finder.*

And yet—from this era too comes the stunning new concept expressed in the phrase *liberty of conscience,* which appeared in the *Catholic Tract* of J. Hay in 1580. The concept was too startling to be taken quite seriously, and the first settlers left it behind; but it was there waiting, soon to be picked up in the great stream of English thought flowing continuously to the shores of America. For the first time, too, the vocabulary made a distinction between *civil* and *ecclesiastical* jurisdiction. Small currents these, but with torrents to follow.

Religious feeling played its part in another contemporary phenomenon that in itself had much to do with the vigor of the language—a rise in national feeling. Prior to the sixteenth century, words of patriotism were notably lacking in English speech; even *nation* referred to a people or a class rather than to the inhabitants of a geographical or political unit. During the Middle Ages and beyond, dynastic claims recognized no geographical boundaries—Hapsburg, Bourbon, and Tudor alike might claim territory in France or the Netherlands, Spain or Italy; and the universal dominion of the Church of Rome made subordinate even the authority of kings. Now, however, the word *national* appeared, as did *patriot, compatriot, fellow countryman,* and *mother country,* the last a term that William Bradford would use touchingly in his letters from Plymouth. *Country,* which had earlier, like *nation,* had only a neutral connotation, acquired the sense of a political unit deserving of one's loyalty. The strength of the concept appeared in the plays and other literature of the period—in Hotspur's "To weepe over his country's wrongs,"[5] and in the conjunction of *patriot* and *country* in Ben Jon-

5. Shakespeare: *Henry IV,* part I, act 4, sc. 3, line 85.

son's *Volpone,* which crystallized the sentiment of the time in the line "Such as were known patriots, Sound lovers of their country."[6]

That pride in language should follow pride in country was inevitable; emotional attachment to one's own tongue has ever been—and is, as we are forcibly reminded in today's contentious world—inextricably related to national identification. Richard Mulcaster, Elizabethan champion of English as a proper language of learning, expressed the growing national feeling thus: "I love Rome, but London better, I favor Italie, but England more, I honor the Latin, but I worship the English."

The colonists, leaving for America, were hardly conscious of such lofty sentiments; English was simply the language one spoke. Because they were Elizabethan Englishmen, creative, adaptive, activist, and imaginative, they quickly set about fitting into that language whatever was needed to serve their needs. That they were introducing innovations which their stay-at-home cousins would later label barbarisms, or that the speech they used so cavalierly and with such rough affection was, with them, beginning a diversionary course, was far from their thoughts. Their only concern was to meet the challenge offered by a new environment and by a way of life beyond any Englishman's earlier imaginings; and they met it verbally as they met it physically, head on.

6. Act 4, sc. 1.

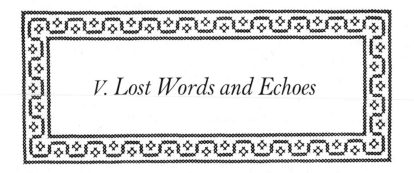

# V. Lost Words and Echoes

"Such a term as *rubberneck*," wrote H. L. Mencken in *The American Language*, "is almost a complete treatise on American psychology; it reveals the national habit of mind more clearly than any labored inquiry could ever reveal it."[1] Graphic and unforgettable, it is a democratic word. There are rubbernecks in the Louvre.

From the beginning of settlement, Englishmen who came to America used language to bring their world to terms. Perhaps because only the less conservative came, perhaps because those "new circumstances" of which Jefferson was to speak demanded expression, perhaps simply because they left England before the climate of restraint set in, these early settlers began at once a bold linguistic assault on their environment. There were few scholars in the wilderness, no sobersides to remind them that the *toothache tree* was a prickly ash or that the *bobcat* was a lynx. With some ancient awareness that to name is to have power, they took possession of the land.

It is difficult to think in terms of "arrested development" of a language in which thousands of inventions have been reliably identified, in which ever-changing meanings and countless new forms tell of continuing vitality, in which the present, like the past, finds turbulent expression. But some

1. 4th ed. (New York: Alfred A. Knopf; 1937), p. 92.

have done so, and not merely the carping critics earlier noted. Many years after those early controversies, when extensive linguistic studies had made possible an analysis of the American vocabulary, scholarly commentators offered unexpected ammunition to its critics. With serene inattention to the vocabulary explosion already taking place in America, and even as Westernisms and industrial terms were enriching the language, the respected scholar J. F. Lonnsbury commented: "The colloquial speech of the educated class in America is to some extent archaic. . . . A tongue carried from one land to another, and keeping up no communication with the tongue of the mother country, undergoes what is technically called an arrest of development. . . . In [the changes occurring in the parent language] the transported speech does not share. It clings to the vocabulary with which it started; and as regards the terms constituting it, and the meanings given them, it is apt to remain stationary."[2] Perhaps if Lonnsbury had not assumed, as he evidently did, that at some time the English in America had "no communication with the tongue of the mother country," he would not have slipped American speech so neatly into the slot marked "isolated languages." Still, his contemporary, M. Schele De Vere, of the University of Virginia, had the same opinion. "The largest part of so-called Americanisms," De Vere wrote, "are nothing more than good old English words."[3] And even Lowell's repeatedly quoted remark defending American speech as Shakespearean implies the retention of old words and ways.

To the last two, at least, the argument of archaism was an argument for merit; pointing triumphantly to prior use by Shakespeare, Chaucer, Gower, Bunyan, Sydney, they defended the legitimacy of such words as *guess* and *homely, greenhorn, daft,* and *flapjack*. They and their allies were reacting to the

2. *The International Magazine* (May 1880). Quoted in George Philip Krapp: *The English Language in America* (New York: The Century Co.; 1925), vol. 1, p. 50.
3. *Americanisms: The English of the New World* (New York: Chas. Scribner & Co.; 1872), p. 427.

still active criticism of American "barbarisms," that collection of bêtes noires which in retrospect seems so singularly small. (All of the criticisms belabor *lengthy* and *belittle, advocate* and *antagonize, plunder,* for baggage, and the universal *clever* and *fix* in Xerox-like repetition.)

Seizing upon the theme that what was good enough for Shakespeare should be honored in the language, the defenders suggested that, in abandoning linguistic treasures, it was the English themselves who were doing the language a disservice. As evidence they cited lines from English writers, the great and the not so great. They countered the *Athenaeum's* denunciation of *magnetic* as a "useless and objectionable Americanism" with Donne's line "She that had all magnetic force alone"; in defense of *mad* for angry or wild, that "vile Americanism," they offered Middleton's "I was mad at him" and Pepys's "Thence by coach with a mad coachman, that drove like mad." *Chore,* they pointed out, was simply Shakespeare's *chare,* as in ". . . the maid that milks / and does the meanest chares . . . ," not only having honorable antecedents in Old English *cierr,* "a piece of work," but also surviving in British *charwoman.* Shakespeare also used *deck* for a pack of cards; *sick* as Americans used it, in the sense of British *ill; flapjacks* (as did Langland in *Piers Plowman*); and the verb *to sag,* whose lost preterit form, *I sog,* was the source of the much criticized "Americanism" *soggy. Scrawny* was simply Milton's *scrannel,* coming through the intermediate *scranny;* and *guess,* so roundly condemned, appeared not only in Shakespeare but also in Chaucer, for Emila's "yellow heer was broyded in a tresse Bihynde her bak, a yerde long, I guess."

Further evidence of legitimacy was presented. Many of the terms that had been disparagingly called Americanisms for a hundred years were still in use in isolated parts of Britain; obviously, therefore, they were not brash new words but respectable old ones. *Skedaddle* and *cantankerous* and *misery* (for bodily pain) still functioned vigorously in Wiltshire, in Ayrshire, in Suffolk. Exactly! cried the critics, rubbing their hands; American speech, save perhaps in Boston, was—like

America itself—provincial. Even in Shakespeare's time, perhaps by Shakespeare himself—who knew?—such provincialism had been condemned by the literati. The sixteenth-century critic George Puttenham had decreed: "Our writer, therefore, in these days shall not follow Piers the Plowman, nor Gower, nor Lydgate, nor yet Chaucer, for their language is now out of use with us; neither yet shall he take the terms of Northmen. . . . He shall, therefore, take the usual speech of the Court, and that of London, and the shires lying about London, within sixty miles and not much above." (Swift and his fellow arbiters, we see, were following a dictatorial tradition.) In the controversy, no one seemed to note how remarkably the definition of provincialism depended upon geography; had *treacle* and *draughts* and *draper* been retained in America and not in England, they, too, would have been considered archaic. The arguments seemed to prove only that in any language, in any place, some words will be kept, some not.

Even as critics and scholars continued the debate about the merits of survivals and provincialisms, their investigations produced serendipitous discoveries inspiring research in other directions. If certain dialectal forms were current in certain colonial areas, conclusions concerning the regional origin of the settlers, and hence of American speech, might be reached. Documentary evidence was slight, and there were almost as many theories as there were scholars. Webster had maintained that New England speech originated in southern England, a belief that would be largely confirmed by later scientific studies. John Russell Bartlett held, with some reason, that the major speech patterns emanated from the north of England. De Vere held that the earlier Pilgrim influences were northern and western but that later settlers from the eastern counties brought to America both their regional vocabulary and "a sound of the voice and mode of utterance" which produced the "New England drawl." That drawl, claims De Vere, is nothing but the well-known Norfolk "whine." Some authorities pointed to Essex as the source of colonial speech in New

England, citing such specifically Essexian survivals as *pesky* and *snicker* and *scrimp;* others favored Kent. Sir William Craigie, whose conclusions in the 1920's were based on studies more scientific than the earlier ones, identified Yorkshire and Lincolnshire, East Anglia, and the southwestern counties of England as its probable source.[4]

Few seemed concerned with the speech of the still earlier settlers of Virginia, where speechways were much the same as in New England; but the surveys begun in 1936 by teams gathering material for the *Linguistic Atlas of the United States and Canada,* under the direction of Dr. Hans Kurath of Brown University, pushed investigations beyond the New England area into other early-settled regions. These findings led Dr. Kurath to point to the speech of settlers from the southern and southeastern counties of England as the most influential in shaping American speechways both in New England and along the Virginia seaboard, with the speech of southeastern England dominant in both areas.[5] However, as George Philip Krapp maintains in *English Language in America,* we cannot with safety—on the basis of a comparison of contemporary dialects—draw definitive conclusions concerning the relations of British and American dialects three hundred years ago. We *can* conclude from the available evidence that the speech of most of the early colonists was standardized English of the seventeenth century, with regional variations. Those whose speech was markedly dialectal soon conformed to the prevailing pattern, contributing, as they did so, their more tenacious terms to the general vocabulary.

The search for the regional genesis of American speech patterns as well as of the colonists themselves has been pursued in other directions too. Genealogical studies tracing the English origins of families settled in various parts of America have been fragmentary at best; but a study of 685 persons re-

4. *The Study of American English.* Society for Pure English, Tract No. 27 (1927), p. 201.

5. *Word Geography of the Eastern United States* (Ann Arbor: University of Michigan Press; 1949), p. 3.

siding in the towns of Plymouth, Watertown, and Dedham in
1652—a probable sampling—suggests that for the roots of
the speech of eastern Massachusetts, at least, we can look to
the eastern dialects of England. A study of place names in
Connecticut—a method found useful in tracing Roman
occupation in early Britain—indicates that a majority of the
settlers were from the southeastern counties, and in lesser
degree from the southwestern, Midland, and northeastern
regions of England. Still another interesting approach is that
of historical deduction.[6] East Anglia, as the principal center
of Puritanism in England, undoubtedly contributed most of
the early colonists; and as they moved south and westward
during the seventeenth century, their speech patterns would
have spread with them throughout New England and into
eastern New Jersey and New York. Pennsylvania, on the
other hand, was settled by Quakers, whose center of activity
and whose range of influence in England were largely in the
north and west; settlement therefore brought northern and
western dialectal forms into that colony. Indeed, a number of
northern English survivals, *dansy* (failing from old age),
*threap* (to argue, to contend), and *smouch* (to salute or kiss)
were noted at an early date as peculiar to Pennsylvania. None
of these approaches has been fully exploited, but in all of
them the role of archaisms as a strong link in the chain of
evidence is clear.

The recognition of this great store of archaisms seemed to
confirm Lonnsbury's thesis of a "stationary" language. If the
American language was in fact "clinging" to the vocabulary
extant at the time of emigration, it was in danger of being
caught in a still water while British English flowed vigorously
past it, outworn terms floating in the backwash. Undeniably,
though, *new* terms had been added to the vocabulary in
America, whether or not they were accepted in England;
obviously, not all the Americanisms cited by critics from
Witherspoon on—*snappish* and *happify, suability, notions,*

6. Thomas Pyles: *Words and Ways of American English* (New York:
Random House; 1952), pp. 56–9.

and *breadstuffs,* for example—were survivals. Jefferson had even accused the inhospitable British tongue of being "stationary" itself for not accepting them. Additions alone, however, would not invalidate the concept of a backward vocabulary with old terms clinging to it like moss.

Then a study of colonial records and other early texts yielded a surprising finding: not only had many seventeenth-century words become obsolete *in* America; some of them, like *tilsom* and *earebred,* had become so obscured that later scholars would have difficulty in reconstructing their meaning. The American language, too, had been racing along, casting aside what was no longer needed, picking up what was, offering its own testimony that, in any living language, terms that are needed only in a certain phase of social or cultural development disappear as that phase passes, suggesting also that, in any given period, the prominence of certain classes of words (for example, topographical, sociological, scientific) reflects dominant social or cultural aspects of that time. It is apparent, then, that for a truly comprehensive insight into the mental atmosphere of an earlier era, obsolete words—wherever retrievable—must be considered along with surviving innovations. In our early colonial records we find a wealth of both.

Reference to land and property transactions is commonplace in public records, but the preponderance of new land-related terms during colonial times confirms the historically attested obsession with land that, for at least two centuries, set the direction of American development. It was the promise of land that brought the first settlers to America; it was the dream of it that inspired later migration; it was possession of it that gave political and economic power.

Where fertile land was scarce and precious, as in New England, the land hunger of these early days was most vividly reflected. *Meadow,* as it came from England, had meant simply grassland annually mowed for hay; the colonists called such grassland *mowing ground* and used *meadow* for those fertile areas, scattered and small and making up only about one-fifth of the available land, which promised rich return.

*Meadow land* was more valuable than house land and worth twice as much as *upland,* where the pesky New England rocks were strewn; like their Anglo-Saxon forebears of centuries earlier, therefore, New England colonists settled first on the rich and fertile land along the river systems. Unlike the colonists of Virginia, where the uniformly rich ground allowed wide dispersal, they clustered around those scarce meadows like bees on a hive, keeping their communities compact and so creating the towns. "The meadow," quotes James Truslow Adams, in *The American,*[7] "was the lifeblood of each New England settlement. . . . These rugged states must be seen in the light of those innumerable spots of vivid green, spots only large enough for a limited number of families in which each one could have an anchorage." *Meadow lots,* a new-coined term, were the most desired, *meadowish land* next. *Meadowish,* an example of the vocabulary's ability to draw fine distinctions, had been coined by 1668, when the Springfield records note that "the Town granted unto Abell Wright fourteen acres of Meddowish Land up the Little River."[8] Derivative words accumulated; combinations now obsolete, like *thatch meadow* and *white meadow, wild meadow* and *marsh meadow,* were joined by those still in use today, *dry meadow, fresh meadow, cane meadow, salt meadow.*

As time went on, *meadow* would come to be associated with swampiness—as in the *Great Meadow* of Maine and the *Hackensack Meadows* in New Jersey—evidently because the settlers, who had come from a smaller and more crowded land where swamps had long been cleared for habitation and cultivation, had no word for swampy ground. The old Teutonic word *marsh* was still in use for extensive areas of wet land, like the great salt marshes along the coast; but in

7. (New York: Charles Scribner's Sons; 1943), p. 42.
8. Quotations from colonial records are, with a few exceptions, taken from Mitford M. Mathews, ed.: *A Dictionary of Americanisms on Historical Principles* (Chicago: University of Chicago Press; 1951). The *Dictionary* is also the principal authority for the dating of Americanisms cited in this study.

the beginning, at least, *swamp* was used primarily for land heavily covered with undergrowth, thicket land—we see frequent reference to the "cleareing" of "undergrowne stuffe," or *shruffe,* on swamp lots. Such terms as *spruce swamp, pine swamp, poplar swamp, beech swamp,* and *maple swamp* attest to a sense of firmer ground than we usually associate with the word. When we are *swamped* with duties, therefore, we are—properly—not mired, but entangled or lost in them.

Many topographical terms in use by the early settlers remain now only in place names or even in sayings whose original meaning has been obscured, sometimes to absurdity. *Hole,* originally a piece of meadow, as in Mr. Howland's "smale hole or acell of meddow neare his land,"[9] came gradually to be used only in the modern sense of a depression or hollow; but *Jackson's Hole* remains with us. Along the heavily indented New England coast, *neck* was used for a section of land; a legal conveyance in the Huntington records of 1663 contains the phrase "my halfe neck of meddow excepted." The usage makes more understandable the expression "neck of the woods" for a section or region of settlement in a woods; and, for those of us not on intimate terms with clams, makes it clear that *littleneck* is a geographical, not an anatomical, label. *Hollow,* not in our modern sense but as a piece of ground somewhat lower than a meadow (and having the wonderful plural *hoolas*), is immortalized in *Sleepy Hollow.* The term evidently could refer to quite large pieces of ground, as "one hollow conteyning one and an halfe Accre" noted in the Hempstead records. It was often used with attributive words; we read of "the wallnut hollow" or "ye chery-tree hollow."

Among the terms that have disappeared or been semantically changed is *interval,* still in use in England and in some parts of New England but replaced quite early by the colonists with *bottom,* which had been lurking dialectally somewhere; for the word is Shakespearean—"a sheepcote . . .

9. Plymouth records I, 46 (1662).

down in the neighbour bottom."[1] The old word *pan* is with
us in the term *hardpan,* a hard substratum of soil that holds
water; *hummock* has shrunk from its original meaning of a
piece of land of about an acre to a mere rise in low ground or
swamp; and *spong* (also *spang* or *spung*), for a strip of meadow,
has disappeared completely. *Doak,* which meant a valley, still
occurs dialectally in England, as does *bevel,* for a piece of
sloping and well-drained ground. Some words we cannot
positively define; *tilsom,* although it occurs several times as a
topographical term in the Hempstead records of 1672, as in
"his fathers tilsom" or "John Carmans toylsum," has defied
precise explanation. An earlier reference to the same John
Carman's "Tille sume" suggests that the word may have been
shortened from some earlier phrase.

Minor etymological mysteries are posed by other terms too,
not all of them topographical. Krapp explores the phrase "to
pine the earebred," used in the Hempstead records in connection with a cart and wheels made by John Jennings.[2] He
speculates that perhaps *pine* is for *pin, bred* for *board,* and
*eare* the Old English word for *plow,* in which case the phrase
might mean "to pin the plough-board." This meaning, however, does not fit well with the cart and wheels, of which the
earebred is apparently a part. Ah, well! One begins to see how
much simpler standardized spelling has made our lives.

Disappearance and change have befallen other terms related to the rustic life. *Stover,* a Shakespearean word meaning
fodder, is occasionally still heard in America; *haver,* which
meant hay, survives in such names as *Haverstraw* and *Haverhill*; and *haysill,* for haying season, has vanished in America
but can still be heard in England's eastern counties. *Driftway*
meant the passage along which cows were driven and can still
be found in Connecticut legal phraseology; *dool,* meaning to
provide with posts or stones to indicate property lines, has
completely disappeared. *Hurry,* or *hurie,* a now obsolete word
for the noun *load,* may have come from northern English

1. *As You Like It,* act 4, sc. 3, line 79.
2. *English Language in America,* vol. 1, p. 87.

dialect; the verb *hurry* in the sense of transport was in use in that area, according to the *Oxford English Dictionary*, as late as 1847. Damage done by cattle was apparently common; we read of *scathes*, which meant the injury done by animals not kept within bounds, and of *stray*, or *strey*, for example, in a complaint recorded in the Plymouth records of 1670 of "great stray and wast of Timber." *Stray* is an aphetic modification of *destroy* and was written as *stroy* by Bunyan and other early authors, while it appears as *stry* in contemporary East Anglian dialect. *Damage* has long supplanted it.

The concept of damage leads logically to steps taken to control it, and we read of the *pounedge* of cattle, which was the responsibility of the *cow constable* or *hog reeve*,[3] hired for "y'e keepint y'e field for the preservation of the corne."[4] The number of combinations made with the word *hog*—some now obsolete, like *hog fence, hog keeper, hog court* (a hog yard), *hogpen creek, hogpen meadow,* and *hog constable,* plus countless surviving ones—tells of the importance of the hog in the colonial economy. Not native to America, except for the distantly related peccaries, hogs were imported from the earliest days of European settlement to provide hardy if poor-quality stock. Foraging for themselves in the forests, they were often rounded up for slaughter, especially in the South, at *hog killing time.* In England, during this early period, the term *hog* was being replaced by *pig* for swine in general; but the Americans kept *hog* and used *pig* usually to indicate young swine. They retained also the Middle English word

3. *Hog reeve* is one of the terms used by Mitford M. Mathews, ed.: *The Beginnings of American English* (Chicago: University of Chicago Press; 1931), p. 7, to illustrate the need for caution in accepting dictionary datings as definitive. The *Oxford English Dictionary*'s first citation of *hog reeve* is dated 1759; it appears in colonial records as early as 1637. Similarly, some of the entries in Mathews: *Dictionary* will be found elsewhere with earlier datings, in spite of exhaustive research. It is important to note also that the date given is for the earliest *recorded* appearance of a word, which usually follows by some time its presence in the vocabulary.

4. Hempstead records I, 235 (1667).

*shoat,* now obsolete in England, for a weaned piglet. The American usage, continued since colonial days, is therefore the traditional one. Two old terms that were not kept, but which figured frequently in colonial records, were *heifer horse* (a filly) and *jade* (a broken-down horse); both now seem whimsical, but *jade,* from which comes our *jaded,* for surfeited or weary, was in poetic use until the twentieth century.

An interesting word no longer used as it was by the colonists is *haunt,* given by them a causative meaning evident in the directive: ". . . none shall hant their hoggs thatt way but haunt them that way where their 2d division lyes" (New Haven records of 1641). Another is *hanker,* which meant much the same as *haunt* does today; the New Haven records of 1637 note that a certain sachem "his counsell and company doe hereby covenant . . .y$^t$ none of them shall henceforth hanker about any of y$^e$ English 'houses.' " It is easy to see how *hanker* acquired from this notion of haunting its modern meaning of longing for. Perhaps our phrase *hanging around* bridges the gap between modern *hanker* and its ancient source, *\*konk-* ("to hang"), from which came ultimately Old English *hangian* and also *hanker*'s immediate source, Dutch dialectal *hankeren* ("to crave"). A rather charming word was *housel,* a weakened form of the compound *household;* and *pillowber,* for *pillowcase,* carries us back to Chaucer and the *pilwe-beer* that the Pardoner tried to palm off as the Virgin's veil.

But even as words disappeared, as the nature of the new environment, the nature of the colonists themselves, or their independence from English speech patterns caused old and formerly useful terms to be left behind, new words took their place. Derivatives multiplied, new forms evolved, semantic change stirred the rushing stream of words that raced along with history. Uninhibited and ingenious, the transplanted Englishmen not only kept what words they needed, at least until the need for them was past, but they also combined and invented, changed form and meaning, shortened and lengthened, and added suffixes or prefixes to make their words more flexible. They experimented, borrowed, and juggled the parts of speech. Principally they used familiar materials to express new concepts, creating phrases and compounds or fitting old words with new meanings. Using the methods their Anglo-Saxon forefathers had used and adding some of their own, they created, with careless eloquence, a vocabulary to fit their needs and fancy.

The colonial records are filled to the brim with new topographical terms: *bluff*, honored in linguistic history as the first target of attack by British critics, with its derivative phrases *bluff land* and *pine bluff*, *sand bluff* and *cedar bluff; barren*, describing open land with little vegetation and forming with attributives such combinations as *oak barren, hickory barren, pine barren*, acquiring the derivative *barreny*, and giving its name to various fauna, like *barren oak, barren pine, barren plum; divide*, the long, low ridge between two river systems; *creek*, meaning not, as in England, an inlet from the sea, but a small running stream; *run*, with similar meaning, as in *Bull Run; watershed; riffle; fordway; pond*, used like Old English *mere* for a small natural body of water rather than for an artificial lake as in England. *Bottom* produced a myriad of derivative terms—*bottom land, oak bottom, bottom lot, bottom sand, beech bottom, swamp bottom, timber bottom*.

The vital importance of soil characteristics for successful planting made the colonists naturalists in spite of themselves; because oak and hickory grew on the best soil for corn and peas, because a stand of spruce pine meant swamp beneath and a stand of chestnut or oak good timber, because cranberries indicated peaty ground and buffalo grass good pasture, they learned to recognize the types of soil and named the land accordingly. They spoke of *hickory land* and *piny woods, thatch grass swamp* and *cranberry marsh*. Without regard to botanical accuracy, they named the trees, some of them with the familiar names of English trees that they resembled; what they called at first the *walnut* was really a hickory tree, and their *palm* was actually a hemlock. Other trees were given new names, *buttonwood* and *sugar tree, cottonwood* and *tulip tree*. It would not have mattered to them, had they known, that the *Jimson weed* (Jamestown weed) was really the *Datura stramonium,* or that the *Johnny-jump-up* should properly have been called the *Viola tricolor.* They pronounced some words carelessly and so changed names: what had been *whortleberry* in England, which itself was an alteration of *hurtleberry,* became *huckleberry*; the sour gum tree was called the *pepperidge tree,* perhaps from association with the old name *piperidge* (a corruption of Latin *berberis*) for the barberry tree, which the sour gum tree is not.

But the word that was most clearly a linguistic declaration of independence was *corn,* running like a dominant motif through the writings of Virginian and New Englander alike. In Britain, "Indian corn," the product discovered in the West Indies and named by the Spaniards *maiz,* from the Taino name *mahiz,* was called—reasonably enough—*maize*; the old word *corn* was to the British, and still is, grain in general —English wheat or Swedish rye, for example. From 1608, however, when John Smith wrote that ". . . it pleased God (in our extremity) to move the Indians to bring us Corne, ere it was halfe ripe, to refresh us,"[5] *corn* meant to Englishmen in America "Indian corn" and no other. The incredible number of early corn-related words—*core* and *husk* (or, as Smith said, *huss*), *leaves, shuck, nubbin, cob* (from dialectal Middle English *cobbe,* meaning a lump or round object), as well as combinations like *corn blade, cornstalk, cornfield, corn fodder, corncrib, corn meal, corn bread, corn snake,* which was "near as big as the Rattle Snake," *corn hill, corn beer, cornflower broth,* and others, many of them now obsolete—tell of the utter dependence of the colonists on the distinctively American grain. Let the English call it *maize* if they liked! The initial confusion caused by the semantic change, however, is reflected in the terms *Indian wheat,* which in England meant corn, and *English corn,* which in America meant wheat.

Creatures of the wilderness acquired picturesque and vivid names; in no other area is the American gift for imagery so

5. *Works* (1884), p. 9.

effectively displayed. Had we never seen them before, we would probably recognize the *lightning bug* and the *razor-back hog*, the *catfish* and the *hoptoad*. The *dauber* wasp is the only remnant of the now obsolete word for plasterer. In the names of the *katydid*, the *chickaree*, the *chickadee*, and the *hummingbird,* the *bobwhite* and the *whip-poor-will*, we hear a woodland chorus; and the *sting ray*—first described by John Smith, after a most painful encounter—the *fiddler crab*, and the *rattlesnake* need little elaboration. Other creatures acquired their names through folk etymology; the *catamount*, the American puma, is probably the old *cat-o'-mountain* of Beaumont and Fletcher and of Shakespeare ("Your Cat-a-Mountaine lookes, your red-lattice phrases"),[6] which was used for the Old World leopard, or "pard," although De Vere suggests the possibility of a Spanish source, *gato* ("cat") and *monte* ("mountain"), as present but less likely. The more usual name for the same animal, and one that acquired overtones of dread, was *painter*, emerging by way of folk etymology from *panther* (Middle English *panter*).

All of these terms, along with others like *garter snake* and *woodchuck, eel grass* and *deer lick, hedgehog* (the porcupine) and *pigeon roost*—for the great nesting grounds of the passenger pigeons, sometimes one hundred thousand acres in area "joyning nest to nest, and tree to tree by their nests, so that the Sunne never sees the ground in that place" (Wood: *New England Prospect*, 1634)—made up a colorful mélange reflecting the wilderness that was the settlers' world, that wilderness which from the beginning was a major element in American history and culture, decisive in the development of both.[7] Because it demanded for survival qualities no longer of prime importance in England, qualities associated, rather, with that earlier time when Teutonic wanderers traversed

6. *The Merry Wives of Windsor*, act 2, sc. 2, line 27.

7. Stanley Williams: *The American Spirit in Letters*, Pageant of America Series (New Haven: Yale University Press; 1926), pp. 1 ff., points to the enormous influence of the wilderness in shaping the themes of American literature and its philosophy.

the northern forests, it produced a society in which independence, resourcefulness, and aggressiveness were glorified, a society of solitary hunters, of families held close by danger, of dreamers moving on. Until the passing of the frontier, hundreds of years and thousands of miles beyond Jamestown and Plymouth, and afterward by means of the ethos it created, the wilderness these words portray shaped in large measure the character and the fortunes of the American people.

The taming of the wilderness, however, was not an end in itself; land for planting, for the grazing of stock, and for the establishment of dwellings was the goal. Because that land had to be divided, a whole special vocabulary arose.

No colonial word has been more durable, no word more continuously prolific, than the old word *lot* (Old English *hlot* > Middle English *lot*), originally a counter, changed in New England to mean an individual grant of land. The usage developed logically from the Puritan practice of assigning land to the planters by *lot*, a method considered most equitable besides having respectable Biblical precedent (Acts 1:24–6). So firmly established was the custom that it continued into the eighteenth century, when the town of Lunenburg, according to its records of 1721, paid for "travil and Expenc When the Lotts Were Drawn at Concord." The land a settler received was therefore his "lot" and, according to its character, a *meadow lot, wood lot, cedar lot,* or the like. The number of derivative terms that have developed from colonial times on is practically inestimable; to such early terms as *hay lot* and *timber lot, hill lot* and *house lot* have been added later ones like *town lot, garden lot, sand lot* (with *sand-lot baseball), movie lot,* even *cemetery lot,* as well as *house-and-lot* in an indivisible phrase. The term came to be used for any large quantity, perhaps because the same method of distribution was used for other commodities in other situations; and Cotton Mather, in *Magnalia,* tells of the "great lot of evil spirits" that possessed a woman in Beverley. Today we have *lots* of fun or *lots* of trouble and other people have a *lot* of nerve, while the singular has become an accepted business term for a specific portion of stocks or bonds or of other commodities for sale.

Two now obsolete words important in the history of New England, at least, were *lotter* and *lot-layer*. These were the titles of officials appointed to supervise the *lotting out* of the land, after discontent over the large acreage mysteriously acquired by the Puritan leaders forced a more equitable arrangement. The *allotters* decided on the disposition of land to the individual inhabitants according to the orders of the court and had extraordinary powers; it was decreed, according to the Boston records of 1635, that "none shall sell their houses or allotments to any new comers, but with the consent and allowance of those that are appointed allotters." The *lot-layers* measured the grants, and one can imagine with what careful scrutiny those land-oriented New England settlers watched them at their work. Land was actually measured not only to inches, but to tenths of inches—a practice that may account for traditional Yankee thrift.

Larger grants were made to groups of settlers for the purpose of founding new *towns*, or *townships*. (To the confusion of strangers, the words were used interchangeably in New England.) Both terms meant specifically, in an entirely new sense, a self-governing local unit. Webster, a century later, would define *town* as "a district of certain limits; also, the inhabitants or legal voters of a town"; but in the early days of settlement, few of the inhabitants were legal voters, the franchise being sharply restricted to church members voted in by other church members. Within that franchise, however, the New England town, through its *town meetings*, initiated the practice of democracy in America. From the later union of the principle of democracy, implemented in New England, with the principle of representative government, already working in Virginia, emerged the American form of government, unique in the world.

At the *town meetings*, the *freemen* (by 1630, the Puritan

leaders, named in the Massachusetts Bay Company charter as *freemen,* or stockholders, had by a remarkable feat of semantic chicanery made the word mean the voting citizens of a state) appointed their administrative officers, the *selectman* and the *town marshal,* as well as lesser officials like the *cowkeeper,*[8] the *wood corder,* and the *fence viewer.* These new terms suggest both the strict regulation and the co-operative nature of the first New England communities; the *commons—cow common, ox common,* and *sheep common*—were held in joint ownership, a custom with medieval precedent in the setting aside of the *waste* for community use.

All planters were expected—in fact, ordered—to *improve* their holdings; in the Massachusetts Bay *Records* of 1632, we read: "If the . . . said John Winthrop shall . . . suffere the said ileland to lye wast, and not improve the same, then this present demise to be voide." A notice in the *Pennsylvania Magazine* in 1675 suggested that "everyone must joyn their Hands, first in Building the Houses, and next in Improving the Land." In these contexts, *improve* is used in logical extension of the sense already extant in England, of enclosing or cultivating wasteland; but in New England, if not elsewhere, it acquired also the meaning of employing or using, applicable to persons or things. An entry in the Connecticut Historical Society *Collections* for 1640 (Series VI, p. 2) notes that individuals have been *improved* "for the killing of woolfs." Perhaps the semantic change is a logical progression from the sense of making better to that of making use of. Krapp believed that the usage appeared too early in colonial writings for it not to be a survival; but Witherspoon cited it as an Americanism, giving as an illustration "He improved the horse for ten days," and so did David Humphreys, who compiled in 1815 what is now known as the earliest glossary of Americanisms. *To improve* is defined as "to make use of" in

---

8. Lest we think of the Puritan scene as drab, a notation in the Massachusetts Historical Society *Collections* for 1643 (4, Series IX, p. 12) tells us that "our cowekeeper here of James City on Sundays goes . . . in freshe flaming silke."

the *Virginia Literary Museum and Journal of Belles Lettres, Arts, Sciences, Etc.;*[9] so those of us who may have wondered how the busy bee improves each shining hour now know.

Fences and outbuildings, like the house itself, were *improvements.* Among them were the *barn,* historically a welded compound of two Old English words, *bere* ("barley") and *ærn* ("place" or "house"), but used here in the sense of a building for storing grain and for housing cattle too; the *barnyard;* the *hogpen;* the *hog court;* and the *cow linter* (lean-to). Hay or forage was stacked around the *stackpole;* and *fodder*—which meant in the North the whole corn ear dried and in the South only the leaves, or blades—was gathered into the barn. *Cattle,* which in England applied generally to all domestic animals used for food or draft, meant only cows, not horses.

The houses themselves were built of *clapboard,* made usually of cedar and cut thinner at one edge than at the other so that, in building, the boards would overlap. *Clapboarding* was used sometimes for entire houses, sometimes, if the structure itself was made of logs, for the roof only. We read of *clapboard houses, clapboard huts, clapboard shutters.* The cutting of *clapboard trees,* cedars suitable for clapboards, as well as of *rail trees,* those suited for splitting into *fence rails,* was carefully restricted; the Jamaica, Long Island, records of 1676 note: "They are to have Liberty to take any timber . . . in our commons except Clappborde trees and Rayle trees under eightene inches." The origin of the word has long interested etymologists; Dr. Alfred L. Elwyn suggested that the term may have been derived from the thin, smooth boards called clapboards on which, in the north of England, a kind of bread is "clapped" and so called *clapbread.* The notion seems fanciful, however; it is more likely that the term was simply a new application of the old term for boards cut thin to serve as staves.

9. The *Virginia Literary Museum* collection of Americanisms is printed in full in Mathews: *Beginnings.*

Sometimes the houses were built in one day in a *raising bee*
or the land cleared in a *clearing bee,* two of the many co-
operative projects expressed in the term *bee.* No word, except
perhaps *bundling,* is more popularly associated with the
colonial scene. We read of *quilting bees* and *husking bees,*
*spinning bees* and *logging bees, chopping bees* and even
*squirrel bees* (for the killing of squirrels). The term was undoubtedly a survival, but few have agreed upon its source.
George Casper Homans traced the custom as a social institution to the Yorkshire *bêan days* and regarded bee as derived
from thirteenth-century *bêan, bene.*[1] Others have ascribed
the term simply to its association with busyness.

*Bundling,* that curious custom which so fascinated European visitors, was not acknowledged by Webster; and Washington Irving wrote of it as a reprehensible practice. According to the *Oxford English Dictionary,* it was brought to
colonial America from the north of England and still exists
in Wales; and there is no doubt of its general acceptance during the colonial period, at least in rural areas. It seems only
reasonable that desperate measures were needed to stay warm
in the cold New England winter, when the wind whistled
through those clapboard chinks; courting is difficult when the
lips are blue. It must have been doubly difficult when all the
family, sometimes including twelve or fourteen brothers and
sisters, was gathered in the one big room, where the *back log*
was kept constantly burning; and new words in the language,
like *cold snap* and *sledding* and *snowshoe* (for "a Rackett
tyed to each foote"), told of climate and terrain that would
hardly have encouraged romance under the moon.

If in the Southern colonies there was no need for such win-
try words, the vocabulary grew with other terms, telling of
life on the rich tobacco land. Until the end of the seventeenth
century, there were few of the great plantations of a later
period; Virginia, like New England, was for the first century

1. *Oxford English Dictionary.*

of settlement largely a land of yeoman farmers working land themselves or, like their Northern counterparts, with the help of indentured servants. Gradually, however, the term *planta-tion,* like the term *planter,* changed under the influence of its usage in the West Indies, where individual sugar planters ad-ministered enormous holdings; the words came more and more to be applied to the one-crop estate and to the one-crop farmer and became associated at last with the extensive hold-ings and great estate owners of the South. In the North, the old word *plantation* was being replaced by *location,* and *planter* by *locater* or the familiar English *farmer.*

Tobacco-related terms—*tobacco merchant, tobacco shop,* even *tobacconist,* for an addict—had long been familiar in England, where the importation and smoking of tobacco had been going on for some time; but with John Rolfe's discovery in 1612 of a process by which tobacco could be more profit-ably produced, innumerable terms related to tobacco growing and marketing began crowding into the vocabulary. *Virginia* was already in use for the choice *Virginia tobacco.* John Smith wrote that "there are so many sofisticating Tobaco-mungers in England, were it never so bad, they would sell it for Verinas . . .";[2] but during the century, distinction was made among *fine cut, Virginia honeycomb,* and other varieties. The problems of the planter were reflected in such terms as *tobacco worm* and *tobacco fly;* and we see, as we did with corn, numerous derivative phrases emerging, among them *tobacco leaves, tobacco stalk,* and *tobacco bed.* The *tobacco house,* a large, airy shed for curing the plant, was called also the *tobacco shed* or *curing house.* From these sheds along the rivers, the planters rolled their product, in *tobacco hogsheads* or *tobacco casks,* down to the *tobacco boats,* which, after loading from the individual plantations, would sail down to the sea to join the *tobacco fleet* that set out on regularly scheduled runs for England. The *tobacco fields,* set out on the fertile spreading

2. *General History of Virginia,* vol. 4, p. 126.

acres along the rivers, prevented close settlement and, consequently, the growth of compact towns like those of New England; the wide acres were enclosed in what from very early days was known as the *Virginia fence*, ". . . made by lapping the ends of rails or poles on each other, turning alternately to the right and left."

Tobacco growing was not the only industry in the South; the Southern colonies were particularly active in the raising of stock. The word *cowpen* came not, as one might suspect, from New England, but from those areas in the South where large enclosures in the forests held great herds of cattle. It is something of a surprise to read: "The ranch system had its beginnings in Virginia and the Carolinas and among the Spaniards of Florida. 'Cowpens,' as they were then called, were established on lands not yet settled, and cattle were herded in droves of hundreds or thousands."[3] *Cowdrivers* drove their herds to Charleston and even as far as the markets of Philadelphia and New York.

Differences in the natural environment gave rise to a multitude of new terms for flora and fauna peculiar to the region. The words *dayflower* and *Virginia creeper, white-tailed deer* and *yellowjacket* show once again the quality of imagery that so notably distinguishes the American vocabulary. *Loblolly,* which gave its name to the *loblolly bay* and the *loblolly pine,* meant a miry puddle or mudhole; it has been called "a good word that shakes in pronunciation like jelly, which is most nearly what it describes." The origin of the word may be a dialectal term for a thick gruel, from *lob,* to bubble or boil, plus *lolly,* for broth. *Stone-toter* captures the imagination; it is a singular name for what J. K. Paulding wrote of as "the most singular fish in this part of the world. [Its] brow is surmounted with several sharp little horns, by the aid of which he *totes* small flat stones from one part of the brook to

3. *Century Magazine* (January 1884). The familiarity of the term in the South is affirmed by the contemporary dialectal variant *cuppin,* occurring in Virginia, Maryland, and North Carolina (Kurath: *Word Geography,* p. 38).

another more quiet, in order to make a snug little enclosure for his lady to lie in safety."[4] De Vere guesses that the fish was actually a stickleback, technically Gasterosteus, or a mullet; but who would prick such a lovely linguistic bubble? The *cottonmouth,* a moccasin, and the *diamondback rattler* are native to the Southern states. Some creatures and plants known elsewhere by their traditional English names were given regional labels, typically metaphorical; the *redbud* is simply a Judas tree, the *marsh hen* a coot.

Whatever the linguistic differences, more striking was the uniformity between Southern and Northern seaboard colonies. The distinction between North and South was not so strong in those early days as that between colony and colony; one spoke of a *Plymothean* or a *Virginian,* a *Pennsylvanian* or even a *Massachusettensian.* The settlers of the Southern colonies, like those at least of New England, had come principally from eastern and southern England, that is, from the same dialectal areas. It is probable that settlers North and South spoke more alike during the seventeenth century and early eighteenth than they would later, after the immigration of other groups and the inland migration of seaboard settlers, with their consequent isolation, would set up distinct speech areas. All along the seaboard, where the separate colonies were more closely bound to England than to each other, speech changes occurring in England were transmitted to North and South alike as new settlers arrived and as a certain amount of correspondence and travel was exchanged. The dramatic change from the flat *a* to the broad *a* in upper-class speech took place in London only at the end of the eighteenth century; it was adopted, with some variation, all along the seaboard but did not influence pronunciation among the inland settlers.[5] Many of the colloquialisms now associated with the South—*reckon,*

4. *Letters from the South,* vol. 2, p. 4. Quoted in De Vere: *Americanisms,* p. 382. The word *tote,* which etymologists have worried for years, was in widespread use in seventeenth-century America.

5. Mencken: *American Language,* pp. 334–5, and Krapp: *English Language in America,* vol. 2, pp. 36 ff.

*right* for very, *heap* for a large quantity (a *heap* of trouble)—
were present in the early days in the North as well. Chances
are that nearly all seventeenth-century Englishmen in America
were using words like *daft* and *spunk* and *techy* and were pronouncing *tea* as *tay* and *palm* as *pam*.

Colonial settlement had begun as a commercial venture.
The first ship that deposited settlers in Virginia returned to
England with a cargo of wooden staves, and the first task of
the colonists was to find gold or in some other way repay
the Virginia Company for its investment. In New England,
nearly all immigrants—with the possible exception of the
Pilgrims—had come to America with more than spiritual
profit in mind; John Winthrop said frankly that the high cost
of keeping servants in England had driven him to make the
move. (He soon found that, although the cost of keeping
servants in America was less, keeping them at all was another
matter—and in the heady American air, they expected to be
called *help,* not *servants.*) In this rich and productive land,
material reward came inevitably to the industrious, and an
equation between virtue and profit—an equation that would
endure long after its validity was past—was established. *Enterprise* and *endeavor,* those new words of Elizabethan England, as well as commerce-related terms like *contract* and
*capital* in their modern sense, *discount, dividend, investment,*
even *bank* with its modern meaning, traveled to America with
the first settlers; and if the practical application of some of
them was not at first possible, the concepts did not fade.

Quite soon there were added to the many agricultural terms
that developed from the dominant pursuit of the settlers other
occupational terms. In the thick forests that grew down to the
sea—suggested in such phrases as *timber swamp* and *timber
land, timber pasture, timber township, wood field,* and *wood
lot*—*sawmill works* were set up to supply England's desperate
need for masts and spars and shingles and staves, as well as to
fill the colonists' own needs. From the miscellaneous nature
of wood products, the old word *lumber,* used in England then
and today simply for disused articles of furniture and for other

cumbrous material that takes up space (cf. *lumber room*), came to mean any cut timber; and as the industry grew, so did the related vocabulary. *Lumber cutter;* the verbs *to lumber* and *to log; lumberer,* for a seller of timber; *lumber carrier; loggers; logrolling* (in the literal sense); *rail timber* and *rail lengths* entered ordinary speech. *Girdling* was the name of a process, learned from the Indians, by which a tree is killed by cutting a circular ring around its trunk.

Not only sawmills, but *flour mills,* too, were set up along the rivers, where there was an abundance of wood for water wheels and for the construction of mills, as well as hard stones for millstones and rushing streams for power; *mill creek, mill slash, mill run, millering* were new terms. A few *iron furnaces* were set up, but the agricultural implements produced were still primitive; American agricultural methods lagged even behind Europe's, at a time when all agriculture was little more advanced than during the Middle Ages.

The importation of textiles from England was costly, and the colonies, according to the mercantilist theory under which they were to produce raw materials only, were not permitted to manufacture. Nevertheless, some wool factories were set up; and *clothiers*—not sellers, but fullers of cloth—pursued their trade. (Oddly, the *clothier*'s place of business was still called a *fulling mill.*) The seller of clothing, called in England a *draper,* became a *dry goods* merchant and his place of business not a *shop* but a *store.* These distinctly American terms developed logically from circumstances. *Goods,* which meant freight, came, reasonably enough, to mean the stock one had on hand, which had come as freight; *dry goods* meant textiles and, by extension, clothing. To the British, the *merchant* was an overseas trader; but because in America the importer was usually the retail seller also, equivalent to the *tradesman* of England, he not only was a *merchant* but also sold from his *store,* or warehouse. To the disdainful amusement of some British visitors, therefore, even the smallest of retail tradesmen was a *merchant.*

The long-established fur trade and fishing industry continued to occupy many of the colonists. *Packhorse trains* traveled to *trucking houses* deep in the wilderness, there to exchange cloth and beads and other *truck* (from Old English *trukken,* "to exchange," "barter") for the valuable *beaver*— the word no longer meant only the animal but the skin as well and, in different context, as it did in England, the elegant hat made by the *beaver maker.* The *packhorse men,* or *pack men,* gained a reputation for debauching the Indians with rum and for their own violent behavior. South of New York, which was already the principal center of exchange, much of the trade was in deerskins; the famous *Trading Path,* extending four hundred miles into the interior, was the scene of bloody fighting between rival pack trains, all seeking the highest prizes to bring back to Charleston, the main Southern port.

Along the coast, the fishing industry, which had been thriving long before colonization, made only minor contributions to the vocabulary during the first century of settlement. English speech was already rich in nautical terms; many of those relating to fishing had entered long before. Some regional contributions, like *jigger,* a small fishing vessel of New England; *dipsy,* as the sinker of a fishing line was called in Pennsylvania; and *dobber,* the New York fisherman's name for a line float, were in use in the early eighteenth century. *Flumadiddle* is cited by De Vere as the name of a long-time favorite dish among New England fishermen but is defined by Mathews (and dated only in the nineteenth century) as nonsense or trifles; since the dish was supposed to contain a variety of ingredients, the two meanings may not be unrelated. The *eel spear* was the American substitute for the English *eel-shear*; and *gigging,* night fishing with a gig, was a term used by John Smith. Probably fishermen introduced in their figurative sense those expressive words *squally* and *keeling over*; and surely they were not mere fishermen but also poets who coined *moonglade* and *grayslick,* the one denoting the soft, silvery track of moonlight on the water, the other, peculiar to the fishermen of Maine, the condition of the sea when the wind has died and the water resembles glass. *Tackling,* for harness, was originally a nautical term, but not —as De Vere and others have held—a new usage in America. Although it is true that the tackling that had been laid up for the winter was used by the colonists for harnessing their horses to sleighs (no vehicles had come with their horses from England), they did not originate the term. Howell, according to the *Oxford English Dictionary,* used it in 1645 (in his *Letters*); but it had become obsolete in England by the eighteenth century. The term is still common in New England and has traveled westward in the horsy compound *tackroom.*

From the lowly *clam,* that shellfish that formed so important a staple for people and stock alike (hogs were put out to forage on the clam banks), came an impressive number of words and phrases. The verb *to clam, clamming* as verb and noun, and *clam bank* were all in seventeenth-century use. Clamming was not a really relaxing occupation in colonial days; a 1676 note in the Massachusetts Historical Society *Collections* tells us that "his father and mother were taken by the Pequts and Monhiggins about ten weeks ago, as they were clamming." The Indians used a *clamshell hoe,* commented on by Wood in *New England Prospect* as superior to the hoes used by the colonists; and the venerable phrase *happy as a clam at high water* is one of our oldest American images.

The transportation of both people and produce was a problem from the beginning; and in the interior most of it was done by *boatable* waterway. Names of vessels designed for river voyaging, like *flatboat* and *barken canoe,* rafts with *setting poles, tobacco boats* and *trading boats*—usually small sailboats or canoes of some kind—abound in early records. Such verb forms as *boating, rafting,* and *keel-boating* were formed from the name of whatever type of vessel was being used; and *carrying places* were those places along the shore where canoes and goods were carried overland around barriers in a stream or from one waterway to another.

Land travel was hazardous and trying. Personal travel was

on horseback or by wagon, and in such new terms as *wagon
ford, ridingway, fordway,* and *rope ferry* we see some of the
difficulties facing the traveler in regions where few roads—
and those few little more than trails—existed. Bridges, except
over small streams, were nonexistent. *Sleighs* were used in
winter; *sleigh ride* and *sledding* tell not of recreation, but of
transportation of goods and persons somehow accomplished
regardless of the season. The only American contribution to
the already large store of English terms for seagoing vessels
in the seventeenth century was *barkentine,* probably a variant of *brigantine* and naming a type of vessel used frequently
for West Indian voyaging.

Another difficulty facing the would-be trader was currency.
Most exchange throughout the first century of settlement
was by barter. Barred from coining their own money (the
pine-tree shilling of 1674 was not technically legal), and with
little coming from England, where most American import
was paid for in goods, the colonists used various *species*—in
the old, medieval sense of the word as *kinds*—of exchange.[6]
*Corn specie, tobacco specie, pork specie* were in common use,
depending on what specie was *merchantable* in specific areas.
The town of Plymouth, for example, agreed to see certain of
its debts defrayed "in such specie as they shall agre with men
for the doing it." Not until the nineteenth century would
the word *specie* acquire its modern meaning of coined money.
In the same sense, *money, pay,* and *payment* were extended;
we read of *corn money, shell money, beaver payment, pork
pay. Country payment* meant produce in general given in
exchange for goods; *current country pay* was whatever was
being presently accepted in a given community. Various
coins that did find their way into the colonies—*Spanish bits*
and *Spanish dollars* (pirates roamed the sea lanes and walked
the streets of New York with equal impunity), Dutch *stivers*
and English shillings—had varying values put upon them; no

6. The phrase *in kind* or *in specie* was in use in England. The *OED*
cites Birch: *Art & Times Chas. I* (1848), I, 131: "Nor will the country
pay money instead of viands in specie." Bacon used *in kind.*

standard existed. That trade was carried on under such vex-
ing circumstances surely indicates early-blooming Yankee ingenuity.

For trade went on. Although agriculture remained the
occupation of ninety per cent of the population well into
the eighteenth century, the enormous number of trading
terms introduced from the days of first settlement signifies
the pervasiveness of the trading spirit. The word *trade* itself,
having come from England in the sense of a business or profession, was converted into a synonym for *swap*—swap itself,
or *swop*, being an archaism against which Dr. Johnson would
later thunder. A single transaction was a *trade,* even figuratively; one *traded* greetings or *traded* blows. Proliferating
derivative combinations testified to the strength of the concept; *trade goods, trade house, beaver trade, Indian trade,
trading post, trade ship* were only some of the earlier ones.
The term gradually replaced *truck* as a verb; but *trucking
masters,* for carrying on a community's trade with the Indians, were still being appointed in the eighteenth century.
North or South, no man scorned buying and selling; the English *gentleman* did not last long in America. In Virginia,
William Byrd, importing goods directly from England to his
plantation, traded pots and pans and rum with the Indians
and sold them guns, too, a practice he justified by noting
what poor shots the Indians were, whereas their aim with
bow and arrow was deadly. In New England, a cobbler
named Nathaniel Hancock and a fisherman named William
Pepperell branched out from their original occupations,
bought land, and planted the seeds of financial dynasties.
Evidently the trading spirit that was already permeating the
air of England had blown across the sea and was picking up
strength in the spacious American skies.

But America was not England, its northern continent not
yet the domain of Englishmen, their speech not dominant.
Men of other nations speaking other languages, Spanish and
French and Swedish and Dutch, came also to the New World
with dreams of conquest or riches and with words that Eng-

lishmen could use. In the consequent mingling of tongues, many words were borrowed and words revised. But stranger still to English ears than the voices of these European new-comers were those of the people whose land this was, of the dusky Indians, who watched uneasily the slow, steady spread of white settlement reaching out like the first waves of an inexorable tide. From these people, and because of them, the English vocabulary in America would acquire not only new terms but a touch of exotic color to mark it as separate and new.

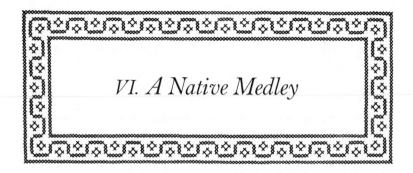

# VI. A Native Medley

Some of our loveliest names are Indian, and some most alien
to our tongue. *Susquehanna, Rappahannock, Shenandoah*—
such names are the stuff of poetry. William Penn knew not "a
language spoken in Europe that hath words of more sweetness
or greatness"; to Whitman, *Monongahela* "rolls with venison
richness upon the palate"; and Paulding, Irving, and Longfellow were among the many who found inspiration in the
Indian names. Even Mencken, rarely rhapsodic, commented
upon their "barbaric brilliancy."

In the translation of some of the names—where such translation is known—in "beautiful water" (*Ohio*) and "daughter
of the skies" (*Shenandoah*) and "place of the great hills"
(*Massachusetts*), the poetry remains; but most are etymologically obscure, and it is clear that the genius of our particular
tongue has chosen and kept them simply for the sound they
make. Some are not even euphonious. Surely *Hoboken* and
*Oshkosh* sing no melody, at least to the ears of most of us;
and *Anasagunticook* and *Mattaggmonsis* (in Maine) are no
less than forbidding. Of the original forms, often doubtful
to begin with, many have been changed according to the
whimsical spelling or pronunciation of the sometimes illiterate transcribers, who were attuned, to begin with, to particular national accents. *Connecticut* was once *Quonaughticot*;
*Missouri, Ouemessourit*; *Michigan, Machigiganing.* The
*Cocheco*, a river in New Hampshire, was variously *Coch-*

*echae, Cuttcheco, Kechceacy,* and *Quocheco* before the official form was finally decided. And for the four-letter word *Iowa,* Hodge's *Handbook of American Indians*[1] lists sixty-four separate spellings. Some names presented such difficulty that even the not easily daunted colonists gave them up after an initial attempt to master them; the names *Pagonchaumischaug, Maushapogue,* and *Wayunckeke* have simply disappeared. That twenty-six states, innumerable towns and counties, hundreds of lakes, and more than a thousand rivers and streams in the United States have Indian names despite their meaninglessness in American speech testifies to the strength of the Indian presence in our land.

If problems were posed in retaining place names—which one expects to be out of the ordinary (after all, the first settlers had come from a land where such names as *Gloucestershire* and *Kidderminster* would have boggled Indian minds)—everyday words were a different matter, and hardly worth the trouble. Some have ascribed the paucity of Indian borrowings in our vocabulary to the traditional relationship between conqueror and conquered[2]—by historical precedent, conqueror does not borrow from the conquered unless and until, as did the Normans and the English, they merge—but it seems far more likely that the essential incompatibility between the languages was responsible for the dearth. John Elyot's heroic efforts at translation in his Bible—*nummatchekodtantamoonganunnonoas* for "our loves" and *kummogkodonattootummooetiteaonganunnonash* for "our question," for example—illustrate the difficulties facing the borrower. Perhaps we should look to some such reason, on a lesser scale, for the always puzzling lack of Celtic borrowings among the Anglo-Saxons.

Consequently, aside from proper names, our whole vocabulary of Indian borrowings that at some time or other

1. Bureau of American Ethnology, Bulletin 30 (Washington, D.C.: Government Printing Office; 1907–10).

2. E.g., Thomas Pyles: *Words and Ways of American English* (New York: Random House; 1952), p. 37.

have had currency as English words consists of a few hundred words at the most; of these, less than forty have entered even the American English mainstream. A few terms from the Indian languages of the West Indies had, as we know, entered English before colonization began. *Hammock* and *savannah*, *maize, potato, tobacco, barbecue* were all brought back by Spanish explorers and made their way through Europe; *cannibal* and *canoe* came from America with Columbus, the first a testimonial to the wishful thinking of a dreamer who interpreted *Cariba*, or *Caniba*—a tribal name meaning "strong men"—as indicating subjects of the Grand *Khan* of Tartary, the second an Arawak word that traveled through French *canot* before reaching England and our own tongue. *Hurakán*, a Taino word defined by Hakluyt in 1589 as a "characteristic West Indian storm," was introduced into the vocabulary from both Portuguese and Spanish, as *furacano, furicanos, hurachana, hericano* (as John Smith spelled it) and in various other forms, its character evidently not clearly understood except by those who had experienced it. (Shakespeare identified a hurricane as a waterspout.[3])

Another word—or pair of words—orthographically but not semantically settled as the seventeenth century opened was *Indian* as opposed to *American*. Which of the two was the correct name for the natives of the New World? *Indian* had at first been accepted as the logical extension of Columbus's *Indies* or the later *Western Inde* but soon came to be recognized as a misnomer; during the sixteenth century, *American* became the favored term. Frobisher's *Voyages*, dating from 1578, tells of "the Americans . . . which dwell under the equinoctiall line"; at century's end, Massinger was using the comparison "worse than ignorant Americans"; and as late as the early eighteenth century, Addison, in *The Spectator*, wrote that "the Americans believe that all creatures have souls." Conversely, in Shakespeare's earlier plays the term *Indian* refers to natives of India; in his later ones, as

3. ". . . dreadfull spout / Which Shipmen doe the Hurricano call." *Troilus and Cressida*, act 5, sc. 2, line 171.

in *The Tempest*, it means a native of the New World. To most of the colonists, regardless of their literary betters, the natives were *Indians* from the beginning; and to W. Brereton's report, in 1602, that on a voyage to Virginia "we saw manie Indians, which are tall big boned men," we ascribe the name's official beginning. *American* was for the most part left in limbo, to be rescued in 1697 (despite the *Oxford English Dictionary*'s delay in acknowledging its existence before 1765) by Cotton Mather and restored to life in its modern incarnation.

The tall, big-boned men whom the first explorers encountered and who became to all of the first settlers, north and south, *Indians* or *injuns* or *engianes* or *Indjons* or *ingens*, according to the orthographic inclinations of the scribe —which suggest strongly the popular pronunciation—were members of a linguistically linked group of tribes comprising, among others, the Arapaho, Blackfoot, Cheyenne, Cree, Delaware, Fox, Micmac, Ojibwa, Chippewa, and Penobscot. It was from their dialects, called collectively Algonquian, that the first Indian loan words in America were taken, many of them entering in several dialectal forms. The American Indian languages, at the time of English colonization, were at a stage passed through by Indo-European languages in ancient times, when a great number of languages were confined each to a limited geographical area and small population. Wide distribution of a few major languages has come relatively late in man's cultural history; the pattern of aboriginal speech as we see it among American Indians suggests the diversity that probably preceded the earliest Indo-European groupings.

This immense diversity in Indian languages was recognized generally for the first time in 1891, with the publication of the work of J. W. Powell, whose classification of aboriginal speech in the United States and Canada remains a classic in its field. Isolating fifty-eight language stocks, of which three were already extinct (two others would subsequently be combined with other stocks), Powell demon-

strated that these fifty-three were not merely separate
languages but separate language *families*, each containing
within itself from one to as many as fifty component tongues.
A generation later, utilizing the methods developed in the
study of Indo-European languages, Edward Sapir regrouped
the stocks into six major divisions, of which Algonquian-
Wakashan, or simply Algonquian, was by far the largest, both
in geographical spread and in the number of its speakers.
It was this Algonquian tongue that John Smith, John Elyot,
Roger Williams, and other English pioneers, as well as the
early French explorers and missionaries who transmitted to
us much of the Indian vocabulary, tried to render into manageable form. Outside of Algonquian, only a few words from
the Muskhogean language in the South, consisting principally of place names (*bayou* and *catalpa* are two of the few
other identifiable borrowings), entered during the colonial
period.

The first Englishman to attempt a systematic rendering of
these Indian terms was John Smith, that amazing adventurer
who played, often simultaneously, the roles of explorer, car-
tographer, soldier, administrator, promoter, scientific observer, writer, and—at least on a minor scale—linguist.
Having more extensive contact with the American Indian
than had any Englishman before him, Smith wrote in *Virginia, a True Relation* (1608), in *A Map of Virginia* (1612),
and in many later works detailed observations on the Indian
and his way of life. He wrote also of the regional characteristics of both Virginia and New England and introduced
some of our earliest Indian borrowings, such as *raccoon,
persimmon, moccasin, muskrat,* and *pone.* Other writers
followed: William Strachey, who also had been at Jamestown,
published a *Dictionary of the Indian Languages* in 1612;
Wood's *New England Prospect,* containing many hitherto
unrecorded terms, appeared in 1634. In all of these works
we see the difficulty that faced the writers in transcribing
Indian speech as heard by English ears. Smith's spelling of
*raccoon* in 1608 was *Raugraoughcun,* as close a rendering

as possible of the Algonquian term, which meant "scratcher"; by 1610, he was writing it *rarowcun*. In 1649, *racoone* was the accepted form, and by 1672 it had settled down into the form we use today. Wood wrote *isquonterquashes* in 1634; by 1672 the spelling was *squontersquashes*; and by century's end it was *squash*. *Skunk* progressed from Algonquian *segankw* or *segongw* to *squunck* in Wood's *New England Prospect*; it, too, had acquired its present form by 1701.

One of the problems facing the translator was that many of the Indian words were not simple words, but combinations of forms. *Tomahawk,* transcribed by Strachey as *tacca hacan* or *tamahaac,* was in many of the Algonquian dialects *tahmahgan*, which was made up of *otamaha*, "to beat," and *egan*, a term used in the construction of all verbal nouns, so that the word meant literally "a beating thing." To complicate matters still further, a word was called in some dialects by a term that had special significance; to the Ojibwa, the raccoon was not *raugraoughcun* or any word resembling it—because tribal tradition held that the curious marks on the animal's fur were the traces of its former existence as a shell, it was called *aisebun*, "a shell it was." It is hardly surprising that many of the words taken temporarily into the language were eventually replaced by simpler English-rooted terms, *shadbush* for *saskatoon*, for example, or that many were simply allowed to disappear as the need for them passed. We cannot, however, ignore these vanished words in studying the relationship between Englishman and Indian during the early days of settlement. Each had its reason for being; and because the sum of all borrowings and the relative proportions of classes of words one to another tell us so much about contemporary interests, it is important that we retrieve what we can.

The Englishman, recognizing and envying the Indian's rapport with the wilderness, which to him was terrifying and mysterious, sought to learn the secret of that harmony. In the early borrowings of animal names like *muskrat* and *opossum* and *quahog* and *terrapin,* of plant names like *tuckahoe* (an

edible root) and *cushaw* (a squash) and *puccoon*,[4] we see suggested the friendly if ambivalent relationship that at first
existed between the newcomers and the original inhabitants
of the wilderness, a relationship in which the settler could
ask, in the handy phrases provided in Smith's mini-Baedeker
that accompanied his glossary of Indian terms: "What call
you this" or "I am verie hungrie? what shall I eate?"

In New England, the Pilgrims signed a peace treaty with
Massasoit, chief of the Wampanoags; and from the Indians
Samoset and Squanto, who had traveled to England on trading ships and spoke English (individual settlers as well as
transient explorers had preceded the Pilgrims in the New
England area), the inexperienced Englishmen learned to
fertilize their cornfields with fish, principally *menhaden*, a
kind of herring that at certain times appeared in incredible
numbers near the shore, or with *alewives*, so that "bad and
sandie ground . . . brought forth exceeding good corne, by
being fished but every third year." *Fished*, now obsolete in the
foregoing sense, was a quite new semantic development. The
etymology of *alewife* has been much disputed. Evidently it
comes from the Narragansett term *aloof* as used by Winthrop
and Baddam; but since the Indian dialects of New England
contained no *l* or *f*, De Vere suggests that the word was more
probably *ainoop*, a form with enough resemblance to English
dialectal *alleys* or *allowes*, for the allice shad, to bring about the
word's conversion.[5] A devious route indeed—but, given the
vagaries of folk etymology, not improbable. *Porgy*, after all,
is difficult to relate to *scuppaug* (Algonquian *mishcùp*) unless
we know that the first syllable was dropped, and so *paugie*
was created and then *porgie*. Then, to make the game fair,

---

4. Most visibly represented by the bloodroot and still in use, *puccoon*
comes from the Algonquian root for "blood" and names a number of
plants yielding red or yellow pigment ". . . for swellings, aches, anoint-
ing their joints, painting their heads and garments." (Smith: *Virginia,
A True Relation*, p. 13).
5. M. Schele De Vere: *Americanisms: The English of the New World*
(New York: Scribner & Co.; 1872), p. 68.

the second syllable was dropped from the original word to produce *scup,* a sister term of identical meaning.

The settlers learned also from the Indians to stalk the *mus,* or *moos,* the "stripper," so called for his habit of peeling bark, and to hunt the *moose deer* Indian-fashion, as described in Josselyn's *New England Rarities*: ". . . the Moose Deer feed much upon them [water lilies], at which time the Indians kill them, when their heads are under water."[6] From *moose* the combinations *moose hide* and *moose horn* were formed, the latter "better for Physick use than Harts Horns." The Englishmen learned the name, too, of the *assapan,* the flying squirrel, which so fascinated King James I that he requested one be brought to him as a pet; of the *cusk,* a large New England fish first commented upon by Smith; of the *opossum;* and of the *woodchuck,* the last coming by way of folk etymology from Algonquian *wejack.*

New Englander and Virginian learned of curious Indian customs and beliefs, of the *manito,* or *manitou,* the definition of which was long a source of dispute. Harriot, in *Briefe and True Report* (1588), was the first to introduce the term to Englishmen, spelling it *Montoac* and stating that such Montoac were "of different sortes and degrees." Some early missionaries equated the manitou of the Indian with the Hebraic God, while others believed that two manitous, one good and one evil, struggled to gain power over nature. The word is generally accepted as signifying simply "spirit"; and every cave or waterfall, every tree or mountain, has, according to Indian belief, its own manitou, to whom sacrifice and petition can be made. The *powan,* sometimes *powwow* or *powaw* or *powwah,* coming from a root word meaning "he dreams," referred to the priest, or prophet, who presided over ritualistic ceremonies. From the name for the priest came application of *powwow* to the ceremonial rites or councils over which he presided; and it was used also as a verb, developing the derivatives *powwower* and *powwowing.* The

6. John Josselyn: *New England Rarities Discovered* (London, 1672), p. 44.

term early became a pejorative among the Puritans; in 1646 they forbade those Indians whom they could control to "paw-waw or p[er]form outward wor[shi]pp to their falce gods."[7] Eventually, however, the word was taken over in popular speech and remains one of our most viable Indian bor-rowings.

The chief was the *sachem*, and his power was carefully de-fined by John Smith: ". . . every Sachem is not a king, but their great Sachems have divers Sachems under their protec-tion, paying them tribute, and dare make no warres without his knowledge, but every Sachem cares for the widowes, or-phans, the aged, and maimed." *Sagamore* was the equivalent word in the Abnaki dialect, and from both words the English characteristically formed derivatives; *sagamoreship* was equiv-alent, in contemporary terms, to an earldom, as in the de-scription of a town lying "in the Saggamooreship, or Earldome of Aggawam."[8] Other titles of rank were *cocka-rouse*, for an outstanding warrior or leader, and *mugwump*, used by Elyot in his Indian Bible as a synonym for *Duke* (in Genesis 36:15) and destined for popularity in nineteenth-century American political campaigns.

The colonists learned of the sacred nature of the *totem*, the tribal mark—carving or other device or amulet—that distinguished the members of each tribe; and as they watched the Indians in their daily life, they took into their speech such words as *wigwam* and *papoose* and *squaw* (*sunck squaw*, too, for chief squaw), *moccasin* and *matchcoat*—which sounds American-made but came from Chippewa *matshigote* and referred to a mantle of fur or feathers. They watched the Indians play *chunkey*, a game resembling today's hockey, and traded with them in *wampumpeag*, the shell money that be-came a medium of exchange among the colonists themselves.

7. Massachusetts Bay *Records* (Boston, 1835–54), III, 98.

8. Edward Johnson: *Wonder-working Providence of Sions Saviour in New England* (London; 1654), p. 56. Quoted in Mitford M. Mathews, ed.: *A Dictionary of Americanisms on Historical Principles* (Chicago: University of Chicago Press; 1951).

They learned of foods, of ways of preparing corn to produce *hominy,* or *rockahominy, samp* and *pone* (*opone* or *poane* or *supawn*) and *succotash,* and of foods like *pemmican* and *johnnycake,* which may come from *Shawnee cake* or *journey cake* or even *Johnny cake* (personalized) but is probably from an Indian word, *jonakin.* And they learned other words now obsolete, *maninosa* (a shellfish), *weequashing* (eel fishing), and *cohonk,* an imitative word for the call of the wild geese, which signaled the beginning of the Indian year.

All of these borrowings, revealing as they are, do not tell the full story of the settlers' first encounters with the Indian; within the vocabulary, however, we find further evidence. Not all of the colonists learned these Indian words; not all knew friendly natives with whom to converse; not all had the same curiosity or the same patience for trying the new words on their tongues. And so, to express whatever called for expression, they fell back on the skill bred in their bones from long ago—phrasemaking, compounding, and inventing. Freely translating supposed Indian terms or combining familiar English ones, they produced combinations like *war paint* and *council fire, medicine man* and *warpath, pipe of peace, paleface, redskin.* They called the communal dwelling or council house of the Iroquois, with characteristic visual directness, a *long house;* they were curious about the *hothouse,* as described by Roger Williams: "This Hot-house is a kind of little Cell or Cave . . . and into this frequently the men enter after they have exceedingly heated it. . . . Here doe they sit . . . sweating together."[9] Cotton Mather later expanded on Williams's description of the New World sauna, adding the information that in the *hothouse* "a crew of them go sit and sweat and smoke for an hour together, and then immediately run into some very cold adjacent brook."[1]

With the word *Indian* itself, the English in America cre-

9. *A Key into the Language of America* (London, 1643). Quoted in Mathews: *Dictionary.*

1. *Magnalia Christi Americana* (Hartford, 1702). Quoted in Mathews: *Dictionary.*

ated so extensive a vocabulary that it alone could tell the story of white man and red. Too numerous to count, and covering areas both material and philosophical, these phrases present a panorama of the wilderness world and the men who had long lived within it. The established cultural and social pattern of Indian life appears in words like *Indian village* and *Indian town, Indian fort* and *Indian nation, Indian barn* and *field* and *hut* and *cabin* and *land. Indian king* and *Indian chief, Indian brave* and *Indian doctor, Indian grave* and *Indian path* and *Indian mound* and *Indian praying village*, like *Indian plantation* and *Indian quarters*, tell of the discoveries of the colonists as they pushed into the wilderness that had been the Indians'. Just as the *powan* could be identified as clearly (or more clearly) to an Englishman as the *medicine man* or the *Indian priest*, so the *matchcoat* could be as reasonably, and more simply, an *Indian coat*. Englishmen spoke of *Indian stockings* and *Indian breeches*, of *Indian boots* and *Indian shoes*, and wore them themselves. An English traveler reports in 1674: "Finding severall flakes of Isinglass in ye paths, ye soales of my Indian shooes in which I travelled glistened like sylver."[2] And when William Hubbard wrote, in 1677, that "Robert Dutch, of Ipswich, having been sorely wounded by a Bullet . . . and then mauled by the Indian Hatchets, was left for dead by the Salvages,"[3] settlers who may never have heard the word *tomahawk* knew what *Indian hatchet* meant. *Indian alarm* and *Indian yell, Indian whoop* and *war* and *warrior* and *arrow* are eloquent of terror; *Indian money, merchant, trader, goods, bowl, basket, tray* tell of trade. Many plants, their Indian names too difficult or their character basically too similar to familiar English types to change their names completely, were given the attribute of *Indian;* the colonists knew *Indian grass* and *hemp* and *bean* and *plum* and *lettuce* and *cherry, pea* and *peach,* and even *Indian weed*. The *Indian dog* was "a Crea-

2. South Carolina Historical Society *Collections* (1897), V, 460.

3. *A Narrative of the Troubles with the Indians in New England* (Boston, 1677).

ture begotten 'twixt a Wolf and a Fox, which the Indian light-
ing up on, bring up to hunt the Deer with."[4]

As the first attitude of curiosity and fear and of a certain
respect and friendliness weakened under the exacerbation
of hostile encounters and of distaste for Indian ways, the
evangelistic fervor evident in such concrete terms as *Indian
church* and *Indian school, Indian college* and *Indian Bible*
was translated into terms of contempt. *Indianize* and *Indianism* appeared in derogatory contexts. "All the while I went on
in Indianisme," we read in an early religious tract, "I was
going from God." To *Indianize* was to adopt the ways of the
Indians, as some did even from the days of Jamestown's
settlement; and Cotton Mather writes sternly, in *Magnalia*,
that "we have shamefully Indianized in all those abominable
things." The figure of an Indian cut out of red cloth was,
like Hester Prynne's A, a brand of shame among the Puritans, marking the woman "suffering an Indian to have carnal
knowledge of her."[5] (The letter *I* was already taken for in-
cest.) Pious antipathy toward the pagan gradually metamor-
phosed into a self-righteous antipathy toward the race; and
during the course of the century, when many Indians were
taken as slaves or hired as servants (in 1670, "Obadia the
engiane was hiered to keepe the cattell"),[6] we see the exploitation of Indian skills in such terms as *Indian scout,
Indian interpreter,* and *Indian guide.* Before 1682, there was
an *Indian constable*, whose duty was to capture runaway
slaves.

The pious English were determined to save the Indian
even if in so doing they had to destroy him. In the process,
they took possession of his land and almost completely ob-
literated from it, in favor of their own, his customs and
culture and beliefs. But they overlooked their own speech.
An eighteenth-century poetess once wrote, in the sentimental

4. Josselyn: *Rarities*, p. 15.
5. John Josselyn: *An Account of Two Voyages to New England* (London, 1674), p. 111.
6. East Hampton *Records*, I, 230 (Sag Harbor, N.Y., 1887–1905).

fashion of the time, of the Indian names that label our rivers and streams: ". . . their name is on your waters; Ye may not wash it out."[7] So are Indian culture and custom and belief and the history of the relationship between Englishman and Indian written in words we speak today; we cannot wash them out, either.

Even as Englishmen in Virginia and New England were learning Indian words and Indian ways, so were others along the eastern seaboard. In the Hudson Valley, Dutch trading posts had dotted the interior since 1610; and in the countryside of Nieuw Nederlandt, up the Hudson, Walloon settlers built their *boueries*, or farms. The *bowery* of the Dutch governors would survive as a place name in a later New York, where its meaning of "garden" would come to seem blackly humorous. On the island of Manhattan (Algonquian *manah*, "island," and *atin*, "hill"), which Peter Minuit had purchased from the Manhattan tribe for sixty guilders' worth of trinkets, the small town of New Amsterdam was a mecca for traders in the area; when the Dutch West India Company opened New Netherland to all the peoples of Europe, men of many nations—Welshmen and Huguenot French, Swiss and Sephardic Jews—added their accents to the community's already cosmopolitan tone. As settlement developed, the topography of what would be the state of New York was labeled with Dutch names—*Zandt Hoek* (*Sandy Hook*), *Helle-gat, Kinderhook, Yonkers, Cape Mey* (*May*). *Kill* ("channel"), *dorp* ("village"), and *clove* ("valley") joined other words to make compounds—*Schuylkill* and *New Dorp* and *Kaatersill Clove*. Some names, like *Nassau* and *Harlem* and *Staten*, would be little changed in later years; others would be hardly recognizable—*Gramercy* as *De Kromme Zee* or *Flatbush* as *Vlacht Bos*. But all would leave the mark of Holland upon the land.

The relationship between the English and Dutch in America was generally friendly; and in busy New Amsterdam,

7. Lydia Huntley Sigourney: "Indian Names" (c. 1822).

English and Dutch, French and Indian and Swede conversed
somehow with one another in the intercourse of trade. They
gathered at the *kermis,* the annual Dutch festival whose
name is still heard in parts of New York, and at the bazaars
and fairs and auctions, called *vendues,* a Dutch borrowing
from Middle French *vendre.* There they bought Delftware
and silverware made by the clever Dutch, and the new Dutch
*landskips,* in frames, to take back to the more elegant of the
colonial homes. Keeping the inevitable tumult of trade and
its accompanying activities under control was the *schout,* the
town officer, who combined the powers of mayor, sheriff, and
district attorney, and whose title may have given us the
phrase *a good scout* for one not unduly harsh.

In the outlying trading areas, however, Dutch and English
interests ultimately conflicted. There were disputes over
boundaries and accusations of encroachments; and after a
period of intermittent military confrontation, New Netherland became an English possession and *New Amsterdam,
New York.* The Dutch, who were more interested in trade in
North America than in dominion anyway, adapted with good
grace to the English regime; and the city remained what it
had been, an apolitical and cosmopolitan center of trade and
conviviality. (When the English assumed control, one-fourth
of all the buildings were "brandy shops, tobacco, or beer
houses," a situation that Peter Stuyvesant had been irritably
and futilely trying to change.) Fairs and bazaars and auctions
continued, and the thunder of *ninepins*—which would become *tenpins* in later years, to evade a prohibition against
the game—rumbled in the Catskills. *Santa Claus (Sinter
Klaas,* or *Saint Nicholas)* entered the consciousness of English
children, to the disapproval of those Puritans who had tried
so valiantly to stamp out pagan feasts.

Throughout the region, but particularly in the vicinity of
Albany, the Dutch clung to their language and customs; Noah
Webster reported hearing a sermon preached in Dutch in
1786. Trade terms were already common coin. Now, as
English and Dutch mingled in the bond of common citizen-

ship, other terms entered the vocabulary, some of them obsolete or reduced to regionalisms today but many of them
part of our everyday speech. Land was no less important to
the settlers in New York than to those in other regions; and
a Dutch measure, the *morgen,* or *morgan,* still current in
parts of New England and meaning slightly more than two
acres, figured in the sale of land—the Hempstead records
of 1658 note a transaction concerning "one Hollands Accre
or Morgen." *Much,* another term of measurement, was used
for quite different purposes; coming from Dutch *mutsje,* it
was a liquid measure amounting to, according to Mathews,
one-fifth of a pint, according to Krapp, one-eighth. As it was
used usually in connection with rum, the difference between
Krapp's and Mathews's estimates could make an important
difference; the same Hempstead records, in 1673, order that
those persons who fail to report for certain assigned duties
in the town are to "pay six muches of Rume to them that
gose." A convivial penalty! *Schepel,* now *skipple,* was a dry
measure, known in New England as a *short bushel* and cal-
culated with the help of a *skipple stone* for counterbalancing.
Some words now regional to the Hudson Valley but in common use during the early colonial period were *speck,* for
pork fat, as in *Speck and Applejees (speken applejees,* or fried
pork and apples); *pinxter,* a kind of azalea; *fly,* for marsh; and
*vlei,* a diminutive of *vellei* (valley). *Frowchey,* applied to a
bonneted elderly woman, came from the staid old greeting
*Vrouwtje,* once in use among the burghers' wives of New
Netherland; and *scup,* from *schop,* for a child's swing, and
*hoople,* from *hoeple,* for a rolling hoop, can still be heard in
the Hudson Valley.

A Dutch borrowing long part of our working vocabulary is
*bush,* from Dutch *bosch,* meaning woods or uncleared forest;
fruitful of derivative terms, it has given us *bush fighter, bush
ranger, bushman, bushmaster, bush league,* and *bush leaguer.*
*Bushwhack,* with the formations *bushwhacker* and *bushwhacking,* has acquired a variety of meanings. Originally it
referred to the practice of pulling a boat against the current

by grasping bushes along the bank or clearing a way through a thicket; later, fugitives from the law hacking their way through the woods were called *bushwhackers;* and during the Civil War, deserters who raided homes or robbed travelers and then retreated to hide-outs in the bush gave to the word even more unsavory connotations. Recently it has found new application in reference to guerrilla warfare. A now obsolete derivative from the same *bosch, bossloper* (Dutch *boschloper*), referred to the Dutch woods runner, the equivalent of the French *coureur de bois.* The term reminds us that the Dutch were more than enterprising traders and hospitable hosts; they were also a venturesome and tough people. Had they, like the Spanish and French, been vitally interested in the colonization of America, the English would have had another formidable rival in the unfolding struggle for empire.

Nevertheless, cozy domesticity is what breathes from most of the words we have taken from the Dutch. *Cruller* (curler) and *coleslaw* and *cookey* and *waffle* are mouth-watering words; they fit into the picture of the gregarious life that was evidently enjoyed by the Dutch burghers. De Vere reminds us that *tea-pumps,* those special pumps in the city that were noted for producing the best water for tea, were long pronounced *tea-pomps,* after the Dutch pronunciation. (As we have seen since De Vere, however, the pronunciation was more likely *tay-pomps.*) *Hot cake* came perhaps from Dutch *heetekoek,* a pancake, although the formations may have been merely parallel; Penn writes in 1683 of "hot cakes and new corn" baked in leaves by the Indians. *Sleigh* is a Dutch word, too, as is *span* (of horses); and the sturdy word *scow,* from Dutch *schouw,* and *keelboat,* from *kielboot,* tell of busy traffic up and down the Hudson.

Domesticity is present too in *stoop,* Dutch *stoep,* the covered or open porch with seats that was a characteristic feature of Dutch houses. It is not difficult to imagine a burgher sitting on the stoop smoking his pipe, with wife and children on the *stoep bancke* by his side, the *vrow* no doubt wearing her *clockmutch,* or *clapmatch,* the traditional Dutch cap seen so often in Dutch paintings. *Slawbank,* another word now obsolete, came from *slaap bancke,* a sleeping bench, and referred to a kind of bedstead used throughout New York, New Jersey, Delaware, and Pennsylvania well into the nineteenth century. And joining all these relaxing terms was *logy,* for lazy, from Dutch *log* ("heavy" or "sluggish"), a congenial companion.

All was not beer and skittles for the Dutch, however, any more than for anyone else in that hard-working age; and the word *boss,* from Dutch *baas,* has spread around the world. It is reported that Lord Carlisle, on a visit to America, was amused to hear from his stage driver: "I suppose the Queen is your boss now?" (Oh, come now, Lord Carlisle, that stage driver surely said *guess!*) And the women's liberation movement might contemplate a passage in M. Philipse's *Early Voyage to New Netherland* in which he remarks: "Here they had their first interview with the female boss or supercargo of the Vessel."[8] Traditionally, the English adopted the Dutch term so readily by reason of distaste for the term *master,* a distaste stemming from the same attitude that replaced *servant* with *help.* John Winthrop is credited with the first use of the term, in 1649, when he reported the arrival of "a small Norsey bark . . . with one Gardiner, an expert engineer or work base and provisions."[9] It is notable that the use of *boss* for the master of a vessel appears in connection with flatboats as well; each boat had its *boss* or *patroon,* the two words evidently being used synonymously. Combinations like *river boss, wagon boss, cow boss, logging boss* developed early in colonial times; and the term was used attributively with *shoemaker, carpenter,* and other occupational terms to indicate superior skill. Other Dutch "worker words" familiar to seventeenth-century Englishmen were *brickstreicker* and *houtkapper* (wood chopper).

8. The two quotations appear in De Vere: *Americanisms,* p. 91; but numerous other references as well suggest the early popularity of this Dutch borrowing.

9. "History of New England," in *Journal* (a. 1649), I, 166.

Just as the attributive word *Indian* gave to many English words an entirely new character, so did *Dutch* testify to the Dutch presence. We see the impact of Dutch architecture on colonial building, and an image of those early structures, too, in *Dutch door* and *Dutch barn*; we feel the warmth of Dutch domesticity in *Dutch blanket* and *Dutch oven*. Some coinages formerly in use have vanished; long before these days of ball-point pens, Benjamin Franklin's reference in *Poor Richard* to *Dutch quills,* which were writing quills hardened and clarified by being plunged into heated sand or passed rapidly through flame, had become irrelevant. Obsolete now are *Dutch sleigh,* a sleigh of distinctive design with two double seats and steel runners, and *Dutch pung,* an interesting combination of English *Dutch* with an Indian borrowing, *pung*— short for *tom pung,* an Algonquian term for a drag or sled made with skin. According to Mathews,[1] the combination was not in use until 1852, when the *New York Weekly Tribune* of January 24 reported that "every kind of sleigh, from the primeval model of the Dutch pung to the last wrinkle of a modern omnibus, was sported in the streets"; but from the context—always essential in a consideration of dating—the object, and hence its name, must have existed long before. *Dutch turnpike,* another obsolete term, was a passway over a swampy place made of the trunks of small trees laid close together, "this called a 'Dutch turnpike,' from the early Dutch settlers first making them."[2] Accompanying all these words, as they weave their picture of colonial life among the Dutch, are the proper names that have become part of our history over the years—*Roosevelt* and *Van Buren* and *Longstreet* (which was *Langestraet* when the General's ancestors arrived in New Amsterdam in 1657). And today, in Albany, descendants of the old Dutch settlers preside proudly over Tulip Time festivities.

A century before Jamestown, perhaps before Columbus,

1. *Dictionary.*

2. John Palmer: *Journal of Travel in the United States of North America and in Lower Canada* (London, 1818), p. 124.

Frenchmen from Normandy were fishing the Newfoundland cod banks. During the sixteenth century, the venturesome *coureurs de bois* began their treks into the northern wilderness; there they established the scattered trading posts that were the harbingers of French empire. As they paddled their *bateaux* along the winding waterways, living with Indian squaws far in the interior, trapping beaver and otter, and trading trinkets with the Indians for skins, they acquired a reputation for lawlessness that soon made them as feared by the settlers as were the Indians. "Necessity of securing the country against the incursion of the Iroquois and the disorders of the Coureur de Bois" is a paragraph heading in a 1672 official document.[3] Along the border between Maine and New France, these men wandered freely, bringing their furs to the great fair at Montreal, where trappers from everywhere gathered, or to New Amsterdam, later New York. Along with the far-ranging French missionaries, they introduced to the English with whom they came in contact French words and French phrases and French versions of Indian terms. *Bateau* soon made its way into the American vocabulary and was applied rather freely to any small boat, although the French-Canadian *bateau* was specifically a light, high-nosed, flat-bottomed boat tapering toward the ends. The word would come later and independently from the French in Louisiana and for many years, in both regions, was spelled in a variety of ways, as *battoe, batteau,* or *batto.* Along with *sault* and *rapids* and *portage,* the last the equivalent of the English *carrying-place,* it tells of a way of life summed up in the evocative term *voyageur,* which later supplanted *coureur de bois.* Of topographical terms introduced by the French, *prairie* (spelled *perarie, priory,* or *peraira*), for a grassy plain, is most notable. We associate the word principally with the West of a later day, and Mathews does not list its entry into the vocabulary until 1770; but *prairie chicken,* obviously a derivative and referring to a now disappearing bird of the Mississippi Valley, where the early French explorers traveled,

3. *Documents of Colonial History of New York* (tr. 1855), IX, 90.

appeared in 1691, evidence that *prairie* was already well
established in the vocabulary. The borrowing was a fruitful
one; when, during the great westward movement, it would
become associated in the national consciousness with those
vast stretches of the central plains, its innumerable derivatives would tell a story of their own.

The more extensive and earlier contact that the French,
especially the missionaries, had with the Indian brought into
English Indian words with a French accent. Place names we
still pronounce in the French way were once spelled cor-
respondingly, a condition that Webster deplored in his *American Spelling Book*. "How," he asked, "does an unlettered
American know the pronounciation of the names, *ouisconsin*
or *ouabasche,* in this French dress?" His complaints helped to
bring about the Anglicizing of some words, at least orthographically, but *Sioux* and *Iroquois* and *Illinois* continue to
be spelled and pronounced as they were when the French
introduced the names to us after changing the original
Algonquian to suit their own vocal inclinations. Still, folk
etymology had its innings on our side; *Bob Ruly* was once
*Bois Brûlé,* and *Bob Low,* an island near Detroit, *Bois Blanc*.
And perhaps just to show the whimsy of its ways, folk
etymology took *Burnt Coast* (on Swan's Island, Maine), which
was a quite literal translation of the original *Côte Brûlé,* and
made of it *Burnt Coat. Brûlé* itself, as a topographical term,
was treated cavalierly: the French coined it to describe burnt-
over ground on which grass had grown, an incipient prairie;
the English took that quite reasonable French word and made
of it the apparently rootless *brooly* (now obsolete).

*Toboggan* came through French. It is from *tobagan,* the
French rendering of an Algonquian word for a drag or sled
made of skin; the Algonquian word itself came from the same
root as did *tom pung,* already noted, and is akin to Micmac
*togâgun. Caribou,* spelled *caribo, carraboo,* or *carriboo* at
various times, came also through French, from an unattested
Algonquian word,*mekālixpowa,* "snow shoveler"; the animal is described by Josselyn, in 1672, as "the *Maccarib,*

*Caribo,* or *Pohano,* a kind of Deer, as big as a Stag."[4] A word
often thought of as Indian, but actually French, is *calumet,*
a French dialectal variant of *chalumeau,* "a straw"; the term
was found useful even by the Indians, who used it in con-
versing with the white man. Father Hennepin described a
*calumet dance* as only one of many ritual ceremonies in which
the calumet played a part. Other words clearly associated with
Indian life but French in origin are *lodge,* from French *loge,*
and the noun *brave,* for warrior. *Lodge* meant not only the
dwelling place of a family of Indians, but also the family itself, so that the size of a tribe could be computed by the number of lodges it comprised. Besides serving this dual semantic
purpose, the word gave rise to English-made combinations
early in colonial times. *Indian lodge* was inevitable, while
*sweat lodge,* a synonym of *sweat house, sweat tepee,* or *hot-
house,* described the building that housed the sauna baths.
Another French borrowing of those early days, not Indian-
connected, calls up the picture of a glow of warmth in the
snowy wilderness—*chowder,* from French *chaudière,* "cal-
dron." De Vere gives the Puritans credit for inventing the
dish, but etymology seems to belie his theory. It may even
have been a later borrowing, coming by way of English settlers
in Nova Scotia after the Treaty of Utrecht;[5] but the word
was evidently well established in New England early in the
eighteenth century.

French speech was heard not only in the North. Huguenots
had sought refuge in the region of the Carolinas during the
sixteenth century, attempting settlement twice and stirring
up the wrath of the Spaniards at Saint Augustine. The
English, united with the French Huguenots in common
hatred of the Spanish, had strong sympathy for the refugees;
and the English colonies were a natural harbor for those
fleeing religious persecution in France. Few French borrowings seem, however, to have come from this source during the
seventeenth century, possibly because most of those entering

4. *Rarities,* p. 20.
5. Steven T. Byington in *American Speech* (April 1944), p. 122.

the language did so in England at the same time or before
and so do not qualify as Americanisms. *Carryall,* from French
*carriole,* for a light one-horse vehicle (and later extended),
is an Americanism, however, and would hardly have come
from the *voyageurs* or even from the missionaries; we can
assume the acquisition was made through urban contact. Its
etymology has been disputed, some contending that it is an
English coinage designed to mean exactly what it says; but
evidence that it developed from *carriole* to its present form by
way of folk etymology is strong. A French word common to
both Dutch and English from earliest colonial times, as has
been seen, was *vendue,* or *vandue;* but it had evidently crossed
the Atlantic with the Dutch. The term was widely used and is
still in use in Pennsylvania and surrounding regions; *vendue
master,* which was a common phrase in colonial times, is now
obsolete, but *vendue crier* is still in regional use. An American-made term that makes it clear that Frenchmen had settled
in the New England colonies in substantial numbers before
1699 is the now obsolete *French Church,* used by Sewall in his
diary—not very happily. "This day," he says, "I spake with
Mr. Newman about his partaking with the French Church
on the 25 December on account of its being Christmas-day,
as they abusively call it." *French-Indian* was a compound used
both for the lingua franca of the northern wilderness and
for an Indian friendly to the French or under their influence.
And *French falls,* or *French fall shoes,* their price set in 1677
as not "above seven pence halfe penny a size for well wrought
[French falls],"[6] suggests that even in early colonial times the
French were already influencing American fashion.

Of the Swedes' short-lived dominion on the banks of the
Delaware (1638–55) only one word has definitely come, but
that a significant one. The *log house*—not *log cabin,* a term
that came much later—was their contribution to pioneer
architecture and to the language. The term appeared early;
that it was authentically Swedish in origin is confirmed in

6. *Connecticut Public Records,* II, 325.

Lawson's *Carolina* (1705), wherein we read of ". . . a House made of Logs, (such as the Swedes in America very often make, and are very strong)." Because of its structural strength and greater resistance to fire, the log house was a favorite type for prison construction; in the Maryland archives of 1663 is the order "that A Logg howse be built Twenty foot Square . . . for a Prison." The term would later be changed to *log cabin* and become a part of the American mythos.

The dearth of Spanish borrowings during the early period testifies to the separation of the English settlers from the vast, thinly spread Spanish empire to the southwest, as well as from that small replica of Old Spain, Saint Augustine, in Florida. Saint Augustine was a target of both French and English raids from the time of its founding in 1565, and some Spanish words did trickle into English awareness—hostile contact brings verbal interchanges, too. A few Spaniards made their way to the empty spaces of New France to compete for the rich fur trade, and in the Southern colonies occasional contact inevitably took place in the unsettled lands. *Pirogue,* which was for us a French borrowing, came from Spanish *piragua,* itself originally a Carib Indian word; *cavort,* according to De Vere, comes from Spanish *cavar* rather than from the usually accepted French *courbetter,* and De Vere's arguments do seem etymologically plausible. *Buffalo* (Spanish *búfalo*) was already in use in Europe for the Indian or African ox; here it was applied, with zoological inexactitude, to the bison, whose name should properly have come from the Old English *wesund* (Teutonic *wisand*), the name of the now extinct wild ox of Europe, the *Bos Urus* of Caesar. Still, it is somehow appropriate that *our* bison, so associated with the Spanish-settled regions of our land, should have a Spanish name.

Few other words entering the vocabulary during the seventeenth century are traceable to the Spanish, although Smith's reference to "a certaine India Bug, called by the Spaniards a Cacarootch," introduces the *cockroach* to literature; and *mosquito,* appearing in Hakluyt's *Voyages* as *musketa,* developed a formidable array of derivative terms in America, such as *mosquito hawk, mosquito bar, mosquito country, mosquito curtains.* Governor Bradford wrote scornfully of those "too delicate . . . that cannot endure the biting of a muskeeto; . . . we would wish such to keepe at home till at least they be muskeeto proofe." And as with the attributive names of other nationalities, the Americans used *Spanish* to form phrases testifying to the Spanish presence. *Spanish oak, Spanish beard* (moss), and *Spanish Indian* were in use quite early, while Spain's economic pre-eminence and—no doubt— the fruits of English piracy are evident in the numerous terms for Spanish moneys, like *Spanish bit, Spanish dollar, Spanish pistole* (or *pistoll*, as Sewall wrote it), which circulated freely in the colonies. But the major contributions of Spanish to American speech would not be made until another century had passed and the English colonies in America had become one nation. During the crucial century ahead, the American language would be busy not only recording vast historical and social change, but also absorbing into its vocabulary much of the speech and the accents of other immigrants from a Europe increasingly aware of the potential of the New World.

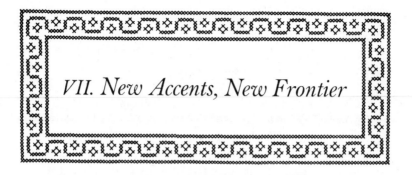

# VII. New Accents, New Frontier

Depending upon our provenance, some of us eat *smearcase;* others eat (or don't eat!) *curds.* In some parts of the land, our children ride the *seesaw,* in others the *teeter-totter* or perhaps the *tilt,* in some—bright word—the *tippity-bounce.* We may promise to arrive at a *quarter of ten* or a *quarter till* or perhaps a *quarter to,* using idiom regionally established more than two hundred years ago.

As the seventeenth century ended, the English colonies, sparsely settled and geographically and politically separate, had not only distinctive social and cultural characteristics but dialectal differences too, these last due to the particular regional backgrounds of the first settlers, to coinage born of local necessities—fishing terms in New England, for example, tobacco terms in the South—and to whatever localized borrowings had been made through contact with other languages. During the early eighteenth century, scattered areas of settlement along the seaboard were gradually joined; pioneers, individually or in small groups, pushed into the interior; and by 1750 an unbroken chain of English-controlled settlement extended from the Penobscot in Maine to the Altamaha in Georgia. This narrow fringe between mountains and sea was the "mother area" not only of American history but also of American speech. Within it were developed, during the colonial period, all the regional and local types of American English that would be carried westward, after the Revolution, to blend into new varieties and be themselves touched and changed by history.[1]

Uniform as is American speech—and compared to the speech of England or France, of Italy or Spain, our "general Volkssprache," as Mencken calls it, is remarkably free of dialect—its differences, even with the leveling impact of radio and movies and TV, are sufficiently marked to be identified within regional boundaries that, in turn, contain within themselves numerous divisions and subdivisions. Popular observation of these differences began with the earliest contact —Sarah Knight, in 1704, was amused at the "dreadful pretty" and "I vow!" of the New Haven people—and during the eighteenth century such astute observers as Bartlett and Webster and Witherspoon commented on local idiom; but the systematic study of dialectal aspects of American speech began only late in the nineteenth century.

With the launching of *Dialect Notes* and the aroused interest of scholars, with the publication in 1919 of the first edition of Mencken's *American Language* (which would eventually go into four editions, numerous reprintings, two *Supplements*, and an abridged edition[2] of all three), with the founding during the twenties of *American Speech* and the commencement of work on the *Dictionary of American English on Historical Principles* (the *DAE*), followed soon after by the initial surveys for the long-term project—still continuing—of a *Linguistic Atlas of the United States and Canada,* American English was recognized as a language of infinite variety and continuing vitality. The *Linguistic Atlas,* a systematic study of American usage whose findings have been published periodically since 1939, reveals dialectal differences as well as similarities, which, Kurath points out, "shed light on U.S. migrations, settlement areas, trade areas, culture areas, and

1. The importance of the Eastern states in the history of American English is stressed in Hans Kurath: *Word Geography of the Eastern United States* (Ann Arbor: University of Michigan Press; 1949), p. vi.

2. Ed. Raven J. McDavid, Jr. (New York: Alfred A. Knopf; 1963).

other aspects of human geography and population history."[3] We see in its maps and guides regionalisms such as *smearcase,* from German *Schmierkase,* and *The bread is all,* a German idiom, occurring not only in Pennsylvania, as testimony to early immigration, but also as far away as Nebraska and Kansas, where Germans from Pennsylvania or their descendants established settlements. *Pail* traveled with New England emigrants to Pennsylvania and Ohio, while *bucket* traveled upward from the South to meet it. Appalachian *poke* (*sack* or *bag* elsewhere) found its way to Texas with emigrants from the southern hill country and even to one small area in northeast Oregon, where descendants of some far-ranging Ozarkians still feel *dauncy,* not *dizzy,* and the *chillun* search for *woodfish* (mushrooms) in the Oregon woods. Occasional oddities emerge; the cattle call *chay,* heard in the vicinity of Williamsburg, South Carolina, is duplicated only—as far as anyone has been able to determine—in County Antrim, Ireland, linking the present residents of a tiny area of the United States with their ancestors in the old country.

It is notable that the vocabulary by which we trace our regional ancestry is rarely that of arts and letters, which unites a supraregional intellectual elite, or of urban sophistication, which is much the same East and West, or of scientific discovery or political jargon. It is that of the intimate, everyday life of home and farm, which even the most cultivated speaker learns in childhood and retains. Sometimes—because urbanization has homogenized the language in cities and eliminated some linguistic demands (who calls cattle in the Bronx?)— terms have been lost except in small speech pockets of the larger area in which they once prevailed. Only in southeastern New England, for example, or from someone who has come from there, is one likely to hear *eace worm,* for an earthworm, or *tempest,* for a storm. Only in the Albemarle Sound area

3. Hans Kurath: "The American Languages," *Scientific American* (January 1950). Reprinted in part in C. Merton Babcock, ed.: *Ordeal of American English* (Boston: Houghton Mifflin Co.; 1961).

are *trumpery room,* for storeroom, and *hicky horse,* for see-saw, commonly heard. Today, with the standardizing of terms, especially for advertised items, some survivals are fast dying out; but the persistence of many of them poses problems for advertisers. Over the years, the Sears, Roebuck catalogue shows *frying pan* winning place over *skillet* and both of them supplanting completely, by 1955, the older *spider;* but the regional tenacity of other terms for *coal hod,* which alone was used in the 1911 catalogue, brought about the inclusion of *coal pail, coal bucket,* and *coal scuttle* in succeeding years so that no potential customer should feel his area slighted. The catalogue writers still vacillate between *shade* and *blind, comforter* and *quilt,* each of which has its regional champions.[4]

Other regional terms still prevailing, according to the *Linguistic Atlas* findings, are *string beans* north of the Potomac and *snap beans* south of it, with *green beans* (which one suspects is gaining ascendancy by reason of its commercial use) in the Appalachian area from the upper Ohio to the Carolinas. *Brook* is a New England and Northern term, *creek* and *run* Middle Atlantic, and *branch* (as in *bourbon and branch water*) peculiar to the South. Cattle are still called even close to Manhattan; in the New York area, the farmer cries, *Boss! Co-boss! Come bossie!,* but in South Carolina he calls, *Cowench! Co-inch! Co-ee!* The *buttonwood* or *button-ball* of New England is the *sycamore* of the South. The *dragonfly* darts around under many names: *darning needle* in most of New England and New York; *snake feeder* and *snake doctor* in the Appalachian area; *mosquito hawk* in most of the South; *spindle, snake guarder,* and other names in scattered speech enclaves.[5] A moral no doubt lies here: let him who would hide his origins avoid dialectologists.

4. Arthur G. Kimball: "Sears-Roebuck and Regional Terms," *American Speech* (October 1963), pp. 209–13.

5. In an article in *American Speech* (February 1968), pp. 51–7, Max D. Smith suggests that the phrasing of questions by *Linguistic Atlas* interviewers may bring misleading answers. "A large winged insect seen

Major change in the American language patterns that had been established in the first days of settlement became inevitable with the great shifting of peoples that began late in the seventeenth century. It was a random shifting, principally north and south, with none of the focal direction of the later westward migrations. The period between the Treaty of Utrecht, in 1713, and the beginning of the French and Indian War, in 1763, has been called by some historians the most "stable" period of American colonial history;[6] it appears, rather, in a perspective that takes in the *back country* stretching from the settled seaboard areas to the Appalachian barrier, to be a time of restless, almost fluid movement, of movement that, in retrospect, moved a fault-finding English critic to admit grudgingly that *immigrant* is "perhaps the only word, of which the circumstances of the United States has in any degree demanded the addition to the English language."[7] At the time he wrote, in 1809, *emigrant,* for either an incoming or a departing person, had long been in use in England; but that word, too, was given new meaning in America, where with its new-coined mirror twin it described not only foreigners leaving other countries and entering America, but also settlers moving from one region to another within it.

Obviously, all of the early settlers had been *immigrants,* and not all of them English. Dutch and German artisans sailed to Jamestown on the *Esther;* and as early as 1633 Governor Winthrop of the Massachusetts Bay Colony wrote—with a tantalizing lack of elaboration—that "a Scotchman by prayer and fasting dispossessed one possessed of the devil."

---

around water" could mean to some—and does in parts of Kansas studied—the *praying mantis,* called also *walking stick* and *katydid.* Smith suggests, somewhat utopianly, that the geographical distribution of insects or other referents should be studied by dialectologists.

6. E.g., Charles M. Andrews: *Colonial Folkways* (New Haven: Yale University Press; 1921), p. 3.

7. Edward A. Kendall: *Through the Northern Parts of the United States in the Years 1807–'8,* 3 vols. (New York; 1809), vol. 2, p. 252.

Dissenting Scots were transported by Cromwell, after the Battle of Dunbar in 1650, to labor in the ironworks at Saugus, Massachusetts; and the *Irish potato* was named for the Scotch-Irish settlers who began its successful cultivation at Londonderry, New Hampshire, in 1719. The *schooner* proverbially owes its name to the Scottish bystander who exclaimed: "Oh, see how she scoons!" (from Scots dialectal term *scun,* or *scoon,* meaning to skim along the surface of the water) when the new-styled craft was launched at Gloucester in 1713. It is clear that the trilled r's of Scottish speech and dialectal terms like *spunky* and *spree* were familiar to English ears early in the colonial period.

Before 1700, Welsh Quakers and Swiss Pietists, Finns and Danes, as well as a great number of Germans, had established flourishing settlements in Pennsylvania, notably at Germantown. German speech, principally the Westricher dialect of the Palatinate that was to become Pennsylvania Dutch, prevailed in the entire region; and advertisements and street signs were printed in both German and English and sometimes (to Benjamin Franklin's disgust) only in German. In New York, the *German Flats,* a region in Herkimer County, near Utica, was occupied as early as 1723; there, too, the German settlers characteristically retained their own speech. Other foreign-speaking immigrants were scattered throughout the colonies. The presence in colonial records of well-known names like *Faneuil* and *Bowdoin, Bayard* and *St. Julien* tells of the rapid rise of the Huguenot French to prominence in colonial affairs, while in South Carolina, where the admission of new counties with largely French populations changed the representational proportion in the assembly, Englishmen asked angrily whether "the Frenchmen who cannot speak our language should make our laws?"[8] In New York, the persistence of Dutch and French as the languages of commerce and of Dutch alone in church and school motivated Anglican missionaries to appeal to the Bishop of

8. James Truslow Adams: *Provincial Society* (New York: The Macmillan Company; 1924), pp. 169–70.

London to forbid the use of either Dutch or French in pulpit or classroom.

Antagonism to non-English elements, however, was not as strong as the desire for *help*, for hands and bodies to labor on the numerous *iron plantations* and in the lumber and flour mills, to till the soil of increasingly larger land grants, to serve as artisans and domestic help for a rapidly growing population. Negro slaves had not become a major factor in the Southern economy—Cotton was not yet King—and were proving unsatisfactory in the North; and so well was the land of the free fulfilling its promise that help was "not to be had at any rate, every one having business of his own."[9] Importation of servants seemed to offer the only solution to the problem. The manner of their importation, however, introduced into the vocabulary a cluster of semantically unpleasant words.

*Servant*, which had for years expressed an honorable and respected concept, took on, in eighteenth-century America, a new and ominous meaning; it was used synonymously with slave.[1] Mathews defines the term as "an immigrant intending or destined to become a servant or indentured servant in America." Note the separation of "intending" and "destined." Many who left their homes with adequate resources and with skills to qualify them for independent living were swindled and robbed and reduced to beggary before departure or on the voyage over; at the mercy, then, of unscrupulous ship's captains or agents, they were forced to join the *redemptioners* (who were redeeming the cost of their passage) and *free willers* (who were selling their labor for a period of years, usually five to seven). We have heard, from Beard and other eminent historians, of the respected status of indentured servants in America and of the rise of many of them to high estate. In many instances, the status and the possibility re-

9. (1711) F. L. Hawks: *History of North Carolina*, vol. 2, p. 215. Quoted in Mitford M. Mathews, ed.: *A Dictionary of Americanisms on Historical Principles* (Chicago: University of Chicago Press; 1951).
1. *Oxford English Dictionary.*

mained; but by the 1720's, the importation of servants had
become big business, eager employers were willing to pay the
high prices demanded by procurers, and exploitation was
rampant. Along with the *free willers* came convicts, who had
chosen or been forced to choose transportation in lieu of im-
prisonment, and *kids,* who had been "Spirited or Kidnapt (as
they call it) into America."[2] *Soul drivers* waited at dockside
to buy in lots those *servants* not yet contracted for and to
drive them around the countryside to sell. The lot of the
steerage passenger was often dreadful to begin with; we read
of cruelty, starvation, raging disease, and even cannibalism
taking place on the voyages over.[3] It is no wonder that many
who survived their terms of servitude left with bitterness
the scenes of their degradation and pushed toward new lands
where they could act and speak as they pleased.

But thousands came. They were not only lured by the
blandishments of *newlanders,* who were sent by the large
landowners to Europe to recruit servants, but were also driven
by the turmoil of continuing wars and religious persecution
in Europe, by economic misery and widespread hopelessness.
Their coming was only part of a great mass movement that
was filling other colonial areas too, pouring the people and
accents of Europe into the West Indies—British and French
and Dutch; into South American colonies like Guiana (a
century earlier, the Pilgrims had almost chosen Guiana as
their place of settlement); into New France and New Spain.
John Law's French-blessed development scheme in Louisiana,
soon to burst as the *Mississippi Bubble,* was bringing not only
Frenchmen but also Germans and Scots and Englishmen into
the Southern regions, to introduce speech that would later
become part of American English. Certainly one *Hans Erich
Roder,* settling on Bayou Teche, had no precognition that, in

2. Increase Mather: *Cases of Conscience* (1862), p. 241.

3. For an account of a typical voyage, see Gottlieb Mittelberger: *Journey to Pennsylvania in the Year 1750, and Return to Germany in the
Year 1754,* ed. Carl Theodore Eben (Philadelphia: John J. McVey Co.;
1898).

a later generation, French-speaking Acadians, also refugees, would change *Hans Erich Roder* phonetically to *Anseriquer Auder,* and that his descendants living in the town of *Des Allemands* (from *Côte des Allemands,* the German Coast) would one day be speaking the colorful "Cajun" dialect of southwest Louisiana, one of the most interesting of American speechways. Colonists in New Spain, occupying those regions that would become Texas and New Mexico, Arizona and California and Florida, were already setting the stamp of Spanish culture and speech on the land, giving to it place names—*Los Angeles* and *Santa Fe, Pensacola* and *Rio Grande* and *Sierra Nevada*—that would trip lightly on the tongues of later Americans and depositing a treasure of ordinary Spanish words to be caught up more than a century later in the spreading stream of American English.

Immigration to the colonies became so massive that European countries were alarmed, some of them passing edicts against emigration; and Americans themselves began to regret their earlier initiative. At Worcester, a mob including "some of the best people in town" destroyed the frame of a Presbyterian church under construction; and Cotton Mather hoped that the coming of the Scotch-Irish should "not prove fatal in the end." Even in traditionally hospitable Pennsylvania, Penn's agent, James Logan, complained in 1729 that "it looks as if Ireland is to send all her inhabitants hither" and labeled all foreigners "surly people." Two decades later, Benjamin Franklin asked querulously why the "Palatine boors" should "be suffered to swarm into our settlements and, by herding together, establish their language and manners to the exclusion of ours? Why should Pennsylvania, founded by the English, become a colony of *aliens,* who will shortly be so numerous as to germanize us instead of our anglifying them . . . ?" *Anglifying* was Franklin's coinage; the concept of *Americanizing* had still to be expressed, or perhaps even conceived. The increasingly multiethnic and multilingual situation is epitomized in a 1744 report that the "inhabitants of Lancaster, Pa., are chiefly High-Dutch, Scotch-

Irish, some few English families, and unbelieving Israelites."[4]
The last were, for the most part, Sephardic Jews from Spain
or Portugal, with names like *Lopez* and *Rivera;* the minority
English probably included emigrant families from New
England. The *High-Dutch* and *Scotch-Irish* were members of
two misleadingly named groups whose imprint on the language was to endure to our own time.

To eighteenth-century Americans, the *Scotch-Irish* were
descendants of those Lowland Scots who had been sent to
*plant* confiscated Irish lands during the political and religious
wars of the seventeenth century; but the separate terms *Scotch*
and *Irish* had traveled on an etymological merry-go-round to
arrive at their American conjunction. *Scotch* was a contraction
of Scottish, coming from Middle English *Scottes* and so from
Old English *Scottas,* a word referring, like Latin *Scotus* and
its ultimate source, Old Irish *Scuit,* to Scot and Irishman both.
Middle English *Irisc(h),* from Old English *Iras,* referred in
the thirteenth century to the Celts alone, but in the sixteenth
to the Gaelic inhabitants of the Scottish Highlands as well.
With all the confusion in its parental background, the analyti-
cal compound *Scotch-Irish* seems a relatively inoffensive com-
promise; but it did not then and does not today satisfy either
of the groups that now claim its elements separately. The
Scots immigrants did not think of themselves as Irish; and
it is ironic that much of the antagonism toward them in
America rose from their nominal association with the Celtic
Irish, who were generally despised on both religious and
ethnic grounds. So prevalent was the confusion and so
onerous its results that a group of Scotch-Irish at one time
petitioned the Massachusetts assembly to recognize them for-
mally as Scots, so that they would be spared the penalties of
the invidious association.

*Dutch,* like *English,* became the name of a people long after
it was the name of a language; and those whom we so label—

---

4. Massachusetts Historical Society *Collections* (1744), I, Series VII, p.
177.

the people of the Netherlands and the Hudson Valley settlers
—never adopted it for themselves. The name takes us far back
in our linguistic history, to the ancient word *teuta-,* "tribe,"
from which came Germanic *theuda-,* with its derivative
*theudiskaz,* "of the people." *Theudiskaz,* reduced to *Deitsc*
in the ninth century, was the equivalent of Latin *vulgaris* and
meant simply "language of the people," as opposed to Latin,
the language of religion and learning. As *Duutsc,* it came into
English and was extended to the Germanic people of Germany, Austria, Switzerland, and the Low Countries, as well
as to their language. Only in modern times, since the United
Provinces gained their independence, was the word *German*
(Latin *Germanus,* "German," perhaps from Celtic, akin to
Old Irish *gair,* "neighbor") restricted to its present meaning
and *Dutch* applied specifically to the language and the people
of the Netherlands. Given the unscholarly genius of the
language and the workings of analogy, it was perhaps inevitable that *Deitsch,* as the Germans called their speech,
should become *Dutch* to their neighbors in America
and they themselves *Dutchmen,* while the attribute *High,*
already in use in English in reference to the language, was
applied to the Pennsylvania people to distinguish them from
the Hudson Valley settlers. Later, *Pennsylvania* was substi-
tuted for *High*; and by the time that purists sought to introduce into common usage the more accurate *Pennsylvania
German,* the popular form had been firmly established. Today, the language and the people of the old German settlement area, like their cooking and architecture and customs,
remain to most of us *Pennsylvania Dutch.*

Franklin's fears that the colony might become Germanized
had historical basis. After all, such great English names as
*Sidney* and *Seymour, Rivers* and *Delaware* had been *St.
Denis* and *Saint-Maure, Des Rivaux* and *La Warre* when the
Normans brought them into England. Now, with *Hubers*
and *Pfoerschings, Linkhorns* and *Krankheits* and *Schmidts*
threatening to outnumber the *Franklins* and *Adamses* and
*Hamiltons,* what might not follow? Most of the *Hubers* soon

became *Hoovers* (however, in French Louisiana they became *Houbres*); the *Pfoerschings, Pershings*. And along with the changing of German names to English ones, German-speaking immigrants began incorporating into their own speech and adapting to it such English terms as *creek* (*krick,* pronounced in the contemporary fashion); *sleek* (*schlick*); *turnpike* (*torn-peik*); and *very* (*weri*) and coined hybrids like *gedscheest* (chased); *gebärrt* (barred); and *vermisst* (missed). Even Franklin should have been satisfied that as much Anglifying as Germanizing was taking place. Anglifying rather than any other kind of -izing was evident also in the transformation of foreign surnames other than German. In New England, *Bon Coeur, Petit,* and *de l'Hôtel* had become *Bunker, Poteet,* and *Doolittle.* Elsewhere, Dutch *Kuiper* had been changed to *Cooper* and *Van Kouwenhoven* to *Conover.* Finnish *Marttinen* was now *Morton.*[5]

Most of these changes in surnames took place, as in many ordinary words, through the processes of folk etymology; and they offer in their instant metamorphoses striking illustration of the nature of those processes. Because three lists of names were made at the port of Philadelphia, one the passenger list itself, another a list of these same passengers subscribing to an oath of allegiance to the British government (as who would not?), and the third a list of those abjuring the Church of Rome—for brotherly love did not embrace Papists, even in Philadelphia—we see in quick succession the changes made by sometimes uneducated officials under the dictation of usually illiterate immigrants. Many of the newcomers progressed into the interior, where other lists were made; these lists incorporated the changes already accomplished and often added to them by way of whimsical or arbitrary spelling. A name like *Bloch* usually became *Block* or *Black*; *Albrecht* was converted to *Albert* or *Albright*; *Katzenellenbogen* somewhat tortuously became *Castle.* Umlauts, as in *Sänger* and

---

5. Mencken discusses surnames and their metamorphoses in great detail in *The American Language*, 4th ed. (New York: Alfred A. Knopf; 1936), pp. 474–505, and in *Supplement II* (1948), pp. 396–461.

*Glück,* were simply dropped; *Kuehle* became *Keeley,* and
*Pfeffer, Pepper.* Bachmann changed to *Baughman* and then
*Boughman* and finally *Bowman; Schnäbele* progressed—or
regressed—through *Snabely* and *Snavely* into *Snively.* In
many cases, the owner of a foreign surname, after settling
down and concluding that having an English name would be
to his advantage, translated his name literally; *Beauchamp*
often became *Beecham,* but in some cases was changed by a
bilingual owner to *Fairfield.* Finnish *Mäki* became *Hill;* German *Vogelgesang, Birdsong.* Evidently, of all national distinctions, surnames have the lowest boiling point in the melting pot.

Drastic change in the Scotch-Irish surnames after the arrival
of their owners in America was less likely and usually unnec-
essary, for many of these immigrants had names already congenial and familiar to English ears, names like *MacDonald*
and *Lewis* and *Davis* and *Patton* and *Campbell.* As speakers
of English, however dialectal, some of these newcomers acquired minor official positions in the interior; and it was
often they who were responsible for the mutilation of the
surnames of their fellow immigrants, especially the Germans.
But they were not particularly fond of the pacifist Germans
anyway.

All of the immigrants, German or Scotch-Irish or Swiss,
had come to America beguiled by the golden promise of land;
but as early as the beginning of the eighteenth century, the
gilt was wearing thin. Most of the new land-related words in
the vocabulary are not the expansive, evocative topographical
terms characteristic of an earlier time, *bluff* and *divide* and
*foothill* and the like; now they spell trouble. Phrases like
*land law* and *land banker, warranted land, patent land, land
warrant, land bill,* and—most ominously—*land speculator*
enter the vocabulary, along with such terms as *pre-emption*
and *pre-emption rights* and *land claim.* (Not coincidentally,
the profession of law, which had been hitherto scorned in the
colonies and had had no professional standards, began the rise
to eminence that would culminate in the brilliant display of

legal talent meeting in Philadelphia in 1774. *Admission to the bar* was a new phrase in the 1760's, when practicing lawyers set up objective qualifications—in Massachusetts, at least three years of study with a barrister—for admittance to practice before the courts.) The increasing density of population, due both to a fantastic birth rate among the English[6] and to the influx of immigrants, was making land scarce in the settled areas, and larger and larger grants were being made to individual proprietors. Formerly, the grantees of a town had been its settlers too, the land their immediate livelihood; the new landowners, obtaining enormous grants either through influence with officials or by means of wealth accumulated from trade, held their shares in a township as a commodity, and many of them never saw the land they held. *Actual settlers*—a term coined to meet an obvious need— tilled the soil and quite literally built the town.

In many cases, those who had settled in a new township and, in common with others, had enhanced the value of the land found their interests suddenly sacrificed, their commons divided and sold, and themselves dispossessed through legal chicanery. Filled with resentment toward the forces of government, which invariably supported the landowners, they joined the migration from one part of the colonies to another that had been going on since the last century. Usually they moved toward the unsettled *back country*, where land was less costly—into upper New England or the Mohawk Valley, into western Pennsylvania and Maryland, toward the Shenandoah Valley, or, from Virginia and farther south, into what was called the *upcountry,* above the fall line, extending into the ridges and valleys of the South. Gradually a belt of new settlement, extending from the Green Mountains and the Mohawk Valley down the eastern fringe of the Alleghenies into the Shenandoah Valley of Virginia and the Piedmont

6. As many as twenty-six children of a single mother are recorded; girls were usually married and several times mothers before they were out of their teens; and second and third marriages were common. Andrews: *Colonial Folkways,* pp. 86–7.

areas of the Carolinas and Georgia, was established between the older seaboard colonies and the great Appalachian barrier. Beyond that barrier lay the French. This line of settlement marked the first American *frontier*; the seaboard one had been English.

*Frontier* has acquired a mystical meaning in America. When the term was brought to this country by the first settlers, it meant, as it continues to mean in England, a boundary between two countries or the territory adjacent to the boundary line on either side; in practical terms, it was the shared defense line of a homogeneous people. We note, in the New Jersey archives of 1671, a report that "if a good Worke were throwne about Matinicock House, and that strengthened with a considerable Guard, it would be an admirable Frontier."[7] Derivative seventeenth-century terms like *frontier settlement* and *frontier plantation* were geographical terms marking location and indicating physical vulnerability. Gradually, however, as settlers moved into the border wilderness that was beyond the frontier, the line between established settlement and outland was blurred; and the word came to define and symbolize that unbroken land of scattered settlement, without even rudimentary roads, which, in the words of historian Frederick Jackson Turner, "constituted the meeting ground of savagery and civilization," or, in the less poetic words of the United States Census, the margin of that settlement which had a density of two or more to the square mile.[8]

Etymologically, the terms that developed in America to identify the frontier are self-contradictory. Frontier comes from Middle English *frountier,* a derivative of French *frontière,* from French *front.* To the colonial American, who was still facing England, the *frontier* was at his back; and the vocabulary is filled with evidence of his attitude. *Back plantations, back counties, back countrymen, back settlers, back people, back farmers, backwoodsmen*—all of the terms con-

7. Archives of the State of New Jersey, Series I (Newark, 1880–1906), vol. 1, p. 76.

8. *Encyclopaedia Britannica,* "American Frontier."

firm the British orientation of those colonists along the seaboard and their ideological attachment to the mother country.
It was inevitable that when those who sought the frontier—
discontented Anglo-Americans, adventurous Scots, devout
Germans—set out in the opposite direction, leaving behind
not only British accents but also British loyalties, which most
of them did not have in the first place, the separation between
them and the seaboard people should be not only geographical, but political and cultural as well.

It is easy to lose sight today of the narrow geographical
limits of this first early migration; a move to western New
York was still pioneering, and the Cumberland Valley was
virgin land. Some of the Palatinate refugees settled first in
New York, on the wide *patroon lands*, a name that would be
used until armed uprising in the mid-nineteenth century
ended the dominance of the great landowners; others, impelled to move on by the grasping policies of the patroons,
pushed on toward already settled Pennsylvania. There they
found land near Philadelphia and other established towns
expensive if not unobtainable; and many continued on toward the *back settlements*, or *frontier places*, of Maryland
and Virginia. Some found work on the great *iron plantation*
developed by Governor Spotswood in western Virginia, where
roaring blast furnaces told of a thriving industry, many settling at the town of *Germanna*, named for them; others,
without the feeling for freehold inbred in Englishmen, became tenants on the plantations of the powerful Maryland
proprietors, the Carrolls and the Dulanys. Often they found
themselves in a trap of their own making; as the value of the
land was increased by their industry, it grew too costly for
them to buy. Names like *New Mecklenburg*, in Virginia, and
*Frederick* and *Fredericksburg*, in Maryland, however, offer
evidence that German settlement was accomplished; *New
Bern*, in North Carolina, was founded by Germans and German-speaking Swiss.

Many regional terms in use today in the old German settlement area are the legacy of these early settlers. *Saddle horse,*

for the near horse (German *saddelgaul*); *fat cakes* (German *fettkuche*); *thick milk* (German *dickemilch*); *snits,* sliced and dried apples (German *schnitz*); and *hommie,* a call to calves (German *hammi*) are some of the expressions prevalent not only in Maryland and Virginia and nearby areas but in Texas and Iowa and farther west where derivative German settlement took place. German surnames remain regionally, too, names like *Kirsch* and *Schreiner*; but some underwent such change as to make them unrecognizable. The name *Upperco,* on the membership rolls of a Maryland parish, was originally *Opferkuchen*; elsewhere *Kirchman* has become *Churchman* and *Neukirch, Newkirk.* The *Fritsche* family of Maryland had its name immortalized as *Frietchie* by a flag-waving daughter named Barbara.

Less industrious but more aggressive, the Scotch-Irish (called *Scots*-Irish, not *Scotch*-Irish, by themselves) took more direct means of acquiring land. Finding their resources inadequate for purchasing the land they sought, some of them proclaimed that it "was against the laws of God and nature that so much land should be idle while so many Christians wanted it to labor on and to raise Bread,"[9] and swarmed over Conestoga Manor, which the Penns had reserved for themselves (they thought). As the law pursued them, they moved into the Susquehanna Valley and the Cumberland, where contemporary sheriff's writs of execution suggest their strategic advantages. "Not executed by stress of water," says one, "and de[fendan]t swore if I did get across he would shoot me if I touched any of his estates; also he is gone out of the country." "Not executed by reason of a gun," reports another; ". . . not executed by reason of an axx."[1]

The situation did not encourage dialogue, but the influence of Scotch-Irish dialect on contemporary speech was nonetheless strong. Most scholars attribute the presence of the strong final *r* and the flat *a* in the speech of the majority of Ameri-

9. Hanna: *Scotch-Irish,* vol. II, p. 63. Quoted in Adams: *Provincial Society,* p. 188.

1. Ibid., p. 219.

cans to Scotch-Irish example, an example that was reinforced by the pedagogy of the many Scotch-Irish schoolmasters who taught reading and writing along the frontier. Kurath calls the Scotch-Irish influence, even though it "cannot be doubted," "surprisingly intangible,"[2] perhaps because many of the Scotticisms once present in the vocabulary have become obsolete. Of the five hundred Americanisms listed by John Pickering in 1816, George H. McKnight identified more than four hundred as Scotticisms; and a study in *American Speech* of the poetry of David Bruce, an eighteenth-century country storekeeper in western Pennsylvania, who wrote in "braid Scots," shows that words like *muckle* and *braw* and *bairn* and *bletherskyte* were understood at least regionally.[3] Most of the terms identified by McKnight—*kedge* (brisk), *clitchy* (clammy, sticky), and *quackle* (almost to choke), for example —are probably no longer in use anywhere in America; but Scotch-Irish expressions such as *comb,* for the crest of a mountain; *cot-betty,* a man fond of woman's work; and *flit,* to move, have been noted not only in parts of Pennsylvania, but in other areas as well.[4] *Bannock,* for a cake made of corn meal (in Scotland it is an oat cake), is heard in the Carolinas and "down East," too; *cracker,* as used in *Georgia cracker,* is Scotch in its original meaning of boaster or braggart.

As the Scotch-Irish and Swiss, the Germans and English and Welsh, and people of other nationalities traveled north and south along the *western frontier,* they began the creation of a vocabulary distinctive of that frontier, a vocabulary that would be for the most part incomprehensible, when it was encountered, to the provincial society of the seaboard. They made it principally of familiar English materials, of old words given new meaning or combined with other words to create a new semantic entity. They invented. They imitated. They changed parts of speech at will. They clipped words or added

2. *Word Geography,* p. 3.

3. Claude M. Newlin: "Dialects on the Pennsylvania Frontier," *American Speech* (December 1928), pp. 104–10.

4. Mencken: *Supplement II,* pp. 16, 206, 207.

to them. They borrowed. They used all the methods of word-making that Englishmen had been using for centuries and used them with an abandon not known since the days of Shakespeare, and with natural genius. Inspiration was all around them.

*Squatting* was probably not their coinage—it was more likely the invention of some disgruntled landowner—but they soon adopted the term and said it proudly. A *squatter* established his right to land by *tomahawk claim*, a claim not recognized in law but bought and sold on the frontier by these pioneers who made laws for themselves. It consisted of marking a few boundary trees by *deadening*—cutting a narrow ring around the trunk—or *blazing out* a claim by cutting initials high on the trunk, marks that would be visible for years. In some colonies, *tomahawk entry*, or *tomahawk improvement*, the planting of a little corn or some other minimal development, was eventually recognized in law as establishing *pre-emption* to public lands. Sometimes referred to as *cabin rights* or *corn rights*, it was usually effective in warding off the claims of other settlers who had no more legal claim than did the incumbent and even of those who did. Often the Scotch-Irish staked a claim, improved the land, and then sold it to the newly arrived Germans, who seemed temperamentally more suited to organized settlement.

Emigrants traveled when they could along *Indian trails* or *buffalo traces, deer traces* or *river trails*, wading through the *pocossons*, as swamps were called even back East, after the Indian term *pâkwesen*. When, as they searched for a *buffalo ford* or a *deer crossing* in some broad, wild stream, they found that an enterprising pioneer had built and was running a *flatboat ferry*, they rejoiced. Sometimes they joined together in groups to build one of the great rafts called *broadhorns* by reason of the great oars or sweeps projecting from either side. More often they *poled off* with their *pushing poles* in their smaller rafts or *gondolas*, a word that had come to the frontier perhaps through *gondel*, the Dutch version of Italian *gondola*, or even through New England's *gundaloe*. When they settled at last, clearing the *timber,* as they called the forest, and established their *German settlement* or *English settlement* or *Irish tract,* they planted either *corn,* which without attribute meant Indian corn, or *German corn,* which meant rye. Sometimes they built *pole houses* and *pole fences;* but their initial dwelling was usually a small square of logs or small tree trunks called a *log pen,* embellished later with lower-roofed attached buildings to become the traditional *log cabin,* that well-known Swedish contribution to the American scene, which was exploited first by the pioneering Scotch-Irish.

The scrubby areas where shrubs and small trees grew, trees too small to be properly part of the *tall timber,* they called the *brush,* perhaps an archaism; the term appears in Australia as early as 1799 and could hardly have traveled there so soon. Along with *brush* came *brush fire;* and perhaps the sight of flames fanned by the wind inspired the use of *brush* as a verb meaning to drive a horse briskly, or even to bring on or force a situation, as *to brush a disagreement.* The *licks* where animals gathered had various attributes. *Salt lick, buffalo lick, deer lick, elk lick,* and *knob lick* were among the familiar terms; and many place names too were formed with the word: *Great Lick, Blue Licks, Bullet's Lick,* and *French Lick* date from the eighteenth century. A *bone lick* was a swamp containing the remains of possibly prehistoric animals; the combination has been noted as an Ohio Valley localism today.[5]

Growing things needed naming. The observant settlers, with their ready imagery, named *bluegrass* and *wire grass, shellbark* and *slippery elm* and *toothache tree,* so named for its effect on the salivary glands. They called a particular kind of locust tree the *honey locust,* for the pulp of honeylike sweetness its large pods contained; and they called a kind of magnolia tree a *beaver tree* because the beaver ate its bark and used its wood for dams. (The Dutch called it a *bever-boom.*) Of special interest was the *bee tree,* or hollow gum

5. W. Bruce Finnie: "Ohio Valley Localisms: Topographical Terms, 1750–1800," *American Speech* (October 1963), pp. 178–87.

tree, which was a favorite spot for bees to build their hives; skill in *lining bees*—capturing one in a honey-filled box and then following it as it made a *beeline* for the rich hive—was the valuable and far from simple accomplishment of the *bee hunters*. So prized was the sweetening that from it came the verb *to honey,* meaning to show affection; *honey-fogle,* or *honeyfuggle,* which meant to obtain by duplicity, to cozen, was perhaps suggested by Lancashire *connyfogle,* to lay plots, but was given a double meaning in its new form. Tar barrels, an important adjunct to pioneer living, could be made from the hollow gum tree; and *busy as a bee in a tar barrel* soon joined *happy as a clam* among classic American figures.

If the bee was sought after, the rattlesnake was feared and ever present; and the multitude of terms relating to it suggests that many a woodsman preferred meeting a hostile Indian. *Rattlesnake den* and *rattlesnake patch,* where numbers of the serpents nested, were places to be carefully avoided; remedies for rattlesnake bite included *rattlesnake weed, rattlesnake master,* and *rattlesnake root.* One who had killed a rattler was dubbed a *rattlesnake colonel,* a title owned with much the same fondness as is *Kentucky colonel* today. And the rattlesnake had its uses; *rattlesnake grease* and *rattlesnake oil* were remedies for gout and other ailments, and childbirth was supposedly hastened by the administration of a powder made from the snake's *rattles.*

Other varmints were the copperhead, called the *rattlesnake's mate;* the lynx, called the *cat* or *bobcat* (the name suggested by its stubby tail); and, of course, the dread *painter,* known from the earliest days of settlement. The vicious wolverine was called by various names: *carcajou,* an Algonquian name coming through Canadian French; *skunk bear; Indian devil;* and *beaver eater,* because it watches "those animals as they come out of their houses, and . . . devours them."[6] Wolves were ever present, and few possibilities were more terrifying than the bite of a rabid wolf; against that

6. Pennent: *Synopsis* (1771), p. 197. Quoted in Mathews: *Dictionary.*

danger, the settlers kept *madstones,* stonelike objects obtained from the stomach of a deer and believed to be efficacious if placed against wolf-bite wounds. *Wolf scalp hunters* brought in *wolf scalps* to receive the bounty offered by nearly all colonial towns surrounded by wilderness—which still meant most of them.

The forest was beautiful as well as deadly, and the creatures and shrubs and other growing things within it were named with the imagination and inventiveness we like to think are still our heritage. *Star root* and *blazing star, silk grass, Carolina pink,* and *tree primrose* are among the lovely names; *eel grass* and *button bush* and *tear coat,* a bush so named for its prickly spines, evoke less lovely images. *Polecat weed* and *skunk weed* need no explanation. *Rafts* of waterfowl were flocks of "all the sorts of small Ducks and Teal, that go in Rafts along the Shoar";[7] among them could usually be seen the *bufflehead,* originally *buffalo head.* Other birds were the *flicker* and the *towhee* (an imitative word), the *thistle bird* and the *teeter,* or *tilt-up,* a sand lark named for its bobbing motions. Pioneer humor shows in the *black flusterers,* also called *old wives,* which were the chattering surf scooters. Insects new named were the *tumblebug* and the *gallinipper,* the large and especially fierce mosquito also called the *Georgia piercer.* Among crawling creatures were the *red-bellied landsnake* and the *glass snake,* the latter not actually a snake but a remarkable lizard with a breakable and renewable tail.

Indian names for flora and fauna were still entering the vocabulary. *Woolyneag* (Abnaki *wulanikw,* "handsome squirrel"), for the fisher mink, and *chipmunk* (Algonquian; cf. Chippewa *atchitamon,* "head first") were first recorded in the eighteenth century, as were *pecan* and *scuppernong.* Through the French, with whom both settler and Indian had contacts hostile or peaceable, came other Indian words. *Babiche,* for thongs of skin, especially eelskin, used in lacing snowshoes, was an old word in Canadian French taken from the Algon-

7. John Lawson: *A New Voyage to Carolina* (1709). Revised as *The History of Carolina* (London: W. Taylor; 1714), p. 150.

quian. *Bayou* was one of the few non-Algonquian Indian words taken into the language in early colonial days; from Choctaw *bayuk,* it came through the French in Louisiana, where New Orleans was becoming an important center of trade. The town was already attracting Anglo-Americans, who traveled there for profit or pleasure, or both, and picked up from the Creoles and from visiting *voyageurs* French words like *crevasse* and *levee* and *lagniappe,* the last an illustration of the importance of trade contacts in the growth of the language. Made up of French *la* plus Spanish *ñapa,* it came ultimately from the Quechuan (South American Indian) word *yapa,* and had from the beginning its still-current meaning of a present ("a little extra") for a customer.

Many of the new terms relating to the Indian—*Indian line* and *Indian frontier* and *Indian purchase*—tell of continuing conflict over Indian lands. As aggressive settlers moved into traditional *Indian hunting ground,* the border terror that had flared only sporadically since King William's War in 1689 increased. European conflicts were reflected in the series of French and Indian wars that climaxed in the 1750's; and the French found willing allies among Indian tribes themselves seeking to stop the English advance. *Indian raids* on *frontier towns* were furious and deadly; and knowledge among the settlers that guns for many of them were supplied by avaricious merchants in Albany aroused bitter feeling against the seaboard commercial establishment.

Whatever the perils of the wilderness, human or otherwise, they had to be faced; for from that wilderness came food and other necessities— deerskin and beaver fur for *hunting jackets* and *beaver blankets,* buffalo hides for *buffalo robes,* furs for trading. The settler learned, therefore, to recognize *signs*— evidence in the form of tracks, broken twigs, or droppings— that warned of danger or promised game; following *bear signs* and *deer signs* and *beaver signs,* he watched warily the while for *Indian signs* that in hostile territory could mean a waiting tomahawk. He learned to lie in wait at a *buffalo beat* and prided himself on *creasing* a deer or a wild horse, cutting the skin at a precise spot on the neck so that the animal would drop down stunned. A really skilled hunter could *bark* a squirrel, striking the bark on the lower side of the tree branch on which it sat, killing it by concussion. *Coon dogs* accompanied the coon hunter—by now, John Smith's *rahaugum* had become simply a *coon*—and *gone coon* had displaced the familiar English expression *gone goose*. From the animal's habit of taking to a tree came the expressions of *treeing* an animal or a person and of *barking up the wrong tree*. The verb *to tree* had another meaning; from the Indian, the American learned to take shelter behind a tree in battle, a technique that would stand him in good stead after Concord.

Fare on the settler's table might include *bear meat (ba'ar mate)*, squirrel, or possum—which, according to a contemporary description, was "very like a little pig"; *hog'n'hominy; greens,* or *salat,* from the truck patch; and *mush and milk* or *Indian bannock,* given the attribute to distinguish it perhaps from the original oat cake. *Sofky,* a Creek word, meant hominy or thin corn gruel; and turkeys were roasted in *bear fat,* which itself was often eaten as a separate dish. For drink there might be *sassafras tea* ("saas tay") or *persimmon beer* ("'simmon beer"), and, for sweetening, the prized honey or, if available, *long sweetening,* as molasses was called, or *Indian sugar,* made of maple syrup.

The utensils for eating were usually homemade. *Dish timber* and *spoon wood* (the mountain laurel) were fashioned into tableware; forks were practically unknown. Refinements were few in the first days of settlement (and not many thereafter) and life was arduous, especially for the pioneer woman, who, besides her unending household chores and frequent childbearing, would "carry a gunn in the woods and kill deer, turkeys, etc., shoot doun wild cattle, catch and tye hoggs, knock down beeves with an ax and perform the most manfull Exercises."[8] When settlement was made in groups or was already established, the individual struggle was lightened by

8. "Boundary Line Proceedings, 1710," *Virginia Historical Magazine,* vol. 10. Quoted in Adams: *Provincial Society,* p. 92.

co-operative *chopping bees* and *building bees* and *raising bees.* From this custom arose a peculiar frontier version of social ostracism called *hating out,* practiced upon those who did not meet community obligations. The offender sooner or later found himself in need of help, which was not forthcoming; subject to general disapproval and moral pressure, he usually moved on to another habitation. For more grievous offenses there were other punishments. *Tarring and feathering,* often attributed to American invention, was a punishment appointed in the time of Richard I for the Royal Navy, whereby any convicted thief should "have his head shorne, and boyling pitch powred over his head, and feathers or downe strawed upon the same, whereby he may be knowen";[9] but certainly it was to be popular in all the colonies during the fury against Tories. *Horse thieves*—the term dates from the mid-eighteenth century—were liable to such summary justice or worse; the increasing number of terms created by combination with *horse*—*horse pen* and *horse swap, horse beat, horse stamp* (where the wild horses gathered), *horse hunting, horse herds, horse sled,* and *horse sled load,* as well as the names for things of nature, like *horse balm, horse mint,* and *horse nettle*—suggests the importance of the horse in that region where no wagons could pass and long distances had to be traveled.

The towns that developed along the frontier consisted usually, as a later French traveler reported, of "a few houses grouped around a church and tavern."[1] Some had been founded by religious groups who left unsatisfactory conditions in their former habitation; the church was central to their lives, and the pastor their leading citizen. The Great Awakening of the 1730's and '40's stirred fervor as well as dissension even in Boston; but by mid-century that fervor had subsided along the seaboard, and the multitude of re-

9. Hakluyt, quoted in M. Schele De Vere: *Americanisms: The English of the New World* (New York: Scribner & Co.; 1872), p. 194.

1. The Marquis de Chastelleux, quoted in Henry T. Tuckerman: *America and Her Commentators* (New York: Scribner & Co.; 1864), p. 64.

ligious labels arising from it—reminiscent of those proliferating in sixteenth-century England—had deep meaning
only in the back country. There, *Separate Baptists* and *Regular Baptists, Seventh Day Baptists* and *Water Baptists,* as well
as *Dunkers,* or *Dunkards* (German *Tunker,* "dipper"), and
*New Divinities,* distinguished between *Sabbath keepers* (the
seventh-day sects) and *Sunday keepers.* Presbyterians had
divided into *Old Lights* and *New Lights;* the latter were particularly prominent along the frontier. Fundamentalism
characterized the theology of all of them, so that even as the
ideas of the Enlightenment were reaching the intellectuals
of the seaboard cities, zeal for the old-time religion in new
manifestations was being strengthened in the back country.

But with all the danger and the seriousness, there was
laughter. We hear now of the *cornstalk fiddle* and the *horse
fiddle,* defined by Mathews as "any one of various noise-
making contrivances," and explained by a later commentator
as being so called "because it is so unlike either a horse or a
fiddle";[2] it figured prominently in *shivarees,* mock serenades
for a newly married couple, a variation of French *charivari.*
We read, too, of a dance called the *Irish trot,* no doubt the
contribution of those Scotch-Irish pioneers, and of *kick ups,*
or dances. There was always the fun of the *husking bees,* introduced by an earlier generation and now—at least, we do
not find the term earlier—made more interesting by the
custom that entitled the finder of a *red ear* among the corn
to give to each girl present a *red ear kiss.* Surely it was a long-
nosed Puritan who wrote in *Yankee,* not many years later,
that ". . . red-ear kisses, field-beds and bundling [are] all of a
piece." *Field beds* were beds four feet wide flanking one whole
side of a house, on which "large parties will range themselves
on opposite sides of the house as economically as candles
in a box."[3] Sometimes the fun could be rough; in the taverns,

2. E. Eggleston: *End of World* (1872), p. 294. Quoted in Mathews:
*Dictionary.*
3. *St. Louis Reveille* (February 6, 1845). Quoted in Mathews: *Dictionary.*

called *ordinaries* in the South, *pumpkin beer* and *molasses whisky* and *New England* (rum) sometimes *brushed* a quarrel. Philip Vickers Fithian, who was employed as a tutor at the plantation home of Robert Carter, noted that in the fights arising among the people of Virginia "every diabolical Stratagem for Mastery is allowed . . . Scratching . . . Biting, Butting . . . Gouging."[4] The Southerners were popularly supposed to be champion *gougers*; *Virginia* and *Carolina gougers* were notorious.

It was as *gouger* or *cracker*, *buckskin* or *buck*, that the people of the seaboard usually thought of the *back country-man*. Stereotyped as a picturesque figure in *deerskin hunting shirt* or *hunting frock*, as the loose jacket was called, wearing *Indian stockings* or *Indian boots*, ". . . made of coarse woolen cloths, much too large for the legs, tied upon their thigh and hang[ing] loose to their shoes,"[5] or *leggins* (a Scotch term), and either *Indian shoes* or homemade shoes of cowhide, he seemed both exotic and uncouth to the sophisticated city man in his *store clothes*, his knee breeches and silver-buckled shoes, or even to the farmer of the countryside in his sober Quaker garb or other clothing of *homespun*. Few outsiders had the occasion, or the adaptability, to don *Indian walking dress*, as did George Washington on his journey to Fort Le Boeuf in 1753; few knew except by hearsay anything of pioneer life and less of the thoughts of those who lived it.

Contemporary comments and the terms used make clear the prevailing urban attitude. *Backwoodsmen*, it is noted in a 1774 letter, are "hunters like the Indians and equally ungovernable." A traveler remarks in his journal: "Buckskins, or Bucks [are] something as it were, betwixt a man and a beast." And a correspondent attempts to explain the term *cracker* to the Earl of Dartmouth (the British were fascinated by exotica Americana) as "a name they have got from being

4. *Journal and Letters, 1767–1774,* ed. John R. Williams (Princeton: Princeton University Press; 1900–34), vol. 1, p. 243.

5. Francis Moore: *A Voyage to Georgia, Begun in the Year 1735* (London, 1744), vol. 1, p. 120.

great boasters; they are a lawless set of rascalls on the frontiers
of Virginia, Maryland, the Carolinas, and Georgia, who often
change their places of abode,"[6] drawing the conclusion, generally concurred in by etymologists, that the name was used
in the earlier north of England and Scottish sense of boaster
or braggart. Some, however, hold that the word in its American sense comes from the term *corn cracker,* for the principal
diet of those to whom it is applied, and that it is equivalent to
*poor white trash* or *sandhillers.* Others ascribe it to the
cracking of a whip over oxen on backwoods farms.

It was certainly in this deprecatory sense that William
Byrd II wrote, in his *History of the Dividing Line,*[7] of the
*borderers,* those "indolent wretches" who "file off to North
Carolina through a thorough aversion to labor and expend
their energy only in begetting." Afflicted by the *country distemper* (yaws) and including *marooners* (fugitive slaves), these
inhabitants of what Byrd called *Lubberland* had not industry
nor decency nor health; and by them Byrd and many others
judged the pioneers in general. It is obvious, however, that
the clearing of forests, the tilling of land, and the building of
settlements were accomplished by people far different from
those so prominent in the popular mind. Much of the developing conflict and dissension between frontier and seaboard might have been avoided had not so many misleading
words stood between them.

Most of the frontier terms would become familiar over the
years to all Americans, just as the new vocabulary of the
seaboard would make its way toward the ever-receding back
country. But in this eighteenth century, even as Dr. Johnson
was speaking disdainfully of American "corruption" of the
language without any awareness of how much "corruption"

6. Letter from Gavin Cochrane to Earl of Dartmouth, June 27, 1766.
*The Manuscripts of the Earl of Dartmouth* (London: Printed for H. M.
Stationery Office by Eyre and Spottiswoode; 1887–96).

7. *The History of the Dividing Line and Other Tracts, from the Papers
of William Byrd of Westover, in Virginia,* ed. Thomas H. Wynne (Rich-
mond, Va.; 1866).

was actually going on, and as British observers were clucking over such barbarisms as *belittle* and *bluff*, the American language was racing in all directions, picking up words cast out by churning social and cultural and economic change. At mid-century, wealthy land speculators and back-country settlers were linked by a common desire to obtain the rich, French-claimed land beyond the Alleghenies; but it was a link they did not recognize. As pioneering *Kaintucks* pushed along the Ohio in what would soon be called *Kentucky boats,* and as some farseeing men like Benjamin Franklin pleaded that the colonies unite in a common frontier defense, Governor James Hamilton of Pennsylvania wrote that "it looks like knowing very little of America to expect that Maryland and New Jersey will concern themselves about what is doing at Ohio."[8]

Why should they? The people of that distant region did not even speak their language.

8. Howard H. Peckham: *The Colonial Wars, 1689–1762* (Chicago: University of Chicago Press; 1964), p. 132.

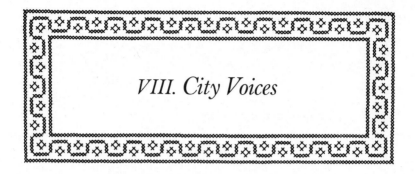

# VIII. City Voices

*Buckshot* and *banjo, chair road* and *tote, Negro mongers, Boston notions,* and *pistareens*—on the eve of the Revolution, American coinage was tumbling pell-mell into the stream of the English language, to enrich or pollute as one chose to look at it, carrying with it its freight of history. Coming from North and South, from farm and city, from frontier and seaboard, ornamented with borrowings from the speech of immigrant and slave and neighboring trader, it varied from formal words like *gubernatorial* to derisive terms like *pumpkin head* (for a New Englander)[1] and sprang from a regional and cultural diversity so great that contemporary observers pronounced united colonial action in any cause unlikely.

"Fire and water," wrote the English clergyman Andrew Burnaby in 1760, "are not more heterogeneous than the different colonies of America." Observing that they quarreled over boundaries and trade and differed in character and religion and custom, he proclaimed that were it not for England's guiding hand, they would engage in civil war "from one end of the continent to the other."[2] Many Americans

1. The Blue Laws of Puritan New England enjoined all males to have their hair cut in the familiar round style. When no cap was available for the shaping, the hard shell of a pumpkin was used.

2. *Travels Through the Middle Settlements of North America* (1759–60). Quoted in Henry T. Tuckerman: *America and Her Commentators* (New York: Scribner & Co.; 1864), p. 179.

agreed. According to Josiah Quincy, there was in the colonies "a prevalent and extended ignorance" about one another's concerns. It was well known that New Yorkers thought Connecticutters "crafty" and were in turn considered frauds, that to Southerners the verb *to yankee* meant to cheat, that New Englanders disliked the Quakers, and that people of western Massachusetts thought Bostonians conceited and vain.[3] And the way other people talked! The *Yankee twang* and *New England dialect* were offensive to Southern ears. *Virginiaisms* like *reckon* and *raise* (for the verb "to rear") were noted disparagingly by Northern visitors, who deplored also the widespread use in the South of *tote*. (Witherspoon would soon include it among American "improprieties.") The British, it appeared, were not fond of American speech, but Americans were not fond of one another's either; only in relation to *Negro English*, also called *Negro*, and to *Indian talk*, both a kind of pidgin that everyone recognized and found useful, did their speech seem quite homogeneous. In one respect, however, they were united: all Americans loved making words.

Most of the words coined in the early days of settlement had emerged from a pioneering and wholly agricultural milieu. Flora and fauna had needed naming, as had unfamiliar features of the landscape and vagaries of the weather. *Wigwams* and *squaws* and *tomahawks* were as new to the Plymothean as to the Virginian, *corn* was Indian corn to both, and *truck house*, for trading house, was a logical combination of familiar English elements. *Town meeting* and *general assembly* expressed different organizational concepts, but both terms came of the characteristically Anglo-Saxon need to establish civil communities in the wilderness. The vocabularies of the separate colonies, varied as they were by reason of English regional background and by factors of the

3. Illustrations of prevailing colonial attitudes, including the quotation from Josiah Quincy, are given in Evarts Boutell Greene: *The Revolutionary Generation,* History of American Life Series (New York: The Macmillan Company; 1934), vol. 4, pp. 185–7.

immediate environment, told therefore of a relatively homogeneous way of life and common interests. And because the pioneering life throughout the colonies allowed only limited options in life style, there had been little need for a lexicon of amenities distinctive of rank.

By 1770, the vocabulary told a different story. New terms for material things and for the appurtenances of urban life reflected the emergence in the seaboard cities of an affluent society, its wealth based in large part on profits from the French and Indian War, which had bloodied the frontier and the sea but not the cities. It was a vocabulary expressing concepts as remote to the wilderness pioneer as were those of *beelining* and *treeing* to a Philadelphia lawyer, their remoteness suggesting the widening cleavage between East and West, between merchant and farmer, which would be only partially bridged during the Revolution. The language told also of divisions among the various colonies, with new terms relating to boundary disputes, conflicting economic interests, and cultural animosity. And although North and South had equally strong cultural and commercial ties with England, it told of the growing divergence between the mercantile interests of the North and the agrarian interests of the South, where a gradually expanding slave economy was creating a unique economic and social milieu.

Like their countrymen to the west, the members of the seaboard society had the English gift for word-making; but they had also the inhibiting influence of close commercial and cultural ties with the mother country. American writers tried to please British reviewers, and purists in Boston differed little from their London counterparts. There was, however, a correlative advantage: words new in England passed quickly across the sea. Urban society in the major port cities of Philadelphia, New York, Boston, and Charleston, and even in such towns as Trenton and Williamsburg and Baltimore, was English-oriented, its trade with England vital, its sons—many of them—educated at Oxford or Cambridge, and its dependence on officialdom heavy. Ideas fashionable in London, therefore, along with the pertinent vocabulary, soon became prominent in colonial speech.

The literati of the cities used the new words *novelist* and *the press* and *literary* (which had formerly meant only alphabetical); the frivolous used such terms as *tea party, entertain,* and the *season.* All tossed off the new *self*-conscious words lately added to the "internalizing" repertoire that had been increasing with each century, words like *ennui* and *egotism, embarrassment* and *interesting.* Social life centered about royal officialdom (in Williamsburg, the governor's mansion was called *the Palace*); and wealthy and influential Anglo-Americans prided themselves on the purity of their speech. According to contemporary English visitors, the speech of Boston was quite like that of "the old country"; that of Philadelphia surpassed "in purity and perfection" all but the "polite" part of London; it was even suggested that the Americans used "better English than the English do."[4] When one considers that the "American dialect" Dr. Johnson thought "corrupt" was this quite conventional language of the seaboard—a language little affected by immigrant words and accents, and, as in the *Geographical Essays* of Lewis Evans that had aroused his wrath, written carefully with an eye to English reviewers—one wonders what splenetic comment would have been his had he visited the frontier.

And yet even this elegant speech was changing too. The extent of the change would not be fully recognized until after the Revolution, when postwar interest in the "American" language would focus attention on coinage minted not by the back settlers "at the Ohio" but by the savants and the wealthy merchants of Boston and Charleston and Philadelphia, whom the democratic genius of the language had been disrespectfully using. No one could suggest that such words as *depreciation* and *legislate* and *dutiable* and *eventuate* came of rural whimsy or frontier simplicity; and purists who sought to stem the tide of words with pedagogic teacups

4. Greene: *Revolutionary Generation,* pp. 183–4.

were themselves swept into the flood. Even such advocates of an academy for policing the language as John Quincy Adams and John Marshall gave currency to coinage that many thought objectionable, Adams to *antagonize*, Marshall to *immigrate* and *dutiable*.

A spate of new-coined terms relating to trade suggests an atmosphere in American cities and their environs reminiscent of that in sixteenth-century England, when the "rich burghers on the flood" began their ascendance. In London, *business* had just begun to be used in its modern commercial sense; Americans immediately went about creating combinations to meet their particular needs, *lumber business, pork business, forwarding business,* and *dry-goods business* among them. *Chamber of commerce* entered the commercial lexicon in New York in 1768, simultaneously with its emergence in England. Because no sharp line separated wholesale and retail traders and few residents lived far from the waterfront, most business was carried on along the *docks,* a word that, in America, had come to mean not the waterways between piers or wharves, as it did in England, but the piers or wharves themselves. *Wharf* still appeared, however, in such names as *Cruger's Wharf* in New York and *Dr. Clark's Wharf* in Boston, where Paul Revere, silversmith, sold the newfangled *teeth powder,* along with artificial teeth. Here were located not only the public markets and the offices of such diverse capitalists as *lumber merchants* and *candle factors* and *book factors,* but also the numerous *storehouses,* a now-entrenched term that included *grocery stores* and *auction stores* and *dry-goods stores,* where *store clerks* waited on customers and *storekeepers kept store.*

In this area was transacted all of the city's business, often made difficult by the troublesome currency problem, a major element of discord not only between colonies but within them as well. *Currency* is marked an Americanism in Johnson's *Dictionary.* Franklin wrote, in 1729: "We must distinguish between Money as it is Bullion, which is Merchandize, and as by being coin'd it is made a Currency";[5] but the word applied also to the paper money issued by the colonies before prohibition of such activity by Britain in 1764. In the commercial centers, the old days of *beaver pay* and *country pay* were over; but the new *currency* was even more confusing. *Philadelphia paper money* had a value different from that of *Georgia money*; *Pennsylvania currency* and *Virginia currency* did not correspond; and the problem was compounded by clever counterfeiting. The English pound sterling, which was the prime monetary standard but was scarce in the colonies, was worth thirty-five *Philadelphia shillings* but only thirty-three of New York's. The *New Tenor* issued by Massachusetts and Rhode Island to replace the *Old Tenor* and the *Middle Tenor* was not accepted in written contracts in Maine.

To get around the paper problem, most trade was carried on in foreign coin, principally Spanish and Portuguese (piracy was still paying well); the *Spanish dollar*, the famous "pieces of eight," was most in demand. The *pistareen* was the Spanish peseta, a small silver coin, so called probably from an unrecorded diminutive (*pesetarin*>*pestarin*>*pistareen*) evolved by non-Spanish speakers. The Spanish real—*half (a) pistareen*, or one part of a bisected pistareen—was called by a variety of names that in themselves suggest the fluctuating value of the coin. To New Englanders it was a *fourpence ha'penny*, to New Yorkers a *sixpence*, to Pennsylvanians a *fippenny bit* or *fip*, the last term still in use in the mid-nineteenth century, when Bartlett defined it as a five-pence and listed it among Pennsylvania "vulgarisms." To the frontier traders who *flatted* their furs and other goods down the Mississippi to New Orleans, the same coin was a *picayune* (French *picaillon*); and the fourth part of a real was a *quartee*, the name taken by the French from Spanish *cuartillo*. (Many of those frontiersmen, who knew nothing of

5. *Writings,* ed. Albert H. Smyth (New York: The Macmillan Company; 1907), vol. 2, p. 149.

Philadelphia *pavements* or New York *sidewalks*, came to feel at home on the *banquettes* of that exciting city to the south and would not be loath, after the Revolution, to take part in the move to found a separate nation in the Mississippi Valley.)

With all the difficulties of exchange, *settling an account* was a much more involved matter than it was in England, where the term referred simply to paying a portion of a bill. In America, it came to mean making final payment and soon took on a figurative meaning; *settling accounts* could mean dire consequences for someone. *Pay*, too, which had acquired so many attributes in colonial times and had high status in an increasingly commercial society, developed so many metaphorical connotations that it became, De Vere suggests, the American *cui bono*. Does it *pay* to be nice to people? we ask. Does it *pay* to get up to watch the sun rise? The idiom provides fodder for rabid anticapitalists to munch on. Other commerce-related coinage included *depreciation*, which became necessary after the already existing terms *appreciate, depreciate,* and *appreciation* were converted to financial purposes, and *obligate*, cited by Fowler as one of those words "which fill the gap or vacancy between two words which are approved,"[6] in this case between *oblige* and *obligation*. Purists hated *obligate*; as late as 1927 George Bernard Shaw brooded over Woodrow Wilson's use of it during the Versailles Conference. Writing in the London *Times* of June 15, he remarked that though a man could use the term and become President of the United States, "we asked ourselves if a man could become King of England if he used [it]. We said at once that it could not be done."

Another business term to which the British objected, and which we would be lost without, is the verb *to run*, for operate or manage, which the *London Daily Telegraph*, a century later, termed an "American locution." Characteristically American, full of bustle, *run* was already versatile when it was

6. *The English Language* (1850). Quoted in H. L. Mencken: *The American Language,* 4th ed. (New York: Alfred A. Knopf; 1936), p. 99

brought from England; Americans made it a word of all work. The noun could mean a stream or a flow of maple sugar, a score in baseball, a stampede, a land rush. As a verb it could mean to manage or to boss, to put forward a candidate or to be one, to navigate a stream. Ads are *run* and accounts are *run* and chances are *run*. We have *running ivy* in our gardens and *running gear* on our machines and had *running boards* on our cars once upon a time. We *run across* people and *run up* a dress, have *run-ins* with our neighbors and *run offs* for our votes, and sometimes give people the *run-around*. Like *pay* and *put* and *lot, run* is one of our very favorite words.

As commerce and population increased, more and more the major port cities dominated the regions around them and inevitably the speech of their inhabitants. The sea and the inland waterways still served as the principal means of transportation and communication; and colonial products like *Maryland wheat, Virginia iron* (and tobacco), *Philadelphia butter, Connecticut shad, breadstuffs* from the middle colonies, indigo and rice from the *indigo plantations* and *rice plantations* of South Carolina, *cypress shingles* and *cedar shingles* from New England had to pass through the ports of Boston or New York, Philadelphia, Charleston, or some other major city, whether destined for the domestic market or for foreign ports.

Goods from the interior were loaded onto the *merchanters* sailing toward England and the West Indies and—under increasingly sharp scrutiny since the end of the French wars— to ports forbidden by the Navigation Acts. Seagoing *packet ships*[7] entered and departed, carrying passengers and mail and goods; and from Baltimore sailed the *Baltimore clippers,* prototypes of the great *Yankee clippers* to follow. *Fishing schooners* fitted especially for codding sailed from Gloucester and Salem and other New England ports; and from Nan-

---

7. Although the *packet ships* were in use in the eighteenth century, regularly scheduled sailings would not become practicable until the next.

tucket and Martha's Vineyard, where geographic isolation would preserve distinctive speechways, were launched the long, narrow *Nantucket whaleboats,* carried now on mother ships to the far haunts of the sperm whale, where the exploits of the whalers would become the stuff of legend. Other, more sinister, vessels sailed from, and into, other ports; they were the noisome ships of the *"Guinea* trade" that was building New England fortunes, the merry trade that went round and round like a nursery tale—*New England rum* to buy the slaves to pay for molasses to make more rum to buy the slaves ta-ta-ta-ta . . . And in and out of the *slips,* as the waterways formerly called *docks* were now called, passed smaller boats, the sloops and *barks* and *Hampton boats* (a modified pink-stern) and *bateaux* and *trading schooners* laden with goods for the interior trade—*Boston notions* and *store clothes, shoe boots* or *bootees* from the factories at Lynn, scythes from the *ironworks* of New Jersey. By almost every vessel, too, came intercolonial passengers, most of whom preferred the coastal voyage to the more hazardous and uncomfortable journey by land. Always in step, the vocabulary continued to reflect the emphasis on water transportation with an increase in nautical terms or their extension. The verb *to ship* spilled over to replace *to wagon* and *to cart* and even *to boat,* so that *shipping* and *shipment* and *shipper* and related terms soon applied to overland transport. *Shipping charges* replaced *wagonage;* and *freight,* which had come in Middle English times from Dutch *vrecht,* for "cargo," was coming into use for goods carried by any conveyance.

Economic dependence upon the port cities inevitably drew rural communities into their cultural orbits; and the influence of these centers upon the speech of the hinterland is thought by some, especially Kurath,[8] to be second only to that of the original settlement in deciding regional speech distinctions and their boundaries. More important, the development led to the setting of a linguistic standard. In the

8. Hans Kurath: *Word Geography of the Eastern United States* (Ann Arbor: University of Michigan Press; 1949), p. 2.

eighteenth century, spoken English was by no means uniform in either England or America; but most educated men of affairs in the colonies—officials, planters, merchants, scholars—knew the literary language of England and spoke at least an approximation of the London standard. Because the enormous variety of spoken English within the colonies was a handicap to communication, the speech of leading personalities and of official correspondence became, as it had in England two hundred years before, the accepted model for the mass of the people, however idiomatic their vernacular. Grammar and spelling and usage in general, especially in the schools, followed the models established by the shared language of the literate; and the trend toward uniformity, which would minimize dialectal factors in giving the American language its character, was well begun.

In the lengthening chain of trade, the middleman—although the term had not yet been coined, *merchant* often taking its place—formed an essential link. *Lumber merchants* differed from "lumberers or fellers of timber," who actually felled the trees, and from *lumbermakers*, who turned the raw logs into lumber for the *lumber trade. British merchants,* factors for English and Scottish concerns, carried on trade with the colonists, especially in the South, buying tobacco and other products (and picking up as lagniappe some American words) in exchange for British products. *Book factors* distributed books to smaller retail outlets; James Rivington advertised in the *Maryland Gazette* "a very great variety of such Books as are usually kept for the Supply of their Customers" to "Country Shopkeepers."[9] *Merchant mills,* at that time probably the finest in the world, were centers to which the countryside farmers brought their grain for sale; there it was ground and shipped to the nearest port as *breadstuffs.* The term *merchant mill* was distinguished from *country mill,* whose products were destined for local consumption—just as *merchant work,* for distribution, was distinguished from *country work,* for local consumption—and its use suggests

9. August 6, 1761.

the growing economic division between the urban centers, involved in increasingly complex trading practices, and the older countryside, where the agricultural life of earlier days continued almost unchanged.

The division was less marked than between frontier and seaboard—these two regions were different worlds—and the economic dependence of the farmer upon his market and of the country store upon its source of supply precluded complete separation. But the gap in life style and in philosophy was widening between city and small rural town almost as much as between town and frontier settlement. The attitude of the urban dweller toward the rural was much like that which developed among the bourgeoisie of seventeenth-century London toward the *country-plain* people; and patronizing eighteenth-century English expressions like *country cousin* and *country-looking* lost no semantic weight in crossing the sea. City visitors were amused at country idiom like *Law you*! (*Law* and *Lawsy* were popular euphemisms for Lord) and *confounded gay* and *peart*; but a boycott of British goods during a pre-Revolutionary belligerent phase found a young woman of New York definitely NOT amused at being forced to wear "horrid *homespun*," which could become "none but a country wench."[1] The *country docket* (at Charleston) was acknowledged by city lawyers to consist of "chiefly trifling causes of debt"; and John Adams complained of annoyance and of time wasted in covering the circuit of *county courts.*[2] Since much legal practice was concerned with the collection of debts owed city merchants, one suspects that Adams, with his *Boston accent* and *Boston manner,* was no more popular with the country people than they with him. Lawyers were villains to the nonaffluent in any case; in 1765, the *Ames Almanac,* which boasted of its readership among the common people, denounced lawyers as "Pettyfoggers" who took up the "most trifling Causes, exciting Quarrels." (Impartially,

1. *New York Post-Boy* (1774). Quoted in Greene: *Revolutionary Generation,* p. 13.
2. Greene: *Revolutionary Generation,* p. 85.

it denounced doctors as well, for their "audacity to practice their Butchery on the human Race.")

But calling a city a *city* did not make it one. The American tendency toward grandiloquence has often given that label to what might properly be called a *town*, just as the name *town* was given, as Chastelleux noted [q.v.], to "a few houses grouped around a Church and tavern." The New Jersey archives of 1747 refer to "this City [Burlington] (as call'd tho' but a village of 170 houses)"; and early in the next century, Frederick Marryat, reporting on his travels through America, commented: "It is strange that the name of a city should be given to an unfinished log house." (He was in Texas, though.) "This city mania," he noted, "is a very extraordinary disease in the United States."[3] Only when certain other words were applicable to a particular community, therefore, could it properly be labeled a city as we think of it today—words like *sidewalk* and *building spot, block* and *square* and *fire wall* and *brick* (house). It is hard now to imagine a time when these words were new, as hard as to imagine that Philadelphia was planned as a "greene, countrie towne." And yet it was only during the eighteenth century that these words entered the American language.

*Sidewalk,* once noted as a particularly felicitous coinage, which "the English obstinately refuse to adopt,"[4] was quite literally at first an elevated *side* walk of boards or planks, which allowed a pedestrian to avoid the mud and filth and dung usually filling the street, as well as the scavenging pigs that were the principal sanitation facilities. Felicitous as the coinage may be, *pavement,* the British term, still prevails in Philadelphia and the region it has influenced; and the French *banquette* (from *banc*), for the benches New Orleans Creoles placed on their sidewalks and occupied in the evenings, is still heard in New Orleans and southwest Louisiana, almost

3. *Travels* (1843). Quoted in Mitford M. Mathews, ed.: *A Dictionary of Americanisms on Historical Principles* (Chicago: University of Chicago Press; 1951).

4. Phipson (1896). Quoted in Mathews: *Dictionary.*

universally among Negroes. *Square,* in the sense of a city block, originated in Philadelphia, where for the first time city lots were laid out in squares. *Block,* influenced by Dutch *blok,* meant originally a connected or compact mass of houses or other buildings, what we would call *row houses* or *town houses* or a *business block.* The word, however, soon acquired the derivative meaning of the area on which the houses were or could be built, as in a *block of lots,* and became synonymous with *square.* Projected to the linear distance along one side, it entered the typically American expressions *down the block* and *two blocks over*—but the contrary Philadelphians still continue to walk a *square or two.* Philadelphia's city *squares* were original but not unique in colonial days; contemporary writings note that Charleston, South Carolina, and New Bern, North Carolina, were so laid out. Hartford, on the contrary, was "a large, scattering town" and New York one with "crooked streets and narrow," which were, however, "pretty well paved." New Orleans was still part of New France; but an eighteenth-century visitor was drawn to comment on its "perfectly straight" streets, which divided the city into sixty-six squares, today's *Vieux Carré.* *Square* was applied also to the open spaces caused by the junction of several streets; and even when such *squares* as Chatham Square and Franklin Square turned out to be triangles, the term endured.

With *city lots* repeatedly divided and subdivided, the sale of property was gradually taken over from owners by agents; and *real estate business* became a major commercial activity. Formerly the sale of property had been a sideline with merchants or lawyers or simply landowners; now the importance of quality and location opened the way for a new business. In colonial newspapers, numbering over twenty by 1770, there appeared ads for the sale of *frame dwelling houses,* of houses of *Philadelphia brick,* of *frame tenements* (the phrase meant simply a dwelling; not until 1835, in New York, would the first *tenement* house, containing several separate dwellings, be built), and of houses with *shops,* meaning workshops, on the ground floor. Such a shop might be a *mechanic's shop* or a *blacksmith's shop* or a *carriage shop*; *shop* in the British sense had been almost completely displaced by *store* and *storehouse*. *Double houses* were advertised; these had rooms on each side of a main entrance hall, a style that was actually an elegant projection of the *double log house* of the frontier, which was made up of two log pens with an open shed for a wagon shelter between them. Some of the more opulent dwellings had *carriage houses* as well as *lightning rods*, or *Franklin rods*, as they were called after their inventor.

Also named after its inventor was the *Franklin stove*, or *Franklin*, originally the *Pennsylvania fireplace*, an improvement over the inferior iron *fire frames* which were replacing the dangerous open-hearth fires. Fire was the nemesis of colonial cities; in some of them, frame dwellings and *shingle* (wood) roofs were banned. Ordinances were not always obeyed, however, and in the close-packed residential and business areas, flames spread quickly; it was not unknown for a hundred buildings to burn at one time. A demand for greater spaciousness and comfort had set a premium on the number of *fire rooms* in a house, and *fireplaces* and *fire hoods* of various kinds had been invented; not many were safe. We read that in Mr. Pierpont's house "a Fire broke out . . . occasioned by the Heat of the Iron Hearth of one of the newly invented Fireplaces, whereby the Floor was set on Fire."[5] Franklin's invention was designed to "avoid the several Inconveniences, and at the same time retain all the Advantages of other Fire-places. . . . It cures most smoaky chimneys, and thereby preserves both the Eyes and Furniture."[6] Despite Franklin's refusal to take out a patent, because "we should be glad of an Opportunity to serve others by any Invention of ours," the stove was given his name; *Franklins* are still distributing cozy warmth in some rural areas today.

5. G. F. Dow: *Everyday Life in the Massachusetts Bay Colony* (Boston: Society for the Preservation of New England Antiquities; 1935), p. 132.

6. Franklin: *Writings*, vol. 2, pp. 256, 257.

Not satisfied with inventing his stove for using fire, the indefatigable Franklin founded the *Union Fire Company* of Philadelphia for controlling it. The company was the first organized in the New World and was soon copied elsewhere; it introduced *fire company* to the language. Related words like *fire club, fire society, fire guard* (warden), *fire sail* (a large piece of canvas used at the scene of a fire for some purpose now obscure, perhaps as a net) tell of the success of the idea if not always of its execution. Rival companies were formed; and so eager were the members for a piece of the action that in fighting off rivals at the scene of a fire they sometimes neglected to extinguish the flames. A *fire bag* was the bag used by firemen to carry things from a burning building; and the most prominent citizens kept one close at hand, along with buckets and the *Society key* that indicated club affiliation.

The homes so valiantly protected were often quite elegant. *Mahogany*, a West Indian word for a wood introduced into England in 1714, to become fashionable there and in the colonies too, joins with two Americanisms, *bureau* and *rocking chair*, to suggest the more elaborate interiors of the period. An ad in the *Boston Evening Post* for July 19, 1751, offered "fashionable furniture, consisting of mahogany, Indian and stone tables, buroes, etc." The *buroes* of this particular ad might have been writing desks with drawers, as the French meaning would have it; but they were more likely chests with mirrors designed for holding clothing, a meaning decided upon by the Americans for reasons unknown. Only in later derivatives like *bureaucracy, bureau of mines,* and the rest of the *bureau* family would the original meaning be retained. Elbow chairs, too, were a feature of colonial homes, and "sophas," as George Washington wrote it; but the most inviting of all innovations, and probably an American invention, was the *rocking chair*. It may be that the enormous increase in reading which occurred during the period came about solely from other, more high-flown causes; but surely the improvement in heating, the better light given by *Nan-*

*tucket* (whale oil) and clear-burning spermaceti candles, and
the comfortable chairs helped to make reading attractive.
Who knows what part the *rocking chair* played in standardizing the language?

That there was a great increase in reading is evident. Many
literary words had come new from England—*magazine* and
*publisher* and the verb *review* and, as noted, *the press*; but
a number of significant terms were coined in America also.
*Book stores*, in business since early in the century, were universally so called, rather than *book-seller's shops* as in England; *book peddlers* or *agents* sold books from house to
house; *book factors*, like Rivington, kept smaller dealers supplied. *Book bindery*, coming from Dutch *boekbinderij*, entered the vocabulary. For the learned there were available
such works as Blackstone's *Commentaries*, Locke's *Two
Treatises of Civil Government*, the classics, many works of
theology, and the works of Hume and Voltaire and other
skeptics as well, so that the vocabulary of eighteenth-century
rationalism was as familiar to thoughtful men in America
as it was elsewhere. Less serious readers enjoyed the novels
of Richardson and Fielding and Smollett and read Lord
Chesterfield's *Letters* and the various almanacs, which, as the
publisher of one of them boasted, were "read by Multitudes
who read nothing else"—and who would not otherwise have
been exposed to the standardizing influence of the written
word.

For those whose resources did not allow extensive pur-
chases or who had not room for large libraries, other facilities
were available. Called variously *library companies* (the first
formed by Franklin in 1751), *social libraries* (a "perversion
of Language," one critic said), and *subscription libraries,*
they increased vastly the *audience* (Franklin's term) not only
for books, but for newspapers and political pamphlets as well.

It is obvious that any study of the eighteenth-century
vocabulary, as any study of American history, must acknowl-
edge the influence of Benjamin Franklin upon it; and yet
Franklin would have been the last to advocate any "Ameri-

canizing" of the language. Linguistically an Anglophile and unsympathetic to the iconoclasm of Webster, who dedicated his *Dissertations on the English Language* to him, Franklin criticized the American usage of such words as *improve, notify, advocate,* and *to progress*—and then went right ahead and innovated himself, besides using in the American way some of the very words he had singled out. Not only did he coin the words and phrases already mentioned—*audience,* for the reading public, *fire company,* and *Pennsylvania fireplace*—but he also introduced *armonica,* for an arrangement of musical glasses he invented (and for which noted composers wrote music), giving it that name in honor of the "musical language" of the Italians. *Battery* and *conductor* were first used in their modern sense in his renowned studies of electricity. He gave currency to the terms *timothy grass* (named for Timothy Hansen, an early grower of it) and *Gulf (Gulph) Stream.* Making one's *pile,* for making one's fortune, appeared first in Franklin's writings, as did *mileage,* for an expense allowance.[7] Other terms arose from the association of ideas or innovations with Franklin. The *Franklin tree* was named in his honor by John Bartram, the eminent botanist; *Franklin spectacles,* the first bifocals, were so called because he invented them, in 1784. A *Franklinism* is a pithy proverb like those he wrote for *Poor Richard's Almanac,* and a *Franklinist* was a follower of his theories of electricity. So widely heralded were his studies of electricity that, as a European noted in 1767, in foreign publications concerned with the subject "the terms *Franklinism, Franklinist,* and the *Franklinian system,* occur in almost every page."[8] Pragmatic and curious, Franklin poked into recesses of knowledge in astonishingly diverse areas and pulled out plums; each called for a name.

In 1743, Franklin founded the *American Philosophical*

7. Originally for members of legislative bodies.

8. Joseph Priestley, in Franklin: *Complete Works,* ed. John Bigelow (New York: G. P. Putnam's Sons; 1887–8), vol. 2, p. 65.

*Society,* an outgrowth of his earlier *Junta.* It drew its membership from virtuosi of all the colonies and became a medium for the dissemination of the thoughts of the Enlightenment. Within it, new terms coming from England, like *rationality* with all its derivatives, *intolerance* (a concept deprecated by free thinkers), *religiosity* (also deprecated), and *enthusiasm,* used as it was by Swift in commenting upon Anabaptist "jargon," expressed the intellectual rebellion against orthodoxy. Adopted terms as they were, they figured large in the context of the American urban vocabulary of the eighteenth century and reveal another cause of the widening rift between city and countryside or frontier, where fundamentalism still prevailed and religion played a central part in community life.

The *Philosophical Society* was only the most intellectual manifestation of the eighteenth-century club movement that had begun in England. A catalogue of the names of some of the colonial organizations—the *St. Cecilia Society* of Charleston, the *Tuesday Club* of Annapolis, the *Physical Club* and the "club at Withered's" of Boston, the *Jockey Club* in Maryland and in Virginia, the *Beefsteak Club* in New York— suggests the variety of interests current among Anglo-Americans in the pre-Revolutionary period and the great interchange of ideas and expression that must have been the rule. As in most clubs today, regardless of purpose, much of the conversation was no doubt focused on some recent *editorial,* "an unpleasant Americanism for leader or leading article."[9] Newspapers, too, were bringing the language into line.

A preoccupation with many colonists was hunting; it was most convenient that the *rifle,* or *riffle,* as the German gunmakers in Pennsylvania called it (from German *riffel,* "groove"), appeared immediately before the Revolution. *Shotgun* dates from the same period. Hunting was a necessity on the frontier; along the seaboard it had become a sport.

9. Richard Grant White: *Words and Their Uses Past and Present* (Boston and New York: Houghton Mifflin Co.; 1899), p. 95.

The great number of hunting terms entering during the period, most of them formed by combining familiar English materials, suggests how rich with game were the forests and how massive the slaughter. *Ring hunt* and *circle hunt* tell of the encirclement of animals by large groups of hunters, *fire hunt* and *fire ring* of the technique by which vast areas of woodland were destroyed. *Pigeon hunts* drove the once great clouds of passenger pigeons deeper into the receding wilderness. *Horse hunting*, described by a visitor to Virginia as "much delighted in by young People, who pursue wild Horses with Dogs, and sometimes without them,"[1] took an enormous toll of the roaming horse population. As early as 1708, New York had established a closed season on the *heath hen* (to no avail; the bird is now extinct), an American grouse named by early settlers when *heath* was still in use; and agitation was developing to protect the *musquash* (Algonquian *musquash*), or muskrat. The qualms of the minority had little effect; *hunting expeditions* continued, as did other sport to which the seaboard colonists were addicted.

Horse racing was a universal passion; the first blooded stallion, *Bully Rock*, was imported into Virginia in 1730. *Quarter race, quarter path*, and *racing path* entered the language, as did *horse jockeying*, for trafficking in horses. Just beginning was another sport, one imported from Scotland, *golf*, or *het kolven*, as its cousin was called in Dutch-dominated New York, where eighty-foot-long malls, called *kolf baans*, were already in use.

For the more passive, there were *spectacles* to enjoy—waxworks, electrical demonstrations, fireworks displays, and Punch-and-Judy shows. Itinerant performers and entrepreneurs toured the colonies, introducing their own regional accents and expressions into the areas they visited. Because *spectacles* were considered respectable even in Boston, where theater was not, the name served to disguise many a theatrical presentation in that Puritan bastion, "until at last the mask was thrown aside . . . and theatres are now built and used

1. Oldmixon: *British Empire in America* (1708), vol. 1, p. 203.

as such."[2] In the Middle and Southern colonies, the theater was enormously popular; Charleston, particularly, was noted for the appearance in its playhouses of noted European actors and actresses. But other terms than those relating to diversion, terms telling of significant economic and social developments and of a new influence upon the language, were entering the vocabulary, especially in the South. They related to the Negro.

Few borrowings from the Negro or terms relating to him entered the vocabulary during the earliest colonial period; and the greatest number of new words—especially acerbic and politically oriented ones—would not be recorded until the nineteenth century. But it was during the eighteenth that the Negro became a pervasive part of the colonial consciousness and made his initial impact on the language. Because by that time he was no longer useful except as a commodity in the North but had become an integral part of the plantation economy, most terms emerged in the context of slavery. *Slave* itself, surprisingly, played only a small part in the early coinage. Because *servant*, as has been seen, was often used interchangeably with it and because, at least early in the century, white indentured servants worked alongside the slaves, *Negro* was a more distinctive term and appeared more often in word combinations. *Negro quarter*, for example, was recorded in 1734, a century earlier than *slave quarter*, which did not make its appearance until 1837.

Distinction among countries of origin made necessary such terms as *Guinea Negro, Congo Negro, Gambia Negro, Gullah Negro. Congo* alone and *Guinea* were used loosely to signify any Negro newly arrived; *African* was in use in the same sense. So were *new Negro* and *salt-water Negro*, terms putting a prospective buyer on notice that the newcomer could not speak English and so was less valuable. Once settled on the plantation, the slave became a *field* or *hoe* or *house Negro*; the *house gang* worked in the vicinity of the plantation owner's home. *Plantation Negro* was a general term; *white*

2. William Ferguson: *America by River and Rail* (1856), p. 8.

*Negro* meant an albino but was sometimes applied to a mulatto (*mulattress* was a new word); and a *dower Negro* was one given to a bride as part of her dowry or owned by her at the time of her marriage. Many *free Negroes,* those emancipated by their owners or the descendants of those so freed, had slaves of their own.

Descriptive terms for dwellings included *Negro house, Negro hut, Negro quarters,* and *Negro cabin; Negro kitchen* was the kitchen in which food for slaves was prepared. Such terms as *Negro boots* and *shoes* and *cotton* and *cloth* (also called *plains*—usually blue for house slaves and white for field slaves) described the special clothing for them; some was made up on the plantation, but much of it was imported, as were *Negro pipes. Negro monger* and *Negro trader* are eighteenth-century words, as is *Negro overseer,* which now entered the vocabulary, to begin acquiring the sinister connotations that would accompany it on its travels through history and fiction. Affectionate terms—*uncle,* for an elderly Negro man; *auntie,* for a woman; *mammy* or *mauma* or *maum,* for the special nurse assigned to a child from infancy on—suggest the intimate intrafamilial relationships bound into the slave culture. The close associations that so many of these words reflect make unreasonable the denial by some linguists that Negro speech could have affected that of Southern whites. Popularly, the influence was long accepted. In 1842, Charles Dickens wrote from the United States to his wife: "All the women who have been bred in slave States speak more or less like Negroes, from having been constantly in their childhood with black nurses."[3] In 1932, the actor Otis Skinner, who was charmed by Southern speech, wrote: "It was inevitable that the Negro mammy should flavor the speech of the white children she brought up and the house slave that of his young master."[4] Mencken, less charmed,

---

3. Quoted in Mencken: *American Language,* pp. 361–2.
4. *New York Times Magazine* (January 10, 1932). Reprinted in C. Merton Babcock, ed.: *Ordeal of American English* (Boston: Houghton Mifflin Co.; 1961), p. 94.

blamed the "bad grammar" of Southern whites, "even in the loftiest circles," on this same association.

In the eighteenth century, no one was concerned about the genesis of *Negro English,* or *Negro;* it was simply accepted, as was *Indian,* as a mixture of imitative English and native idiom, having its own accent and tone. The earliest reference to the dialect, and one suggesting that it had already acquired identifying characteristics, is that of the observant Miss Sarah Knight in her journal in 1702. Telling of the very informal "trial" of a Connecticut Indian for a minor offense, she notes that one judge complained that the other was speaking *Negro* rather than *Indian* to the accused; "I'le ask him," the first volunteers, and addresses the Indian in different but equally mixed terms.[5] Both forms of address, consisting as they did of a kind of pidgin English, evidently required a discriminating ear to distinguish between them, and evidently, too, some terms overlapped. Although the testimony of Tituba in the Salem witch trials was given, according to the records, in typical Negro speech, the first literary attempt to set down the dialect was Cotton Mather's reproduction of his Negro slave's description of smallpox inoculation: ". . . People take Juice of *Small-Pox*; and *Cutty-skin,* and Putt in a Drop; then by-nd by a little Sicky, Sicky."[6] Mather's rendition was ridiculed by contemporary critics, but other attempts, made in early plays, were little different. *Dis* (this), *gemmen* (gentlemen), *berry* (very), *cawra* (call), *axa* (ask) were commonly used; the sounds represented were characteristic of the Gullah speech of the coastal Carolina region rather than of the "plantation" or "Virginia" speech used by later writers like Harriet Beecher Stowe and Joel Chandler Harris. Franklin's rendering of the Negro's observation that *"Boccarorra* [the white man] make de black man workee, make de Horse

5. *The Journals of Madam Knight and Rev. Mr. Buckingham, 1704–1710* (New York: Wilder and Campbell; 1825), p. 38.
6. *The Angel of Bethesda* (1721), in *Works of Cotton Mather,* ed. Kittredge. *Proceedings* of the Massachusetts Historical Society. XLV. 431 (1912).

workee, make de Ox workee, make ebery thing workee; only de Hog,"[7] shows similar idiom, as does the dialect used in the works of Cooper and Paulding and other early-nineteenth-century writers.

During the nineteenth century, Negro dialect presented on stage and in fiction gradually became stereotyped in the later tradition; and the tenet that it was merely ungrammatical English, poorly pronounced, came into vogue. De Vere, writing immediately after the Civil War, ascribed the accent and pronunciation to physiological characteristics of the Negro that prevented his perception and reproduction of the "more delicate modifications of sound" in English speech. While emphasizing that Negro minstrelsy exaggerated the dialect and that the Virginia house servant spoke better English than the "Yorkshire yokel, or even the thorough-bred Cockney," he maintained that "the most successful among the well-educated negroes, who have risen to honorable positions at the bar, retain nevertheless certain peculiarities of sound, of utterance, and accentuation." The possibility that the Negro in any way influenced the speech of his white masters or their children he dismissed in accordance with the traditional and academically respected doctrine that the slave occupied too subordinate a position to do so.[8]

The first scholarly denial of Negro dialect as unique came from Krapp, in his *English Language in America,* published in 1925. Krapp's exhaustive study of regional pronunciations in the United States, of phonetic spellings recorded in early colonial records, of guides to pronunciation given in old spelling books and dictionaries, and of words meant to rhyme in early verse gave convincing evidence, if it was needed, of the instability of pronunciation as a speech element. In tenaciously pursuing his thesis that all American speech is merely an extension of regional English speech, he applied his

---

7. Benjamin Franklin: *American Museum* (1787), vol. 2, p. 212.

8. M. Schele De Vere: *Americanisms: The English of the New World* (New York: Scribner & Co.; 1872), pp. 148–54.

findings even to Gullah, holding that imitative expressions learned by the original slaves had simply become archaic by the time that critics took notice of them in the slaves' descendants. Gullah's peculiarities of syntax, he maintained, had been established in much the same way as in pidgin English, whereby superiors address inferiors in a simplified, infantile speech. "So far as language goes," Krapp wrote, "there is very little evidence to show that the negroes are a special class in America, that they have developed a special idiom of their own or are addressed in a special idiom by their white fellow-citizens."[9] Hans Kurath, writing more recently, after years of work preparing the *Linguistic Atlas,* agreed with Krapp. "By and large," Kurath wrote, in *Word Geography of the Eastern United States,* "the Southern Negro speaks the language of the white man of his locality or area and of his level of education."[1] While disagreeing with Krapp about Gullah, in which Lorenzo Turner (since Krapp's time) has identified many terms as well as speechways derived from African languages,[2] Kurath believed that the speech of uneducated Negroes exhibits the same regional and local variations as does the speech of the illiterate white.

The conclusions of these linguists and others of like mind were challenged in the 1960's by a number of scholars, notably William A. Stewart, now president of the Education Study Center in Washington, D.C. In many articles, books, and lectures, Stewart has pointed out the survival of African cultural patterns, including linguistic, even among inner-city children, and the educational handicap these patterns create. Articles by others have appeared in linguistic and educational journals; the publication of Raven McDavid's abridged edition of Mencken's *American Language*[3] brought on a flurry

9. George Philip Krapp: *The English Language in America* (New York: The Century Co.; 1925), vol. 1, p. 162.

1. P. 6.

2. *Africanisms in the Gullah Dialect* (Chicago: University of Chicago Press; 1949).

3. (New York: Alfred A. Knopf; 1963).

of scholarly attacks on the "Mencken-McDavid treatment" of what has come to be called *Black English*.[4] The 1972 publication of J. L. Dillard's *Black English*[5] has most recently attracted popular attention to the genesis and nature of contemporary Negro speech.

Most of the controversial conclusions concerning Negro dialect have been based upon the evidence of syntax and pronunciation. No one denies that Negro speech, however "different," uses the same basic vocabulary content as does any other in America.[6] Only since Turner's work, however, has the contribution of African languages to that vocabulary been recognized in any degree. De Vere could find only three words to identify as African loan words: *buckra*; *swanga*, meaning elegant or bright-colored; and *moonack*, a mythical African animal. He denied the African genesis of either *tote*, which Webster had noted as probably of African origin, or the common Negro name *Cuffy*. Krapp denied any borrowings, managing to trace even *yam* (Gullah *nyam*, related to the Fulani for "to eat") to the English imitative *yum-yum*. Mencken could do little better, although by the time he wrote *Supplements I* and *II* he had profited by Turner's earlier studies and acknowledged the relationship at least of Gullah to various African languages. Turner had identified no fewer than six thousand African words in Gullah.

Even before the eighteenth century, *Cuff*, or *Cuffy*, and *Sambo* had entered American English as common and even generic names for Negro servants; but few who used them— often as one used *George* in Pullman-porter days—were conscious of being influenced by West African naming practices. We read in Hempstead's diary (1755): "An Indian freewoman, wife to Mr. Tilley's Negro Cuff died" (a pertinent quotation

4. E.g., Beryl Loftman Bailey: "Toward a New Perspective in Negro English Dialectology," *American Speech* (October 1965), pp. 171–7.

5. (New York: Random House; 1972).

6. As in relexification generally, "the vocabulary items themselves come from the European languages, but the different grammatical functions derive from another source." Dillard: *Black English*, p. 175.

for those interested in connecting Negro and Indian linguistically). The name was from *Kofi*, the name given by natives on the Gold Coast to a boy born on Friday. *Sambo* appears as early as 1704 and is traced by Turner to Hausan (northern Nigerian) *sambo*, meaning "second son." This kind of name is still used in Africa; the first name of *Kwame Nkrumah* indicates that he was born on a Saturday.

*Banjo* was once thought to be either a mispronunciation of *bandore*, a Latin name for a musical instrument, or a corruption of Spanish *bandurria*; but it was brought from the West Indies by slaves as *banjil*, *banjor*, or *banger* and is an African word. The instrument is noted in Cresswell's *Journal* (1774) as played by Negroes at a party in Virginia. *Voodoo* entered the language through Louisiana French and was written variously as *vandoo*, *vandous*, or *vandou*. (*Hoodoo* is a later corruption.) It comes from Dahomey *vodu* and meant originally an intermediary spirit, tutelary deity, fetish, or demon. Coming with it was *gris-gris*, which had traveled to Louisiana not only from Africa, by way of the Spanish West Indies, but also directly from Spain, where its Arabic form, *hirz acihr*, "amulet of enchantment," remained from Moorish times. Also connected with Louisiana—and surely discovered with delight by those early visitors to New Orleans—was *gumbo*, from *kingombo*, a native name for okra in the Bantu of central or northern Angola. It is perhaps the only African borrowing that has developed numerous derivatives and semantic metamorphoses, but not all are traceable to the same source. *Gumbo soup* and *gumbo filé* (*filé* is the French name for a powder made from sassafras leaves), like *gumbo* (soil) and *prairie gumbo*, are obviously related; but the term *gumbo* for a person of mixed blood—French and Indian or French and Negro—is probably from Congo *nkombo*, which meant a runaway slave. *Gumbo French* is a derivative. *Gumbo box*, a kind of drum used at the *gumbo balls* held twice weekly in the French-held territory around Cahokia, Illinois, was from still another word, Congo *nkumbi*.

*Jazz* has a long history of etymological controversy. The

*Oxford English Dictionary* concedes cautiously that it is "generally said to be Negro." Krapp considered it an English dialectal word (naturally) corresponding to the *English Dialect Dictionary*'s *jass,* meaning violent motion or the sound produced by a heavy blow. Others have connected the word with the name of a dancing slave, *Jasper,* on a plantation near New Orleans; Mathews states noncommittally that it is "often regarded" as being of African or Creole origin and suggests that it may come from *jasm,* equally obscure, which meant energy or enthusiasm. Some have connected it with a Louisiana French verb, *jaser,* meaning to speed up. Mencken, coming to no conclusion, notes that the verb has long had a sexual meaning in folk speech and that its transfer to orgiastic music came about naturally. *Juke,* a related term, is traced by Turner to Wolof *dzug,* or *dzog,* which means to lead a disorderly life or to misbehave.

Africanisms extending beyond the Gullah area are *goober* (Congo *nguba*), a peanut, and—to a lesser extent—*cooter,* a box turtle. More localized are *cush,* or *cushie* (Gullah *kush*), a corn-meal cake, coming from the original Arabic through Hausa *kusha* and probably the same word as the *Oxford English Dictionary*'s *cuscus,* or *couscous*; and *poor joe,* or *poor Job,* the great blue heron, a name that appears in the Vai dialect of Liberia and Sierra Leone. A New Orleans word, *jambalaya,* the name of a Creole seafood that is often applied to a miscellaneous mixture of anything, seems obviously to be from French Provençal *jambalaia*; but J. M. Carriere tells of tracing the related *jambolail* of the French settlement area of Illinois to an African source.[7] Also contradicting traditional etymology is Dillard's identification of *buckaroo* as an Africanism, an identification based on a not very convincing article by Julian Mason[8] that traces it to *buckra* (white man), rather than to the semantically identical *vaquero* (sometimes spelled *bakhara*). Dillard may be stretching as strenuously to support his thesis as Krapp was to support his.

7. *American Speech* (April 1939), pp. 109–19.
8. *American Speech* (February 1960), pp. 51–5.

Whatever the Negro's influence on the language and whatever the nature of his speech, there is no question that by the time of the Revolution he was an integral part of American life. Slavery was not yet the sectionally divisive element it would later become; in the South, such men as Jefferson of Virginia and Carroll of Maryland favored emancipation, as did George Washington, while in the North, the slave merchants were reluctant to see a profitable enterprise ended. Nevertheless, the issue was already provoking acrimonious exchanges and aggravating tensions among a people already at odds. It is no wonder that the Reverend Burnaby found a voluntary coalition so "difficult to suppose." And yet it is in the very words of division that we can detect the factors that would make this coalition possible.

A hundred years earlier, no such phrases as *Yankeeism, Yankee trickery, Virginiaism, Boston manner, Georgia vocabulary, New Yorkism* were coined because there was too little contact among the colonists to bring differences to anyone's attention. Only when the settlement area had extended into a chain of contiguous settlements and such words as *mile post, post stage, stage road, post guide, wagon road,* and *chair road* marked the clatter of wheels along the new highways; only when improved communication called for the coinage of *post rider* and *mail boat, mail stage* and *inferior* (provincial) *post office* to tell of the delivery of correspondence between cities and into the interior, some of it coming, by way of Charleston or New York, from overseas; only when the gazettes, with their thought-provoking *editorials,* or *newspaporials,* could disseminate foreign news and political opinion throughout the hinterland; and only when such terms as *Yankee peddler* and *country trader* carried their connotations of the exchange of gossip and outside news along with *notions* —only then could sectional and regional differences enter the general awareness and so the language.

Most observers who visited the towns and small villages of America noted the intellectual curiosity of even the most isolated settlers and their universal interest in politics. In-

evitably, along with the recognition of differences had to
come an awareness of common grievances and common loyalties. *Northward* and *Southward,* as they were called, were
alike affected by the restrictions of the Navigation Acts; and
*back settlers* and *land speculators* alike resented the closing
of the *wild lands* to settlement after the French and Indian
War. Moreover, the *Yankees*—which to the British meant all
Americans—had received scant thanks for their part in defending what George III called his *farms.* Few Americans
were unaware of the British contempt for American soldiers,
whom General Wolfe once described as "the dirtiest, most
contemptible cowardly dogs that you can conceive";[9] few
from Virginia forgot the laughter of General Braddock's
troops at the Virginia *bobtails* with their ridiculous short
coats. For Americans to call one another names was one thing;
for the *lobsterbacks* to do so was quite another. The speech
of the frontiersman following an *Indian trace* might differ
from that of the New Yorker walking around the *block*; but
all of it was *American,* as the British, with their talk of "barbarisms," were so sharply proclaiming. And so, when the die
had been cast and the struggle for political independence
begun, it was only fitting that the linguistic gauntlet should
be flung down also.

A committee appointed by the Continental Congress to
arrange for the reception of the French minister recommended that "all replies or answers" should be "in the language of the United States." In 1782, the Marquis de
Chastelleux wrote, in his *Travels in North America in the
Years 1780, 1781 and 1782*: "Here they avoid using these
expressions; *you speak English well, you understand English
well.* I have often heard them say: *you speak American well.*"[1]
And in 1789, Noah Webster issued his declaration of linguistic independence. The American Philological Society, formed
in 1802, declared its goal to be the ascertainment and im-

9. Willson Beckles: *Life and Letters of James Wolfe* (1900), p. 392.
1. (1786), vol. 2, p. 202.

provement of the *American tongue*. And in that same year, in the records of the First Session of the Seventh Congress of the United States, the phrase *American language* appeared. Samuel Johnson's *American dialect* of 1756 had come of age.

The validity of the phrase *American language* was properly challenged—our language is still English, with all of its English heritage intact—and even Webster later used *American English* instead. But the phrase expressed not so much a faulty concept as an attitude. Discussion of the merits and defects of American English, or whatever one wished to call it, continued; but hardly anyone cared. By the time that Pakenham's forces fell at New Orleans and the lumbering Conestogas started across the mountains, the language, like the country, was no longer looking toward England. Its frontier was ahead.

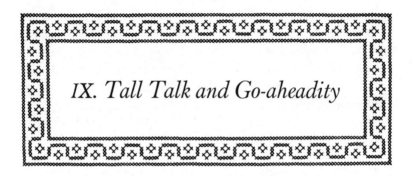

# IX. Tall Talk and Go-aheadity

In 1821, the new Academy of Language and Belles Lettres, its membership including, among others, James Madison, John Quincy Adams, Chief Justice John Marshall, and Daniel Webster, its aim admittedly to drive "doubtful" or "bad" words and phrases into disrepute, offered its honorary presidency to Thomas Jefferson, who declined the office. Writing to the academy's corresponding secretary, William Cardell, Jefferson suggested that it was fortunate that such an academy was not formed "in the days of our Saxon ancestors, whose vocabulary would illy express the science of this day." "Judicious neology," he wrote, "can alone give strength and copiousness to language, and enable it to be the vehicle of new ideas."[1] The members of the academy were obviously not in accord with Jefferson's views, but the people in general were; already neologizing with joyous abandon (if not judiciously), they were giving more "strength and copiousness" to the language than even Jefferson dreamed of. Some of their more fanciful innovations, like *questionize* and *happify* and *ramsquaddle* (to overcome, to "use up [a person] bodaciously"), would eventually lie discarded on the receding shores of history; but in controlling the national idiom at least for a time they gave to it its distinctively American character.

A few years after Jefferson's statement, Webster's *American Dictionary of the English Language* appeared. Of its seventy

1. From Monticello, January 27, 1821.

thousand entries, thirty thousand were new terms or definitions not in accord with Johnsonian precedent; and it was
obvious that Webster's attitude toward authority was unchanged since the old curmudgeon, with a shrug, had written
to John Pickering some years earlier: "How can the English
*locate* lands, when they have no lands to *locate?*"[2] A year after
the publication of the *Dictionary*, the *Virginia Literary
Museum and Journal of Belles Lettres* published a list of
Americanisms including such familiar words as *blizzard,
cavort, caucus, notions,* and *educational,* along with more
venturesome terms like *to squiggle,* which is defined as "to
move about like an eel," and *ripsnitious,* which meant smart
or "spruce." During the same period, writers like Paulding
and Seba Smith and Longstreet were introducing American
dialects—New England, "Virginny," and Negro—into literature; and even such noted authors as Cooper and Poe and
Emerson, who were bound in their writing to English example, gave at least lip service to the principle of linguistic
development. By the time that James Russell Lowell published *The Biglow Papers* in 1848, the American vernacular
had achieved literary respectability.

Since 1787, when Jefferson's *belittle* had so incensed British critics, innovations like *noncommittal, jeopardize, immigrant, constitutionality,* and *governmental* had been appearing in the writings of educated men as well as in the
*Congressional Record;* and English visitors lamented that
not only the "operative class" (factory workers) but even
lawyers and public officials in America used such reprehensible terms as *right away* and *reckon* and "perpetrated
other conversational anomalies with remorseless impunity."[3]
Most deplorably, some of these anomalies were infiltrating

2. *Letter to the Honorable John Pickering on the Subject of His
Vocabulary, or Collection of Words and Phrases Supposed to be Peculiar
to the United States of America* (Boston: West and Richardson; 1847).
3. Captain Thomas Hamilton: *Men and Manners in America,* 2 vols.
(Edinburgh, 1833). Quoted in H. L. Mencken: *The American Language,* 4th ed. (New York: Alfred A. Knopf; 1936), p. 23.

respectable literary circles in London! Coleridge, even as he
fulminated against *talented* (which was not really an Americanism to begin with), adopted *influential* and *reliable* and
*leniency; lengthy* appeared in the writings of Jeremy Bentham
as early as 1816 and in the writings of Scott and Dickens
later; and William Pitt himself used the political term *floor,*
which had been introduced by John Quincy Adams in 1774.
No King's-Englishman, however, even attempted to imitate
—or stooped to criticize—such gibberish as could be found
in some American writing: words like *jimberjawed* and
*hornswoggle* and *quiddle* and *flunkt,* and dialogue like "I
should like to shoot the holl gang, by the gret horn spoon!"[4]
or "Ax'd me out a flopper with my tom-axe in no time . . .
jumped in . . . and came down the falls like a cob in a corn-
van."[5]

Many of the new words were strange to some Americans,
too, but not for long. A prolific source of neologisms was
politics; and because "all American conversation must finish
with politics,"[6] and because the strident, polemic newspapers,
constantly increasing in numbers and influence, quoted the
uninhibited stump speeches of backwoods politicians, terms
like *silk-stocking gentry* and *ruffled-shirt gentry, crawfishing,
whitewash, electioneering,* and *districting, logrolling* and
*campaign* became the stuff of ordinary conversation. *Gerrymander* caught the public fancy by way of a caricature circulated in Boston and representing an imaginary dragonlike
creature, the *Gerrymander Beast,* based on the outline of an
election district devised for party purposes; the word combined the name of Governor Elbridge Gerry with "sala-
mander." Gilbert Stuart, for whom the drawing must have
been quite a change of pace from presidential portraits, is

4. James Russell Lowell: *The Biglow Papers* (1848), series I, no. 5,
stanza 2.

5. R. M. Bird: *Nick of the Woods* (1837), vol. 1, p. 218.

6. Marquis de Chastelleux: *Travels in North America.* Quoted in
Henry T. Tuckerman: *America and Her Commentators* (New York:
Scribner & Co.; 1864), p. 67.

credited with adding head, wings, and claws to the outline
when he saw it hanging in a friend's newspaper office.

Serious terms like *nullification party* and *nullifier, anti-
nullifier* and *nullificatory* (Jefferson had coined *nullification*
and *nullify* in 1798) were tempered by nicknames like *nullie,*
for one favoring nullification; the pervasiveness of politics
labeled even such unrelated items as footwear—a *nullifier*
was "a sort of shoe, made like a decapitated boot, brought
into fashion in the 'nullification' times." *Heroites* were supporters of Andrew Jackson, the *Hero of New Orleans,* as were
*Hickory Men* and *Old Hickoryites. Logrolling,* noted as early
as 1812 as a Kentucky political term, was used by Davy
Crockett; it came from the custom of co-operative effort in
the logging camps, where loggers helped one another to
roll the great logs down to the water on which they would
be floated downstream. *Lobby,* in the collective sense of
lobbyists, was used at least by 1808; and its many derivatives—*to lobby, lobbying, lobby member, lobbyer,* and
*lobbyist*—followed soon after. The word itself comes from
German *Laube,* a bower or small summerhouse, and signified
originally nothing more than a small hall or entry room outside a larger room; now it means not only the antechamber
of a legislative hall but all the power of a political pressure group. *Bunkum,* from which comes *bunk,* meaning nonsense talked to impress the listener, apparently originated in
a speech in Congress by Felix Walker, a congressman from the
county of Buncombe in North Carolina. When colleagues
protested at the length of a tiresome speech and left the
chamber, he declared that their departure did not disturb
him; he was speaking not to the House but to *Buncombe.*
A later English writer suggested, in *Blackwood's* of April
1861, that the word and associated parable could most bene-
ficially be set up over the Speaker's chair in Parliament.

Along with topical terms like *hard currency, gold standard, paper aristocracy, abolitionist, abolitionize* (to imbue
with the principles of those favoring the abolition of slavery),
*antislavery men* (also *antislavery element, paper, ticket,* and

so on), *Negro party, antitariffites,* and *wildcat bank*—which, topical as it was, has left us a legacy in the term *wildcat* for any unsound venture[7]—there were the words and phrases still so much with us today, like *favorite son* and *split ticket, political machine*—shortened to *machine*—*banner state, third party, platform, plank, to stump,* and many others. The notorious *half-horse, half-alligator* frontiersman entered the contemporary political glossary; the Columbia *County Register* of September 7, 1830, reported: "Each party kept a half dozen bullies under pay—genuine specimens of Kentucky Alligatorism—to flog every poor fellow that would attempt to vote illegally," a co-operative effort that must surely have made for honest elections. Some of the coinage was whimsical; an ornithologically oriented observer gave the name *politician* to the white-eyed vireo for its habit of "feathering its nest by the use of even the commonest materials,"[8] and opponents of the Embargo Acts turned the word around to call them the *O-grab-me Acts.* Americans evidently have had linguistic fun with politics from the beginning; former Vice-President Agnew's *nattering nabobs of negativism* has a long tradition behind it.

All such words and phrases, along with others like *on the fence* and *to bolt the party,* became common coin in this critical time when the character of American politics was changing, when the old, largely elite political establishment was being challenged by men from that back country which had once seemed so far removed. The political situation had also an indirect effect upon the American vocabulary. Because political reportage and popular controversy were concerned with a new breed of men, and because the popularity

7. The term *wildcat bank* apparently originated in Michigan, where a bank had on its notes a large vignette representing a panther, there called a wildcat. After the bank became insolvent, the name was applied to all irresponsible banks, and later to any unsound venture.

8. Mitford M. Mathews, ed.: *A Dictionary of Americanisms on Historical Principles* (Chicago: University of Chicago Press; 1951).

of such men as Jackson and Crockett introduced a new
dimension to the language even in the conservative East,
nonpolitical terms that would otherwise have been limited
to remote areas entered the national arena. To the domesti-
cated Easterners, the West, that early West of Kentucky and
Tennessee and the extending West of Missouri and Kansas
and Texas and beyond, was exotic, the exploits of frontiersmen like Daniel Boone and Davy Crockett legendary. *Texas
fever, California fever, Oregon fever,* all part of the strong
pull of the West, were in the national blood stream; and those
who would not or could not go there were fascinated by the
experiences of those who did. Moreover, the popular books
of James Fenimore Cooper were imprinting sharply on the
national consciousness the traditions and the character of the
frontier. The pattern of Western speech, therefore—authentic
or apocryphal—helped to shape the general vocabulary.

Davy Crockett, who was sent to Congress in 1827 and
earned immortality nine years later at the Alamo, once declared defensively that even in the West he had never met a
man who actually used such terms as *bodyaciously, teetota-
tiously,* and *obflisticated.* But the first two appeared in the
*Congressional Globe* of July 21, 1840, along with *exflunctified*
(from *exflunct,* to overcome or to beat thoroughly); and
Crockett himself was quoted, accurately or otherwise, by the
*New York Sun,* on June 5, 1834, as swearing ". . . he'd be te-
to-natiously [sic] obfusticated if he would take the office on
any condition." It would have been surprising had he not
used some of those terms so popular on the frontier, such as
*rambunctious* and *hornswoggle* and *absquatulate* (to decamp
precipitously); the trend showed up even in Boston, where the
*Transcript* of June 24, 1831, quoted a Bostonian as saying:
"Come, gentlemen, let's liquor and then I'll *explaterate*
more," the word no doubt being a humorous blending of "explanation" and "elaborate." Crockett has been given credit
for *sockdolager* and *ripsnorter* and for such picturesque
phrases as *root hog or die, singing psalms to a dead horse,*

*quicker than hell could scorch a feather,* and *fine as silk.* That a *ring-tailed roarer,* "a most violent fellow," was equated with a *Crockett* was, of course, not his doing, nor was the expression *a sin to Davy Crockett,* which meant whatever was exceptional or extraordinary.

Jackson, although somewhat better educated (hardly a challenge—Crockett's schooling consisted of one hundred days of tutoring), was nevertheless a Philistine, an Anglophobe, coming from the still raw land where tall talk and grotesque ornaments of speech were commonplace. In Tennessee and farther west, where in many communities *lynch law,* or *Lynch's Law*—called also *Judge Lynch, General Lynch,* and *Captain Lynch*—prevailed (*lynching, lyncher, to lynch,* and *lynchy* were also in the vocabulary), the way of life was reflected in such terms as *rough and tumble, gander-plucked* (having an ear bitten off), *make the fur fly, rotgut* and *red-eye* (for whiskey), *gouging scrape, claim jumper,* and *land pirate.* Jackson could not have gained the support of his back-country constituents had he talked like Henry Clay. His most direct contribution to the vocabulary, however, was in the lending of his name as an attribute. It occurred in so many combinations—*Jackson men, Jackson party, Jackson banks, Jackson money* (gold), *Jackson coats, hats, jackets, trousers, shoes, slippers*—that the *Albany Evening Journal* of August 8, 1834, complained that the rage for naming everything after Jackson was evidence of his "bloated reputation." *Jacksonian men* and *Jacksonian democracy, Jacksonize* (to defeat in battle, as at the Battle of New Orleans) and *Jacksoniana,* the name proposed for a state to be carved out of portions of Kentucky, Mississippi, and Tennessee, were other terms coined by the *Heroites.*

Bloated reputation or not, these two men, political opponents, epitomized the vigorous, explosive spirit of the times, the spirit of a people who, in the space of little more than two generations, had won three wars, humbled pirates, declared two continents off limits to the rest of the world, doubled and then tripled their territory, crossed mountains, built bridges, conquered rivers, dug canals, and begun the laying of tracks that, so visionaries claimed, would reach the Pacific. Above the territory of the United States of America—the *American Republic,* the *American Empire*—the *star-spangled banner* flew splendid and free; the *American eagle,* that "proudest bird upon the mountain," soared into the limitless sky. In that clear first half of the nineteenth century, a man could look ahead and see forever; and the wagons rolled across the plains, across the mountains, into Oregon, into California. Jefferson had called for pure *Americanism*; now it emerged full-blown, and the *Manifest Destiny* of the Republic made not only just but imperative the removal of the Indians, the annexation of Texas, the occupation of Oregon, the war with Mexico, the acquisition of the great Southwest. Twenty-three million people saw glory around them and glory ahead, and they expressed their jubilation in a national idiom that soon broke down the defenses of the purists.

Reaching for new heights of imagery, of expression, the language grew tall; in a country bigger than life, speech could not be laggard. Splendid became *splendiferous*; a man was *whole-souled* or *true-blue;* he might have a *heart as big as all outdoors* or be *savage as a meat ax*; people were not just *crazy* but *plumb crazy.* The excitement, the wonder of new ways of travel—of canals and steamboats, of roads and railroads, of the whole transportation revolution that was bringing the products of farm and factory to distant markets, countrymen to the city, emigrants westward, politicians to the stump, and representatives to Congress—inspired extravagant comment in Easterner and Westerner alike. Edward Everett of Massachusetts, speaking at a railroad promotional meeting in the thirties about the flow of goods from the West, proclaimed: "The country, by nature or art, is traversed, crossed, reticulated (pardon me, sir, this long word; the old ones are too short to describe these prodigious works) with canals and railroads, rivers and lakes. The entire west is moving to meet us; by water, land, and stream, they ride, they sail, they drive, they paddle, they whiz—they do all but fly down towards us."[9] It was all too much, too fast, too huge, this kaleidoscopic, pushing, pulsating nation; the existing language, as Everett sensed, could not contain it.

But the language managed; its genius could cope. Into the vocabulary came words never before heard, at a rate precedented, perhaps, only in Elizabethan England, words used in new ways, words combined, words clipped, words blended, words borrowed, words adapted to this new world in which everyone was riding, sailing, driving, paddling, whizzing . . .

From the beginning, candidates in the United States did not *stand* for election, as in England; they *ran*. Not only aspirants to public office but even the average man in nineteenth-century America seemed to be running. Visitors were amazed at the alacrity, even eagerness, with which the people moved from place to place and noted that "even when in prosperous circumstances [they can] contemplate a change of situation which, under our old establishments and fixed habits, none but the most enterprising would venture upon." Morris Birbeck, who traveled by stage and on foot along the road to Illinois, compared the "scene of bustle and business" to "the internal movement of a vast hive."[1] Along the *macadam* roads, most of them *turnpiked* and built by *turnpike companies,* hurried the *buckboards* and *accommodation coaches,* the *buggies* and the *rockaways* and the *Concords,* guided by signposts that were popularly called *preachers* because "they point out the road but never travel it."[2] Sup-

9. *Reticulated,* although "long," was not new, as Everett implied (nor were old words necessarily short); but he made his point. The peroration is quoted in Marcus Cunliffe: *The Nation Takes Shape, 1789–1837* (Chicago: University of Chicago Press; 1959), p. 108.

1. Both comments come from Birbeck: *Notes on a Journey in America* (London, 1818). Reprinted in part in H. S. Commager and Allen Nevins, eds.: *Heritage of America* (Boston: Little, Brown and Company; 1945), pp. 259–61.

2. Royall: *Pennsylvania,* II (1829). Quoted in Mathews: *Dictionary.*

plementing the macadams, of which the principal one was the
*Cumberland* or *National Road,* were the more numerous
*plank roads* and the *corduroys,* made "of small trees, stripped
of their boughs, and laid touching one another,"[3] a type of
road characteristic of the frontier and still used in remote
areas. The importance of the *corduroy road* is apparent in the
many related terms in use: *corduroy* or *corduroying,* for the
material used; the verb *to corduroy;* and the compounds
*corduroy road* and *corduroy bridge,* the last sometimes called,
with comparable visual imagery, *gridiron bridge*—on such a
surface, according to a contemporary traveler, one ran the
risk "of having his bones dislocated." Always, too, there were
the *dirt roads,* many of them little more than trails, whose
name still puzzles Englishmen; *dirt* in British usage means
filth, not earth; *pay dirt* is as American as a word can be.

Where the roads ended, the *moving wagons* kept on rolling
across the unruled land, the *prairie carts* and the *Pittsburghs,*
the *family wagons* and the *Conestogas,* which would arrive at
their destinations with bronze harness bells jingling, to give
rise to the expression *I'll be there with bells on.* Traffic moved
on the right rather than on the left as formerly and as in
Britain today because of the Conestogas, which were best
guided from the left and so afforded a clear view ahead only
when driven on the right side of the road. Drivers of other
vehicles found it not only wise not to argue but convenient to
follow in the ruts made by the heavy wagons, and habit soon
became law.

The "bustle and business" (busyness, surely) were not
limited to the roads and the beckoning frontier. In the cities,
the people, according to observers, *moved* continually, *moving*
in the sense of changing lodgings being a peculiarly American
term. *Moving Day* was established in colonial times and had
become an institution by which, according to Washington
Irving, "this most restless of cities is literally turned out of
doors on every May-day."[4] In the *New York Mirror* of May 12,

3. Blane: *Excursion* (1824). Quoted in Mathews: *Dictionary.*
4. *Knickerbocker's History of New York* (New York, 1809).

1832, a mournful correspondent lamented: ". . . the fashion of *moving* (is it not a wretched New Yorkism?) has all my life given me a great annual disturbance." De Vere suggests that the custom of having an annual moving day came to the New World with the Dutch settlers; for in parts of Holland and Belgium the same custom and same date—in New York, for many years, it was the first of May—prevail. Its congeniality to the American character, however, must have given it strong reinforcement. De Vere comments also that this tendency to *move* is often looked upon as a sign of instability in the national character but may be explained by the "marvellous facility of locomotion which this country affords by its network of railways, rivers, and canals . . . to which must be added the temptation held out by countless openings for all in the newer States."[5] Not only did people themselves move; the vocabulary tells us also that *house movers,* whose business was literally to move houses, carried on their business in the city. With the new *horse cars* competing with other traffic on the cobblestoned streets, it is easy to imagine the clatter of hooves, the clanging of bells, the rumble of wheels, and the shouts of drivers creating a din worthy of our own times.

Whoever moved did so with one object in mind, to *get ahead*; and every American was supposedly equipped with the *go-ahead* for doing so. The phrase *go ahead* reverberated in the brisk mental atmosphere. As a verb it had imperative force, expressing assent and approval. "We say to our Clay friends, 'go ahead,' . . ." read a political notice in the Harrodsburg, Kentucky, *American* of March 25, 1831; "Dear Sir—" read a letter from Davy Crockett to a young man who had asked his permission to marry a relative, "I received your letter. Go ahead. David Crockett."[6] As a substantive it became *go-ahead, go-aheadness, go-aheadedness, go-aheadativity, go-aheadativeness, go-aheadity.* Irving wrote of "our state of

5. M. Schele De Vere: *Americanisms: The English of the New World* (New York: Scribner & Co.; 1872), p. 93.

6. Possibly apocryphal. The story was related by the *Political Examiner* of Shelbyville, Kentucky, April 20, 1833; the style, at least, is authentic.

society in America with . . . its helter-skelterism and go-aheadivity";[7] Cooper used *go-aheadism;* and in the spirit of the times, the *New Orleans Times-Picayune* of April 23, 1837, commented: "The voyage, like unto all voyages upon flat boats in these days of steam and go-aheadity, was necessarily tedious."

Along with these words appeared the phrase *self-made man,* a speaker in the congressional debates of 1832 declaring: "In Kentucky, almost every manufactory known to me is in the hands of enterprising self-made men." The sentence strikingly juxtaposes the new phrase with the Elizabethan term *enterprising,* which, in America, had as a companion the verb *to enterprise* (since lost). *To progress,* that earlier Elizabethan term, had been revived or newly coined in America and after two centuries was returning to England as a recognized Americanism; Southey was among those adopting it. In such an atmosphere, time was dear; William F. Harnden, a conductor on the Boston and Worcester Railroad, founded *Harnden's Express,* nucleus of the railroad and steamboat express services to follow, which undertook "the personal bearing of parcels and executing commissions between New York and Boston." America had begun to *hustle,* a word that came to be universally associated with the American spirit before the century was done.

The hustling was done to the throb of pistons and keynoted by the shrill whistle of steam; its background music was the hum of the new machines that marked the coming of the Industrial Revolution to America. That revolution would not have marked impact economically and socially until after mid-century, but already the vocabulary was full of the sound of it. Eli Whitney had introduced the concepts of interchangeable parts and the division of labor in his musket factory at New Haven in 1798, an innovation hardly less important than his invention of the *cotton gin,* which revolutionized the economy of the South. Muskets were the first product

7. *Knickerbocker's History,* XXIV, 73.

referred to as *assembled*; they point straight ahead to the auto-mobile assembly line of today. McCormick's reaper, patented in 1836, gave new impetus to agriculture and was followed by a variety of inventions that combined *machine*, meaning formerly a fire engine (as in *running with the machine*), with functional attributes. There were now *barrel machines* and *harvesting machines* and *cotton machines* and *mowing machines* and *planing machines* and even *milking machines*. There were *power presses*, too. And in 1846 Elias Howe patented that invention which would ease labor in the home and stimulate it in the factories; the pattern was cut for Bertha the *Sewing Machine* Girl. With the invention of the power loom in the same year, factories put in *weave rooms* and *weave shops*; mass production became a goal, and *factory cotton* and *factory thread*—even *factory homespun!*—entered the language.

From *factory villages*, despite the admiration for them expressed by Dickens and by Harriet Martineau, rose a cloud of smoke no bigger than a man's hand, portent of strife to come. *Labor reform* was in the vocabulary; so was *scab*, both as a noun and as a verb, transitive and intransitive. *Worky* (or *workey*) meant a factory worker, with *workeyism* its derivative to describe a political doctrine upholding the rights of labor. "They . . . get up the cry of workeyism," complained the *New England Magazine* in 1835, "as if, forsooth, every man in New England did not work." In the South, where the *cotton gin* was combining with the *steamboat* to make King Cotton supreme in the land, the proliferation of terms like *cotton country, cotton region, cotton interest, cotton broker, cotton harvester, cotton picker,* and *cotton droger,* along with related terms like *baling press* and *ginner* and *ginnery,* promised bitter struggle when that kingdom would be threatened with destruction.

But inventions and industry and improvements in agriculture meant little without transport. It was the canals and the steamboats, the roads and the railroads, that in this first half of the nineteenth century transformed the direction—physically, politically, and economically—of America. The *Erie Canal—Clinton's Ditch* or *the Big Ditch*, as it was called at first—was the most significant; but it was only one of the canals constructed to link section to section, port to port, producer to consumer. The Erie was to be, according to *Niles' Register* of 1823, "a chain to bind together rich and populous territories, far distant from each other"; and it fulfilled its promise well, offering new and easier access to the Western lands, making New York the leading port of the nation, booming the economy of the middle states. It is difficult today to imagine the impact of canal construction; the language, however, in the many new terms entering during the period, suggests its dimensions. *Canal commissioner, canal policy, canal scrip, canal grant, canal land, canal department*—each has behind it a story of political battles, of economic and often social concern. *Canal boats* carried passengers and freight, towed other vessels, and often served as living quarters for the *canallers* who worked aboard them. They traveled sometimes in caravan; we read that "tow-boats . . . are large vessels, which are lashed on each side of the steam-vessels, and to the stern of the former are frequently two heavy canal-boats . . . sometimes one or more each side. They carry heavy luggage, and passengers too . . ."[8] *Canal packets* were run by a *canal packet line* on a regular schedule, and for years natural horse power was their motive force. The use of horses, led by *canal drivers* along the towpath beside the canal, continued into the twentieth century, despite the competition of a parallel railroad.

The fortuitous conjunction of canal construction and the development of the *steamboat* enormously magnified the effectiveness of both. *Steamboat canal* makes its first appearance for the record in 1830; but before that time, "curious-looking machines . . . like factories that had broken loose, and taken to the water"[9] were churning the waters of canals

8. *Letter from Tradesman* (1835). Quoted in Mathews: *Dictionary.*
9. *Edinburgh Journal* (1844), I, 230.

and rivers, lakes and coastal waters. During the first half of the nineteenth century, not only did these curious-looking machines dominate the economy, the agriculture, the commerce, and the social life of the middle area of the United States; they also accelerated the movement westward, afforded new markets for the products of Eastern factory and Southern plantation and Western farm, and gave to the language some words and phrases that keep their magic still. Surely none of us hears the phrase *river town* without envisioning a steamboat coming in to land, and *steamboat whistle* stirs some remembered quickening in our collective memory.

The expected utilitarian combinations entered the vocabulary in the first decades of the century; *steamboat laws, steamboat inspector, steamboat locks, steamboat basin, steamboat landing, steamboat engineer, steamboat navigation*—all are familiar terms in official documents and in correspondence. The vessels themselves, *steamboats* in general (*steamer* was usually reserved for ocean-going ships, except in combinations like *steamer edition* and *steamer issue*), were particularized as *steam galleys, steam flats, steam ferryboats, steam towboats, side-paddle-wheelers, stern-wheelers, wheelbarrow boats, wheelbarrows*—many of these terms, of course, overlapping. Some called them *swimming volcanoes,* and with reason. Boiler explosions were a constant hazard, aggravated by the competitive spirit of *steamboat captains* and their passengers too. Many an impromptu race strained engines beyond their capacity, and the cheers of passengers were drowned out as the deafening roar of explosion proclaimed another disaster on the waterways or at sea. No one knows how many thousands lost their lives in the rivers and on the seaport-to-seaport runs; reports of such disasters were common in the newspapers of the day. Along the Hudson, *safety barges,* passenger boats "towed by a steamboat at such a distance from it as to avoid all apprehension of danger to the passengers,"[1] obviated the hazard; confident passengers could indulge in *steamboat*

1. Bartlett (1859), p. 376.

✗ I remember The riverboats on the Ohio as a boy but never travelled on one. I did travel from Washington ↓ Baltimore on the Old Bay Line.

*cotillion parties,* described as "an elegant summer amusement."[2]

The well-known danger of explosion, as well as additional hazards posed by the treacherous shoals and currents of the Mississippi, lent drama to the introduction of the steamboat to inland waters in 1811, when the steamboat *New Orleans,* built under the direction of Nicholas Roosevelt, made her maiden voyage down the great river with the Roosevelts aboard. The courage of Mrs. Roosevelt in the face of danger and inevitable hardships—the voyage would last five months—as well as the perennial fascination of the river itself, captured the imagination of the nation. Had the public —or the Roosevelts—anticipated the violent earthquake that nearly brought a sad ending to the expedition at New Madrid, Missouri, there would have been even greater suspense. But the voyage was completed, and the *Mississippi River steamboat* embarked on its half century of glory.

Our image of the *floating palaces,* or—as some called them —*floating wedding cakes,* is a romantic one, but the reality was evidently not always so. Mrs. Trollope warned her readers in 1823: ". . . no one who wishes to receive agreeable impressions of American manners, should commence their travels in a Mississippi steam boat."[3] On even the finest vessels, wrote another observer, *deck passengers,* the equivalent of steerage passengers, "were herded like cattle among the freight . . . accorded the treatment which their poverty and lowly estate deserved."[4] Sometimes called *standees,* they included immigrants from Europe, flatboatmen going upriver (their flatboats broken up and sold in New Orleans and their profits perhaps dissipated in a New Orleans *gin mill* or *groggery*), poor traders, emigrants from the Eastern states, and the genteel poor, all crowded against the cotton bales, which were piled sometimes as high as the *hurricane deck,* or upper

2. Howison: *Sketches* (1821), p. 325. Quoted in Mathews: *Dictionary.*

3. *Domestic Manners of the Americans,* 2nd ed., I, 19.

4. Herbert Asbury: *Sucker's Progress* (New York: Dodd, Mead, and Company; 1938), p. 201.

deck, a term surely ironic—the mildest of hurricanes must have laughed.

But if the *stateroom passengers* traveled in greater comfort, even in fantastic luxury, they were no more exempt than the standees from danger. *Snag* seems an innocuous term to us, especially since we have made it a figurative term; but to *steamboat men* it meant a deadly menace, a tree embedded in the river's bottom and capable of ripping like a knife through the hull of a steamboat. Contemporary accounts tell of wrecked vessels, of lost passengers, of irreparable damage caused by collision with these obstacles. "We passed the wrecks of two steamers," relates one, "which had been sunk by striking snags."[5] In one mishap, described by the *New Orleans Times-Picayune* of March 29, 1839, the "snag went through the guards, cabin and hurricane roofs, destroying six or seven berths." Equally dangerous were the *sawyers,* long familiar to keelboatmen and flatboatmen on lesser rivers, those uprooted trees sawing up and down in the river's current, threatening whatever sought to pass them by. Some steamboats were equipped with a watertight compartment, called the *snagroom* or *snagchamber,* built into the hull; sometimes double-bottomed *snagboats* were sent ahead to remove such obstructions in the steamboat's path. And always, to keep one in mind of the close prospect of eternity, there belched forth the sparks and the great columns of smoke from the *boiler deck,* located not below but above the main deck, to tell of the latent volcano below.

The boilers, with their great maws, were greedy, calling for frequent stops at *wooding places* along the shore to *take in* wood. The refueling stops became traditionally the occasion for passengers and crew to step ashore and have refreshments, and for many years *let's wood up* was a popular euphemism for *let's have a drink.* From this need to wood up came, too, the expression *independent as a wood sawyer,* still heard in areas where people know what a *wood sawyer* is; so important was

5. Falconer: *Letters and Notes* (1841). Quoted in Mathews: *Dictionary.*

the fuel and so high the sawyer's wages that his self-assurance was noted for turning to arrogance.

In the *pilothouse,* the *river pilot,* that man of skill and daring who *learned*[6] Mark Twain the intricacies of his calling, guided the vessel through its always unpredictable channel. On the *Texas deck,* so called because staterooms were given the names of states and *Texas* seemed appropriate for the largest, were the officers' quarters. And from the *hurricane deck* the privileged passengers watched the curving shore. A kingdom of itself, presided over by the *steamboat captain,* whose word aboard was law and whose status abroad was high, the steamboat world was a smaller country of their own for those who lived within it; it is not surprising that the captains, in their *retiracy* (or with it—the term applied both to seclusion and to a *competency,* or retirement fund), were inclined to build their homes in a style that came to be known as *Steamboat Gothic,* reminiscent of the glory they had known.

For half a century the steamboat held sway, traveling the great river highway, docking at the New Orleans water front to become part of a brilliant tableau of proud vessels sometimes extending four or five miles along the shore and two or three boats deep. But even as the glory continued, an ominous note was sounding in the distance, the clanging sound of *ironing,* or laying track. The steamboat men scoffed; but as the *steamboat trains* made connections and carried freight and passengers to distant destinations, they saw the shadow of those twin tracks cutting across their future.

*Railroad,* according to Mencken, is effectively an Americanism; the accepted English term, *railway,* has usually been applied in America to other forms of rail lines than steam—electric or horsedrawn, for example. And despite the parallel development of railroading in the two countries, the related vocabulary is sharply different, suggesting that by the early nineteenth century the American language was asserting its

6. *Teach,* Twain said, was not in the river vocabulary. *Life on the Mississippi* (1883), in Mark Van Doren, ed.: *Voice of America* (Cleveland and New York: World Publishing Co.; 1942), p. 367.

independence not only in expressing purely American concepts or phenomena but for more general notions, too. The
national style was evident in the earliest coinages; *cow-
catcher* and *frog* are more in character than the sober English
equivalents, *fender* and *crossing-plate*. Independent coinages
also were *steam car,* instead of the English *steam carriage;
boxcar; hotbox; switch,* instead of *shunt,* with many combinations, like *switchyard* and *switch track; sidetrack,* which acquired figurative meanings; and *jerkwater,* also transferable
and coming from the practice of branch trains of stopping for
water at trackside creeks, where a bucket brigade would be
formed. *Depot,* from the French but without the accents,
was adopted in place of the English *station,* to De Vere's
disgust. "Why we should ever have exchanged the sensible
*station* of the English for the absurd *depot* of the French,"
he exclaims, "is perfectly unaccountable; . . . and we must
needs call it *dee-po,* and thus add to the absurdity."[7] Passengers' belongings were not *luggage* but *baggage—plunder* had
become provincial—and numerous derivatives were formed,
*baggage room, baggage check, baggage agent,* and so on.
*Checking* named an innovation typical of the go-aheadative
Americans; the practice was soon adopted elsewhere.

In keeping with American devotion to nautical terms, much
of the nomenclature of the steamboat was retained. At the
cry of *all aboard,* passengers got *on* the steam cars, not *in*
as in England. The conductor was at first called a *pilot;* and
the *locomotive engineer,* rather than *driver,* as the English
called him, was considered the counterpart of the *steamboat
engineer. Freight,* not *goods,* was shipped, often on a *gondola
car,* which resembled a large flat-bottomed boat. Even the
*caboose,* a term unknown in England, came from Dutch
*kombuis,* which had lent its name, as *caboose,* to a ship's
galley. (Mathews connects the term, in the sense of a hut or
poor dwelling, with Low German *Kabuse,* without the intermediate Dutch term.) Trains built with double decks, the

7. *Americanisms,* p. 355.

upper one called a *hurricane deck*, were *double-deckers*, a term much with us today in reference to many things, from buses to sandwiches. We cannot speak and deny our seagoing heritage!

In the more formal railroad terms developing before the Civil War and afterward can be traced the political and social problems that followed the track of the railroad—*railroad land, railroad prospector, railroad pool, railroad lawyer, lobby, king, commission, lobbyist, lobbying, magnate, president.* And it is evident that railroad construction was ecologically damaging for more reasons than its gobbling of land; the term *railroad fire*, for those great prairie fires and other fires caused by sparks and cinders from the passing engines, encapsulates a history of the destruction of thousands and thousands of acres of forest and grassy lands, of the loss of great herds of cattle, and of enormous property damage. As with the steamboat, disaster to passengers also was common; contemporary newspaper accounts of collisions in which cars and engines *telescoped* into one another tell a tale of gore comparable to that of our own highway statistics.

While the transportation revolution itself was demanding so many new words, new phrases, new ways of speaking, the vast new land it was opening up called for expression beyond anyone's earlier imaginings. The sight of mountains and plains and desert, the revelation of creatures and phenomena hitherto unknown, the demands of a new kind of pioneer life offered a linguistic challenge to test even American ingenuity. In the first decades of the half century, the frontier lay principally in the Mississippi Valley—in Indiana, in Illinois, in Missouri; and as New Englanders and Virginians, New Yorkers and Pennsylvanians pushed on across earlier-settled regions—the pre-Revolutionary frontier east of the mountains and the Ohio Valley lands beyond—they were struck by the unfamiliar expressions and diction of the *back-country* people.

Many of the differences noted were a consequence of survival in the back country of older forms, lost in the East; others came of independent linguistic developments. Timothy

Flint, a New England clergyman who traveled to Ohio in 1815, remarked on some of the expressions unfamiliar to him.[8] The terms of navigation, he noted, were "as novel as are the forms of the boats. You hear of the danger of 'riffles,' meaning probably ripples, and planters, and sawyers, and points, and bends, and shoots, a corruption, I suppose, of the French 'chute.' " On this last, Flint is supported by the *Oxford English Dictionary* and other authorities, who agree that French *chute,* meaning a fall or rapids in a river or a precipitous channel, displaced, through *voyageur* influence, the English *shoot,* which meant a short cut or a new channel formed by a river; the term was gradually extended, however, to include the original English sense and was spelled *shoot* and *shute* as well as *chute.* Flint noted other curious usages. *Reverend* meant strong or firm, he said, as in a *reverend* set of the boat pole; but he did not mention the common use of *reverend* or *reverent* for strong or pure in reference to whiskey ("jist reverend, without water"). *Plunder* remained the usual term along the frontier for baggage, a usage that we know dates from early colonial times; and boats moved *fernenst* the stream. Flint was struck by the phrase *to get religion,* an expression common still, and one that became practically universal in the back country during those days when the *camp meeting* or *tent meeting* was the scene of prolonged and frenzied religious gatherings and men felt *the power.* It is strange to note the juxtaposition, in so religious an atmosphere, of the humorously cynical *preacher,* already noted, of *reverend* in its hardly respectful usage, and of the verb *to deacon,* which meant to put the best fruit on top of the basket.

Another emigrant from New England, Christiana Holmes Tillson, moved to Illinois in 1822 and in her letters home described some of the strange customs of the frontier people.[9]

8. A portion of Flint's *Recollections of the Last Ten Years* (1826) is reprinted in Van Doren: *Voice of America,* pp. 322–33.

9. *A Woman's Story of Pioneer Illinois,* ed. Milo Melton Quaife (Chicago, 1919). Also reprinted in part in Van Doren: *Voice of America,* pp. 334–42.

She was most taken aback by the Sunday-morning visitors who arrived regularly to spend the day, be fed, and inspect all of one's belongings, making appropriate comments (of her shelf of china plates—"Whart's this 'ere fixin'? . . . never seed so many together"). She noted the custom of covering the heads of newborn infants with calico caps that were not removed for months; at the supposedly favorable time, the cap was removed and the accumulated crust cleaned gradually with *bar's grease*. Mrs. Tillson's neighbors were surprised that she did not resent being known as a *Yankee*, which, in Illinois as elsewhere, meant until the Civil War a New Englander and, at least figuratively, a seller of wooden nutmegs. One young woman confided: "I allus knowed youens were all Yankees, but Billy said 'don't let on that we know it, kase it'll jest make them mad.'" The Yankee newcomer commented on the pronunciations of *gwine* and *brile* (broil), and on the use of *reckon, his'n, heap* as an adverb, *common doin's* for an ordinary meal and *chicken fixin's* for a company one. One is struck by the correspondence of the dialect recorded with that of some rural areas today.

The comments of Mrs. Tillson and others remind us, however, not only of the differences, but also of the potential for linguistic uniformity as the newcomers settled down among these dialectal groups. Undoubtedly Mrs. Tillson's grandchildren and the grandchildren of her visitors spoke much the same.

Most of the emigrants of the first half of the nineteenth century were English-speaking Americans; and because immigration from Europe had dropped after the Revolution and those immigrants who did come stayed mostly in the cities, in New York and Philadelphia, in the developing towns of Cincinnati and Saint Louis, the linguistic tendencies of the American character were given full scope to expand. Beginning about 1840, the frontier moved rapidly westward, across the Great Plains, past the Rockies, on to California; and as *land seekers* and *gold hunters*, bankrupt merchants and adventurers assembled in their wagon trains on the banks of the Missouri, to be ferried across on *scow* or *wagon box* or *ferry flat* or—if they hit the right month—the *steamboat ferry,* as they branched off toward the *Santa Fe Trail* or the *Oregon Trail,* they left behind them the inhibiting restraints of convention and habit, of established schools and bookish clergymen, but not their rich store of words and the creativity of which that rich store had come. Word-making was in the air, phrase-making the prerogative of every man; and an exaggerated country demanded a vocabulary to match.

There was little of verbal subtlety among these pioneers, whom Mencken likens to the Okies of the 1930's,[1] but there was unconscious eloquence. Ready humor, disdain for precedent, and an almost childish delight in the sounds of words were natural to them, and with these tools they achieved not only expressiveness but sometimes poetry as well. *To clear out, to heft, to squiggle, to stump, to scoot, to boost, to splurge* were some of the vivid action words they coined or converted, *wrathy* and *high-falutin, scary* and *beatingest* some of the descriptive ones. *Scamper-down* is as joyous a name for a dance as has yet been invented. *Swellhead* and *big head, small potatoes* and *squirt* were among the kinder epithets, while *scrumptious* and *hunky-dory, spondulix, kerflop* (along with many other *ker-*prefixed words), and *scalawag* were some of the invented ones. Beside these hardly lofty words, though, were others, like *looking-glass prairie* and *hermit thrush, Shining Mountains* (the Rockies), *morning glory, paint* (for a horse), and *honeysuckle,* that have the freshness of mountain dew upon them. And some of the popular metaphorical expressions, like *keeping a stiff upper lip, a hard row to hoe,* and

1. "Most of them," he says, "were bankrupt (and highly incompetent) small farmers or out-at-heel city proletarians, and the rest were mainly chronic nomads of the sort who, a century later, were to rove the country in caricatures of automobiles." From *Supplement I* (New York: Alfred A. Knopf; 1945), p. 234. Mencken's harsh generality seems contradicted, however, by the writings of such pioneers as Mrs. Tillson and "Grandmother Brown," whose inspiring story was told by her granddaughter in Harriet Connor Brown: *Grandmother Brown's Hundred Years* (Boston: Little, Brown and Company; 1931).

*contented as pigs in clover,* remind us of Lowell's remark that vulgarisms are poetry in the egg.

The principal way in which the resources of the English language have been augmented in this country, Mathews notes in the preface to his *Dictionary of Americanisms,* has been by forming new combinations; and no word, native or borrowed, has been more useful or more prolific than the topographical term *prairie,* borrowed during the eighteenth century from the French settlers of the Mississippi Valley. Inconspicuous in its beginnings, it was, like the words *chute* and *rapids,* reflective of the early possession by the French of that heartland which was to become the Middle West. In that region, French power predominated for a hundred years and more; there the *coureurs de bois* wandered, and there some of them settled down, to beget the families whose descendants still inhabit such communities as Cahokia and Kaskaskia and Prairie de Roches and still speak French. And there the *prairies* began.

Webster omitted the word from his *Dictionary* in 1828, but contemporary documents indicate that *prairie* was in common use before the Revolution. By the mid-nineteenth century, it had become so Americanized in its new combinations that it is impossible to imagine what those westward emigrants would have done without it. Even excluding the terms that are no longer in use, the *Dictionary of Americanisms* lists approximately one hundred and fifty that are current and common; and the numbers increase.

The whole saga of the westward movement can be traced in the progressive appearance of the various combinations. Although Lewis and Clark had brought back a number of coinages from their great expedition of 1804, principally for flora and fauna, such as *prairie lark, prairie cock, prairie bean, prairie buffalo,* and *prairie bird,*[2] the first topographical combinations appeared, early in the century, in connection with

2. A complete study of the Lewis and Clark vocabulary appears in Elijah Harry Croswell: *Lewis and Clark, Linguistic Pioneers,* University of Missouri Studies, XV, 2.

the Mississippi Valley area. *Prairie region, prairie land, prairie island, prairie ravine, prairie hill, prairie farm* come from the region of the Missouri; *prairie cottage* appears first in the advertisement of an Indiana builder, who states that "we have prepared a plan . . . of a house or 'Prairie cottage' for the western settler."[3] *Trembling prairie,* or *prairie tremblante,* a term one still hears in the marshlands of Louisiana, was the wet land without firm surface found near the lower river lands. *Chocolate prairie* and *mulatto prairie* were found in Texas, *chocolate* in the Arkansas region. The combinations multiplied: *open prairie, rolling prairie, sunken prairie* joined those terms in which *prairie* itself became the attribute, like *prairie grass* and *prairie marsh* and *prairie state.* Animals and insects, birds and plants were distinguished as *prairie cattle, prairie cricket, prairie fly, prairie hare, prairie wolf, prairie rattlesnake,* and so on. Many of these terms were English translations of French names, for French influence in begetting this great family of *prairie* terms was not limited to the original word; early explorers of the West relied frequently on the skill and experience of French *voyageurs,* called *engagés,* to guide them on their travels, and they accepted much of the French terminology. Zebulon Pike mentions, in 1808, in his *Sources of the Mississippi*: "I caught a curious little animal on the prairie, which my Frenchman termed a *prairie mole,* but it is very different from the mole of the States." And John Frémont, in the account of his exploration of the Rockies, wrote: "I have collected . . . twenty-one men, principally Creole and Canadian voyageurs, who had become familiar with prairie life in the service of the fur companies in the Indian country."[4]

Vehicles and implements especially adapted to the prairies were named appropriately; we read of *prairie carts* and *prairie breakers* (plows) and *prairie wagons.* That two-word poem

---

3. Ellsworth: *Valley of the Wabash* (1838), p. 52. Quoted in Mathews: *Dictionary.*

4. *Exploring the Rocky Mountains* (1843), p. 9.

*prairie schooner* figures large; it was called also a *prairie frigate* or *prairie ship*—here we go again, back to the sea! Independence, Missouri, was known as the *prairie port*; and travelers talked of *making port* and of the *prairie ocean*. There were *prairie islands,* groves or clumps of trees; *coves,* strips of prairie extending into the woodland; *bays,* tracts of prairie or open land partially surrounded by forest; and *capes,* pieces of timberland projecting into a prairie. The Reverend Cartwright described his travels as a Methodist preacher in the prairie country, where "there was no guide to be had, no road to follow, but the traveller's only resource was to sight a line from one cape to the other, and thus to cross the bays, no other landmarks being visible as far as the eye could reach."[5]

They go on and on, the combinations, beyond enumeration, telling of hardship and humor and the day-to-day effort—*prairie fire, prairie twister, prairie burner, prairie cocktail* (a raw egg in whiskey), *prairie coal* (*buffalo chips*—itself a new term), *prairie itch.* The adjective *prairied* was formed; and *prairillon,* little prairie, is still heard in its French form in some of the once French-held lands. A splendid word, this *prairie.* Had the French given us no other, our language would still owe them much.

But if the French had strong influence on the Western and so eventually on the national vocabulary, the Spanish had even more. American English has borrowed more words from Spanish than from any other Continental language; and the great interchange that took place between the descendants of the early Spanish settlers and the emigrating Americans is confirmed in American Spanish, which has been studied extensively by Spanish-American philologians.[6] In it they have discovered archaic Castilian terms like *agora* and *ansi, naidien* and *trujo* (which correspond to our own archaisms like *fox-*

5. *Autobiography,* ed. W. B. Strickland (1857). Quoted in De Vere: *Americanisms,* p. 103.

6. Mencken discusses the findings of these scholars and the effect of American English upon the Spanish spoken in America in *American Language,* pp. 647 ff.

*fire, homespun, andiron,* and *ragamuffin*) mingling companionably with American expressions given Spanish pronunciation and spelling. *Jamachi* is American *how much, olraite* is *all right, espeche* is *speech.* Such terms are a corporate part of American Spanish just as *lariat* and *lasso* and *bonanza* are part of American English.

But the American language took more than it gave. For two hundred years, the Spanish settlers had familiarized themselves with the terrain and the inhabitants, the creatures and the climate of the region and had named them, borrowing some terms from the Indians, creating others from Spanish materials or roots; and the Americans wisely saw little need to change what was good. Spanish borrowings from the Indian, like *coyote* and *mesquite* and *avocado,* sounded no more difficult as the Spanish pronounced them than did the purely Spanish words, like *mesa* and *arroyo* and *mustang. Cañon* was easy, although those who tried to spell it used *kanyon* and *kenyan* and several other forms before they settled on *canyon.* Not only topography but also the way of life that had developed had its own vocabulary; and the Americans adopted many of the words that went with it. They retained the Spanish pronunciation and spelling for many words, *sombrero* and *peon* and *siesta,* for example, but Anglicized others, like *rancho* and *calabozo,* which they made *ranch* and *calaboose.*

*Ranch,* which we now associate with large holdings and great herds of cattle, meant originally a hut or camping place for the *vaquero* (herdsman) or the traveler. The variety of meanings and derivatives it developed over the years makes it impossible to know precisely what it meant at all times; quotations of the mid-nineteenth century and beyond give it such differing meanings as trading house, tavern, small farm, or even village. As a verb, the Americans used it in the sense of both operating a farm and putting an animal on such a place. *Rancher* was apparently pronounced in the Spanish way, at least at first, if we can judge by Lowell's use of the word in *The Biglow Papers*; Hosea Biglow tells us that "these fellers [the ranchers] are very propilly called Rank Heroes, and the more they kill the ranker and the more heroick they bekim." Americans soon simplified the form to *rancher,* as they had *rancho* to *ranch,* continuing, however, to use for many years Spanish *rancheria* for an Indian village or a collection of huts and for the buildings of a ranch, including the *hacienda,* or main house. *Ranchito* was a small ranch or farm. Other terms connected with the cattle industry—unchanged Spanish borrowings like *corral* and *rodeo* and *bronco* and Anglicized ones like *stampede* (from *estampida), lariat* (from *la reata),* and *chaps* (from *chaparejos)*—remind us that those activities we think of as so distinctively American, branding and trail driving and roundups, even the cattle themselves, originated with the Spaniards in America. *Vaquero,* which from its alternate spellings of *bakhara* and *buckhara* we made eventually into *buckaroo,*[7] is older in our land than *cowboy.*

As the emigrants mingled with the Spanish of the Southwest, observing the architecture of the Spanish towns and learning of Spanish foods and Spanish customs, they adopted not only the names but often the styles and the foods as well. *Adobe* was to the West what *clapboard* had been to the colonial East. New towns were built with *plazas* and *haciendas* and *patios.* The *padre* became a familiar figure; as the territories became states, his flock, too, would become Americans. The energetic newcomers found the *siesta* did not fit well with *go-aheadity,* but it was difficult to continue working while one's servants were not; at least they adopted the word, if not the habit. Some wore *sombreros* and even ate *tortillas* and deplored the indulgence in *tequila* that led many a *vaquero* before the *juzgado,* or court, which would eventually be called the *hoosegow* or even the *jug. Vamos,* vigorous and succinct, appealed to the Americans; unconcerned with its first-person-plural character, they converted it to a general-utility verb and pronounced it *vamoose. Mosey* came of it,

7. This etymology, as noted, is disputed by those who trace the word to American Negro *buckra,* for white man (*Efik* [*m*] *bakara*).

too; the term at first meant to move quickly, to get away fast, but somehow it slowed down over the years.

Other foreign borrowings during this first half of the nineteenth century were minor in comparison. Even the Indians of the Northwest seemed not to have much to add to the rich store of Indian borrowings acquired in the East. *Chinook jargon*, or *Oregon jargon*, an amalgam of Chinook proper and various other Indian languages combined with a smattering of French, English, and probably Russian, was the lingua franca of trade in the Northwest; a few terms have been credited to this source. *Chinook*, besides referring to an Indian of that tribe or his language, means a warm wind characteristic of the region; its opposite, a cold east wind, is the *Cayuse*, also the name of an Indian tribe. As an attribute, *cayuse* was applied to an Indian pony and colloquially to any horse. The only other terms generally familiar that were borrowed from the Northwest Indian languages—*tillicum* and *potlatch*—are, for the most part, book terms, the first meaning friend and popular in the mock-Indian rituals of girls' camps, the second coming from *patshatl*, "a gift," and signifying a feast with gifts. *Muck-a-muck*, "to eat" or "food," led to the expression *high-muck-a-muck*, or *high-muckety-muck*, as it is sometimes pronounced. Mathews quotes Charles A. Lovell, writing in *American Speech*,[8] as having traced the word to Chinook jargon *hiu*, "plenty," "a lot," and *muckamuck*, "food," "to eat," "drink." The combination, meaning plenty to eat, gradually developed into the sense of a person of importance, a "bigwig." The connecting idea that only such a person could afford to give his guests plenty to eat does not seem a foreign idea today.

All of these words, the old and the new, the borrowed and the converted, became a part of Western speech. With the great surge westward that began in the late forties, with the accelerating pace of communication, and with the admission of new states that made Washington the governmental focus

8. (April 1947), pp. 91 ff.

of the far-flung lands and brought Western representatives eastward, they became a part of the speech of all the people. The joining of the Union Pacific and the Central Pacific railroads in 1869 was more than a meeting of tracks; it united not only a people and a nation but their language too. Mark Twain wrote later of the accomplished fact: "Our changed conditions and the spread of our people far to the South and far to the West have made many alterations in our pronunciation, and have introduced new words among us and changed the meaning of many old ones."[9] That these alterations and coinages were of the kind they were—bold, independent, unconfined—was due to the happy (happy if we like our language the way it is) conjunction of an independent linguistic attitude and an expansive historical situation. Because the people moving westward were linguistically homogeneous, they were able to add enormously to their speech without disturbing the underlying linguistic heritage. By the time other elements entered the formation of the language in the later nineteenth century—a lessening of nationalistic fervor, linguistic restraint, class distinctions marked by speech, greater foreign influence—the basic character of the American language was set. It could not return, if it would, to what it had been.

9. "Concerning the American Language," in *Stolen White Elephants* (Boston, 1882).

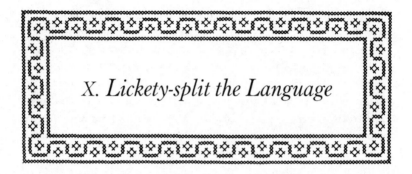

# X. Lickety-split the Language

From distant events—a potato famine in Ireland, revolution in Germany, a pogrom in Russia—have come shock waves carrying new words and speechways to our shores. When, in the 1840's, starving Irish streamed toward the land of plenty; when, in the same period, troubled Germans sought escape from violent political turmoil in their land; and when, little more than a generation later, persecuted Jews fled eastern Europe in an exodus of Biblical proportions, they brought with them their living languages. As their descendants gradually left old words and ways behind, they retained in their speech elements of these ancestral tongues; and the American language, ever hospitable, reached out to take them in.

For two generations after the founding of the Republic, immigration from abroad was not an important factor in the development of either the nation or its language, although the people of New York, where most newcomers settled, might have argued that point—and did, with unsuccessful attempts at restrictive laws. Immigrants numbered only some twenty thousand a year, to total, after seventy years, hardly a million and a half in a population of a little over twenty million. Then suddenly, in a period of seven years—just seven!—there arrived in the United States almost three million people,[1] the first of the great waves that would bring,

1. This number is great only in relation to preceding numbers; a

within the next two generations, an astounding total of some thirty million people from across the sea. Such a migration, enormous by any historical standard, had to affect the language.

Two invasions, the Irish and the German, began shortly before mid-century. By 1860, the Irish, who in the first national census (that of 1790) had numbered a minuscule 44,273, constituted the largest body of foreign-born residents in the land, 1,611,304, or 38.93 per cent of the foreign-born population. Close on their heels came the Germans, 1,276,075 of them, or 30.83 per cent, but, as a people, hardly Johnny-come-latelys. Since colonial times, Germans had constituted the largest body of non-British stock in America. Along with the Scotch-Irish, they had formed the dominant element in the population of the colonial frontier; and in the normal course of linguistic history, their presence should already have had marked effect on American English. Surprisingly, it had not. Unlike the easily assimilated Welsh and Scotch-Irish, the Germans in heavily German areas had continued to use their own speech and had contributed little save regional terms (q.v.) to the vocabulary. Even in 1861, De Vere could write of them: "Their press is powerful and high-toned, their potent voice is heard in State Legislatures and in the national Senate. Their influence is felt in every State, and their vote is decisive in great crises. And yet they have not enriched our language by a dozen important words!"[2] The massive influx of new Germans, therefore, had much the same effect on non-Germans as an earlier one had had on Benjamin Franklin. Just as he had complained, in 1753, that the printing of street signs, legal instruments, and other public papers in *Dutch* (German) along with English would contribute to *Germanizing* the colony,[3] so nineteenth-century Americans labeled

---

million immigrants would enter in *each* of several years in the early twentieth century.

2. M. Schele De Vere: *Americanisms: The English of the New World* (New York: Scribner & Co.; 1872), p. 139.

3. In a letter to Peter Collinson, in London. Quoted in H. L. Mencken:

the now spreading German speech and accent both obtrusive and laughable.

Dialectal writing, brought into high favor with *The Biglow Papers*, was already in vogue, as was a new type of humor based on poor grammar, bad spelling, and slang—for an example, "the biggest phool in this world haint bin born yet; thare iz plenty of time yet." (Tastes do change!) From such writing, it was only a step to using as literary material whatever dialect—Irish, German, or Negro—happened to strike the national funny bone. *Hans Breitmann's Ballads*, by Charles G. Leland, supposedly presented the speech ("I schpeaksch English") of the typical German immigrant, who was caricatured in *Harper's Magazine* of June 1861 wearing a beer barrel for a coat, smoking a porcelain pipe with a long stem, and carrying a long sausage and a sheet of music under his arm. Parodies like "Mudder, may I a schwimming went? Nix, my grosse dotter!" were thought hilarious. Sometimes no distinction was made between German dialect and *deitschmerish*,[4] the broken Yiddish and German accepted then and much later, even by Yiddish theater companies, as typical Jewish speech; and the association of Yiddish with low comedy prompted those Jews who were able to do so to avoid it in favor of German. The latter, however, already contained some Jewish loan words (generally attributed to Yiddish, but possibly direct borrowings from the Hebrew); and a number of them entered American English through this medium. *Kosher* and *mazuma* were in our language early; and the parallel between *mazuma*'s literal translation from the Chaldean, the "ready necessary," and the common frontier expression *the needful*, for money, suggests an early Hebrew influence.

German loan words were already entering American English from a source more intellectually respectable than dialectal comedy—extensive cultural exchange between Ger-

*The American Language, Supplement I* (New York: Alfred A. Knopf; 1945), p. 140.

4. Ande Manners: *Poor Cousins* (New York: Coward, McCann and Geohegan, Inc.; 1972) so labels the German-larded Yiddish of the period.

many and America. As early as 1848, Bartlett commented on the "peculiarities" of the literary language of the Bostonians, due, he said, to "the great extent to which the scholars of New England have carried the study of the German language and literature for some years back, added to a very general neglect of the old masterpieces of English composition."[5] For more than a generation, Americans who studied abroad studied in Germany, from Edward Everett of Massachusetts in the early part of the century to John Pierpont Morgan at midpoint; the awarding of the degree of doctor of philosophy, begun by Yale University in 1861, was in direct emulation of German custom. Most of the German newcomers of this period, moreover, were well educated, with special interest in music; among the 1849 immigrants was Henry Engelhard Steinway (originally *Steinweg*), who established the firm of Steinway and Son in New York in 1853 and excited the musical world with his innovations in pianoforte construction. The term *Liederkranz*, for a singing society made up of men of German extraction (hence *Liederkranzer*), became familiar to music lovers; the now obsolete word *dumb-bull* was introduced for a musical instrument "prepared to lend dignity to the music"; and our continuing use of *concert-master*, rather than the British-preferred *concert leader*, is due to the influence of the German *konzertmeister* of the period. A respectable German verb, *spielen,* "to play" (an instrument), had a tortuous history. First used in American English with the same meaning, it gradually suffered a sad semantic decline; and the supercilious attitude in some areas toward the German language may have been responsible. In 1870, the *Territorial Enterprise* of Virginia, Nevada, announced, on July 16: "The new 'circus' is to be seen at the corner of D street and Sutton avenue—down var der orkan goes a spielin'." It took only two decades for the word to acquire the sense it has now, of talking persuasively or

5. Introduction to *Dictionary*. Reprinted in part in Mitford M. Mathews, ed.: *The Beginnings of American English* (Chicago: University of Chicago Press; 1931), pp. 149–50.

colorfully, as does a barker or pitchman; to be used as a noun; and to develop derivatives, *spieler* and *spieling*. Happily, the term has not completely lost its original meaning; as recently as 1947, George Perry's *Cities of America* used it in reference to the Denver Symphony (*not* pejoratively).

The sausage, the pipe, and the beer in the *Harper's* cartoon were as authentically German as was the sheet of music. A great number of German loan words in more mundane areas entered the American vocabulary; and, despite their late start, their number is exceeded only by the Spanish. The etymology of some has been disputed; *landlaufer* as a source for *loafer* has competition in English dialectal *louper*, for vagabond, as well as in Dutch *loof*, for weary or tired. *Bummer*, which gave rise to *bum* (unrelated to British *bum*, slang for buttocks) as verb, noun, and adjective, plus *bumming* and *bummerish* and *bummy*—and ultimately to such far-flung combinations as *bum deal* and *beach bum*—is apparently from German *bummler*, an agent noun from *bummeln*, "to waste time"; but Mathews cautiously marks it "origin obscure." That the term was surely associated with Germans in the minds of Americans of the nineteenth century is evident in a quotation from the *Portland Oregonian* of January 27, 1855: "Come, clear out, you trunken loafer! Ve don't vant no *bummers* here!" *Fresh* in the sense of saucy or impudent is related to German *frech*. Of undisputed German origin are the many words for food and drink, with their related terms, which evoke an image of the beer-barreled, sausage-toting German and which Americans have adopted with gusto: *pumpernickel* and *dunking, lager, pretzel, stein, beer garden* (German *biergarten*), *bock* (German *bochbier*), and *prosit*. Late in the century, as German *delicatessens* (German *Delikatessen*, "dainties," from French *délicatesse*) offered their wares to a wider public, other terms came into the language—*frankfurter* and *wienerwurst,* the latter quickly becoming *wiener* or *weenie,* and *Hamburg steak,* destined for a great future. Changed to *hamburger* at the turn of the century, the word eventually entered into numerous combinations such as *hamburger stand, hamburger bun,* and *hamburger steak* and contributed to the language that suffix-of-all-work *-burger*. The contribution has made possible not only *cheeseburger* and *chickenburger* and all their relatives, but even *Mexiburger*, an unlikely etymological mating indeed. *Hamburger* survived the attempt during World War I to de-Germanize the language; its suggested substitute, *Salisbury steak*, never really made it except as a euphemism on the menus of expensive restaurants.

Other late German contributions were the suffix *-fest*, familiar to nineteenth-century Americans in *saengerfest* and *volksfest* and soon utilized to create compounds like *talkfest*, *gabfest*, and *funfest*, and even the solidly American *slugfest*. Also traceable to German are some of our idiomatic expressions, like *so long*, from German *so lange*; *nix*, from *nix*, *nichts*, "nothing"; and *hold on*, probably influenced by German *halt an*. Our numerous expressions using the prefix *ker-*, such as *kerplunk, kerflop, kerchunk,* and so on, are, most authorities agree, related to the German prefix *ge-* and may have come of attempts to create German verbs by analogy, as *geflop* and *gesplash*. *Dumb,* meaning stupid, is related to German *dumm* in the same sense; *dummkopf* meant blockhead and fit in nicely with such characteristic coinage of the period as *dumbflustered* and *dumbfoozled*. Some terms made of English materials, like *Dutch treat, beat the Dutch,* and *in Dutch,* may be German reference points rather than Dutch; the indiscriminate use of *Dutch* for both ethnic groups makes it sometimes impossible to distinguish which was meant. During Gold Rush days, all Europeans "save French, English, and 'Eyetalians' were classed under the general denomination of Dutchmen."[6] Whatever the linguistic uncertainties, there is no doubt that one of the most important influences of German upon American English has been the reinforcement of the compounding tendencies already pre-

6. Borthwick: *In California*, p. 311. Quoted in Mitford M. Mathews, ed.: *A Dictionary of Americanisms on Historical Principles* (Chicago: University of Chicago Press; 1951).

sent. Compounding is more common today among Americans than among British, and the enrichment of our vocabulary thereby is evident in the whole history of American English.

The southern Irish brought to America, along with little wealth and less education, the old Jacobean pronunciation that had become provincial in America. They said *tay* for *tea* and *jine* for *join* and *sass* for *sauce*, *agin* for *again* and *chaw* for *chew*, just as the most elegant English had been doing a century earlier and as Americans on the frontier were doing still. Undoubtedly, they gave new vigor to the old forms; and most of us are more likely to get *riled up* than *roiled*, even when we would not think of *jining up*. Mencken believes that the effect of Irish speechways upon our language was far greater than that of the German, both directly and indirectly, although their contributions to the vocabulary were few.[7]

Irish habits of speech, of pronunciation, of syntax, even of grammar, were not only survivals from an earlier stage of English but were partly the fruit of efforts to translate the idioms of Gaelic into English. Gaelic employs the definite article before nouns, as does French or German, so that an Irishman will say "I am good at the Latin"; and today an American is more likely to say "I have the measles" than simply "measles." The prefix *a-* before various continuing verbs, like *a-going* and *a-riding*, while native to English, is more common in the Irish dialect because of the parallel Gaelic form, and is—or was at an earlier period—more common in American than in British English usage. Intensifying prefixes and suffixes, already commented upon as typical of the frontier vocabulary, happened to fit remarkably well into Irish speechways, or vice versa. If many of the intensives of the period, like *yes siree* and *no siree* and *teetotal*, were not taken from Irish example, they do demonstrate a close affinity between the two languages; and *dead* as in *dead right* and

7. *The American Language*, 4th ed. (New York: Alfred A. Knopf; 1936), pp. 160 ff.

*dead sure* has been definitely traced to the Irish.[8] A pattern of speech not borrowed but recognized by all as characteristically Irish appears in the sentence "John is dead and him so hearty!" Here the Gaelic form, in which the accusative is permissibly interchangeable with the nominative, is preserved. Around the Erie Canal, where many Irish immigrants worked, the pronunciation of *b'hoy* for *boy* continued until late in the century, with *g'hal* coined as its feminine counterpart; and in 1855, the general abandonment of *shall* for *will* in the New York area was ascribed by Charles Astor Bristed to Irish influence.[9] Wherever they went, wherever they worked—on canals and on railroads, from Nevada to New Orleans—the Irish carried their idiom with them, giving a touch of the emerald to American speech.

*Paddy* (for Patrick) was disliked as soon as he began coming in numbers, and the attitude he encountered is graphically expressed in the term *dumb Paddy*. Frederick Law Olmsted, in *Slave States* (1856), compared the Negroes to ". . . what our farmers call dumb Paddies—that is, Irishmen who do not readily understand the English language, and who are still weak and stiff from the effects of the emigrating voyage." Poor, Catholic, aggressive, noticeable, and noisy, the Irishman aroused an antagonism that brought into full flower, and into the vocabulary, the latent *nativism* of long-settled Americans. Political parties opposing further immigration and the franchising of the foreign-born were organized, among them the *Order of the Star-Spangled Banner*, the *Native American Party*, and the *Know-Nothings*, who, when interrogated about their organization, would profess to know nothing. All engaged in political activity and sometimes in violence, protesting the presence of the Irish as agents of a foreign power, the Roman Catholic Church; it was the era of Maria Monk, of the *church burners*.

8. Mencken: *American Language*, p. 162.

9. "The English Language in America," *Cambridge Essays, Contributed by Members of the University* (Cambridge: Cambridge University Press; 1855).

The attitude of most Americans, however, was more contemptuous than hostile; and as the immigrants became ditch diggers or domestic help in an increasingly affluent society, social scorn found expression in derisive terms. *Paddies* or *micks* (from *Michael*) and *biddies* (from *Bridget,* for the women) found themselves facing the caveat "No Irish Need Apply" on houses to let and on office doors. A shovel or spade was called an *Irish spoon,* a wheelbarrow an *Irish buggy,* defined in a stock witticism as an invention that had taught Irishmen to walk on their hind legs. Their reputation for contentiousness had crossed the sea with them; to *Irish beauty,* listed in Grose's *Dictionary of the Vulgar Tongue* as a woman with two black eyes, Americans added *Irish confetti,* for bricks, and *Irish hoist,* for a kick in the rear. *Irish* to indicate anger, as in the phrase *getting one's Irish up,* was in the vocabulary as early as 1809; Davy Crockett used it in reference to his prospective mother-in-law.[1] The term was used with pride by the Irish themselves, just as the equivalent *Dutch* was used by the Pennsylvanians. But the terms introduced to describe the mid-century immigrants were not meant to be flattering, the attribute *Irish* being understood to give at once an invidious or contradictory meaning. *Irish promotion* meant a demotion, *Irish nightingale* a bullfrog, *Irish dividend* an assessment on stock.

A few loan words probably Irish did enter the vocabulary. *Shebang,* related to Irish *shebeen,* an illegally operated drinking place, and coming in its turn from Gaelic *sībīn,* "bad ale," was applied originally to a poor dwelling place or hunter's lodge. Over the years, it came to be used variously for an engine house, a student's room at Yale, a conveyance, and finally "any matter of concern, thing, business; as tired of the whole *shebang.*" *Shenanigan,* with its fine Irish flavor, may indeed be from Irish *sionnachuighim,* "I play tricks"; but it has been attributed also to German *schinagel* or *schinaglen,*

---

1. *Autobiography,* ed. Hamlin Garland (1923). Reprinted in part in Mark Van Doren, ed.: *Voice of America* (Cleveland and New York: World Publishing Co.; 1942), p. 318.

and to Spanish *chanada*, a trick or deceit. *Lallapalooza*, while not Gaelic or even English, is a County Mayo provincialism for a sturdy fellow and comes, according to P. W. Joyce, from French *allez-fusil*, which means "Forward the muskets!" —a memory of the French landing at Killala in 1798.[2] Some words and expressions, like *shillelah* and *begorrah*, are widely known but rarely used by non-Irish save in after-dinner jokes about Pat and Mike, now outmoded in our sensitive, humorless age. (Archie Bunker *had* to come.)

German and Irish were only the most ubiquitous of the alien tongues at mid-century and beyond; there were many others. So many speech enclaves existed, in fact, that Bartlett predicted in 1848, in his introduction to his *Dictionary*, that the German language in Pennsylvania and Ohio would doubtless exist "for centuries," that the Norwegian language would be preserved for a long time to come in Illinois and would engraft on the regional speech a Norwegian dialect, that Creole French would remain strong in Louisiana, and that in Pennsylvania and in New York, where in Oneida County one could "travel for miles and hear nothing but the Welsh language," Welsh loan words would enter the American vocabulary. The "tendency of a people of common origin to cling together," Bartlett wrote, ". . . the publication of newspapers, almanacs, and books . . . will tend to preserve the idiom and nationality of the people." It was his belief that in some parts of the United States "dialects will spring up as marked as those of Great Britain . . . and where a dialect has once become firmly established, a thousand years will not suffice to eradicate it."[3]

We have seen to how meager an extent Bartlett's predictions have been fulfilled; and the meagerness was evident long before our own era, in which mass-media communication has tended to standardize speech. Although localisms remain, as do regional dialects in a few isolated areas (the

2. *English As We Speak It in Ireland.* Quoted in Mencken: *American Language*, p. 160.

3. Quoted in Mathews: *Beginnings.* pp. 141 ff.

Ozarks, for one),[4] the difficulties of the task faced by research groups in isolating differences show how basically uniform is the American *Volkssprache*, far more uniform than our history and geography would suggest. Foreign elements, save in the speech of newcomers or perhaps of first-generation Americans, have been largely obscured or assimilated. How did this uniformity come about? What factors deflected the common tendency "to preserve the idiom and the nationality of the people"?

Geographical mobility was obviously a leading factor in dispersing dialectal groups and homogenizing accents, bringing about uniformity not by suppressing provincialisms but by spreading them. Associated with that mobility were other effects of the transportation and communication revolutions. Even before the Civil War, North, South, East, and West were engaged in interlocking economic and social relationships that demanded mutual comprehension and shared terms. More important than any other factor in developing a truly national idiom, however, was the emergence of the public-school system as we know it today (or have known it up to now), which, after long struggle, appeared in its main outlines during this period of greatest pluralism. Immigrants, who saw in mastery of English the key that would open doors of opportunity, encouraged their children—or ordered them, it being the era it was—to apply themselves; and although social mobility may not have been as absolute as the champions of democracy claimed, the vision was there. Every German had heard of John Jacob Astor; and if for every Meyer Guggenheim or Andrew Carnegie there were many who lived their lives in quiet desperation, even those who had attained modest success as policemen or storekeepers or minor officials inspired emulation.

Within the schools, therefore, with the *dunce block* awaiting them in the corner, the children studied the first volume

4. The reference here is, of course, to dialects of American English, not to foreign languages or patois still spoken in bilingual areas.

of Webster's *Grammatical Institute of the English Language*, the *American Spelling Book*. Learning to spell the Websterian way, to pronounce the Websterian way, to syllabify the Websterian way, they engaged in *spelling matches* or *bees* or *tournaments* or, as Mark Twain called them, *spelling fights*, trying to *spell up* to the head of the line or at least to avoid being *spelled down* to its foot, developing the habit of careful separation of syllables that distinguishes American pronunciation. The influence of Webster's "Little Blue-Backed Speller" was enormous; for nearly a century it maintained its authority, selling ultimately more than seventy million copies and being peddled by Yankee peddlers along with tin pans and nutmegs. In 1848, at the beginning of the great surge of immigration, the annual sale of the spelling book was more than a million copies—this in a population of less than twenty-three million. Almost as important as the *Speller* in establishing linguistic conformity, and to a great extent philosophical conformity as well, was McGuffey's *Eclectic Reader*, consisting of four volumes published in the 1830's and a fifth and a sixth added in the next two decades. The most widely used readers in the nation's schools, *McGuffey's* sold ultimately over 122,000,000 copies; with the *Speller*, it formed the educational staple of generations of American and American-to-be children before a multiplicity of textbooks and changing educational theories drove it out of print.

By the time of the Civil War, then, the vernacular had achieved respectability in speech as it almost had in literature. Not only was the talk American in tone at *ward clubs* in the city and at *mining camps* in the West; it was also so at *Congressional caucuses* and in college *eating clubs*, reflecting, along with the writings of Lowell, the poetry of Whitman, and the work of Bret Harte and Mark Twain—just beginning—the multifaceted, vigorous, turbulent life of the period. And across the addresses, letters, and daily speech of that most American of men, Abraham Lincoln, there "streamed . . . the new words of the American language," their author caring not "a cornhusk for the literary critics."[5]

Much of the coinage of the period reflected the great split dividing the nation, sad and best-forgotten words like *bluebellies* and *graybacks, rebel spies* and *copperheads, scalawags* and *seceshers* and *Sherman's bummers*. But most of the coinage was of things of every day, of the occupations men pursued, and women, too, often far from the scene of national agony. During the war years, baseball terms proliferated; *baseball,* for the ball itself, *base line, liner, to baseball, baseballer,* and similar terms suggest the unflagging devotion that made of the game, imported in a rudimentary form from England, an American institution. Many industry-related terms were brought into the vocabulary quickly because of need created by the war. *Oil* combinations, like *oil well, oil belt, oil drill, oil speculation, oil strike, oil derrick, oil fever,* came from the rich oil fields of Ohio and Pennsylvania; Texas and Oklahoma were still to be heard from, and a sage noted, in *Harper's Magazine* of December 1864: "It is certain that great oil strikes are no longer looked for." New railroad terms like *railroad men, railroad freight, railroad engine, round trip,* and *commute* increased the railroad lexicon; in 1865, *commuters' roads,* "running chiefly for the accommodation of city business-men with suburban residences,"[6] were established. The discovery of the *Comstock Lode* in Nevada in 1859 had drawn men to the *Silver Land; bonanza,* from the Spanish, which had meant the accidental discovery of a rich vein of ore, came to be applied to the vein itself. In the agricultural field, farmers bought the new *headers,* reaping machines that cut the heads off standing grain; *combines,* which headed, threshed, and cleaned the grain too; *hay rigs; hay loaders*. On the urban scene, *brownstone front* became a familiar synecdoche for the mansions of the wealthy, where

5. Carl Sandburg: *Abraham Lincoln: The War Years,* vol. 2. Quoted in Mencken: *Supplement I,* p. 323.

6. *Atlantic Monthly* (1865), XV, 82.

*parlor girls*, probably Irish, "did" the silver and china, and
*house girls* or *house help* labored over the new *wash benches*,
manufactured and sold, along with ironing tables, under the
label of Cram's Patent Folding Furniture.

To many, the war was a sometime thing. Mark Twain,
after spending a few weeks in the Confederate militia in the
spring of 1861, moved on to Nevada to mine for silver with
his brother, there to begin the career that would make him
if not the largest single contributor to the American vocabulary, at least its finest recorder. For the purpose, he was
moving just in time. The West retained its supremacy as
the fountainhead of neologism for only a quarter of a century
after the Civil War; but during that period, the call of land
and of gold and silver was still strong. From all sections of
the country men came, to blend their various accents into
a rich mélange and be challenged to linguistic invention by
the demands of their new surroundings. Former soldiers of
the Confederate army left their ruined homeland to seek
their fortunes; New Yorkers and New Englanders, disturbed
by the swelling competition of industrial life, moved toward
the still free lands; and small groups of immigrants continued past the East Coast to join relatives or friends in
Western communities. Nevertheless, the pioneer movement
was losing momentum. Space was running out; and the
center of word-making, in its bondage to history, was preparing to move East.

But not quite yet. In August 1869 the *Overland Monthly*
published a study of "South-western Slang" by an observer
calling himself "Socrates Hyacinth."[7] He had made his notes
—far more extensive and inclusive notes than the title indicates—"in the course of a rather leisurely walk through
Texas and then across the continent with a company of
emigrants." According to Hyacinth, Texas itself was "a
bundle of crooked and stupendous phrases, tied together

7. The article is reprinted in full in Mathews: *Beginnings*, pp. 151–62.

with a thong of rawhide," his metaphor for a land where "rabbits have somehow gotten the body of the hare and the ears of the ass; the frogs, the body of the toad, the horns of the stag-beetle, and the tail of the lizard; the trees fall up-hill, and the lightning comes out of the ground." There, towns were named *Lick Skillet* and *Buck Snort, Hog Eye* and *Possum Trot*; revolvers, *Meat in the Pot* and *Mr. Speaker*; oxen, *Presbyterian* and *Filibuster*. But aside from these extravagances, there were utilitarian words and phrases, too; and they tell something of the aftermath of the Civil War and the nature of the land. Texas sentiment, as well as that of the soldiers moving westward, was reflected in the popularity of the term *Confederate* to express strong approval, as in *You're mighty Confederate! Slow bear* and *mud-lark,* euphemisms for the hogs clandestinely killed and smuggled into camp by short-rationed soldiers, were still in use; *Josh,* for a man from Arkansas, and *tarheel,* for a North Carolinian, both nicknames acquired during the war, would become permanent. Many Texans still believed that Confederate money, if not the South, would rise again; the author said the bills issued by the Confederacy, called *bluebacks* in general and *Blue Williamses* (fifty-dollar bills) in particular, were being kept against the day when they could be exchanged for *greenbacks*. Even *greenbacks*, federal issue, were not particularly welcome in hard-money Texas; west of Marshall, when a price was named it was meant to be paid in *spizerinctums,* or hard money (corrupted from our old friend *specie*).

The Southerners had brought some of their regional expressions into Texas. *Cush,* for corn meal fried in grease, the Arabic-African-Gullah term, was evidently new to Socrates; so were *blue John,* for skim milk, *collards* (from *colewort*), *kettlings,* evidently a variant of *chitterlings* or *chitlins,* and *puddings,* a kind of pork sausage. Terms peculiar to Texas were *jimpsecute*, for a sweetheart (female); *juicy-spicy*, for her beau; and *scads* or *oodles,* for much or many, or, in combination, *scadoodles*. Occupational terms relating to cattle-breeding were numerous: *mulley cow,* for a cow without horns;[8] *pointers* and *siders*, for herders on a cattle drive; *on herd*, for on and off duty; *cutting out*; *cow-whip*; *ox-whip* (which differed from the cow-whip in the length of the stock); *maverick. Mustang*, after Mexican Spanish *mestango*, or *mesteño*, which meant a stray, occurred in frequent combinations: *mustang cattle, mustang cavalry* (dating from the Mexican War), *mustang hunter, mustang range*, and *wild as a mustang*, for a wild or uncultivated person. Mustangs could be *religious*, meaning well-behaved, or *buckers*; most of them, in the opinion of cattlemen, were not *worth shucks* and were likely to run *skygodlin* (obliquely) or to go *scallyhootin* and stop *suddent. Scallyhoot*, an equivalent of *skedaddle*, may have incorporated Welsh *hwt* ("hoot"); if so, it suggests a Welsh presence rarely evident in American English, despite Bartlett's prediction. The verb *to june*, used in describing the mustang's dancing movement, apparently came from German *gehen*, a source made likely by the presence of a large colony of Germans in western Texas. Still another word of alien origin was *moke*, for a Negro. Socrates Hyacinth suggests as its source Icelandic *möckvi*, "darkness," and attributes Cymric affinities to it as well; it was introduced, he says, by Welsh recruits who had drifted into the army in New York City and were serving in the West. His suggested etymology is far from definitive; if the Icelandic attribution is correct, the word may well have come from Icelanders settled in Utah as early as 1855.

Other words and phrases expressive of Western life were still pouring into the language. *Homestead* had already come a long way from its earlier meaning of a modest lot with the buildings upon it; now it meant, in accordance with the *Homestead Law* and *Homestead Acts*, a lot of at least 160 acres, or a quarter section, and sometimes as much as 640 acres. The word became a verb and took on suffixes, to form *homesteader* and *homesteading*; in combination it joined *bill* and *claim* and *grant, entry, exemption clause*, and

8. Mathews: *Beginnings*, p. 162, points out that the author contradicts himself on this point.

*settler.* An element of conflict is reflected in the increase in numbers of sheep-related terms; *sheep-growers* were moving in to offer competition to the *cattlemen,* whose *trail drivers, riding the range,* found much of it *sheeped off,* or grazed out, and *range wars* became common as the *sheepmen* and *sheep ranches* spread out over the seemingly crowded land.

*Cowboy* in the Western sense was new. It had been used in the East during the Revolutionary War for Tory guerrillas because of their trick of luring victims into the bush with cowbells. Irrelevant or forgotten in the original sense, it was newly coined in the West, first written as two words, then hyphenated, then joined. It soon acquired a suffix to form *cowboyism* and entered into combination with *boots* and *hat* and *land* and *saddle* and *town. Range* was combined with *boss* and *cattle* and *herding* and *horse* and *rider* and was used in phrases like *riding the range* and *on the range;* it acquired suffixes to form *ranger* and *ranging* and *rangy. Trail* took on *rider* and *outfit* and *work* and *boss* and *cinch, herd* and *herder; trailing through* meant to drive cattle overland. There were mining terms, some to become figurative—*strike* and *pay dirt, gold brick, grubstake.* There were countless words telling of other aspects of Western life: *vigilante,* from the Spanish, sometimes shortened to *vigy; tenderfoot; blue norther; jack-leg* and *jack-legged* (a Texas coinage); *Boot Hill; jack rabbit; silvertip grizzly; soddy* (a sod house). The Western fountainhead of neologism seemed inexhaustible. Gradually the terms made their way east; and Easterners adopted them timorously, a little abashed. In *Harper's Magazine* for October 1886, we read: "It hasn't—ah—'panned out.' He involuntarily made a droll face as he uttered the Westernism."

But the center of word-making was moving east. The *silver spike* that marked the joining of the Union Pacific and the Central Pacific railroads was driven in 1869. With the destruction of the great buffalo herds and the extension of cattle country, with the Indians retreating to reservations, with *barbed wire* (*bob wire*) fencing the once open range, the frontier—save for a few last vivid splashes of color, as in Oklahoma—was fading. New demands in the East, new challenges, a changing economy turned American English into new channels, opened new springs; and the well of pure American undefiled, true-blue, whole-souled, egalitarian, became a little murky in the backwash.

As far back as 1837, Washington Irving had coined the phrase *almighty dollar*. The terms *millionism* and *millionairism*, "the state of being a millionaire; the social order prevailing where millionaires are numerous" (Mathews: *Dictionary*), appeared before the Civil War. In 1858, Oliver Wendell Holmes referred to "people in the green stages of millionism"; *multimillionaire* appeared in the same year. And in 1884, William Dean Howells translated *nouveaux riches* from the French to make *new rich* a permanent part of the American vocabulary. The terms summed up a developing phenomenon on the national scene.

Since before the Civil War, the expansion of the railroad and its alliance with the newly invented *telegraph*, as well as other economic factors, had made possible the concentration of vast wealth in the hands of a few. In the eighties, millionaires numbered at least in the hundreds, multimillionaires (including a congressman with an annual salary of $5,000) somewhat fewer. The names *Morgan, Gould, Astor, Vanderbilt, Rockefeller* dominated not only the financial world but the political and social as well. New abstract, imageless terms in the vocabulary, *merger* and *trust* and *consolidation*, suggested esoteric practices hidden from public view; and the average man, who in a simpler time had understood *merchant mill* and *wagon shop* and *dry-goods store*, began to feel put upon, somehow tricked.

*Wall Streeters* spoke a specialized vocabulary, what Timothy Flint, in referring to boating terminology (*bushwhacking*, for example), had earlier called a *technic*. They spoke of *holding the market*, of *margins up* and *margins down*, and of what showed on the *stock ticker*, that peculiar device invented by young Thomas Edison. No longer was a *combine* only that wondrous aid to farming which had appeared in American fields in the fifties; now it had sinister connotations, and in 1886 the word was used in the trial of a New York alderman for bribery. That politicians could be bought became common knowledge; and *boodle*, for property or goods, from Dutch *boedel*, which had been in the language for almost two hundred years and had entered the argot of counterfeiters in the fifties, came to signify political bribes and loot. So pertinent was the word that it spawned a number of derivatives, *boodleize, boodler, boodlerism, boodleism. Capitalistic* and *monopolistic* entered the language; and *labor candidates* talked on the stump of *moneyed institutions* and *sweat shops*, of the *interests* and of the various *trusts*—the *Coal-Oil Trust*, the *Railroad Trust*, the *Sugar Trust*. Counterpointing these terms in the vocabulary appeared *antitrust* and *antimonopoly* to fill in the outlines of strife, along with a coinage having a frontier sound, *trust buster*. The small cloud that had hovered above the factory villages of Lynn grew heavy; and the forces that in the next decade would bring *Populism* into the vocabulary, along with *Populist, Populite, Populistic, Populization, Populist Party, Poplocrat,* and *Poplocracy,* added fuel to the already heated political turmoil in which *silver beetles* and *gold bugs* were fighting the currency battle. *Labor* acquired new connotations, was used in new contexts, became an attribute, itself gained attributes, entered into combinations. It was *organized*, had *organizers; labor reformer, labor baron, labor convention, labor party* were new terms. Not much earlier, *Union man* had meant one opposed to secession; now it meant one who held a *union card* in a *labor union*.

The rich, growing richer, acquired the patina of royalty. To gather material for a new department in the newspapers, *society editors* sent *society reporters* to cover the comings and goings of the *Four Hundred*, a term coined by Ward McAllister for the only people "that one really knows" and given currency by Cecil Allen of the *New York Sun*. Their travels, to the South in winter, especially to *health resorts* in the

Carolinas or Georgia, and to *summer resorts*, were faithfully noted; "Not all of 'the 400,' " reported the *New York Tribune* of April 8, 1888, "have yet returned from the South." The *Social Register* was published for the first time in 1886. The private vocabulary of this select group—and perhaps a few others—included such terms as *receptioning*, both for being received and for attending receptions (James Russell Lowell writes of being busy "dining and receptioning");[9] *ball cards; lap teas; reverse Newport* (a dance); *Newport fashion; dancing receptions*. Unfashionable people or unfashionable practices were labeled *tacky*, a word originally applied to small, insignificant horses or North Carolina marsh ponies and by extension to hillbillies; now, for some obscure reason, or none, it was the chic word of the "in" group. No more easily could a blacksmith understand the jargon of this group than he could that of Wall Street.

This growing fragmentation of vocabulary content among special groups was symptomatic of an increasing fragmentation within society. No longer was it divided simply into large classes or regions or divisions but into smaller segments, social, intellectual, economic, even—because of the new scientific developments—occupational. Thomas Jefferson and the humblest Virginian (or New Englander) could have discussed farming; men were linked by the land and the language relating to it. Now, as the first shadows of technological specialization appeared, communication faltered. What, for instance, did an *electrician* do? The word had meant earlier, according to Webster in 1806, "one versed in electricity," a man who, like Franklin, studied and experimented with *electric fluid*, that dangerous substance which concerned the average man only when it traveled menacingly from the sky. Now, an *electrician* made or *fixed* (repaired) anything powered by that mysterious element, which was not a fluid, after all, and which preachers were using as an analogy for God—you couldn't see it, but its effects told you it was there.

9. *Letters* (1889), II, 407.

*Electric bells* rang at the press of a button; *electric arc lights* brightened the streets, although they were somewhat obscured by clusters of *electric light bugs,* which, it was believed, were spontaneously generated in the arc carbons and had a bite as deadly as a tarantula's. *Electric cars* were traveling too fast for public safety, as numerous editorials pointed out; but *electric railroads* or *railways,* using *electric locomotives* run by *motor-neers* (by analogy with *engineer*), clearly had an advantage over coal-burning trains in such places as tunnels and mines.

All of these electricity-related terms had been created, in the old-fashioned American way, by combination with *electric,* which, although foreign, had been in the language too long for change. Now even such linguistic simplicity was threatened. Since mid-century, scientists had been introducing words with classical roots, and the average man accepted them; after all, he knew little of invention and could not fault the scientist for seeking verbal precision. *Electro-chronograph, stereopticon, kinetoscope, phonograph, telephone, photophone*—such words seemed uncomfortably exotic but evidently answered some scientific need. In 1889, however, there rose a situation that showed in what threatening depths the American genius was floundering. *Notes & Queries,* on May 11, appealed to its readers: "A New Word Wanted.—Correspondents of American Notes and Queries are requested to send suggestions for a word that shall express execution by electricity." The appeal was accepted as a linguistic challenge not only by the somewhat scholarly readers of *Notes & Queries,* who began juggling classical roots, but also by others whose response shows a deliberate departure from traditional spontaneity. The *North American Review,* plunging with zest into the etymological pool, suggested *electrolethe* (Greek *ēlectro-* and *lēthē,* "forgetfulness"). The *Saginaw Evening News* introduced *electricide.* The *Century Magazine,* noting some use of *electricution,* termed it "recent and colloquial." In the *Congressional Record* of August 9, 1890, reference was made to electrical execution as the *Kemmler process,* dubiously honoring not its inventor but the first criminal to experience its final solution. And—most disturbing!—the *Chautauquan,* journal of that organization which appealed to the middle-class, middle-American, middle-educated citizen who spoke good honest vernacular without conscious ornament, made a downright subversive suggestion: "A Latin word for execute, to go with electric, or a Greek word to go with electro is wanted. The Latin word execute makes electri-execute, which would contract into electricute." *Electrocute,* a hybrid of Greek *electro-* plus Latin *-cute,* eventually won out. But the folk had the last word. Before long, criminals were simply *sent to the chair*; and everyone, in the American way, got the picture. In a final fillip at all the formalism having to do with electricity and related mystifying elements, *electrified* came to be used for moderately drunk.

This deliberate search for etymological roots suggests the entrance of a new element in American word-making. The exuberant, adolescent spontaneity that had dominated the language and the American spirit for half a century and more was being challenged by a more urbane, self-conscious urge toward correctness. The *Brahmins* of New England had glorified *Boston culture;* increasing cultural contact with Europe and travel abroad gave greater sophistication to language; and impressive imported words like *gestalt* and *phonetician* and *phenomenology* and *orthogenesis*, with all the concepts involved, were becoming familiar in intellectual and scientific circles and leading their members toward like verbalization. Emerson's *transcendentalism* and James's *pragmatism*—or, in the form given it later by C. S. Peirce, *pragmaticism*—were in keeping with the trend. Moreover, Darwinism had shaken frontier fundamentalism, and with it some of the breezy self-confidence that was reflected in the frontier vocabulary.

The American idiom, nevertheless, had gained too much strength during its growing-up years to be intimidated. Henry James was writing, but so was Mark Twain; and his introduction of words and phrases relating to nearly every area of American life and made in the American way—compounds like *stockholder* and *typesetter* and *hayride;* parts-of-speech

combinations like *gilt-edged* and *dead broke* and *all-fired;*
verbs and adjectives made into nouns—*stake* and *jockey* and
*husky;* expressions like *take it easy, close call, eat crow, get
even*—gave reassurance that the American vernacular had
lost none of its vigor. The work of Hamlin Garland, of
William Dean Howells, of Owen Wister and other writers,
with its emphasis on the American scene, inevitably incorporated American speech and speechways. Consequently,
along with the expansion of the vocabulary to contain the new
medical, botanical, physical, mechanical, and other technical
terms, there continued the same busy, ingenious, metaphorical
development of the vocabulary at another level. Before the
turn of the century, the language had absorbed an array of
colorful coinage including *smarty; uplifter; rubberneck;
knicker* (from *knicker-bocker*); *ad* (from *advertisement*, fought
vigorously into the 1930's by advertising men, who considered
the form "beneath the dignity of men of the advertising profession");[1] *flyer* (financial); *sleeper*, both for a sleeping car on
a railroad and, figuratively, for something unnoticed that suddenly attains value; *night owl; shantytown; sand lotter; sinker*
(doughnut); *spellbinder; bonehead; sissy; dude;* and countless other words in the vernacular tradition. Expressions like
*to pass the buck, chip in, square away, keep one's eyes peeled,
know-it-all, neck-and-neck,* and *like fury* were in common use.

One of the most socially significant coinages was *bachelor
girl*, whose latchkey, it was said, was "her prized possession
and mark of identity."[2] The distance between the coinage of
*sewing-machine girl* not many years earlier (the sewing-machine girl was not yet an endangered species, even in 1900)
and of *typewriter girl* in the nineties was far greater than any
could be between traditional *Miss* or *Mrs.* and *Ms.* (surely
our genius—female, of course—can do better!). The *typewriter*, as much as any suffragist movement, gloriously
liberated the female dependent relative, the unpaid sitter,
housemaid, cook, who was sometimes loved but often a burden

1. Mencken: *Supplement I*, pp. 374–5.
2. *Tid-Bits* (September 8, 1899). Quoted in Mathews: *Dictionary*.

and aware of it. As the *cash register,* the *adding machine,* and other inventions joined the *typewriter* in transforming business methods, the *bachelor girls*—*typewriter girls* and *telephone girls* (*hello girls,* Mark Twain called them) and *salesgirls*—rode the new electric *trolleys* toward the *business offices* of America, changing as drastically as were the new *skyscrapers* the American scene.

But even as the native idiom was being enriched and strengthened, additional exotic elements were crowding into it. Between 1880, when the population stood at something over fifty million, and 1910, when it reached almost ninety million, the flood of immigration became a tidal wave. Along with the English, who continued to come in moderate numbers, along with the Irish and Germans, with the scattered Swedes and Hungarians and Finns and Italians and Welsh and French and Lithuanians, came the eastern European Jews, pouring in at the rate of one thousand, two thousand, five thousand a month, increasing the Jewish population from two hundred and fifty thousand at the beginning of 1881 to almost three million by 1910. As they moved into New York and made of the Lower East Side by 1890 perhaps the most congested area on earth, they disturbed not only Anglo-Saxon Americans but also Sephardim and German Jews, heretofore called *Hebrews* or *Israelites,* who had established themselves as leading citizens and who felt their status threatened by the unwelcome presence of their unimpressive relatives.[3] To them, as to other Americans, the newcomers were *Yids,* from Russian *Zhyd,* a pejorative, or *kikis,* for their names, which usually ended in *-ki* or *-ky* (from which comes *kike*). The attitude was contagious; other foreigners were given other labels. *Bohunk* (from *Bohemian* plus *Hungarian*) soon was applied to any laborer of foreign birth. *Dago,* from Spanish *Diego,* had formerly been applied to Mexicans but was displaced by *greaser* during the Mexican War; now it labeled

3. The embarrassment this enormous immigration caused these Jewish Americans and their heroic efforts to aid and Americanize their exotic relatives form the principal theme of Manners's *Poor Cousins.*

the Italians, with *wop,* from Neapolitan *guappo* (a showy, pretentious fellow), soon giving it competition. Immigrant Germans were commonly called *sauerkrauters,* often spelled *sour-krauters* and soon shortened to *krauts.* In California, agitation against the *Chinks,* the "heathen Chinee" of Bret Harte, had been going on for years; the Chinese Exclusion Act was passed in 1869.

Oblivious to the feelings of its speakers, the language picked up the alien speech, tried it out, kept some of it. German loan words, as noted, continued their steady flow into the main stream. Spanish, now the tongue of a whole segment of the American population, mingled its words with American in the Southwest; *chili, tamale, tequila, marihuana* entered the language, as did *fiesta,* no doubt reinforcing the German suffix *-fest.* Earlier Spanish borrowings had become so much a part of the language that they began taking on English affixes (for example, *peon* > *peonage*), while some Spanish word elements were found to go nicely with English words. From *cafeteria* (Spanish *cafetería*) which seems to have been introduced at the Chicago World's Fair in 1893 and was enthusiastically adopted—four *cafetirias* (so spelled) were listed in the Chicago city directory in 1895—the suffix *-teria* was extracted to convey the self-service concept. *Marketeria, luncheteria, washerteria,* even *casketeria,* have been listed among its many progeny; *laundeteria* seems to have been the most successful.

Italian immigrants began entering in considerable numbers only at the end of the century. They spoke a variety of dialects, of which Neapolitan and Sicilian were most prevalent. Settling principally in New York, but moving on also to such widely scattered cities as Chicago, San Francisco, and New Orleans, they added new terms like *spaghetti, salami,* and *chianti* to the familiar *macaroni,* as well as to the rich store of Italian borrowings already in English from pre-American times. Their major influence on American English, however, would not come until later.

The arrival of the Jewish immigrants, if only by weight of

numbers, had a more immediate effect. In 1882, Abraham Cahan broke precedent by addressing his Jewish audience in true Yiddish, unlike the German-larded type used earlier, and gave to it a status it had never had in America; he also launched, in Yiddish, the long-lasting *Jewish Daily Journal.* *Kosher delicatessens* featured *bagels* and *lox* and *gefilte fish,* Germanic words all; and Jewish jokes, with *oy-oy* as the principal dialectal ingredient, entered the non-Jewish repertoire. Such expressions as *I'm telling you, I should worry,* and *did I say no?* made their way from Yiddish idiom into American, although some who used them would have abandoned them had they known their source. A few German words came through Yiddish, as Yiddish ones had come through German; *kibitz,* that useful term which has made itself at home in American and British English, too, and has acquired the derivatives *-er* and *-ing* and even *-ee,* for a player kibitzed, was originally Austrian army slang for a staff officer.

But there were other things to think about at the turn of the century than foreigners and their language; most Americans had little contact with either. The center of population was moving steadily westward; by 1900, it was in Indiana, and the "average" American spoke with a Midwestern twang of which he was proud. Despite his feeling that *they*—big business? government? foreigners?—were trying to *put something over* on him, his vocabulary in general showed him to be a reasonably happy man. The Chicago World's Fair in 1893, attended by over twelve million people, and so splendidly done that even the aesthetically oriented Henry Adams said that "as a scenic display, Paris had never approached it," broadened cultural horizons, made Americans aware of their own achievements, and gave pride in the knowledge that others recognized them as well.

In its wake, the concept of city planning, if not yet the term, was in the air;[4] people demanded *city parks,* rare till

4. The fairgrounds were designed by Frederick Law Olmsted, whose artistry is still evident in the grounds surrounding the Capitol in Washington, in Central Park and Riverside Park in New York City, in

then; the classical lines of the fair's buildings improved the
national taste in architecture; and interest in the arts was
stimulated (among those arts—the *hootchy-cootchy*). In response to demand, the fare offered theatergoers at the turn
of the century was spectacular. *Theater parties* were made up
to attend the performances of John Drew, Richard Mansfield,
Minnie Maddern Fiske; Sarah Bernhardt was making her
numerous "farewell" appearances; Maude Adams played
*Peter Pan.* Madame Schumann-Heink sang, as did Nellie
Melba; Paderewski played. There was the new *light opera.*
On a less elevated level, *minstrelsy* was still popular; and the
*Tommers,* who played only *Uncle Tom's Cabin,* appeared
everywhere—the play was still, in 1901, "the greatest money-
maker of any attraction on the stage of New York City."
Buffalo Bill's *Wild West Show* thrilled Americans whose older
relatives may have fought Indians on the plains. *Song and
dance* acts delighted many; it was the era of Weber and
Fields, of the one-liner, of jokes, of *jollying people along,* of
the beginnings of *ballyhoo*—Anna Held's milk baths captured
the attention of the public more than did her marriage to
Florenz Ziegfeld. *Show business* was becoming big business;
and into the language came figurative expressions like *to run
the show, the whole show,* and *song and dance,* for an elaborate and fictitious explanation.

Other shows attracted the public. Baseball continued its
pull, with new terms constantly entering the vocabulary—
*ball team, ball park, ball game, bobble.* Football was becoming the college game; spectators talked of *kickoffs* and *safeties.*
In the ring, "Gentleman Jim" Corbett and other fighters wore
their hair in a *fighting clip,* much imitated; Corbett himself
attained the distinction of putting a dictionary word, *solar
plexus,* into the mouths of many who thought he invented
the term. On *music stands* in the parks, bands played Sousa's
new marches against the counterpoint of *carrousel* tunes (a

Mount Royal Park in Montreal, and in many other landscaping
achievements.

French borrowing) nearby. And on summer evenings, boys and girls gathered at the *ice-cream parlor* for an *ice-cream soda,* while their parents might be having an *ice-cream supper* or sipping the popular new *iced tea* at home. Groups gathered in the parlors around *pianolas* to sing such songs as "The Bowery" and "On the Road to Mandalay" and "A Hot Time in the Old Town Tonight" and "After the Ball," while others, more daring, went to the *concert saloons* (night clubs), where the bands played *ragtime* and everyone knew the *cakewalk,* that imitation of the "darkey strut" or "walk-around" which traditionally earned a cake for the dancer showing the fanciest step.

Those who spent time reading were discovering the familiar and comfortable scenes and vernacular of Mark Twain, of Mary E. Wilkins, of Sarah Orne Jewett, of William Dean Howells, or the high romance (also expressed in comfortable and familiar language) of Richard Harding Davis and Charles Major. They laughed at the comments of "Mr. Dooley," that early Will Rogers created by Finley Peter Dunne. The passage of the International Copyright Law in 1891 was a boon to American authors, whose work could now be profitably published—royalty-free foreign works had been favored earlier—and the American idiom profited with the authors. American authors coined distinctively American words and phrases—George Ade's *glad hand* and *panhandler* and *tightwad,* Jack Conway's *push-over* and *high hat.* A new kind of entertainment was being talked about, too, but had not yet caught on. Mr. Edison had invented what he called the *kinetograph* and some called the *biograph* or *cinematograph.* The device showed pictures of objects actually in motion; the average simplistic American thought *moving pictures* a better name—he would soon reduce it to *movie.*

No entertainment, however, was as diverting, as popular, as utterly delightful, as *biking.* Since the invention in 1889 of the *safety bicycle* with two wheels of equal size, soon modified so that young ladies could *go for a wheel* without loss of modesty, sewing-machine companies and arms companies alike had gone into the manufacture of it. Different makes had different slogans: the *Pierce* was "a study in vibration"; the *Barnes* was "like a trusted steed"; the *Sterling* was "built like a watch." *Cycleries,* or bicycle shops, rented *machines* by the hour. Office buildings offered *parking* space. Bicycle clubs had *Century* runs on Sundays and holidays; in the *Pullman Road Race,* from Chicago to Pullman, Illinois, as many as a thousand riders participated, some of the women, not suffragettes, wearing *bloomers.* "Daisy Bell" ("Daisy, Daisy") was the accompaniment to the times.

As they *biked* along, riders looked curiously at the new motor-driven carriages, which, like the steam carriages and electric cars, were beginning to appear on the streets. Already they were being raced in Paris; by 1898, *Cosmopolitan* noted: "It is scarcely an exaggeration to say that Paris is becoming 'automobilized.' " There was some indecision as to the name of the vehicle. The French were using *automobile,* meaning self-moving, as an adjective; it seemed a good word too for the vehicle itself, as well as for the related verb. *Locomobile,* however, the trademarked name of a steam model, showed signs of catching on as a generic word, both for verb and noun; and *bubbling,* according to the *New York Journal* of November 11, 1900, was "the fashionable slang for automobling or locomobling or whatever you choose to call it." The *Boston Herald,* recognizing a linguistic vacuum, made its own suggestion: "If we must Americanize and shorten the word [the *Boston Herald* knew its people], why not call them 'autos.' " In fact, a later column pointed out, "we should have the new words . . . autobus . . . autocab."[5] Already the *New York Auto-Truck Company* was in existence; *truck* had come a long journey from its home in fourteenth-century England, when it was *trukken,* "to trade," and had touched many bases, in Indian country and elsewhere, in the meantime. Many people called the new vehicles simply *machines;* the word had a nice, optimistically purring sound.

5. July 4 and 12, 1899.

In accepting as a foregone conclusion that "we must Americanize and shorten the word," the *Boston Herald* conceded, as the *North American Review* and the *Chautauquan* had not, that Americans were going to make their language in their own way. Doers and tryer-outers, they wanted their words not just to work, but to appeal to their by now instinctive sense of the vernacular. The contemporary vocabulary—forceful, picturesque, colloquial, often playful, retaining the innovative, unconventional quality that had come to distinguish it from British English—reflected the personality of its makers. When President McKinley said that he would not be *jingoed* into war, adding a new verb to the language, the average American would have been shocked to know that the word was a euphemism for Jesus and came from "By Jingo!" in the refrain of an English fighting song; but the word had a good American sound—by jingo! Theodore Roosevelt's response that the President had "no more backbone than a chocolate éclair" delighted the average man too.[6] *Backbone* was true-blue American; politicians had been using it for years, attacking, among others, President Lincoln and General McClellan for lack of it. *Chocolate éclair*, familiar enough to show with what ease foreign terms were now slipping into the vocabulary, was not only a perfect image of the backboneless, but la-de-dah foreign besides. When, in 1892, a Harvard-alumnus author used typically American imagery in relating a Harvard anecdote—"I was on the box-seat driving, you know—lickety-split, to beat the band"[7]—it was clear that the last bastion of purism had been breached. American idiom was on the box-seat driving, lickety-split, to beat the band.

6. Both remarks are cited in Mark Sullivan: *Our Times*, vol. 1, *The Turn of the Century* (New York: Charles Scribner's Sons; 1928).

7. Flandreau: *Harvard Episodes* (1897). p. 223. Quoted in Mathews: *Dictionary*.

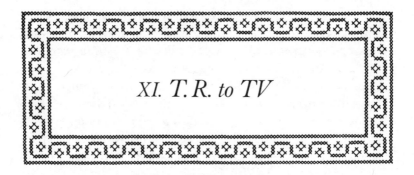

# XI. T. R. to TV

Addressing his subjects on March 1, 1936, King Edward VIII used the word *radio* instead of the preferred British *wireless*. In so doing, he disturbed even further those of his subjects already displeased by his predilection for things American; *radio* had been denounced in the *London Daily Telegraph* only a year earlier as one of a number of "bastard American expressions" sullying the pure English stream.[1] Originally *radiotelegraphy* (from *radi[ate]* plus *telegraphy*), the term had been suggested as the mark of the wireless telegram by the International Radio Convention at Berlin in 1906, had been adopted by the United States Congress in 1912, and since 1921 had been expanded by the American people to cover a broad spectrum of related concepts—the wireless medium itself, the equipment for receiving or transmitting or a combination of both, a message transmitted or received. It was used as a verb both transitively and intransitively; it was a modifying element, as in *radio frequency,* and a compounding element, as in *radiogram.* Critics felt that its indiscriminate use made for ambiguity in the presence of like combinations relating to the increasingly important element *radium* (Latin *radium,* "ray"). Who knew which concept entered into *radiogenic,* for example, which was ostensibly analogous to *photogenic?* Which into *radiograph?* No doubt about it—the word

1. By a correspondent named John C. Mellis, on March 2.

was less precise than *wireless*. But neither sweet reason nor bitter scorn seemed able to dislodge it.

Other terminology making headway in the King's English was even more disturbing, and not only the King was using it. The Archbishop of Canterbury had been heard to use *up against* in a public pronouncement; Stanley Baldwin, the Prime Minister, had introduced *backslider, best seller,* and *deliver the goods* into Parliamentary debate; in the same forum had been heard *debunked* and *to pass the buck.* Respected British writers, who usually scorned the vulgate of their own land, seemed to find some piquancy in Americanisms like *highbrow* and *gate-crasher* and *glad rags*; and in the everyday conversation of Englishmen one could hear such expressions as *nothing doing, stand for, boom, crook,* and *under the weather.* Clearly, the words coming from America were no longer those principally concerned with American phenomena, like *canyon* and *backwoods* and *blizzard,* nor were they only business and political terms, like *to corner* and *gerrymander*; no longer, indeed, were they scarce and noticeable enough to be caught at the water's edge and scooped up by purists—they were coming in waves. The two streams of English, mother stream and branch now grown to flood, were converging; and perfectly good terms for the same notion were beginning to run together and compete for place. London *sweet shops* were sometimes called *candy stores*; *chemists' shops, drugstores*; *multiple shops, chain stores.* Theaters boasted *box offices* rather than *booking offices*; and drama critics wrote, without blinking, of *flops. So long* often displaced *cheerio,* and English toddlers pointing at railway engines were as likely to say *choo-choo* as the traditional *puff-puff.* The trend seemed to bear out Sir William Craigie's observation that the course of neologism had run westward for only two centuries after Jamestown; in the early nineteenth century it began reversing direction and in the twentieth was firmly oriented.[2]

2. *The Study of American English.* Society for Pure English, Tract No. 27 (1927), p. 208.

Radio, or wireless, despite its important role, was not the principal medium of passage. Since World War I, by an accident of history, American movies had been projecting verbiage into British consciousness. Because cellulose nitrate was not only the base for film but also an important ingredient in explosives, British film makers found themselves, in the early stages of the war, with a shortage of materials. American producers filled the gap, and by the time the war was over had made their product dominant in the field. Capturing the attention of the common people with larger-than-life and distorted pictures of America, the *movies*—or *cinema*—spread abroad an idiom designed to appeal to the broadest possible audience. Some film makers tried at first to placate British critics by furnishing "English translations" of the *captions,* as the subtitles were then called, substituting *madhouse* for *nut factory* and *put-up job* for *frame*; but when it became clear that the "American" versions were more popular, even these concessions were dropped. The Cinematograph Films Act of 1927, which put a high duty on American films and required a certain quota of British-made films to be shown, seemed to promise relief to the purists. But alas! Along came the *talkies,* and the British people, already accustomed to the American way with words through American fiction and pulp magazines and comic strips, welcomed American musicals and gangster films with undiscriminating joy. It is hardly surprising that an International Conference on English, held in London in 1927, did little but provoke the ire of the hosts; Dr. Henry Seidel Canby's blasphemy in equating *Anglicisms* with *Americanisms* prompted *The New Statesman* to remark tartly that "Anglicisms are English *tout court.*"

Unfortunately—or fortunately for the separate identities of both English and American idiom—there was little *quid pro quo.* The American public found English speech difficult to understand and associated it with the Boston accent, against which regional prejudice already existed; consequently, films imported from Britain made little profit. What Briticisms did enter the American vocabulary came in largely on the upper level of usage, and there they usually stayed. Scientific, economic, and other specialized terms were shared internationally. The days when medical dictionaries, for example, could list as many as twenty synonyms for one anatomical name, as had been the case before publication of the *Basle Nomina Anatomica* in 1895 (which reduced fifty thousand terms to 5,528), were long over; advances in communication had made standardization both possible and necessary. On the vernacular level, however, British and American retained their separate identities, the differences between them offering a fertile field for study by some curious student of national psychology. Americans accepted *civil service* from the British but not *civil servant,* preferring *government worker. Weatherman* is as clearly American as *clerk of the weather* is British. American taxis *cruise*; British taxis *crawl*. An American *dump* is a British *refuse tip*; an American *newsstand,* a British *kiosk* (French *kiosque,* from Turkish *köshk,* "pavilion"). Why *atomizer* and *elevator* were retained in America in preference to the clearly superior British *scent spray* and *lift* is a mystery; the latter two have (with our apologies· to the British) an American smack. By the end of the nineteenth century, that "smack," as Mencken dubs it, was identifiable if not definable; and new forces were acting upon the idiom to individualize it even more. One of the most potent of these was a new kind of journalism.

The *yellow journalism* of the 1890's, so called for the *Yellow Kid* cartoons that brought to a focus the fierce rivalry between Joseph Pulitzer's *New York World* and William Randolph Hearst's *Journal,* had created a market for sensationalism as well as tremendous readership. To satisfy both, newspapers and many magazines changed in content and in style. Plunging boldly into matters of heated contemporary controversy like corporate privilege and political corruption, they made contact with a crusading spirit already stirring. Lincoln Steffens's "Tweed Days in St. Louis" and Ida M.

Tarbell's history of the Standard Oil Company, appearing in *McClure's,* were only the first of a plethora of *probes,*[3] some sincere and effective, some libelous, exposing the dealings of companies and individuals, of elected officials and appointees. The sensational articles not only gave expression to the problems disturbing the American people; they also attracted the reader to unrelated materials appearing in the same publications and so verbalized for many the new and exciting concepts—scientific, political, social, and technological—that were emerging on the world scene. And the style in which the articles were written made its own impact on the general vocabulary.

*Newspaper English,* terse, idiomatic, and neologistic, dates only from the end of the last century. Prior to that time, journalistic style was flowery and full of euphemisms, the headline often running halfway down a column, yet constituting a single sentence. When the custom arose of setting headlines in self-contained banks, it became necessary to fit them to the column; and copyreaders began squeezing. The resultant headline vocabulary influenced newspaper style in general; and back formations, clipped forms, and initial abbreviations became so familiar to readers that they entered popular speech. *Crash* and *blast* replaced *collision* and *explosion*; *edict* became a standard substitute for *command, injunction,* or—unreasonably—*order; slate* meant a program or agenda of any kind, *plea* a petition or request. Shortened forms like *exam, gas, mart, photo,* and *quake* (*quake* was screaming in the headlines in 1906) became routine, as did short verbs like *nab, quit,* and *snag,* along with a few short compounds like *prewar, firebug* (not shorter but more graphic than *arsonist*), and *comeback. Headline* itself became a verb —but then, everything in America becomes a verb! At the same time, *sportswriters,* already noted for the "peculiarities"

3. "Few words are commoner in newspaper headlines," wrote *Christendom* (May 9, 1903), "than 'probe,' which is newspaper English for an investigation of alleged abuses."

of their diction,[4] were introducing terms like *shutout* and *muff* and *kayo* and *bunt*. And comic strips, with dialogue made up largely of *grrr, wow, zowie,* and *whap,* were reinforcing the American tendency to use short and to-the-point expressions. Illustrative of this abbreviating tendency is the failure of 1912 film makers to change what they considered the undignified term *movie* to one more acceptable. The coiner of *photoplay* won twenty-five dollars in a promotional contest, but the American people would have none of it.

The press influenced the language not only directly, by word-forms and style and by the wide exposure given political, scientific, and other specialized terms in the Sunday-magazine type of article, but also indirectly. *Muckraker* came of Theodore Roosevelt's anger at David Graham Phillips's series "The Treason of the Senate." Roosevelt's comparison of irresponsible writers to the "Man with the Muckrak" in *Pilgrim's Progress,* "who could look no way but downward," gave to Lincoln Steffens and his colleagues a coinage they seized upon happily; *muckrake, muckraking,* and *muckraker* gained wide currency. Who invented *sob story, sob stuff,* and *sob sister* no one knows; they have certainly become part of the language. *To release,* in the sense of to give out for publication, came into use in 1904; by 1907, the *New York Evening Post* of July 15 could note that a report "was given to the press associations . . . labelled 'confidential,' with a fixed date for 'release,' before which no part of it was to be used." The term was denounced in England when it was used in connection with films as "an abominable Americanism"; but even the Manchester *Guardian* defended it as having no satisfactory equivalent. The *confidential* label suggests the related *off the record,* but despite the use of *on record* early in the century, its counterpart had to wait for Alfred E. Smith. *Slant,* for point of view, came along in 1905.

Roosevelt—*T. R.* to the press—was a master of vernacular;

4. "Chronicle and Comment," *Bookman* (October 1901).

262 OUR OWN WORDS

and he popularized if he did not coin many of our familiar expressions. *Rough rider* and *lunatic fringe* are evidently his coinage; Mark Twain's *square deal,* which fitted admirably his own vigorous, colloquial style, was a favorite phrase, as was *one hundred per cent American.* The well-known *big stick* image originated, according to him, in a West African proverb; *big sticker* developed from it. Roosevelt's forthright and characteristically "American" speech, along with his heroic stature and recognized integrity, undoubtedly encouraged popular support for his crusades. Many who had been hesitant to endorse the ideas promoted by academics and *do-gooders,* not to speak of known radicals like the *Wobblies* (the IWW), went along when T. R. led the way. Not only did *trust busting* become fashionable; so did numerous other causes that left their legacy in the language. Conservation fervor introduced, along with related terms, *forestation* and *forest management, forest manager* and *forester.* Child welfare projects, encouraged by the first White House Conference on Children, brought *child welfare* into the vocabulary, to join *welfare center, welfare administrator,* and like combinations, *welfare* being used for the first time in its modern sense at Dayton, Ohio, in 1904.[5] *Employers' liability, workmen's compensation, industrial safety* became articulated concepts prior to World War I. *Female suffrage,* first expressed in the 1860's and derided in *Harper's,* in April 1893, as an "incoherent and fantastic dream of social improvement," became more and more common in popular speech. *Pure food laws* were passed and so named. There were any number of organizations of *anti-*'s, whose christening required no linguistic effort: *anti-saloon leaguers, antiprohibitionists, antivivisectionists,*

5. According to the *Westminster Gazette* (January 28, 1905): "The home of 'the welfare policy' is the city of Dayton, Ohio." Quoted in Mitford M. Mathews, ed.: *A Dictionary of Americanisms on Historical Principles* (Chicago: University of Chicago Press; 1951). Ernest Weekley's *Something about Words* (London: J. Murray; 1935), p. 63, states: "*Welfare* . . . was first used in this special sense in Ohio in 1904." Also quoted in Mathews: *Dictionary.*

even *antismoke* advocates—pollution is not our discovery. Pre-World War I Americans were convinced that with the right kind of *go-head* any reform could be accomplished.

The great strides in medical knowledge being taken all over the world were adding new terms to the medical lexicon; American pioneers in the field contributed their share. *Anesthesia* and *anesthetic, appendicitis* and *appendectomy* had been earlier contributions; isolation of *hookworm (Necator Americanus)* meant new life for countless debilitated victims. The National Tuberculosis Association was formed in 1904, as part of a world-wide battle against the disease. Universally called *consumption* before the German Robert Koch's discovery of the tubercle bacillus, and provincially in America called *breast complaint, tuberculosis* was soon reduced by Americans to *TB*. In the field of mental health, Dr. Henry H. Goddard, impressed by the new Binet intelligence tests and believing that the widely used *feeble-minded* had become generic, coined *moron* (Greek *mōron*, neuter of *mōros,* "foolish") for the higher grade of mental defective. Used correctly in professional circles, the word was unfortunately widened in popular idiom to include not only other grades of mental defectives but sexual deviates also and people one didn't like. *Behaviorism,* which begat *behaviorist,* was the coinage of psychologist John B. Watson. That scientific coinage has an international flavor is suggested by the term *epinephrine,* a Greek-derived word coined by a Japanese scientist working in an American laboratory.

Other crusades introduced other expressions. *Vice crusaders* —or *vice hounds,* as their critics called them—sought legislation against *white-slave traders,* who were a very real threat, especially against female immigrants; they were believed to infest the primitive *movie parlors* of the day and very likely did. The *Mann Act,* passed in 1910, was a direct result of the vice crusaders' efforts. *Opium fiends* and *cigarette fiends* were thought by some to be equally evil (not yet by the surgeon general of the United States); perhaps because the word was thus overused, *fiend* gradually lost its ancient and sin-

ister meaning to enter into combinations of hyperbole like
*baseball fiend* and *dance fiend* and *fiend for punishment.*
Many Americans, troubled by the swarming and increasingly
troublesome immigrants, demonstrated their awareness of the
correlation between language skills and achievement by ad-
vocating not only *vocational training* but also better language
teaching; in 1891, a pioneering article in *Voice* had noted:
"Their [the immigrants'] inability to handle the American
vernacular . . . will cause the aroma of foreignership to cling
to them always." The statement incidentally introduced the
awkward word *foreignership,* which proved ephemeral but
expressed a concept that was bothering a great many people.
Another type of crusade emerged in the *service clubs,* founded
on idealistic tenets of community service and good fellowship;
*Rotary,* so called because its members met at various homes
in rotation, was founded in 1905.

Concern with causes, however, did not dominate American
speech any more than it did American life. The people continued to enrich the language with expressions from newspaper and stage, from popular songs and sports, from current
happenings and passing fads. The pre-World War I era saw the
emergence of *Tin Pan Alley,* so called for the kind of piano
generally found in music publishers' cubbyholes, which were
originally located on Broadway. *Ragtime* still prevailed, and
the *jazz age* had not begun; but in 1907 W. C. Handy wrote
his first *blues,* and, soon after, *jazz bands* were playing a new
kind of music, described in *Harper's Weekly* of May 11, 1913,
as having "the rhythm of African tom-toms . . . or of ragtime
down on the levee—the swaying, sensuous syncopation that
is characteristic of the black man everywhere." Other descriptions were less lyric; "Jazz music," wrote the *Literary Digest*
in 1917, "is the delirium tremens of syncopation."

People danced. Irene and Vernon Castle captured the
hearts of their audiences with the sinuous grace of the *Castle
walk* and the *fox trot,* the latter a name already given to the
smooth and easy trotting gait of a horse. Irene's *bobbed hair*
was a little too daring for most women to imitate, but some

were already indulging in the new *permanent wave,* introduced by Charles Nessler in London. As a consequence, *beauty parlors* and *beauty shops* were proliferating; they were run by *beauty operators,* who would become *beauticians* only after *morticians* (who had already advanced from *undertakers* to *funeral directors*) led the way.

From sports came other terms. Ever-popular baseball continued to contribute expressions quickly made figurative; *out in left field, grandstand play, off base, hit and run, southpaw* (from the position of left-handed pitchers in the old baseball park on Chicago's West Side), *go to bat for* were among them. From boxing came *punch-drunk* and *shadowboxing* and *punk,* from racing, *backing a winner* (or *loser*). The enduring *four-flusher* came from poker,[6] along with *ace-high* and *ace in the hole* and *full house* and *chip in.* The stage contributed *fall guy, barnstorming* (borrowed by politicians, preachers, and flying circuses), *upstage, bring down the house,* and numerous other expressions. *Hot dogs* were introduced at the New York Polo Grounds by an inspired caterer named Harry Mozely Stevens, who gave credit for the name to the sports cartoonist T. A. Dorgan *(Tad).* Dorgan, the story goes, was not sure how to spell *dachshund sausages,* as Stevens had christened his creation. The inference that dog meat was the principal ingredient so incensed the Coney Island Chamber of Commerce that, in 1913, it forbade the use of the term by concessionaires on the *boardwalk.*

From other areas of diversion or occupation or environment came innumerable miscellaneous expressions: *lay off* and *boob* (short for *booby*); *off his trolley*—still used, despite the demise of the trolley; *panhandle* and *panhandler*; and *loan shark.* The change in living patterns brought about by ever-increasing urbanization appeared in *walk-up,* a typically American verb phrase made noun, and *kitchenette.* The fondness for initials continued; *O.K., C.O.D., n.g.,* and *P.D.Q.*

6. "There is a good, plain, honest virtue in the word 'four-flushing' . . ." commented a writer in *Saturday Evening Post* (February 6, 1901), ". . . it draws its name from the poker table."

were popularly noted as following only *hell* and *damn* in the primer of immigrants; and *GOP, FFV, GAR, on the q.t., B.V.D.,* and *L* (for *Elevated,* later *El*) were but a few of the abbreviations in wide use before 1910. It was only appropriate, therefore, that an invention, or phenomenon, or development, destined to change the habits, language, and future of American society should be named the *Model T*.

When Henry Ford presented the *Model T* in 1908, automobiles were playthings of the wealthy. Woodrow Wilson had proclaimed in 1906 that "nothing has spread socialistic feeling in this country more than the automobile," nor was anything, he said, more expressive of the "arrogance of wealth." Twenty years later, when investigators were gathering data for their sociological study of *Middletown, USA* (Muncie, Indiana), women of small income declared that they would rather give up clothes or the bathtub than their cars.

No prancing steed, no elegant carriage, was ever better loved than the *flivver,* or *tin Lizzie,* which meant to many the mobility and to some a status long denied them. *Flivver* had meant failure or to fail ("a human flivver" appeared in H. L. Wilson's *Ruggles of Red Gap* in 1917) and was at some time passed on to the Model T by an exasperated owner or some jeering nonowner. It soon became a term of affection and was extended eventually to any contrivance small and inexpensive; in World War I, the smaller class of destroyers was so named, and since then so have been small planes and even helicopters. *Tin Lizzie* may have come from *lizard,* a sledlike contrivance designed to haul logs or other heavy objects, with *tin* as the obvious attribute. By 1915, the expression was familiar enough to become part of the folk saying that the successful man was one who could "make a tin lizzie out of the cans they tie to him."

Whatever its label, the *Model T* soon signified not only a possession but a way of life. The larger economic implications of the *eight-hour day* instituted by Ford, of his *five-dollars-a-day wage,* of his perception of the dynamic logic of mass production, of the vast new market opened for steel and oil and gasoline were enormous. But equally so were the social and cultural implications of a phenomenon that added immediately to the vernacular such terms as *filling station* and *gas* (for *gasoline*), *spark plugs* and *hood* and *detour*; and, over the years, *parking lot* and *back-seat driver* and *tourist court* and *suburban sprawl* and *traffic engineer* and *mobile home* and *two-car family.* New expressions abounded; people *flew along the road,* they *stepped on the gas,* they shouted at *road hogs. Joy riding* became so much a part of the language that, in 1916, a viewer called *Birth of a Nation* "a joyride through history."[7] *Harper's* commented on the excellent word sense of the Bostonians, "supposedly sesquipedalian of speech," who had reduced "a pedestrian who crosses streets in disregard of traffic signals" to the compact *jaywalker.*[8] So engrossed were Americans in the automobile that they had little but passing attention to pay to news of another kind of vehicle when it was belatedly described by excited reporters in Dayton, Ohio, also in 1908.

Various persons in several countries had been experimenting for some time with *flying machines,* or, as they were also called, *aerial ships, aerial machines,* or *aerial steam carriages.* In 1897, there was excitement over what Samuel Langley called his *aerodrome,* or "air-runner" (Greek *aerodromos*), a steam-driven airplane, which had shown promise but failed in a launching test over the Potomac. Professor Langley, however, a distinguished scientist and inventor, secretary of the Smithsonian Institution, and even the coiner of the impressive term *aerodynamics,* had an international reputation; the Wright brothers were mere mechanics. Their success in keeping a power-driven, heavier-than-air craft in the air for fifty-nine seconds at Kitty Hawk, North Carolina, in 1903, was hardly noticed; and their subsequent efforts to obtain financial backing for their experiments failed. Not until 1908 did

7. *Out West* (December 1916).
8. (June 1917).

some newspaper editors take note of the curious stories
coming out of Dayton and send experienced reporters to the
scene. Their startling news electrified the world; those Wright
brothers had accomplished a real stunt! It would, most
people thought, have little practical application.

The word *aeroplane*, which had been coined in England
in 1866 to describe a wing, or "a plane in the air," and later
an aircraft of any kind, including gliders and airships, was
soon restricted to the power-driven, heavier-than-air kind of
craft the Wrights had successfully pioneered; several years
later, the United States government officially simplified the
spelling to *airplane*. And in 1909, the *Westminster Gazette*,
describing the international *air meeting* at Reims, France,
took note of a significant new word. *Aviator* (French *aviateur*,
from *aviation*), it remarked, had "forced itself into the vocabulary." So would a great many other terms within the next
few years; as *barnstorming* flyers (*flying fools*, the people
called them) did stunts at fairs and *flying meets* all over the
country, expressions like *nose dive* and *tail spin* and *bail out*
and all the other argot of the air entered the vernacular,
much of it to be transmitted into popular imagery.

Wireless telegraphy did not make much of an impression
at first, either, on American life or language. Amateur experi-
menters bandied about terms like *loop aerials, crystal detectors, reflex circuits,* and *rotary sparks*; and at sea, wireless
operators depended upon the universally adopted call of
distress, *CQD*, which used D for danger in combination with
the standard "all stations" call (eventually replaced by the
Morse mnemonic *SOS*). The press used wireless for some of
its dispatches; and a few of the more farsighted among the
military, which was already interested in the reconnaissance
possibilities of the airplane, were considering the potential
uses of wireless in warfare. But to the average man, the concept of sound transmitted without wires was not merely
mysterious but remote; when David Sarnoff, assistant traffic
manager of the Marconi Wireless Telegraph Company, suggested a *radio music box* in 1916, even his peers paid little

attention—little more than anyone had paid to another new concept, initially verbalized in *Engineering Magazine* in 1910, *air conditioning.*

Popular attention, though, was no longer its own master. At about the same time that sensationalism in the press was attracting greater readership, a new force was beginning its campaign for control of the public mind—mass advertising. S. H. McClure was the first to recognize in the equation between expanded readership and advertising profits a new formula for success; and as other publishers of mass-circulation magazines, *Saturday Evening Post, Ladies' Home Journal,* and others, followed his lead in advertising *zippers* and *Dictaphones* and *thermos bottles* and all the other products appearing helter-skelter in the market place, they collaborated with industry to add a new dimension to the language.

Manufacturers had been using all the tricks of word-making for many years. *Kodak,* which has entered all the Continental languages, was a purely arbitrary coinage registered by George Eastman in 1888; *Oldsmobile* was a blend of the name of maker R. E. *Olds* with *mobile, Reo* a combination of his initials. In the effort to create distinctive and memorable trade names, other such inventions and blends and combinations appeared, along with derivatives from proper names, compounds, and diminutives. Over the objections of the honoree, *Listerine* memorialized the name of Lord Lister, the English surgeon who introduced aseptic surgery. *Orangeade* utilized a common suffix, *Wheatena* a new one. *Chiclet* and *Toasterette* were typical diminutives, *Uneeda* and *Holsum* phonetic spellings, *Palmolive* and *Spearmint* simple compounds. *Cuticura* and *Nabisco* were typical blends. All were flaunted, with pictures and slogans, in newspapers and on *fliers* inserted therein, in magazines, on posters, and on signs in urban and rural grocery stores, so that farmer and city slicker alike called for *Corn Flakes* and *Nabiscos, Jell-O* and *Shinola, Vapo-rub* and *Coca-Cola,* the familiarity of the names and their common use suggesting a growing and certainly democratizing standardization of taste.

Some names were almost too successful. If a product had wide popular appeal, and particularly if it was completely new, its name was likely to become common or generic. *Zipper* was coined by the Goodrich Company in 1913 as the name for a slide fastener on overshoes; after numerous lawsuits, the company retained the exclusive right to the use of the name on footwear, but to what avail? *Zipper* belongs to us all. The *Coca-Cola Company* had been plagued by imitators using both *Coke* and *Cola* ever since the registry of its trademark in 1893. Not until 1930 did the company win the exclusive right to the informal *Coke*; but the United States Supreme Court decided at the same time that *cola* had become a descriptive name. So successful was the *Victor Talking Machine Company* in promoting its product that the phonographs of its competitors were soon called *victrolas*, too.

Interviews—the *interview* was noted as early as 1894 as "peculiarly an American product"[9]—reinforced the power of advertising in creating consumer demand. In the *Good Housekeeping* of October 1912, Thomas Edison presented a prospectus of household wonders soon to join the *electric iron* and *vacuum cleaner* already available. With a notable lack of linguistic inventiveness, the great inventor predicted *electric kitchens, electric laundries, electric chafing dishes,* and various other electrical devices, which would "change the housewives of the future from drudges into engineers." In an approach prophetic of women's liberation (but hardly flattering to his audience), Edison theorized that such contributions would halt the "retardation" that had been women's lot through the ages. Other experimental inventions he described but gave no name to were home movies and stereophonic music.

As the *ads* continued to show more and more products of American invention, and as articles and interviews promised more and more marvels to come, complacency about American *know-how* increased. So did the crusading fervor that was

9. Edwin L. Shuman: *Steps into Journalism* (Evanston, Ill.: Correspondence School of Journalism; 1894), p. 68.

sweeping the country. In 1917, this zestful combination inspired Americans with both zeal in their mission to make the world safe for democracy and confidence that it could not fail.

The confident *Yanks*, coming from every region of the land, speaking American and believing that English was the same, were in for a cultural shock. Speech differences between British and American had been noted by scholars for years, and foreign countries recognized American as a distinct language; many published "guides" to it. The practical difficulties affecting the English-speaking people themselves, however, appeared only with the arrival in England of the American *doughboy*. (*Doughboy*, explained in as many ways as there are etymologists, may have come from the resemblance noted between a type of doughnut served to sailors and the brass buttons on infantry uniforms.)[1] Men of the *AEF* found such difficulty in understanding the lingo of the *Limeys* that the only successful shopkeepers in London were those who put up signs saying "American spoken here." In Paris, the YMCA attracted American soldiers into its clubhouse by promising "American" speech. In fact, so much ill will was engendered among the Allied soldiers by linguistic misunderstanding that the military on both sides learned a lesson; in World War II, each would put out a glossary for the other.

When the Yanks finally returned home, therefore (those who did), they brought back with them only a few terms borrowed from their English counterparts. *Shell shock* was one of them, a far more vivid and evocative expression than the *battle fatigue* of World War II. *Over the top*, with all it contains of terror and courage and the immediacy of battle, of the drama of Saint Mihiel and Château-Thierry and Belleau Wood, epitomized in a phrase the nature of the war these

1. Mathews: *Dictionary* offers alternative etymologies, and Mencken suggests still another in *The American Language,* 4th ed. (New York: Alfred A. Knopf; 1936), p. 575. The "doughnut" source, stated very positively and said to have been recognized during the Civil War, comes from Elizabeth Custer: *Tenting on the Plains* (1887), XVI, 516.

men had fought; *cootie* told of its minor discomforts. (The British had brought back *cootie* from their own far-flung expeditions; the word comes from Malay *kutu,* "louse.") The *tank*, a product of World War I, was named by British Colonel (later General) Sir Ernest Swinton. The hull of the experimental vehicle, which was being assembled secretly and in parts and was described as a "water carrier for Mesopotamia," was referred to by workmen as "that tank thing." It occurred to Colonel Swinton that the phrase suggested a desirable code name. The seagoing nomenclature connected with the tank—*hull, turret, deck, hatch,* and the like—came of its sponsorship by the Admiralty rather than the War Office.

The immediate postwar period in America was a time of unrest and fear. The Russian Revolution had cast its shadow over the world; and some anarchistic incidents, inextricably mingled with violent labor disputes, occurred in the United States. *Bolshevik, bolshevize,* and related terms (coming from Russian *Bol'shevik,* "one of the majority"), along with the typically American adaptation *bolshie* and the weighty phrase *Red menace,* told of the suspicion and even panic that held the people in thrall. By the time of Harding's election in 1920, however, the fears were beginning to subside, people were becoming more concerned with struggling out of a financial depression than with the vague threat of socialism, and the country felt reassured by the new administration's promise of a return to *normalcy* (Harding's coinage)—although no one was quite sure just what *normalcy* was. Those who remembered the patriotic fervor and the crusading zeal of the prewar period were sure that it was NOT whatever was being expressed in the behavior and speech of the *Lost Generation.*

The vocabulary of the twenties, like the era it portrayed, was frenetic, staccato, its tone set by Hollywood, the comic strips, radio, and the sportswriters. It echoed in the strident voices of *flaming youth,* the rat-a-tat-tat of *tommy guns,* the crescendo of *honking horns.* (Few in that decade remembered or cared that *honking* had once meant only the call of wild geese passing in a cold, gray sky.) The line between slang and conventional speech was drawn less sharply than ever before; old and young alike talked of *bathtub gin* and *necking* and *big shots*. The oft-heard *flapper*, label of that symbol of the *jazz age*, was actually a British word.[2] In 1892, it had meant in England a very young prostitute or simply, according to Partridge, an immoral young girl in her early teens. By 1910, it was in use in the United States but carried a sense of brashness and frivolity rather than immorality. It was only fitting that it should reach its heyday, then, in what has been called both the *Decade of Bad Manners* and the *Age of Play*.[3]

The last thrust of the crusader's sword in 1919 had produced the Nineteenth Amendment, but suffrage seemed the least consequential of freedoms to women a few years later; and, along with their long skirts and corsets and long hair, they were tossing away the traditional restraints on feminine speech. Fitzgerald's *jazz babies*, with their *boyish bobs*, drinking from their *boyfriends' hip flasks*, dancing the *Charleston* and the *black bottom*, were parroting the Freudian terms introduced earlier but only now becoming common currency—*libido* and *complex* and *ego* and *repressed*. Those who knew not *Freud* from *Fred* were buying like hot cakes *confession magazines*, which told in titillating terms of *petting parties*—usually coming to a bad end to please the censor but terribly exciting while they lasted. Stage plays like *What Price Glory?* and novels like *The Sun Also Rises* and *Dark Laughter* presented topics and dialogue once unacceptable. A 1927 observer of the female vocabulary noted not only the presence of a high proportion of words that

2. Mencken discusses the word fully in *Supplement I* (New York: Alfred A. Knopf; 1945), pp. 514–15.

3. "The Decade of Bad Manners," in Frederick Lewis Allen: *Only Yesterday* (New York: Harper and Row; 1931), p. 111; "The Age of Play," in Robert L. Duffus: "The Age of Play," *Independent* (December 20, 1924).

formerly "no lady could use," but also its restrictiveness; *damn* and *hell* were routine, and *lousy* a word of all work.[4]

Whatever limitations to expansion of the vocabulary existed, however, were more than canceled out by the emergence of the greatest word disseminator since printing, *radio broadcasting*, which began with the transmission of the Harding-Cox election returns in 1920. By the mid-twenties, a radio-mad public was absorbing like a sponge the words and phrases, bright or dull, of radio *broadcasters*. (*Broadcaster*, like the noun *broadcast*, is evidently British in origin, but America claims the verb.) In news reports, in the songs of Tin Pan Alley played by *big bands* and sung by *crooners*, in made-for-radio drama, in merchandising slogans and sales pitches, but most of all in *play-by-play* accounts of the sporting events that were the nation's madness, Americans were exposed as never before to a torrent of verbiage, in which the neologism of today became the popular idiom of tomorrow.

The nation's preoccupation with sports, with games, with its own national pastimes was the inevitable aftermath of postwar disillusionment. The apparently fruitless sacrifices of the war and the *Red scare* following it had brought a revulsion against involvement in Europe and against foreigners and their speech, even the *Limeys* and the *Frogs* with their *blighters* and their *parley voos* and their complaints about *Uncle Shylock*, who only wanted his loans repaid. The immigrant population was blamed for the Bolshevist terrorism, which had been greatly exaggerated; and Americans, withdrawing into themselves and jilting the League of Nations, established immigration quotas that more and more reduced the number of foreign-born Americans and consequently the foreign language element in cities and towns. Politics was of little interest; trivia held the stage. No one knew or cared that *mah-jongg* meant "house sparrow" in Cantonese or found it ironic that isolationist Americans should be calling out *pung* and *chow* as they set up ivory

4. Mary Agnes Hamilton, quoted in Allen: *Only Yesterday*, p. 112.

and bamboo tiles on green baize tables in living rooms all over the land; they knew and cared only that *mah-jongg* was fun. They turned from that game to *crossword-puzzle books,* insuring the fortunes of a young man named Schuster and his friend Simon, who were the first to publish one; so universal was the crossword-puzzle craze that the sale of dictionaries and of Roget's *Thesaurus* hit an unprecedented high. They followed in *sporting columns,* on the *air waves,* and in *captions* on movie screens the exploits of Jack Dempsey and Babe Ruth and Helen Wills; radio presented fascinating sound effects to go with the excited tones of Graham Mc-Namee or Grantland Rice. (No fan would ever forget the spiraling *psr-r-r* of a foul ball, the hard, clean *whack* of a hit.) The names of the *Four Horsemen* were on everyone's lips.

And yet—beneath the light and flippant words, the joyous and profane ones, under the surface of everyday life, could be heard, like a left-hand beat or a Greek chorus, the drumming of other words that told of a phenomenon new to America, universal flouting of the law accompanied by organized crime. Blunt, harsh terms like *rumrunner* and *rumrunning* (noun and adjective), *highjacker, rub out, bump off, taken for a ride, on the lam, trigger man* were rising from their murky habitat to enter the vernacular. *Racket* was an old word in the English argot of crime; Americans added *racketeer* and *racketeering*—the *Daily Express* of· London noted the latter, in 1928, as "the new word that has been coined in America to describe the big business of organized crime."[5] Most of the terms came from the underworld, but some were the contributions of industrious news gatherers and reporters. An anonymous former friend of Al Capone wrote, in *True Detective* of June 1947, that *syndicate* was "picked up by Al from the newspaper stories about him."

There were other words, too, less obtrusive, but telling of better things, of accomplishment and invention and of the everyday working life of the people. *White-collar* comes of

5. September 14.

the twenties; so does *electronics,* at first for theoretical and applied work involving the movement of electrons in a vacuum, but gradually extending to the whole science and technology of electronic phenomena. One of the most important developments of twentieth-century science has been the production of "artificial silk," which began early in the century in Europe and America but was not brought to practical perfection until the twenties, when the National Retail Drygoods Association chose the name *rayon* to replace the earlier *glos.* The achievement was the prelude to later advances in the production of *miracle fabrics.* Touching the lives of people more immediately and carrying far greater social implication, however, was the production in mass of the *sedan,* the closed automobile, which brought new comfort, new appeal, and new and undreamed-of possibilities to the already beloved automobile. Americans to whom the *Charleston* was for others and *bathtub gin* abhorrent savored the delight of *going for a drive* on Sunday. So much did the automobile become a part of everyone's life that when Ford unveiled his *Model A,* in 1927, the event was advertised in two thousand daily newspapers, which ran full-page advertisements for five days; one million people—according to the *Herald-Tribune*—tried to get into Ford headquarters in New York; and in Cleveland mounted police had to be brought out to patrol the crowds. Coolidge prosperity had put money in people's pockets and they were ready to buy. The competition for that money gave to the salesman a new role in American life, and to many familiar words a new role in the language.

The rivalry between Chevrolet and Ford for the automobile market was but one phase of the competitive selling spirit that gave to salesmanship in the twenties a revivalist, even religious, character; the Puritan tenet that material success meant godliness was resurrected in glory. Indeed, the line between religion and business was sometimes difficult to perceive. "Advertising the Kingdom through Press-Radio Service" was the title of a clergyman's address; "Knock and it

shall be opened unto you" was the text offered at a salesmanship meeting.[6] Action and aggressiveness were the keys to
success, and success meant the big sale. Symptomatically, the
vocabulary was filled with action words more than ever
before: *contact,* as in *contacting a prospect,* appeared as a
verb, to begin its long history of offending purists; a real
*operator put over* his product and might even *put it all over*
a rival. *Promote* took on a new meaning; with the right kind
of *promotion,* a book could *make* the best-seller list. *To sell*
acquired new objects; one sold not only commodities but
also an idea or himself. *Boost* and *booster* took a new lease on
life and a signification of virtue; it was honorable *to boost*
one's home town, *to boost* one's product, one's company,
one's church. The *booster club* came into being—and so did
George F. Babbitt. The cynics were watching.

The cynics were the intellectuals. Counterpointing all the
optimism and bustle and frivolity and prosperity of the
twenties was an attitude summed up in a word—*debunk.*
According to H. L. Mencken, one of the greatest and least
subtle *debunkers* of all time, the term was popularized by
W. E. Woodward, who published a novel called *Bunk* in 1923
and a *debunking* life of George Washington in 1926; but
Woodward made no claim to having coined it. A *debunker*
was defined in *The Nation,* in October 1923, as a "pricker
of bubbles"; a less poetic observer, in *Word Study* the same
year, defined *debunking* as "simply taking the bunk out of
things."[7] In the twenties, the debunkers were taking the
bunk not only out of the taken-for-granted ideals, beliefs, and
traditions of the American people and out of national heroes
like George Washington and Benjamin Franklin but out of
God and the whole-souled, true-blue American himself as
well.

Many people did not know until the *monkey trial* in Dayton, Tennessee, that they were *fundamentalists*—the word

6. Allen: *Only Yesterday,* p. 179.
7. XX, 5/1.

had been coined in 1909 in a defensive series of pamphlets called *The Fundamentals*. They did know that the enormous publicity surrounding the trial, the accounts of the exchanges between Clarence Darrow and William Jennings Bryan, the attitudes expressed by many of the observers who gathered from around the world introduced new and disturbing concepts into their thinking; phrases like *Darwinism* and *natural selection,* already familiar to the erudite, reached into the hinterlands. There were other terms. The average man did not read Mencken's *Prejudices* and so was spared the discomfort of being knowingly called *Boobus Americanus, homo boobiens,* and—if resident in rural America—*gaping primate.* But inevitably there filtered down to popular awareness some of the critical attitudes compiled in such volumes as Harold Stearns's *Civilization in the United States,*[8] in which American taste, American speech, American architecture, and (sacrilege!) American humor were attacked by writers like Deems Taylor and George Jean Nathan and Frank Moore Colby. Ruth Suckow and Sherwood Anderson  and other "village" writers attacked the *village virus,* the narrowness and provincialism in the small communities that had traditionally been considered the nation's strength. Some who read *Main Street* and *Babbitt* laughed, but uncomfortably; others could not understand why to some people George Babbitt seemed such a bad guy. It was all very disturbing; and, defensively, Americans decided that if they were the ones, after all, who could make the money and lick the world and swim the Channel and even, in 1927, fly the Atlantic solo, well—why worry? Why not go off on a *toot, get in on* the Florida real-estate boom, visit the *speakeasies, look out for number one, play the market,* in fact, be a *Wall Street plunger?* The expression was still only figurative in 1928, when Herbert Hoover was elected on a platform of "four more years of prosperity."

Just as rubberneck "reveals the national habit of mind," so the words that entered the vocabulary during the Depression

8. (New York: Harcourt, Brace and World, Inc.; 1922).

tell much of the national spirit under stress. In 1931, a favorite expression, *Oh yeah,* became the title of a book[9] quoting the glib and optimistic prophecies of bankers and statesmen at the onset of the Depression. The phrase grates; it is unpleasant. And yet it bespeaks a defiant cynicism born of hardship; there is no submission in it. The sardonic humor of *Hoovervilles,* named after the President, for the makeshift shelters cast up by the homeless; the flippancy of *Okies,* for the desperate migrants from the *Dust Bowl;* the upbeat sound of *tin-can shows,* for movies to which one brought a can of food for the needy, suggest that the sustaining humor which accompanied an earlier generation into terror and trial was not lost. With cardboard in his shoes, his farm foreclosed or his city job gone, the American retained along with the spirit of survival the careless facility of expression that could still produce such enduring terms as *double cross* and *gang buster* and *ad lib* and *boondoggle.* The average American was little concerned with linguistic status during the Depression —if ever he was—but it was in this dark, dreary period that the American language was gaining its ascendancy all over the world.

Some of the attention given it obviously had ulterior motivation. The Russians, who urged that students learn American rather than English because it was more "democratic" as well as "alive and picturesque," were constrained to mention also that the latest industrial techniques were finding their highest development and expression in the United States.[1] Those Japanese who advocated its preference as an official second language "despite the increasing haughtiness of the United States" noted that "common sense teaches us the wisdom of deciding for the majority where the question concerned is that of greater utility."[2] Still, there is no doubt that having a good language to begin with helps.

9. By Edward Angley, New York, 1931. Cited in Louise Tanner: *All the Things We Were* (New York: Doubleday and Co., Inc.; 1968), p. 300.

1. Mencken: *American Language,* p. 88.

2. Mencken: *Supplement I,* p. 150.

The impact of the language abroad was only one aspect of its role in the thirties. More immediately than ever before, perhaps, because words were pouring forth so prolifically and were so quickly spread, they were telling the national story. It was a story of remarkable contrast—not of the physical contrast so evident in the eighteenth century between city and country, rich and poor, region and region (the Depression was a great leveler), but within the national spirit itself. In a time of hardship suggested in such expressions as *farm relief, shed towns, street-corner apple sellers,* and *exodusters* (revived from a half century earlier, when it meant migrating Negroes, but given special pertinence in its application to *Dust Bowl refugees*), one expects to find words of dissension like *Red-baiting* and *Jew-baiting* and *rotten rich* and *pinko* and *fascist* (without the capital). What one does not expect are such incongruous expressions of frivolity as *beach pajamas* and *cocktail lounge, café society, glamorize,* and *jitterbug,* or lilting terms like *swing* and *musical* (as a noun) and the refreshingly honest *tunesmith,* or a joyous phrase like *tickled pink.*

Some of the terms of the time were self-limiting and are now historical. *Rent parties,* to which everybody brought two dollars to help pay the rent, are, like *tin-can shows,* happily no more; *fireside chat* was F. D. R.'s term for his addresses to his radio-oriented society; *New Deal* itself combined the *square deal* of Theodore Roosevelt with the *New Freedom* proclaimed by Wilson; *Brain Trust,* first as *Brains Trust,* was the invention of James M. Kieran, a reporter for the *New York Times,* and was applied originally to F. D. R.'s speechwriters. All the New Deal ingredients, the *National Industrial Recovery Act* (the *Industrial* was eventually dropped), the *Works Progress Administration,* the *Civilian Conservation Corps,* and countless other agencies combined to create what Al Smith called the New Deal *alphabet soup* as they were reduced impatiently to the *NRA,* the *WPA,* the *CCC,* and every other possible alphabetical combination. As the WPA provided work or a facsimile thereof for artists and writers, laborers and teachers, social workers and students, the enduring term *boondoggling*—originally coined by Robert H. Link and applied to the leather braiding done by Boy Scouts—came to describe the innumerable useless and often repetitive tasks performed by recipients of governmental largesse. The jargon of bureaucracy was given a tremendous boost. Administrators *expedited, finalized, implemented, processed* ad infinitum, while social workers, already famed for euphemism, called their investigators *case workers*, dispensed *relief* rather than a *dole*, and spoke of *clients* instead of *applicants* and *underprivileged* instead of the *poor*, thereby dooming already overloaded words to hopeless ambiguity. One does not wonder that *New Dealophobia* entered the vocabulary at the same time.

Radio, reaching its apogee of appeal and influence, continued to contribute the terms now so much a part of our lives, many of them since transferred to TV—*network* and *hookup, station break, mike, commercial, static* (quickly made metaphorical), and—permanent memorial to the sponsors of the daytime tear-jerkers—*soap opera. Sportscasters* (not yet so called) kept up their saturation coverage of the exploits of contemporary idols Bobby Jones, Lou Gehrig, Babe Didrikson, Joe Louis; more and more, the vernacular borrowed expressions from sports—*par for the course, stymie, rhubarb, tee off. Newscasters* and *commentators* (the latter apparently a cut above the former) joined newspaper pundits in disseminating the coinage of the New Deal, the terminology of science, the latest political phrase. Radio diction was, after 1931, carefully "general American." Prior to that year, announcers had preferred—or used under orders—the British pronunciation favored by the American Academy of Arts and Letters and other such groups. Complaints from listeners, however, had prevailed; and the major networks set up schools for instruction in the speech demanded by the public —concrete evidence of the consumer's power.

Economic anxieties were seldom allowed to intrude on the entertainment scene, but more personal ones were fulsomely exploited. In magazine ads and radio commercials, publicists cast madly about for the catchword that would sell the product. *Halitosis* (Latin *halitus*, "breath," plus *-osis*) appeared in 1926; but *athlete's foot, irregularity, tattletale gray, B.O., pink toothbrush, lordosis* (New Latin, from Greek *lordosis, lordos,* "bent backward")—which could be remedied by the right foundation garment—are all products of the anxious thirties. The most vulnerable radio audience was the daytime matron, who heard between the agonies of "Helen Trent" and "Portia Faces Life" the happy voice of the woman who had switched to Fels-Naphtha *soap flakes. Soap flakes* "made" it into Webster's in 1936. The matron's husband, whose desire for a car or for a good smoke was assumed to supersede domestic anxieties, was beguiled between segments of "Fibber McGee and Molly" or World Series games by descriptions of the latest-model automobile or a "great" smoke. Terms like *convertible, power brakes, overdrive, no-draft ventilation,* as they entered the vocabulary, recorded the evolution of the automobile; *streamlining,* a 1934 development that made the classic square radiator obsolete, entered the language to become an indispensable adjunct to advertising for innumerable products, from cameras to cruisers; *freewheeling* lost little time in its conversion to metaphor. The advertisers did not mention one kind of car that many were buying, the *jalopy,* spelled variously as *jallopy, joloppy,* or *jaloopy.* The etymology of the word is obscure; Mencken, presenting eight "horrible examples," declares them all "highly unpersuasive."[3] Newspaper classified ads did mention other terms suggesting that the fancy new automobiles in *desert tan* or *carmine red* or *cigarette cream* were not accessible to everyone; *reconditioned, rebuilt, repossessed,* and *used* were among the euphemisms for the supposedly demeaning *secondhand.* No one thought of Cadillac's current *previously owned.*

In the thirties, no one had yet voiced objection to the use of dialect; if any were offended by the "I'se regusted" of

3. *Supplement II,* pp. 725–6.

Amos and Andy, stars of the most popular radio show of all
time, or by the "Chust listen to me!" in the heavy *echt-
Deutsch* dialect of the Katzenjammer Kids comic strip, the
resentment was unexpressed. The now defunct "Reg'lar
Fellers" comic strip had Puddinhead Duffy and his brother
and all their Irish-surnamed friends saying "yestiddy" and
"foist"; but no Irishman protested. And there was Prissy in
*Gone with the Wind.* Ethnic sensitivity had not yet surfaced.

At the movies, *air-cooled* in summer and wonderfully warm
in those Depression winters (ten cents in the balcony), a
few foreign terms were making subliminal impressions; along
with *It Happened One Night* or *Naughty Marietta* might
appear a newsreel showing *Nazis* and *swastikas* and the
*Fuehrer,* whom most people laughed at for his Chaplinesque
posturings. From radio and newspapers and such magazines
as *Time,* one learned of *concentration camps,* of *Brown
Shirts* and *Black Shirts.* One learned also what was happening
in the Spanish Civil War, which was engaging the energies
of literati and other intellectuals, even their physical parti-
cipation; most people, though, could never get quite straight
the difference between *Loyalists* and *Royalists.* Such terms
as *pinko* and *fascist* were being bandied about; and late in
the thirties, German *-bund,* which had been a respectable
suffix, acquired a pejorative connotation as the FBI began
cracking down on *Bundists.* In Cincinnati and other cities
where Americans of German ancestry predominated, the
people stopped calling their building association the *Bauverein.* But to most, the principal interest of words having to
do with the European situation was their relationship to the
demand for arms and supplies, which was lifting the clouds
of Depression in America.

When the New York World's Fair opened in 1939, with
sixty-three nations participating, prosperity had returned
sufficiently to permit many to travel toward the *World of
Tomorrow,* where GM's *Futurama* and Billy Rose's *Aquacade*
vied for attention with GE's complete *television studio* and
Du Pont's sensational *nylon stockings,* and where one could

sample such foreign delicacies as *sukiyaki, poulet farci en cocotte, borscht,* or the variety of a Swedish *smörgåsbord.* When, in November of 1940, the visitors to the Fair heard Marshal Pétain broadcasting greetings from Vichy, none foresaw that within a few years *The New Yorker* would be suggesting that *crème vichysoisse* be changed to a name with less unpleasant associations or that the lowly herring christened *Bismarck* would almost have its name changed to *Eisenhower.*[4]

No one could keep up with all the new words, anyway, even the lexicographers. Each new invention produced numbers of related and derivative terms; *radio* and *electronics* alone offered infinite possibilities. Music, entertainment, social change, philosophy—all made their contributions to the language either directly or through other tongues. Year after year, thousands of words, many of questionable status, clamored for inclusion in the dictionaries. In increasing numbers, words went abroad. By the time the GI went off to war, after December 7, 1941, innumerable linguistic heralds had preceded him. The dean of them all was *OK.*

No other term in any language has had the universal imprimatur so freely given to it. In use in England in popular songs of the 1880's, understood in other Western countries and in some Asian ones by the early 1900's, appearing in the London *Times* in 1935, becoming a popular substitute for *Salud!* during the Spanish Civil War, made official by the Judicial Committee of the British Privy Council in 1935, and put on the record by Lord Beaverbrook at the Moscow Conference in 1941,[5] it is the most successful Americanism of all time.[6] It can be a noun, a verb, a predicate adjective, an

4. Mencken: *Supplement II,* p. 430.

5. As recounted by him in "The Moscow Conference," *Listener* (London; October 16, 1941), p. 320.

6. *OK* has been exhaustively discussed by etymologists. Allen Walker Read's series of articles in *American Speech* (February 1963–February 1964) discussing its history and folklore is accepted as the definitive statement on it.

interjection, even an adverb. It has been spelled *O.K., okay, okeh* (by Woodrow Wilson), *okey*; it has become *okey-dokey, oky-doke, o-ke* (in Liberia), and *ole kalla* (in Greece, where it found a congener). Lieutenant Colonel W. E. Dyess noted its use by Japanese guards at the prison camp at Davao during World War II; American troops heard it from their Moslem allies in North Africa. One can imagine that it evoked a bittersweet nostalgia in many a GI far from home.

The liking for the short form that popularized *OK*, however, was absent from wartime bureaucracy. Following New Deal precedent, circumlocutory and euphemistic terms abounded. So prevalent were expressions like *directive, finalize, channelize,* and *utilization of factors* that the Honorable Maury Maverick coined the felicitous *gobbledygook* for the whole family of them, ordering the Smaller War Plants Corporation to "stop *pointing up* programs, *finalizing* contracts. . . . No more *patterns, effectuating, dynamics.* Anyone using the words *activation* or *implementation* will be shot."[7] Asked about the source of his coinage, Maverick said it "must have come in a vision" after his attendance at an exceptionally wordy committee meeting. "Perhaps I was thinking," he speculated, "of the old bearded turkey gobbler back in Texas who was always gobbledygobbling and strutting with ludicrous pomposity. At the end of this gobble there was a sort of gook."[8] Many lengthy titles of agencies, civilian and military, however, ended up in the *alphabet soup* with their predecessors, especially if the initials made a pronounceable name, as with *Seabees* (for Construction Battalion) or *Waves* (Women Accepted for Voluntary Emergency Service). But even a Demosthenes could do little with such a name as the Economic Intelligence Division of the Enemy Branch of the Office of Economic Warfare Analysis of the Board of Economic Warfare, which appeared as *EIDEBOE-WABEW.*

7. Please—American-style joke!
8. *New York Times Magazine* (May 21, 1944), p. 11.

Many neologisms were the product of GI slang; *snafu*, the acronym for "situation normal, all fouled up" (the genteel translation), spread through the ranks quickly. *GI* may have stood for *general issue*, the label for all uniforms and equipment; but its etymology has been disputed. *Pin-up girl* appeared first in *Yank*; *jeep* had been in use earlier for a more primitive type of vehicle, and the claims and counterclaims for the invention of the jeep itself are as conflicting as those for the coinage of its name. Many terms associated with World War II were in use in earlier wars but had not had as good a press; *dog tag, KP, pup tent, gook,* and *booby trap* were all inherited. *Walkie-talkie* was obviously a new coinage, as was *bazooka*, named for the horn used by radio comedian Bob Burns. Some GI expressions have been taken to the heart of the civilian vocabulary; *goofing off, snow job,* and *sack time* are happy spin-offs, and *gizmo,* for a mechanical device or part of one without a known name, has made its way into the dictionary in two forms, spelled with either z or s.

The perennial words of pain—*death, casualty, prisoner of war*—remained the same; only the methods of dealing death required new labels. *Robot bombs,* the *V–1* and *V–2* (German *Vergeltungswaffe eins* and *zwei*—"vengeance weapon one" and "two"), raining their terror over London, were the world's introduction to a new and frightening weapon with horrifying potential. The *kamikaze* (Japanese "divine wind": *kami,* "god," plus *kaze,* "wind"), plunging to destruction in suicidal attacks on navy ships in the Pacific, taught Americans a Japanese word they would rather not have learned. *Flame throwers,* name and device, were American—*napalm* came of that time—and so too, ultimately and decisively and awesomely, was *atomic bomb.*

The acceleration of applied technology brought about by the war, the many new scientific concepts, and the refinement and extension of communications had introduced defense workers as well as the military to technical terms. The more forbidding ones were reduced to manageable linguistic proportions—*dichloro-diphenyl-trichloroethane*, for example, to *DDT*—but the impact of postwar discoveries on everyday life made terms like *cortisone* and *detergents, transistor* and *computerization* a part of everyone's speech by the fifties. The names of new professions—*computer programmer, petro-chemist, electronics engineer*—appeared even in help-wanted ads. The mystery to the uninitiated of heard terms like *input, output, components,* and *cybernetics,* combined with popular articles suggesting a cybernated future, created a sense of vague dis-ease similar to that felt when the mysterious *electrical current* had first been captured by science.

Even the presidents of corporations found themselves unable to master the intricacies of plant operation; and technological experts became essential to the *Organization,* as did professional *Management,* now spelled with a capital. Wide dispersal of ownership spelled the death of the monarchial *tycoon*; and as the strength of labor and agriculture, grown strong through the New Deal and the war years, balanced corporate power, observers suddenly discovered that *capitalism* as hitherto defined was a misnomer for the existing American economic system. *This Week* magazine, perhaps inspired by a series of articles in *Fortune* entitled *U.S.A.: The Permanent Revolution,* asked its readers to suggest a substitute term;[9] fifteen thousand readers responded. Unfortunately, the American genius rarely produces dynamic words on order; none of the suggestions, such as *democratic capitalism, economic democracy,* and *industrial democracy,* quite rang the bell, and we still await the definitive term.

The changed nature of the *System* (bête noire of the next decade) and the problems relating to it did give rise to other cerebral phrases that made surprising inroads into the vernacular. Articles in the popular *Reader's Digest*; increased readership of news magazines like *Time* and especially picture-news ones like *Life*; a minimal interspersal of news and commentary sandwiched between entertainment programs

9. March 4, 1951.

on television, just getting into its stride; and headlined news stories that brought attention to matters affecting lives and pocketbooks introduced to the general public terms like *power politics, urban renewal* (prior to and connected with the U.S. Housing Act of 1954), *planned obsolescence,* and even the new mathematical term *googol*.[1] *Bus boycotts* in the South and the decision of the United States Supreme Court in *Brown v. Board of Education* focused attention on the looming desegregation crisis and made *interposition* a Southern catchword.

More and more, the language seemed to be prescribed from above; but paralleling such solemn phrases as *corporate society* and *electronic surveillance* were *rat race* and *bugging. Hot rod* and *drag race* countered the technical terminology of the automobile, now more than ever a *status symbol,* especially among *teen-agers,* who in the prosperous fifties took on new status themselves. Newly discovered by sociologists as a subject of study and by fashion magazines and manufacturers of assorted products as a potentially rich market, adolescents in the mass expected and often had cars of their own, or at least the use of the family's; the car key was both security blanket and virility symbol. *Drag races,* races between cars to see which could accelerate faster from a standstill, took place even on city streets, with sometimes lethal consequences. *Chicken,* popular and equally lethal, was a sport in which youthful drivers competed to see who could longer postpone swerving aside from the edge of a cliff or— head on—from each other. (*Chicken out* as a verb form still lingers.) When not involved with speed—still in the literal sense—teen-agers were busy creating the cult of popular music that would pave the way for the Beatles and The Grateful Dead. Significant terms were *rock 'n' roll,* new at mid-decade, and the combination *country-and-western;* both suggest the direction in which the devotees were to move. The jargon of jazz and swing, which had reached its peak

1. The number 10 raised to the power 100 ($10^{100}$). It was coined by Edward Kasner, an American mathematician.

in Harlem in the forties, continued to thrust its esoteric expressions into the light of day; and some gained new shadings of meaning thereby. *In the groove, cat,* used on the campus as counterpoise to *frat, icky, creep* were commonly used; *hip* through some alchemy became *hep,* only to revert later. Such words, the "coinage of the teen-agers and the jive and hepcat," were labeled *exuberant words* by Max Lerner in his two-volume *America as a Civilization*[2] and equated with *functional* and *synthetic* words as one of the three great sources of vocabulary enrichment.

One counterword of the next decade, *alienation,* had no place in the youthful lexicon. The young were not yet questioning the values of an *affluent society* in which—if their fathers were *organization men* (the Babbitts of the fifties)— they lived in a *ranch-type* house or a *hi-lo* in *suburbia* and played *rock 'n' roll* records, probably the new *long-playing* ones, on the *hi-fi (high fidelity)* in the *rumpus room* or danced on the *patio,* which might be a few flagstones at the back door and hardly recognizable to the Spaniards who had generously contributed the name. Their younger siblings, the first generation born into the *television age,* watched the cartoons on Saturday morning, and at school during the week were subjected to the *audiovisual aids* that were the new passion of the educators and the means of a coming de-emphasis on verbalization in communication.

Their parents were concerned with the political issue of *McCarthyism.* Senator Joseph McCarthy, instigator of what some called *witch hunts* and others considered crusades designed to root out Communist infiltration in government and in academic circles, gave his name to his time of tenure. The *McCarthy era,* during which there developed a divisive bitterness and controversy that has not yet disappeared, promises to be as enduring a term historically as *New Deal* or *Reconstruction.* The domestic confrontation was but one phase of the *Cold War,* that rivalry between the Soviet and American

2. (New York: Simon & Schuster; 1957), vol. 2, p. 810.

blocs which sent chill warnings of its coming almost immediately after World War II. The Korean War was its major overt manifestation. Never called a *war,* but euphemistically a *police action* or *emergency,* the operation was baffling and frustrating to the American people; that it had little actual impact on everyday life in America, however, is indicated by the paucity of words coming out of it. *Brainwashing* was the most enduring—and most significant.

*Brainwashing* appears to have the mark of the American genius upon it. Vividly metaphorical, creating a new semantic unit from simple, familiar elements, it belongs in the tradition of *streamline* and *logrolling* and *sidetrack.* And yet it is a direct translation from Mandarin Chinese *hsi nao* (*hsi,* "to wash," plus *nao,* "brain"). The reality it expressed, made painfully visible by the increasingly powerful medium of *TV* (as it was now called), was so unacceptable, so contradictory to the held belief in the integrity of man's mind and the strength of American patriotism, that the spectacle of American prisoners of war violating military codes and even choosing exile infected the people with a national malaise. Already, terms like *hydrogen bomb, radiation sickness, fallout shelter* had created an unprecedented feeling of fatalism, especially among youth; now a new and frighteningly intangible force was abroad. And then, in the chilly atmosphere of the *Cold War,* a new word flashed across the horizon on its way to the moon—*sputnik.* Its echoes reverberated over the land.

The name itself struck some Americans as oddly flippant for so awesome an object. Yiddish *nudnik,* slang for a bothersome person or pest, was familiar to many; *-nik,* like many other Yiddish elements, had become a jocular adjunct in such expressions as *no-good-nik* or *hold-up-nik. Beatnik* (*beat* plus [*nud*]*nik*), was just becoming popular for the new-style Bohemians of the postwar *Beat Generation* (who played the part but lacked the talent of the *Lost Generation* of the twenties). A moon rocket called *sputnik?* The name did not seem to fit. But to some, it was a striking illustration of the historical thread winding intricately through language. *Sputnik,* literally "fellow traveler" (of earth), not only held within it the agent suffix *-nik,* which had traveled from Poland to America a century earlier in *nudnik* (Polish *nudny*); but the elements of *sput-* itself were the prefix *s[o],* congener of the Greek root *syn,* from which comes our *syn-* (as in *synonymous*), and *put',* for path or way, descendant like Old English *pæth* of the Indo-European root *\*pent-,* "to tread" or "go." The alien word, so seemingly strange, illustrates how inescapably present in the language is a common cultural past.

# XII. A Legacy of Words

A *trip* in the sixties could have been to the moon—or to a *mind-blowing high*. Old words were acquiring new meanings, new words multiplying beyond the counting in every area of American life. By the end of the decade, they reflected a multi-faceted scene wherein ". . . rapid accumulation of knowledge [was] dividing history, even current history—as it [had] already divided science—into a thousand specialties."[1] Not only did scientist communicate with scientist in esoteric terms like *nucleosynthesis* and *technetronic* and *selenodesy* and *pulsar* and *gigahertz* to express concepts once undreamed of; members of other groups and social enclaves also were creating specialized vocabularies going far beyond the traditional boundaries of trade argot or slang.

From the *counterculture*, that vaguely defined mélange of *drug scene* and *rock*, of *psychedelia* and *hippiedom* (spiritual realm of the *flower children*, who had trailed the beatniks into Haight-Ashbury), came words and phrases like *acid* and *crash pad* and *be-in* and *flower power*, with Hindi *guru* and *karma*, new in popular awareness, providing exotic color. From city streets and college campuses came terms like *honky* and *rip-off*, *Mace* and *trashing* and *Black Power* to tell of violent *confrontation*, while the urban panorama itself produced *megalopolis* and *low-rise*, *slumism*, *roofscaping*, *ghet-*

1. William Benton, in the introduction to *Britannica Book of the Year* (1972), p. 3.

*tologist,* and *urban blight.* The long, dreary war in Vietnam, with its domestic repercussions, gave new meaning to *escalation* and *overkill* and introduced, among other terms, *punji stake* and *people sniffer, draft-card burner, peacenik, fragging,* and the vividly metaphoric *telephone pole,* for the SAM missile. Economists talked of *econometrics* and industrialists of *conglomerates,* educators of *educational alternatives* and *interfaces* and home builders of *cluster planning* and *utility cores.*

So distinctive were the jargons that observers coined new labels for some of them: *criticalese,* for the style and language of professional critics; *missilese,* for that of the guided-missile experts; *transatlantese,* for the mixed British and American idiom used by those whose business and cultural ties dislodged them from their local bases; *mediaese* or *mid-Atlantic* for the preferred speech of the public-information and entertainment media; even *childrenese,* a special vocabulary recommended to parents for communicating with their children "tactfully and authoritatively."[2] The more lightsome educators labeled their own jargon *pedageese.* One wondered if there was an American language still, or if—the personality of its genius shattered—it reflected only blurred afterimages of the habit of mind that had created a national idiom.

If we judge only by the *content* of contemporary coinage, it becomes clear that the American people are not of one mind—but a habit of mind is a different thing. The language gives striking evidence that all of us, however divided by *life style* (that contemporary term) or interests, share a linguistic approach that is in itself a psychic bond. At all cultural levels, and available to the newest immigrant, we hold in trust the legacy of that English speech whose "riches, good sense, and terse convenience" were noted by Jacob Grimm a hundred years ago and whose "clarity, directness and force" make it—according to Otto Jespersen (male chauvinist!)— "positively and expressively masculine." It has lost in our possession none of the flexibility that allowed Dr. C. K. Ogden, in composing his vocabulary of *basic English* in the

2. *Britannica Book of the Year* (1969), "Words and Meanings, New."

1930's, to include only fifteen "primary" verbs, which by combination with simple operational words could be made to serve practically any verbal need. In the tradition of that flexibility, we continue to create our own verb phrases—*lay off, cop out, pay off, sit in*—and then extend their usefulness by converting them to substantives. We utilize, too, all those other devices for word-making—semantic change and invention and borrowing and adding and clipping and conversion of parts of speech—that have been characteristic of the English language throughout its history. And we make full use, changing and modifying and augmenting, of those "marvellous" English monosyllables whose "fidelity," according to the Spanish critic Salvador de Madariaga, "is so perfect that one is tempted to think English words are the right and proper names which acts are meant to have . . . *splash, smash, ooze, shriek . . . sweet* a kiss in itself."[3]

All of these qualities—the flexibility, the force, the convenience, and of course the words—are familial possessions; we share them with parent British English and with our linguistic siblings of Australia and Canada and all those other areas where the English stream has cut new channels. But it is the uniquely American qualities that interest us. Do we have still the distinctive and unifying marks of our own idiom, the "restless inventiveness," the "fancy for the terse, the vivid . . . the bold and imaginative," long noted as characteristically American? Or has uniqueness been lost in the homogenizing climate of the mass media, in the linguistic interchange inevitable in today's *multinational economy*, in the exchange of films and fashion, in the adoption of speechways and words from exchange students and foreign diplomats and English novels and from contacts in travel around the world, in—most particularly—the de-emphasis on national identity, at least for ourselves? Do we coin words with the same careless ingenuity, find congenial the kinds of words we

3. *Englishmen, Frenchmen, Spaniards* (London, 1928). Quoted in H. L. Mencken: *The American Language,* 4th ed. (New York: Alfred A. Knopf; 1936), p. 602.

did before, show the tendencies in our word-making that reflect a still-homogeneous habit of mind? The evidence of our vocabulary suggests that we do.

First of all, we continue to combine madly. All Germanic languages, along with some others, are compounding languages; German itself constructs some awesome chains of linked words—Pei cites *Kriegsgefangenanentschädigungsgesetz*, "law for the compensation of war prisoners," as an example.[4] But the American enthusiasm for throwing together helter-skelter whatever words express a meaning most effectively, from the early *sourwood* and *butternut* and *backlog* and *selectman* and *salt lick* to contemporary *folk rock* and *splashdown* and *think tank*, an enthusiasm that Mark Twain called the American "compounding disease," has lost none of its force.

It comes naturally to us still to form combinations of words and elements expressing what has not been expressed before, to make of unrelated words a single semantic unit that may or may not be eventually hyphenated and later joined. (*Life style* is currently separated in Webster's, hyphenated in *Time*, joined in the *Saturday Review*; in whichever form, it is obviously a new creation that is more than the sum of its parts.) So with other recent coinage: *flower child, jetliner* (sometimes joined, sometimes not), *pantyhose, speed freak, table hopper* —all are synergistic combinations that express completely new concepts. The raw materials of coinage may be very old; the components of *no-knock, workfare, water bed, wayout* (from which has come *wayoutitude*), for example, belonged to the Canterbury Pilgrims no less than to ourselves. All the materials may be—but rarely are—new, as in *teenybopper* or *creepybopper*. Often they are a hybrid of new and old, as in *funk art*. They are made up of all parts of speech, can become any part of speech, and often develop their own derivatives: *skydive* is both noun and verb and has produced *skydiver* and *skydiving*; from *tripsit*, to sit with someone on

4. *The Story of Language*, 2nd ed. (Philadelphia and New York: J. B. Lippincott Company; 1965), p. 162.

an LSD trip, have come *tripsitter* and *tripsitting. Swing-by, rip-off, hang-up, phase-out,* and other substantives were originally verb phrases and, uncompounded, still are. *Piggyback,* both adjective and adverb, a metaphor for trailer-on-train transportation, has inspired the analogical *birdieback,* which means air-freighted. Some components of combinations may be words already processed, as in the double contractions *radic-lib* and *sculpfest.* The possibilities are endless, and advertisers seem to find the coinage of compound adjectives irresistible; one suspects that appliance salesmen would be speechless without *solid-state, two-level, slide-out, no-frost, fine-tuning, quick-on,* and *built-in.*

Derivative coinage using prefixes and suffixes remains fantastically active. *Micro-,* old in English, was revitalized with the development of *microelectronics;* now we have *micro-engineering, microcircuitry, microbook, micrometeorite, microencapsulate,* and similar terms. *Micro* unadorned is a trade name for a small calculator. *Mini-,* more the layman's term, became enormously popular after the introduction of the *miniskirt* from Carnaby Street; *mini-mini* and *micro-mini* left their legacy of *mini-* consciousness in the vernacular as the styles they named left their legacy of permissiveness in fashion. Today the vocabulary runs the gamut from *miniburger* to *minination,* with *minibus, minicomputer, minibike,* and countless other *mini-*prefaced terms in between. *Multi-* continues vigorously. *Multinationals* are corporations with branches in many countries (*macroeconomics,* as opposed to *microeconomics,* is much concerned with them); and the *multipurpose minicomputer* is fast becoming a standard fixture on the small-business scene. *Mega-,* best known in common speech in the fun-associated *megaphone,* entered after Hiroshima into an unholy alliance with *ton* to form *megaton,* for use in estimating the destructive power of atomic bombs. It has since become part of other frightening combinations: *megacorpse,* for a body count of one million, was adopted in the late fifties for calculating probable casualties in a postulated nuclear war; *megadeath* joined it.

In refreshing contrast, the increase in terms incorporating *bio-* and *eco-* reveals the dominance in contemporary thought of environmental and biological concerns; however, most of them are international in usage and not identifiably American. *Ecology*, from German *Ökologie*, (from Greek *oikos*, "house"), has largely displaced the earlier French-derived *bionomics*; in a game of etymological musical chairs, the United States Air Force in 1960 adopted the name *bionics*, which had once belonged to histology, for the application of biological principles to the study and design of engineering (especially electronic) systems. *Ecosystem* and *ecomanagement* emerged from the activities of the European Conservation Year of 1970; but *ecofreak*, for an ecology zealot, *had* to come, and does, from America. The space program has contributed a great number of *bio-*prefixed terms, many of them, like *bioacoustics, bioinstrument, bioastronautics, biosensor,* and *biosatellite,* telling of exciting new scientific developments. The impressive-sounding *biomorphic,* however, refers to contemporary "body-fitting" furniture.

Other affixes, *para-* and *-ac* and *tele-* and *-ology* and *-ist* and *-ee* and *-cide,* continue their role in the language, two or more of them often serving the same root. *Suicidology* is a recently initiated study, while *ecocide, biocide, urbicide,* and *urbicidal* come of our concern with environment. *Magnicide* italicizes recent political history; it means the murder of a prominent leader or ruler. (*Scubacide,* though, does not mean a slaughter of scubas.) The old and honorable prefix *eu-,* which had been entering into few combinations of late, has now contributed to *euphenics,* meaning the biological improvement of human beings after birth, and rounds out a triad with *euthenics* and *eugenics. Telelecture, telediagnosis,* and *telefacsimile* reflect new advances in communication; the prefix is one that will inevitably remain active in today's *global village.* To the dismay of purists, *-wise* retains its popularity; *stylewise, fashionwise, ecologywise,* even *comparisonwise* occur not only in the vernacular but in relatively learned prose. A new linguistic element, *cyber-.* entered the language in 1948, when

Norbert Wiener sought expression for a revolutionary scientific advance, the control of electronic, mechanical, and biological systems by means of informational analysis and guidance. Coming from Greek *kubernētēs*, "pilot" or "governor" (from *kubernan*, to "steer," "guide," "govern"), *cybernetics* has given rise to *cybernate, cybernetic, cyberneticist,* and *cybernation* (control by computer). The potent combination of two revolutionary concepts, bionics and cybernation, is expressed in *cyborg,* that science-fictional-sounding "cybernetic organism," which means man plus machine or other artificial agent to produce an organism or system superior to either.

All of us continue to give new meanings to old words in the cavalier fashion noted by Alexis de Tocqueville, as early as 1835, as the "most common" device of vocabulary building "among democratic peoples." Blithely we change parts of speech, calling nouns into service as verbs, adjectives as nouns. *Jawboning,* used first to describe President John F. Kennedy's tough approach to national business and labor leaders in an appeal for price and wage restraints, made an action word of an ancient substantive. *To trash,* used formerly only in the restricted sense of lopping off the outer leaves of sugar cane, seems far more descriptive today than does its predecessor, *to vandalize. To moonlight,* for working at two jobs in shifts, is a brilliant and vivid invention. Much of the semantic change entering the vocabulary occurs first in slang; if, as with *mugging,* the new usage fills a contemporary need, it becomes respectable and enters the dictionaries. *Grass, acid* (with all its derivatives, *acid head, acid high, acid rock,* and so on), *hit, bag,* and *speed* are all drug-related terms; some will endure. *Cool, dig, trash* (as a verb), *straight* (meaning not hip), *rumble* come from the street. The once lovely *gay* has been kidnaped by homosexuals. *Camp* (noun and adjective) is gaining stature, along with *campy;* both refer to the banal or artificial appreciated for its humor.

But not all changed meanings have lowly origins; from such lofty sources as the space program come kindred terms.

*Go* has become an adjective: *all systems are go* means clear sailing—or rocketing—ahead; similarly, *no-go* is a predicate adjective or noun. *Scrub, burn, launch* have new meanings relating to space travel; and *booster* has traveled a long way from George Babbitt's Rotary Club meetings. The space and computer industries together have produced *hardware,* which means the actual physical equipment for a flight or for a computing process, while *firmware* fills a gap for computer technicians, who needed a name for "software designed as an integral part of hardware." A venerable word that has served many masters over the centuries, *sophisticated*—which meant, in the first stages of its journey from Greece, simply "deprived of primitive simplicity, falsified, not straightforward"—acquired favorable connotations during the jazz age, when the quality, or at least the appearance, of blasé worldly wisdom was valued. Technology has now taken the term to mean intricate or complicated and applies it to weaponry and other mechanical systems. Most *donnant à penser,* perhaps, is the extension of the verb *to program;* from the meaning of providing a computer with instructions for solving a problem, it has come to be used speculatively for the genetic and psychological conditioning of humans. The thought of a *programmed cyborg* gives one pause.

If, as Jespersen says, the essence of language is activity, ours is in no danger of atrophy; never have we been busier at wordmaking. Not only do untraceable inventions like *kook* (possibly from *cuckoo*) and *grok* (to enjoy what is happening) emerge in the vulgate and even in the rarefied atmosphere of science (*glitch,* for example, has to do with the varying periodicity of pulsars); more traceable ones proliferate also. Youth, as always, has its own language, and some of that language enters the general vocabulary, at least for a time. *Vibes,* a term popular among the young on both sides of the Atlantic, refers to those mystical vibrations stirred by rock music; the term carries over, with attributive *good* or *bad,* to the feelings aroused in any given situation. *Grubs* are ragged, short-cut blue jeans, obviously from *grubby. Weirdo,* which developed from the earlier *weirdie,* was heard for a while even among adults; but, according to Ellen Peck's widely read column, it has been replaced among hip teen-agers by *wacko* (which, Ms. Peck assured an anxious seeker after the bon mot, means someone not quite as weird as a *weirdo* and may even have a faintly complimentary aura). Youthful invention would be more abundant were not the present generation so hung up on once-taboo obscenities and scatologies. As all-purpose expressions, they leave few gaps for inventiveness to fill.

From other areas come other words: *fragging,* from the military, for the tossing of a fragmentation bomb at a disliked military officer, and *grunt,* for the slogging foot soldier, which together epitomize much of the history of the war in Vietnam; *the blahs,* inspired coinage from a television commercial; *fen,* invented by science-fiction *(sci-fi)* fans as a plural for themselves. Abbreviations, many formed by acronyms, remain popular. The familiar *scuba* comes from *se*lf-contained *u*nder*w*ater *b*reathing *a*pparatus; *laser* stands for *l*ight *a*mplification by *s*timulated *e*mission of *r*adiation; *ZIP,* for the Post Office's *z*one *i*mprovement *p*rogram, has the advantage of semantic appropriateness. *Comsat* signifies *Com*munications *Sat*ellite; *mascon,* discovered by orbiting spacecraft late in 1960, are *mas*sive *con*centrations of rock embedded beneath the moon's circular maria; and *COBOL,* for *co*mmon *b*usiness *o*riented *l*anguage, like *FORTRAN,* for *for*mula *tran*slation, describes a specific computer language. Closely allied to abbreviation in general are such synecdochic expressions as *The Pill,* which everyone knows means birth-control pill *(fertility pill* must be expressed in full); *hard-hat,* for a blue-collar man with, it is implied, programmed social attitudes; *a Fulbright,* for the scholarship; and *white tie,* for formal attire (an expression pertinent only in square circles).

Blends, or portmanteau words, show linguistic sophistication and at their best achieve the quality of inevitability. *Snowmobile, sexplosion, sexploitation, astrowives, glasphalt* all seem to come naturally; so do *electrodelic, communiversity, leotites, sociopath,* and *datamation* (referring to all forms of data processing). Whoever contributed the ill-fated *demogrant* to the McGovern presidential campaign of '72 was no doubt acclaimed, at first. Analogy plays an important role in the development of blends. *Surfari, seafari,* and *snowfari* owe their being to the earlier *safari; moontel, skytel,* and *floatel* copy *motel; carbecue,* a large oven for melting away the unsalvageable materials of an automobile while it is turned on a spit, shows not only analogy but vivid metaphor.

As counterpoint to the vivid coinages—and notable for nondistinction—we have vogue words or counterwords. "There is an inverse ratio," writes Joshua Whatmough, in discussing "Semantics in Linguistics," "between frequence of usage and affectivity";[5] words too can become clichés. No word in our contemporary vocabulary has become more meaningless than *meaningful,* none more irrelevant than *relevant* (which usually stands alone, unoriented). Particularly cherished by college students, the two join *alienation* as grist for *dialogue,* a term that lends great dignity to any discussion. Sometimes *dialogue* becomes *confrontation,* a word that in its turn is extended by the media to signify anything from a face-to-face encounter on "Meet the Press" to a bloody street riot. The predicative phrase *all about* has been for some years pervasive and inescapable; statements like "this is what politics (or education, or life, or love, or fame, or work, or whatever) is all about" do away with such old-fashioned expressions as "politics is concerned with . . ." or "the main purpose of education is . . ." Even such writers of conservative prose as political reporter Theodore White, with "but this, after all, was what campaigns were all about,"[6] and columnist James Kilpatrick, with "that was what *Engel* v. *Vitale* was all about,"[7] have spread the *all about* gospel, as has Senator Ted Kennedy, with his statement that ice-skating with Bedford-

5. *Encyclopaedia Britannica.*

6. *Britannica Book of the Year* (1972), "The End of the Postwar World," p. 21.

7. *New Orleans Times-Picayune* (December 15, 1972).

Stuyvesant children at Rockefeller Center is "what Christmas is all about."[8] Almost—but not quite!—in the same counter-word class is the phrase *credibility gap,* which, since its overexposure during the Johnson administration, has been stretched to mean anything from lack of faith to a poor media image. Fortunately, counterwords and counterphrases collapse eventually of the weight put upon them.

If any one aspect of language reveals a culture, it is that of imagery. From the time of primitive man, when language and myth were so closely intertwined that abstractions like justice and peace and war were personalized, leaving as testimony in the language the genders of the nouns, the words of a people have been enduring artifacts of its philosophy. Only in a time-conscious, Westernized society could the contemporary phrase *biological clock* be coined—*seasonal rhythms* or *laws* might have been the choice in an earlier day or in a less clock-driven society. Only after electricity was captured could getting a *charge* out of something have meaning. In colonial days, when nature was all around and the sea close by or remembered, imagery evoked the familiar, as it does today; and *spread-eagle, mosquito hawk, prairie schooner, stumped, to crawfish, to backwater, to follow a bee-line* related directly to experience. Much of this early imagery is still part of our speech, inherited; but for few of us is the original inspiration—the eagle, the hawk, the schooner, the beeline—part of our experience; metaphors we originate reflect a different milieu.

The *nuclear family, chain reaction, in orbit*—all come of a mental atmosphere never before present in the world; *inner space,* for the deep, unknown recesses of the mind, is counter-point to *outer space* as we today conceive it, mysterious but there to be explored. The counterculture's *plastic* to describe as artificial and false our contemporary society (the term changed, in an interesting semantic development, from its original sense of pliable and easily molded, which refer to the

8. *New Orleans Times-Picayune* (December 23, 1972).

raw materials, to that of hard, rigid, and imitation, which refer to the product) shows that even those who protest against a society are culturally captive to it. Emphasis on sensation, a notable aspect of our milieu (cf. McLuhan's *total sensorium* concept), appears in the ubiquitous drug metaphors *speed* and *downers* and *uppers;* and *uptight* and *hanging loose* strike responsive chords in all of us. *Crunch,* for a showdown point, financial or otherwise (*energy crunch* was new in 1973), has not only tactile but auditory associations and belongs with the ever-growing family of auditory metaphors. With sophisticated sound systems capturing the fancy and the financial resources of a generation expert on *rockomastics* (the study of the names of rock 'n' roll performers), and with all Americans becoming familiar with such impressive terms as *quadraphonic sound systems* and *discrete disc demodulators,* metaphorical expressions like *tune in* and *turn on* become singularly appropriate. The imitative *blip* refers to the erasure of sound from tape; *beep,* used already as verb and noun for an electronic signal (*beep-beep* is for roadrunners), has been used to form the derivative *beeper,* for an individual who flies a pilotless aircraft by remote control; even such neologisms as *woofer* and *tweeter* (electronic devices on sound systems to bring out low notes and high) emphasize the audiovisual character of our world and the electronic domination of our lives. One begins to listen to the doomsayers who predict the demise of the written and even the spoken word.

More traditional is the metaphorical coinage of automobile manufacturers, of owners of sports franchises, even of militant organizations, all of whom know the magic of a name and the power over the public mind of semantic association. In a television age, however, the seen is the remembered. *Cougar* and *Wildcat, Viking* and *Saint* carry contemporary associations; it would be a rare American child indeed who would not define a *mustang* as a car. From space travel, the great adventure of our age, we should expect new words of poetry; but perhaps because so many of the literal expressions relating to it would not long ago have been pure imagery—*moon walk* and *spaceship, space walk, moon buggy, skylab*—the vocabulary of space turns to mundane experience for speech figures. *Scrubbing* a flight means canceling it; a *burn* is one firing of a rocket; *umbilical cord* is the lifeline between spaceship and space-walking astronaut. *Barbecuing,* for the rolling of a spacecraft about its long axis in relation to the sun's heat, comes straight from suburbia; and the *Donald Duck effect,* for the voice change taking place in space, reminds us that our astronauts were brought up on Disney cartoons and comic books. The *Gulliver,* an instrument for reporting on microbial life, commendably weds science and the humanities.

So internationalized has our language become that foreign borrowings merge into the vernacular almost unnoticed. Accustomed as we are to Italian and French and German and other terms for food and fashion, sports and political concepts, more and more used to seeing advertising that incorporates foreign words, learning at least simple expressions from travel to far places or from reading about them, we accept with ease such terms as *karate* and *shish kebab, machismo* and *détente.* American *aficionados* watch the bulls in Barcelona, American *schussers* ski at Kitzbühel and Mont Tremblant, American *hippies* (the word has traveled with them) clutter the streets of Amsterdam; *multinational* corporations set up foreign-language schools for their employees; one even hears it whispered that Russian and German expressions have infiltrated the CIA, with *dubok,* Russian for oak tree, in use for a secret "drop," and *treff,* from German *treffen,* for a clandestine meeting place.[9] *Comsat* and *Telstar* not only carry Americanisms to foreign lands but their expressions to us; and as we hear and watch Alistair Cooke narrating the story of America for the BBC in cultured *mediaese* and as *posh* schools appoint *headmasters* and *headmistresses* who take a *dim view* of certain things, even British speech and American draw closer together.

9. H. L. Mencken: *The American Language,* ed. Raven J. McDavid, Jr. (New York: Alfred A. Knopf; 1963), p. 729.

No longer do great waves of immigration, however, bring new accents to our shores; major influences upon our language come from speech groups already here. The prominence of Jewish actors, writers, and other professionals, especially in the communications media; the phenomenon of the *Jewish novel*; and the popularity of plays and television programs like *Fiddler on the Roof* and "Bridget Loves Bernie" contribute to the continuing Yiddish influence on the language, especially on speechways. Turns of phrase once familiar only in the New York area or in trade and literary circles become widespread—expressions like *he should live so long; so I'll pay for it; he's complaining yet.* Words like *schlimazel* and *schlock* and *shtick,* while not commonly used, are recognized even in Peoria. For a period in the sixties, rhyming pairs with the *sch-* plus consonant prefix were popular, as in "Oedipus Schmoedipus, so long as he loves his mother," leading some linguists to postulate the admittance to American English of *sch-* plus consonant as a new pejorative prefix;[1] a recent and interesting coinage, however, *schnorrologist,* for a successful fund raiser for an educational institution, belies the "pejorative" label (depending upon one's attitude toward fund raisers). A derivative of Yiddish *schnorrer,* meaning beggar or one who takes advantage of the generosity of friends, its source is the earlier *schnorren,* which means to beg while playing a pipe or harp and which came from Middle High German *snurren,* "to hum" or "to whir." So do words tell tales! The suffix *-nik,* so popular since *sputnik,* continues to be reinforced by Yiddish influence. *Computernik, spacenik,* and *spudnik* (a potato in space) are among recent additions to the family, while *sicknik* means one mentally ill, and *Mitnik,* according to the *Encyclopaedia Britannica* of 1970, is a "transformational linguist trained at the Massachusetts Institute of Technology."

The black American's part in shaping the language is

1. Pei: *Story of Language,* p. 178; and Mencken-McDavid: *American Language,* pp. 262–3.

greater than ever, and comes from several directions. Adapting to his particular needs the old Anglo-Saxon words—which are his by adoption as they are those of all Americans, of whatever descent—he has given to many of them a new eloquence. *Soul,* which has no true equivalent in any African language, was ready at hand to become for a basically spiritual people the expression of personal identity, of a concept defined by Claude Brown as "bein' true to yourself. . . . [It is the] uninhibited self-expression that goes into every Negro endeavor."[2] Vividly evocative, *soul* has entered standard speech, despite the contention of some Negroes that the term is not fully understood by whites. As an attribute, it gives a special character to *brother, sister, music, session,* even *food.*

Greater likelihood of misunderstanding arises from the semantic development of *black,* another ancient Germanic word (*\*blakaz*), once used substantively only in the sense of color. Now preferred by many Negroes as an identifying term for themselves, it has come also to mean Negritude, or blackness in reference to Negroes, as in "Black is beautiful." Because the change is not spontaneous but imposed, principally by the news media, and because not only regional but also class usage differs (*colored* has long been preferred to *Negro* or *black* by both Negro and white in the South, as it has by the NAACP), the term has not gained easy acceptance; to many it is insulting. Nevertheless, persistent use of it by the media and its promotion by some militant groups seem to insure its permanence; attributively, in *Black Power, black history, black culture, black theater, black consciousness,* and similar phrases, it has already displaced the earlier *Negro.* An expression also originating in the Negro community and received with ultimate enthusiasm in the vernacular, despite some resistance to it during the protest movements of the sixties, is *right on,* an interjection of approval and encouragement that can be heard in quite unlikely places.

A few African words, like *dashiki,* or *daishiki,* are entering

2. Quoted in *American Heritage Dictionary.*

general awareness; and some individuals active in separatist movements have adopted African names. Various black organizations, too, have introduced African terms along with cultural innovations like the *Kwanza* (Swahili for "first fruits") Festival in Harlem; but the average *Afro-American* is no more comfortable with his ancestral tongue, which is rarely Swahili to begin with, than the average descendant of Dutch or Welsh or Russian immigrants is with his, and the likelihood of extensive African borrowing at the present time is remote. Some linguists are discovering evidence of West African origins in a number of already existing Americanisms, however. The slang term *cat*, for a person or man, as well as *hip* (hence *hippie*) and *hepcat*, may have come from Wolof *hipicat*, "man who is aware or has his eyes open."

That such expressions originated in the entertainment subculture seems undeniable, and the emergence of others from the same milieu is likely. In a review of Sam Shepard's *The Tooth of Crime*, critic T. E. Kalem talks of the "crossover culture . . . the place and time where private black lingo, black clothing fashions, black drugs and violence and black music become part of some whites' life-styles." "Everyone attending the play," Kalem cautions, "should be provided with a text before they enter the playhouse."[3] However questionable his premise sociologically (Should lingo and violence and clothing fashions be equated? Are drugs black?), and however dismaying his caveat grammatically, the linguistic implications are clear. Just as *jazz* and *juke* crossed into the standard vocabulary at the interface between social and cultural levels, so is much of the black "private" vocabulary entering the vernacular—and black customs the mental atmosphere. The verbal-musical encounter scene in *Tooth*, in which words and music are weapons, represents both the quasi-ritualized game of verbal insult called *jonin'*, *sounding*, or *the dozens* among young blacks and the game of *cuttin'*, a jazz term for defeating in a musical contest. The words must follow.

3. *Time* (November 11, 1972), p. 73.

More significant to the future of American English than any isolated borrowings is the increasingly vocal demand—and not only from the black English apostolate—for linguistic pluralism in our schools. In New York, the Puerto Ricans demand that classes be taught in Spanish; in New Mexico, the *Chicanos*[4] demand the same. The chairman of the Polish-American Historical Association states that his people want to preserve their own language.[5] Chinese parents fight for the right to continue having their children taught in Chinese. In support of all of them, some linguists advocate bilingualism, trilingualism, or no-special-lingualism; and historical debunkers attack the "myth" that compulsory use of English in American schools has brought about national unity. Americans who have long taken for granted the rightness and the value of one national language see the specter of linguistic separation creating bitterness and even bloodshed, as it has in other lands, and wonder if we are quite sane.

So under attack is traditional education itself, and so controversial the alternatives proposed for it, that to isolate and treat the linguistic problem is not easy. Efforts are being made, nevertheless, by thoughtful educators who recognize the problems of the linguistically different but recognize, too, the greater problems that linguistic fragmentation would create. Among the many experiments tried has been the teaching of English as a second language or a second "dialect" (*ESD*) in the public schools of Detroit and Los Angeles, at Hunter College in New York, and elsewhere. Nonverbal educational testing that does not put the non-English-speaking child at a disadvantage has been introduced in many places. In New Orleans, where nearly one hundred thousand Latin Ameri-

4. *Chicano,* from *chico,* "fellow" or "chap," promises to become a label for all Spanish-speaking Americans, as *Dutch* did for all German-speaking ones. The older *hispanos* of New Mexico, like most of the refugee Cubans, strongly oppose the name.

5. The Reverend M. J. Madaj, of Chicago, who believes that Polish-Americans have not been sufficiently vocal in the past. *New Orleans Times-Picayune* (December 29, 1972).

cans, including many Cuban refugees, have settled, the "pairing" of Spanish-speaking with English-speaking children, in which each learns the language of the other, has brought "exciting" and "phenomenal" results.[6] For the specific problems of black children, men like William A. Stewart have urged an acceptance and understanding by teachers of their speechways and a "working around" them; and the Educational Study Center has introduced experimental textbooks written in parallel black English and standard English versions, basing the project on the principle (as yet unproved) of transference.

No one of the programs is a panacea, none the ultimate solution; but together they are an acknowledgment—and a promise. They are an acknowledgment that American English, like our rivers and our streams, is a national treasure owned by no one group, earned by no right of prior place, accessible to all. The promise is that it shall so continue, undiverted, undiminished. Rich with the accumulation of many centuries and contributions from many tongues, holding within each single word some essence of our history, it will gather into itself the coinage of our times, minted by all of us whatever our ancestral past, and carry it as our legacy to the children of America's tomorrow.

6. Thought-provoking were some parental comments—reported by Chuck Lob in the *New Orleans States-Item* (December 28, 1972)— which suggested that the program existed more for the benefit of parents who feared a generation gap and a culture loss than for the benefit of the children. "After three years," Alberto Fowler, director of international relations for the city's Human Relations Committee, has said, "any Latin child is fluent in English." His own son, who was three when he came to the United States, refused to speak Spanish after only three months of studying English in the public schools.

# Suggested Readings

◄▨▨▨▨►

Any suggestions for reading about American English must begin with the classic *The American Language* of H. L. Mencken, 4th edition (New York: Alfred A. Knopf; 1936). There are other studies, many more recent, some more scholarly, others more detailed; no other has its style. Provocative, wide-ranging, and rich in philological and human interest, the book is a celebration of the genius of the language in America—and the index is superb. *Supplements I* and *II,* published in 1945 and 1948 respectively (also by Knopf), reflect the sharp increase in professional literature about American English after 1936 and present an enormous amount of etymological information and speculation as well as observations on regional differences. Valuable as they are, however, the later works lack something of the élan of their predecessor; the author's scrupulous consideration of every etymological possibility proposed by earnest contributors makes sometimes for tediousness. An abridgment of the three volumes by Raven McDavid (New York: Knopf; 1963) is a well-arranged and useful book, adding information not available at the time of the earlier publications. It is, of course not Mencken.

An early work cited by Mencken as furthering his interest in the language is M. Schele De Vere's *Americanisms: The English of the New World* (New York: Charles Scribner & Company; 1872). Never again reprinted (it had been pub-

lished first in 1871), the book remains one of the most engaging and valuable studies of the early American vocabulary.
Little scientific investigation of the language had been made
at the time it was written and some of its etymologies have
been amended; but it offers a wealth of information about
loan words, archaisms, and neologisms arranged in categories:
Natural History, The Great West, The Church, and so on.
Other works of the nineteenth century, principally glossaries,
and such notable works of the early twentieth as Richard H.
Thornton's *An American Glossary,* 2 volumes (Philadelphia:
Lippincott; 1912) and a later volume (Madison, Wisc.: American Dialect Society; 1939); George Philip Krapp's *The English Language in America,* 2 volumes (New York: The Century Co.; 1925); William A. Craigie and James R. Hulbert's
*Dictionary of American English on Historical Principles*
(*DAE*) (Chicago: University of Chicago Press; 1936–44); and
the preliminary work on Hans Kurath and associates' *A
Linguistic Atlas of the United States and Canada* (Providence:
Brown University Press; 1939–41) are all noted by Mencken
in *Supplement I* and listed in many bibliographies; but a
particularly compendious and useful guide to reading for
anyone interested in American English appears in *The Ordeal
of American English,* edited by C. Merton Babcock (Cambridge: Riverside Press; 1961), a publication of the Houghton
Mifflin Research Series. The paperback itself, a judicious
selection of short articles and excerpts from larger works ranging all the way from Noah Webster's *Dissertations on the
English Language* and entertaining samples of colloquial
speech to contemporary *New York Times* book reviews, could
easily get a reader hooked on language. Its Selected Bibliography separates general works such as Thomas Pyles's *Words
and Ways of American English* (New York: Random House,
Inc.; 1952) and Albert H. Marckwardt's *American English*
(New York: Oxford University Press; 1958) from dictionaries
and glossaries and these in turn from topical books and
articles on regional idiom, slang, and contemporary usage.
The bibliography omits De Vere's *Americanisms,* perhaps be-

cause of its general unavailability, although two selections from it appear in the text.

The most comprehensive and up-to-date dictionary of Americanisms and one on which I have leaned heavily is Mitford M. Mathews's *A Dictionary of Americanisms on Historical Principles* (Chicago: University of Chicago Press; 1951). Freely acknowledging its debt to its predecessors, the *OED* (*Oxford English Dictionary*) and the *DAE* and the *EDD* (*English Dialect Dictionary*), the work is indeed what its editor claims: "an index of the history and culture of the American people." Less ponderous than the *DAE,* available in either one or two volumes, and attractively illustrated, the book is an invitation to browsing and to historical speculation. The same author's small book *The Beginnings of American English* (Chicago: University of Chicago Press; 1931) traces by means of essay selections and commentary the genesis and recognition of American English.

Most books written on the English language or on language in general, at least in this century, give a certain amount of attention to its upstart child; but to attempt to list even a representative number of such books would be a formidable task. Lincoln Barnett's *The Treasure of Our Tongue* (Knopf, 1965); Mario Pei's *The Story of Language,* 2nd edition (Philadelphia and New York: J. B. Lippincott Company; 1965) and *The Story of the English Language* (Lippincott, 1967); Charles Barber's *The Flux of Language* (London: George Allen & Unwin, Ltd.; 1965) are among recent books that incorporate discussion of the American language into their general studies; while Ernest Weekley's *The English Language* (London: Andre Deutsch; 1952) contains a chapter on American English by John W. Clark. Professor Clark contributed also the American section in Eric Partridge and his *British and American English Since 1900* (New York: Philosophical Library; 1951), wherein he takes Mencken to task for his delight in recording "nauseating novelties" and "every revolting freak" in the language. (As one would guess, the American section projects a strong whiff of academe.) Eric

Partridge has given American English its due in much of his writing, although his statement in *World of Words* (London: Hamish Hamilton; 1948) that the English language may be said to have come to America on the *Mayflower* (that tardy ship!) would bar him forever from Virginia. For those who are led by these readings to seek more knowledge about language itself, a convenient bibliography for the lay reader is provided in Pei's *Language for Everybody* (New York: Devin-Adair Company; 1957), in which works are graded for complexity, from Pei's own *All About Language* to the works of Jespersen and Bloomfield and Sapir and Entwhistle.

No retrospective writing gives the flavor of contemporary observation. Such anthologies as *The Ordeal of American English*, already mentioned, as well as documentary histories like Henry Steele Commager and Allan Nevins's *Heritage of America* (Boston: Little, Brown and Company; 1945) or Mark Van Doren's *The Voice of America* (Cleveland and New York: World Publishing Co.; 1942) give brief selections from the comments of early travelers—Madame Sarah Knight, William Byrd II, Anne Royall, Mrs. Trollope, and other astute observers—on the vagaries of speech among Americans. *Quest for America, 1810–1824,* ably edited by Charles L. Sanford (New York: New York University Press; 1964), one of the *Documents in American Civilization* series edited by Hennig Cohen and John William Ward, contains a number of selections that weave vernacular into the history of a time when American speech was most brashly asserting its independence. And many of the dated quotations in *A Dictionary of Americanisms,* discontinuous as they are, give a sense of presence found only in words fresh from the mint.

Of the many splendid historical writings that tell of the past reflected in our words I have named only a few in my footnotes. Charles and Mary Beard, James Truslow Adams, Arthur Schlesinger, Henry Cabot Lodge, and other historians of note or sometimes not of note could keep one forever reading. Informal histories such as Mark Sullivan's *Our Times,* 6 volumes (New York and London: Charles Scribner's Sons;

1928–35) and the popular and impressionistic books of the family of Frederick Lewis Allen's *Only Yesterday* (New York: Harper & Row; 1931) and Louise Tanner's *All the Things We Were* (New York: Doubleday & Company, Inc.; 1968) re-create scenes still echoing in our speech.

Our own new-minted words are telling their own tales, carrying into the stream of American English the record of our times. If we would hear what they will say of us to the readers of tomorrow's books, we need only listen to ourselves.

# Index of Americanisms

a (pronunciation of), 105
a- (prefix), 232
abolitionist, 199
abolitionize, 199
absquatulate, 10, 201
-ac (suffix), 297
accommodation coach, 204
ace-high, 265
ace in the hole, 265
acid, 292; - head, - high, - rock, 298
actual settlers, 150
ad, 270
adding machine, 249
ad lib, 279
admission to the bar, 150
adobe, 223
advocate, 85, 182
A.E.F., 271
aerial: machine, - ship, - steam carriage, 267
aerodrome, 267
aerodynamics, 267
aeroplane, 268
affluent society, 289
aficionado, 304
African, 185
Afro-American, 307
Age of Play, 273

air: conditioning, 269; -cooled, 283; - meeting, 268; - waves, 275
airplane, 268
alewives, 119
alienation, 289, 301
all aboard, 214
all about, 301
all-fired, 248
alligator, 75
allotter, 99
almighty dollar, 243
alphabet soup, 280, 285
American, 115, 116, 194; - dialect, 195; - eagle, 203; - Empire, 203; - English, 195, 203; - language, 195; - Republic, 203; - tongue, 195
Americanisms, 6, 258
Americanizing, 146
Anasagunticook, 113
andiron, 222
anesthesia, 263
anesthetic, 263
Anglicisms, 258
Anglifying, 145
Anglo-Saxon, 38
antagonize, 85, 170

anti -, 87; - monopoly, 244;
  - prohibitionists, 262; - saloon
  leaguers, 262; - smoke, 263;
  tariffites, 200; - trust, 244;
  - vivisectionists, 262
anti-slavery element, 199; - men,
  199; - paper, 199; - ticket, 199
appendectomy, 263
appendicitis, 263
appreciate, appreciation, 172
armonica, 182
arroyo, 222
assapan, 120
astronaut, 3
astrowives, 300
athlete's foot, 282
atomic bomb, 286
atomizer, 259
audience, 181, 182
audio-visual aids, 289
auntie, 186
automobile, 254
aviator, 268
avocado, 222

babiche, 158
bachelor girl, 248, 249
back, 151; - country, 141, 150,
  215; - countryman, 151, 163;
  - county, 151; - farmer, 151;
  - people, 151; - plantation, 151;
  - settlements, 152; - settlers,
  151, 194; -woods, 257;
  -woodsman, 151, 163
backbone, 255
backing a winner (or loser), 265
backlog, 102, 295
backseat driver, 267
backslider, 257
backwater, to, 302
bag, 298
bagel, 251

baggage, 214
bail out, 268
bairn, 154
baling press, 208
ball: - game, - park, - team, 252
ball card, 245
Baltimore clipper, 173
banjo, 166, 191
banner state, 200
bannock, 154
banquette, 172, 177
Baptist, 162
barbecue, 75, 115, 304
barbed wire, 242
bark, 160, 174
barken canoe, 109
barkentine, 110
barking up the wrong tree, 160
barn, barnyard, 101
barnstorming, 265, 268
barren, 95
barreny, 95
baseball, to, 238
baseballer, 238
base line, 238
bateau, 131, 174
bathtub gin, 273, 276
battery, 182
battle fatigue, 271
Bauverein, 283
bay, 221
bayou, 117, 159
bazooka, 286
beach pajamas, 280
beans, 181
bear, 159–60
bear's grease, 217
Beat Generation, 290
beatingest, 218
beatnik, 290, 292
beautician, 265
beauty: - operator, - parlor, - shop,
  265

beaver; 108; - blanket, 159;
- eater, 157; - maker, 108;
- pay, 171; - sign, 159; - tree,
156
bee (insect), 21, 156, 157, 168
bee (project), 102, 161, 162
beeline, to follow a, 302
beep, 303
beer garden, 230
begorrah, 235
behaviorism, -ist, 263
be-in, 292
belittle, 85, 165, 197
bevel, 92
b'hoy, 233
biddy, 234
big: - bands, 274; - head, 218;
- shots, 273; - stick, 262;
- sticker, 262
bike, to, 254
biking, 253
bio-, 297
biograph, 253
biological clock, 302
birdieback, 296
Bismarck herring, 284
black, 306; - bottom, 273;
- consciousness, 306; - culture,
306; flusterer, 158; - history,
306; Power, 292, 306; - Shirts,
283; theater, 306
blahs, 300
blast, 260
blazing out, 155
blazing star, 158
bletherskyte, 154
blind, 140
blip, 303
blizzard, 197, 257
block, 177, 178, 194
bloomers, 254
blue: - back, 240; - bellies, 238;
- grass, 156; - John, 240;

- norther, 242; - William, 240
blues, 264
bluff, 5, 95, 149, 165
B.O., 282
board, 92; -walk, 265
boat, to, 174
boatable, 109
boating, 109; keel -, 109
bobble, 252
bobcat, 83, 157
Bob Low, 132
Bob Ruly, 132
bobtails, 194
bobwhite, 97
bock, 230
bodies politic, 74
bodyaciously, 201
Bohunk, 249
boiler deck, 212
Bolshie, 272
bolt the party, to, 200
bonanza, 222, 238
Bon Coeur, 148
bonehead, 248
boob, 265
Boobus Americanus, 278
booby trap, 286
boodle, 244
book: - agents, - bindery,
- peddlers, - stores, 181; factor,
170, 175, 181
boom, 257
boondoggle, 279; - ling, 281
boost, to, 218, 277
booster, 277, 299
bootees, 174
Boot Hill, 242
borscht, 284
boss, 129
Boss! Co-boss!, 149
bossloper, 128
Boston: accent, 176; culture,
247; manner, 176, 193; notions,

Boston (*continued*)
    166, 174; people, 167
bottom, 91, 95
bourbon and branch water, 181
bowery, 125
bowl over, to, 61
box car, 214
box office, 257
boy friend, 273
boyish bob, 273
Brahmins, 247
Brain Trust, 280
brainwashing, 290
branch, 140
bread is all, the, 139
breadstuffs, 173, 175
breast complaint, 263
brick (house), 177
brickstreicker, 129
bring down the house, to, 265
broadcast, 274; -er, 274
broadhorn, 155
bronco, 223
brook, 140
brooly, 132
Brown Shirts, 283
brownstone front, 238
brûlé, 132
brush, 156, 163; - a disagreement,
    156; - fire, 156
bubbling, 254
buck, 163; -shot, 166, -skin, 163
buckaroo, 192, 223
buckboard, 204
bucker, 241
bucket, 139
buckra, 190
Buck Snort, 240
buffalo, 135; - beat, 159; - chips,
    221, - ford, 155; - robe, 159;
    - trace, 155
bufflehead, 158
bugging, 288

buggy, 204
building spot, 177
built-in, 296
bum, 230; beach -, - deal, 230
bummer, 230; -ish, 230
bumming, 230
bummy, 230
bump, 64; - off, 275
- bund, 283
Bundists, 283
bundling, 102
bunk, bunkum, 199
Bunker, 148
bunt, 260
bureau, 180
burg, 73
-burger, 231
burghers, 40, 73
burn, 299, 304
Burnt Coat, 132
bus boycotts, 288
bush, 127; - fighter, 127; - league,
    127; - leaguer, 127; -man, 127;
    - master, 127; - ranger, 127;
    -whack, 127, 243
business, 170; - block, 178;
    dry-goods -, 170; forwarding -,
    170; lumber -, 170; - office, 249;
    pork -, 170
bustle, 64, 205
busy as a bee in a tar barrel, 157
butternut, 295
buttonball, 140
button bush, 158
buttonwood, 95, 140
B.V.D., 266


cabin rights, 155
caboose, 214
cafe society, 280
cafeteria, 250
cake walk, 253

calaboose, 222
California fever, 201
calumet, 133; - dance, 133
camp, 298; - meeting, 216; -y, 298
campaign, 198
canal, 209
canallers, 209
candle factor, 170
candy store, 257
cannibal, 75, 115
canoe, 75, 115
cantankerous, 85
canyon, 222, 257
cape, 53, 221
Cape May, 125
capital, 73, 106
capitalism, 287
capitalistic, 244
captions, 258, 275
carbecue, 301
carcajou, 157
caribou, 132
carmine red, 282
Carolina pink, 158
Carolina gouger, 163
carrousel, 252
carryall, 134
carrying place, 109, 131
cart, to, 174
case workers, 281
cash register, 249
Castle, 148; - walk, 264
cat, 157, 289, 307
catalpa, 117
catamount, 97
catfish, 97
cattle, 22, 101; -men, 242
caucus, 197; Congressional -, 237
cavort, 135, 197
Cayuse, 224
CCC, 280
cedar, 44; - bluff, 124; - shingles,
   173

chain reaction, 302
chain store, 257
chair, sent to the, 247
chair road, 166, 193
Chamber of Commerce, 170
channelize, 285
chaps, 223
chare, 85
charge, 398
charivari, 162
Charleston, 273, 276
chay, 139
check, to, 214
chemists' shops, 257
chianti, 250
Chicano, 308
chickadee, 97
chickaree, 97
chicken, 288; - fixin's, 217; - out,
   288
Chiclet, 269
childrenese, 293
child welfare, 262
chili, 250
Chink, 250
Chinook, 224; - jargon, 224
chip in, 248, 265
chipmunk, 158
chitterlings, 240
chocolate éclair, 255
choo-choo, 257
chore, 85
chow!, 274
chowder, 133
chunkey, 121
church burner, 233
chute, 216, 219
-cide, 297
cigarette cream, 282
cigarette fiend, 263
cinema, 258
cinematograph, 253
circle hunt, 240

city, 177; - lot, 178; - park, 251
civil service, 259
claim jumper, 202
clam, 109; - bank, 109; - shell hoe, 109
clam, to, 109
clapboard, 101, 223
clapbread, 101
clear out, to, 218
clergy, 43
clever, 85
clients, 281
clitchy, 154
clockmutch, 128
cloister, 47
close call, 248
clothier, 107
clove, 125
cluster planning, 293
coal: - bucket, hod, - pail, - scuttle, 140
cob, 96
COBOL, 300
Coca-Cola, 269, 270
Cocheco, 113
cockarouse, 121
cockroach, 135
cocktail lounge, 280
C.O.D., 265
cohonk, 122
cold snap, 102
Cold War, 289, 290
coleslaw, 128
collards, 240
colonize, 8
colored, 306
comb, 154
combine, 238, 243
comeback, 260
comforter, 140
commentators, 281
commercial, 281
commons, 100

communiversity, 300
commute, 238
commuters' roads, 238
competency, 213
complex, 273
components, 287
computerization, 287
computer programmer, 287
Comsat, 300, 304
Comstock Lode, 238
concert: - leader, 229; - master, 229; - saloon, 253
Concord, 204
concentration camps, 283
conductor, 182
Conestoga, 205
Confederate, 240
confession magazine, 273
confidential, 261
confounded gay, 176
confrontation, 292, 301
conglomerates, 293
Congo, 185
Connecticut, 113; - shad, 173
consolidation, 243
constitutionality, 197
contact, 277; - a prospect, 277
contented as pigs in clover, 219
contract, 74, 106
convertible, 282
cookey, 128
cool, 298
coon, 160
cooter, 192
cootie, 272
cop out, 294
copperhead, 238
corduroy, 205
core, 96
corn, 96, 156, 167; - cracker, 164; German -, 202; - rights, 155
corner, to, 257
Corn Flakes, 269

corn stalk fiddle, 162
corporate society, 288
corral, 223
cortisone, 287
cot-betty, 154
cotton, 207–8
cottonmouth, 105
cottonwood, 95
Cougar, 303
council fire, 122
counter-culture, 292
country, 81; - cousin, 176;
   - distemper, 164; - docket,
   176; - looking, 176; - mill,
   175; - pay, 171; - plain, 176;
   - trader, 193; - work, 175
country-and-western, 288
county court, 176
coureur de bois, 128, 131,
   219
cove, 221
cow, 30; - catcher, 214;
   - constable, 93; - drivers, 104;
   - keeper, 100; - linter, 101
cowboy, 223, 242
Cowench! Co-inch! Co-ee!, 140
cowpen, 104
coyote, 222
CQD, 351
cracker, 154, 163–4; corn -, 163;
   Georgia -, 154
cranberry marsh, 95
crash, 260; - pad, 292
crawfish, to, 302
crawfishing, 198
creasing, 159
credibility gap, 302
creek, 95, 140, 148
creep, 289
creepybopper, 295
crevasse, 159
crew cut, 381
criticalese, 293

Crockett, 202; a sin to Davy -,
   202
crook, 257
crooners, 274
crossing plate, 214
crossword puzzle books, 275
cruise, 259
cruller, 128
crunch, 303; energy -, 303
crystal detectors, 268
Cuff, Cuffy, 190
cuppin, 135 *n.*
curds, 137
currency, 170, 171; hard -, 199;
   Pennsylvania -, 171; Virginia -,
   171
cush, 192, 240
cushaw, 119
cushie, 192
cushion, 53
cusk, 120
Cuticura, 269
cuttin', 307
cutting out, 241
cyber-, 297–8
cybernetics, 287
cyborg, 295, 299
cyclery, 254

daft, 84, 106
dago, 249
damage, 93
damn, 266, 274
dancing reception, 245
dansy, 88
darkey strut, 253
darning needle, 140
Darwinism, 278
dashiki, 306
datamation, 300
dauber wasp, 97
dauncy, 139

day, 31; -flower, 104
DDT, 287
deacon, to, 216
dead, 232–3; - broke, 248
deadening, 155
debunk, 257, 277
Decade of Bad Manners, 273
deck, 55, 85, 272; boiler -, 212;
  hurricane -, 211, 213, 214;
  passenger -, 279; Texas, -, 279
deer: - crossing, 155; - sign, 159;
  - traces, 155
deerskin hunting frock, 163
Delaware, 147
delicatessen, 230, 328; kosher -,
  251
deliver the goods, 257
demogrant, 301
depot, 214
depreciation, 169, 172
Des Allemands, 145
desert tan, 282
détente, 304
detergents, 287
detour, 267
dialogue, 301
diamondback rattler, 105
Dictaphone, 269
Did I say no?, 251
dig, 298
dim view, 304
dipsy, 108
directive, 285
dirt: pay -, - road, 205
discount, 106
discrete disc modulators, 303
dish timber, 160
districting, 198
divide, 95, 149
dividend, 106
doak, 92
dobber, 108
dock, 55, 170, 174

dog tag, 286
dole, 281
Donald Duck effect, 304
dool, 92
dorp, 125
double cross, 279
double-decker, 215
double house, 179
double log house, 179
doughboy, 271
downers, 303
dozens, the, 307
draft card burner, 293
dragonfly, 140
drag race, 288
driftway, 92
driver, 214
drug scene, 292
drugstore, 257
dry goods, 107
dubok, 304
dude, 248
dumb, 231; -bull, 229; -flustered,
  231; -foozled, 231
dummkopf, 231
dump, 259
dunce, 80; - block, 236
Dunkards, Dunkers, 162
dunking, 230
Dust Bowl, 279, 280
Dutch, 25, 130, 146–7, 231;
  - barn, 130; beat the -, 231;
  - blanket, 130; - door, 130;
  in -, 231; -men, 147; - oven,
  130; - pung, 130; - quills, 130;
  - sleigh, 130; - treat, 231;
  - turnpike, 130
dutiable, 169, 170
dynamics, 285


eace worm, 139
earebred, 89, 92

eat: - crow, 248; -ing club,
237
eco-, 297
ecology, 391; - freak, 391
econometrics, 293
editorial, 183, 193
educational, 197; - alternatives,
386
-ee, 297
eel: - grass, 5, 97, 158; - spear,
108
effectuating, 285
eggplant, 5
ego, 22, 273; -tism, 169
eight-hour day, 266
Eisenhower, 284
El, 266
electioneering, 198
electric: - fluid, 245; - arc lights,
- bell, - cars, - light bugs,
- locomotives, - railroads,
- railways, 246; - chafing
dishes, - iron, - kitchen,
- laundries, - vacuum
cleaners, 270
electrical current, 287
electrician, 245
electrified, 247
electro-chromograph, 246
electrocute, 246–7
electrodelic, 300
electronic surveillance, 288
electronics, 276, 284; - engineer,
287
elevator, 259
embargo (imbargo), 75
embarrassment, 169
emergency, 290
emigrant, 141
employer's liability, 262
endeavor, 106
engagé, 220
engineer, 246

English, 38, 39, 146; - corn, 96;
- settlement, 156
ennui, 169
enterprise, 106
enterprise, to, 207
entertain, 169
enthusiasm, 183
entrance, 67
epinephrine, 263
escalation, 293
eu-, 297
eventuate, 169
exam, 260
exflunctified, 201
exodusters, 280
expedite, 281
explaterate, 201

factor: book -, 170, 175, 181;
candle -, 170
factory, 208
fall guy, 265
fall-out shelter, 290
farm, 194; - relief, 280
fascist, 280, 283
fat cakes, 153
favorite son, 200
feeble-minded, 263
fellow countryman, 6, 81
female suffrage, 262
fen, 300
fence: on the -, 200; - rails,
101; - viewer, 100
fender, 214
fernenst, 216
ferry flat, 218
fertility pill, 300
-fest, 231, 250
F.F.V., 266
fiddler crab, 97
field bed, 162
fiend, 58, 263–4

fiesta, 250
fighting clip, 252
Filibuster, 240
filling station, 267
finalize, 281, 285
fine as silk, 202
fine-tuning, 296
fip, fippenny bit, 171
fire, 179, 180, 182, 184
firebug, 260
fireside chat, 280
firmware, 299
fish, 25; -ing schooner,
    173
fished, 119
five dollars a day, 266
fix, to, 85, 245
flame-throwers, 286
flaming youth, 272
flapjack, 84, 85
flapper, 273
flat, to, 171
flatboat, 109; - ferry, 155
Flatbush, 125
flicker, 158
flier, 269
flit, 154
flivver, 266
floatel, 301
floating: - palace, - wedding
    cake, 211
floor, 198
flops, 257
flower: - child, 292, 295;
    - power, 292
flumadiddle, 108
flunkt, 198
fly, 127
fly along the road, to, 267
flyer, 248
flying: - fools, 268; - machines,
    267
fodder, 101

folk rock, 295
fordway, 95, 110
foreignership, 264
forestation, 262
forest management, 262
FORTRAN, 300
four-flusher, 265; -ing,
    265 n.
Four Horsemen, 275
Four Hundred, 244
foxfire, 221
fox trot, 264
fragging, 293, 300
frame, 258; - dwelling house,
    - tenement, 178
frankfurter, 230
Franklin, 147, 179; - rod, 179;
    - spectacles, 182; - stove,
    179; - tree, 182
Franklinism, 182
frat, 289
Fredericksburg, 152
freemen, 74, 99
freewheeling, 282
free will, 59; -er, 143, 144
freight, 55, 174, 214
French: - Church, - falls, - fall
    shoes, - Indian, 134
fresh, 230
frog, 214
Frogs, 274
frontier, 151; - places, 152;
    - plantation, 151; - settlement,
    151; - towns, 159; western -,
    201
frying pan, 140
Fuehrer, 283
Fulbright, 300
full house, 265
fulling mill, 107
fundamentalist, 277
funk art, 295
Futurama, 283

gallinipper, 158
gander-plucked, 202
gangbuster, 279
gaping primate, 278
G.A.R., 266
garter snake, 97
gas, 260, 267
gate-crasher, 257
gay, 298
gazette, 68
gefilte fish, 251
general assembly, 167
Georgia; - money, 171; - piercer, 158; - vocabulary, 193
German, 147; - corn, 156; - Flats, 142; Pennsylvania -, 191; - settlement, 156
Germanizing, 227
Germanna, 152
gerrymander, 198, 257
get: - ahead, 206; - even, 248; - in on, 278; - religion, 216
g'hal, 233
ghettologist, 292
G.I., 286
gigahertz, 292
gigging, 108
gilt-edged, 248
gin mill, 211
ginner, ginnery, 208
girdling, 107
gizmo, 286
glad hand, 253
glad rags, 257
glamorize, 280
glance, 69
glasphalt, 300
glass snake, 158
glitch, 299
glos, 276
go, 299; - for a drive, 276; - for a wheel, 253; no -, 299; - to bat for, 265

go-ahead, 206, 263
go-aheadity, 206, 223
gobbledygook, 285
gold: -brick, 242; -bug, 244; -hunter, 217; -standard, 199
golf, 184
gondola, 155; -car, 214
gone coon, 208
gong, 76
goober, 192
goods, 107, 214
goofing off, 286
googol, 288
gook, 286
G.O.P., 266
gouger, 163
gouging scrape, 202
government worker, 259
grandstand play, 265
grass: blue-, 156; eel -, 5, 97, 158; silk -, 158; timothy -, 182; wire -, 156
grayback, 238
grayslick, 108
greaser, 249
greenback, 240
greenhorn, 84
greens, 160
gridiron bridge, 205
gris-gris, 191
groggery, 211
grok, 299
groove, in the, 289
grubs, 299
grubstake, 242
grunt, 300
gubernatorial, 166
guess, 84, 85
Guinea, 185; - trade, 174
Gulf Stream, 182
Gulliver, the, 304
gumbo, 191

gundaloe, 202
guru, 292

hacienda, 223
half horse, half alligator, 200
halitosis, 282
hamburger 230, 231
hammock, 75, 115
Hampton boat, 174
hang around, 94
hanging loose, 303
hang-up, 296
hanker, 94
happify, 88, 196
happy as a clam, 63, 109, 157
hard, 66; - hat, 300; -pan, 92;
    - row to hoe, 218; -ware, 299
Harlem, 125
hatch, 272
hating out, 161
haunt, 94
haver, 92
Haverstraw, 92
Haverhill, 92
hay: -loader, 238; -ride, 247;
    -rig, 238; -sill, 92
header, 238
headline, to, 260
headmasters, -mistresses, 304
health resorts, 244
heap, 106, 217
heart as big as all outdoors, 203
heath hen, 184
Hebrew, 249
hedgehog, 97
heft, to, 218
heifer horse, 94
hell, 44, 266, 274
Hell Gate, 125
hello girl, 125
help, 106, 129, 143
hep, 289; -cat, 307

hermit thrush, 218
Heroite, 199, 202
He's complaining yet!, 305
He should live so long!, 305
hickory, 95
Hickory men, 199
hicky horse, 140
hi-fi, 289
high, 24, 292; -brow, 257; -hat,
    253; -falutin', 218; -jacker,
    275; -muck-a-muck, 224
High Dutch, 146, 147
hi-lo, 289
hip, 289, 307; - flask, 273
hippie, 304, 307; -dom, 292
hit, 298; - and run, 265
Hoboken, 113
hog, 93, 101; - 'n' hominy, 160;
    razorback -, 126; -wallow, 63
Hog Eye, 240
holding the market, 243
Hold on, 231
hold-up-nik, 290
hollow, 91; Sleepy -, 120
Holsum, 269      .
homespun, 163, 176, 222
homestead, 241–2
hominy, 122
hommie!, 153
homo boobiens, 278
honey, to, 157; -fuggle, 157;
    - locust, 156; -suckle, 218
honking, 273; - horns, 272
honky, 292
hoochy-koochy, 252
hoodoo, 191
hook-up, 281
hoolas, 120
hoople, 127
hoosegow, 223
Hoovervilles, 279
hoptoad, 63, 97
hornswoggle, 10, 198, 201

horse, 161–2, 184; - car, 206
hot: -box, 214; - cake, 128;
  - dogs, 265; -house, 122, 133;
  - rod, 288
house, 27; carriage -, 179;
  curing -, 103; double -, 179;
  double log -, 179; frame
  dwelling -, 179; - gang, 185;
  - girl, 239; - help, 239;
  -hold, 94; - movers, 206;
  pilot-, 213; row -, 178;
  store-, 179; town -, 178
housel, 94
huckleberry, 96
hull, 272
hummingbird, 97
hummock, 121
hunky-dory, 218
hunt, 184
hunting: - frock, 163; - jacket,
  159
hurricane, 115; - deck, 211, 213,
  214
hurry, 92
hurtleberry, 125
husk, 96
husking bee, 162
husky, 248
hustle, 207
hydrogen bomb, 290

ice cream, 253
iced tea, 253
icky, 289
ill, 48, 85
I'll be there with bells on,
  205
Illinois, 132
immigrant, 141, 197
immigrate, 170
implement, to, 281
implementation, 285

improve, 70, 100, 182
improvement, 70; -s, 101
I'm telling you, 251
in, 214; - specie, 110 *n.*
independent as a wood sawyer,
  212
Indian, 115, 116, 123–4, 130,
  159, 160, 163, 187
Indian corn, 96
Indian devil, 157
Indianism, 124
Indianize, 124
Indian talk, 167
Indian trace, 194
Indian trail, 155
Indian wheat, 96
industrial safety, 262
influential, 198
inner space, 302
input, 287
interesting, 169
interests, 244
interfaces, 293
interposition, 288
interval, 91
interview, 270
intolerance, 183
investment, 106
Iowa, 114
Irish, 146, 234
Irish potato, 142
Irish tract, 156
Irish Trot, 162
iron, 28; - furnace, 107;
  - plantation, 143, 152;
  -works, 174
ironing, 213
Iroquois, 132
irregularity, 282
I should worry, 251
Israelite, 249
-ist, 66, 297

jack-leg, jack-legged, 242
jack rabbit, 242
Jackson, Jacksonize, 202
Jackson's Hole, 120
jade, jaded, 94
jalopy, 282
jambalaya, 192
jawboning, 298
jaywalker, 267
jazz, 191–2
jazz age, 264, 273
jeep, 286
Jello, 269
jeopardize, 197
jerkwater, 214
jet liner, 295
Jew-baiting, 280
Jewish novel, 305
jigger, 108
jimberjawed, 198
jimpsecute, 240
Jimson weed, 96
jingoed, 255
jitterbug, 280
jockey, 248
johnny cake, 122
Johnny-jump-up, 96
jollying people along, 252
jonin', 307
Josh, 240
joy riding, 267
jug, 223
juicy-spicy, 240
juke, 192, 307
june, to, 241

Kaatersill Clove, 125
kamikaze, 286
karate, 304
karma, 292
katydid, 97, 141 *n.*
kayo, 261

kedge, 154
keel-boat, 128; -ing, 109
keeling over, 108
keeping a stiff upper lip, 218
keep one's eye peeled, 248
Kemmler process, 246
Kentucky boat, 165
Kentucky colonel, 157
ker-, 218, 231
kermis, 126
kibitz, 251
kick-off, 252
kick-up, 162
Kidderminster, 114
kike, 249
kill, 125
kind, 143; in -, 143 *n.*
Kinderhook, 125
kinetograph, 253
kinetoscope, 246
kiosk, 259
kitchenette, 265
knicker, 248
know-how, 270
know-it-all, 248
Know Nothing, 233
Kodak, 269
kook, 299
kosher, 228; - delicatessen, 251
K.P., 286
kraut, 250
Kwame, 191
Kwanza, 307

L, 266
labor, 244; - reform, 208
lager, 230
lagniappe, 159
Lallapalooza, 235
land, 149; - pirate, 202; - seeker,
    217; - speculator, 149, 194
lands, wild, 253

landskip, 126
lap tea, 245
lariat, 222, 223
laser, 3, 300
lasso, 222
launch, 299
Law!, Lawsy! Law you!, 176
lay off, 265
learned, 213
leaves, 96
leggins, 163
legislate, 169
legislator, 72
lengthy, 85, 198
leniency, 198
leotite, 301
Let's wood up, 212
levee, 159
libido, 273
library, 181
lick, 156
lickety-split, 255
Lick Skillet, 240
Liederkranz, 229; -er, 229
life style, 293, 295
lift, 259
lightning bug, 97
lightning rod, 179
light opera, 252
like fury, 248
Limey, 271, 274
Listerine, 269
literary, 169
littleneck, 91
lizard, 266
loafer, 230
loan shark, 265
loblolly, 104
lobby, 199
lobsterbacks, 194
locate, 197
locater, location, 103
locomobile, 254

locomotive engineer, 214
lodge, 133
log, to, 107
loggers, 107
log cabin, 134, 156
log house, 134
log pen, 156
logrolling, 107, 198, 199, 290
logy, 129
long: - house, 122; -playing,
    289; - sweetening, 160
looking glass prairie, 218
look out for number one, to,
    278.
loop aerials, 268
lordosis, 282
Los Angeles, 145
Lost Generation, 272, 290
lot, 98, 173
lotter, lot-layer, lotting out, 99
lousy, 274
low, 48; -rise, 292
lox, 251
Loyalists, 283
Lubberland, 164
luggage, 214
lumber, 106–7, 170, 175
lunatic, 57, 68; - fringe, 262
lynch, 202


macadam, 204
macaroni, 250
Mace, 292
machine, 200, 208, 254
machismo, 304
macroeconomics, 296
mad, 6, 85; -house, 258; -stone,
    158
magazine, 181
magnetic, 85
magnicide, 297
mah jongg, 274

mahogany, 180
mail, 193
maize, 75, 96, 115
make, 277; - the fur fly, 202
Mammy, 186
Management, 287
Manhattan, 125
Manifest Destiny, 203
maninosa, 122
manitou, 120
margins, 243
marihuana, 250
marooner, 164
marsh, 26, 90; - hen, 105
mart, 260
Maryland wheat, 173
mascon, 300
Massachusettensian, 105
Massachusetts, 113
master, 45, 129
matchcoat, 121, 123
Mattaggmonsis, 113
maum, mauma, 186
Maushapogue, 114
maverick, 241
mazuma, 228
McCarthyism, 289
meadow, 63, 89–90
meadowish, 90
meaningful, 301
Meat in the Pot, 240
mediaese, 293, 304
medicine man, 122, 123
mega-, 296
megalopolis, 292
melancholy, 57
menhaden, 119
merchant, 107, 175; - mill,
    175–6, 243; - work, 175
merchantable, 110
merchanters, 173
merger, 243
mesa, 222

mesquite, 222
Michigan, 113
mick, 234
micro-, 296
Mid-Atlantic, 293
Middle Tenor, 171
mighty words, 41
mike, 281
mileage, 182
mile post, 193
mill, 107; country -, 175;
    merchant -, 175
millering, 107
millionairism, 243
millionism, 243
mind-blowing, 292
mini-, 296
mining camp, 237
minstrelsy, 252
miracle fabrics, 276
misery, 85
missilese, 293
Missouri, 113
mobile homes, 267
moccasin, 117, 121
Model-A, 276
Model-T, 266
moke, 241
molasses whisky, 163
money, 110, 171
moneyed institutions, 244
monkey trial, 277
Monongahela, 113
monopolistic, 244
moon: - buggy, 304; -glade, 108;
    -tel, 301; - walk, 303–4
moonack, 190
moonlight, to, 298
moose, 120
morgen, 127
morning glory, 218
moron, 263
mortician, 265

mosey, 223
mosquito, 135–6; - hawk, 140, 302
motel, 301
mother country, 81
motorneer, 246
move, 205–6
movie, 253, 261; - parlors, 263
movies, 258
Moving Day, 205
moving: - pictures, 253; - wagon, 205
mowing ground, 89
Mr. Speaker, 240
Ms., 326
much, 127
muckle, 154
muckrake, 261
mud-lark, 240
muff, 261
mugging, 298
mugwump, 121
mulattress, 186
mulley cow, 240
multi-, 296; -millionaire, 243; -national economy, 294; -nationals, 304; -purpose minicomputer, 391
mush and milk, 160
music, 58; -al, 280; - stand, 252
muskrat, 117, 118
musquash, 184
mustang, 222, 241, 303

nab, 260
Nabisco, 269
Nantucket, 180; - whale boat, 174
napalm, 286
Nassau, 125
nativism, 233
nattering nabobs of negativism, 200

natural selection, 278
Nazis, 283
neck, 91; - and neck, 248
necking, 273
needul, the, 228
Negro, 167, 185–6, 187, 306; - English, 167, 187; - monger, 166, 186; - party, 200
network, 281
New Amsterdam, 126
New Bern, 152
New Deal, 280, 289
New Dealerophobia, 281
New Divinities, 162
New Dorp, 125
New England, 162; - rum, 174; - dialect, 167
New Freedom, 280
newlander, 144
New Lights, 162
New Mecklenburg, 152
Newport, 245
new rich, 243
newscasters, 281
newspaper English, 260
newspaporial, 193
newsstand, 259
New Tenor, 171
New York, 126; -ism, 193
n.g., 265
night owl, 248
-nik, 290, 305
ninepins, 126
nix, 231
no-draft ventilation, 282
no-frost, 296
no-knock, 295
noncommittal, 197
normalcy, 272
Northward, 194
nose dive, 268
No sirree, 232
nothing doing, 257

notify, 182
notions, 88, 193, 197
novelist, 169
N.R.A., 280
nubbin, 96
nuclear family, 302
nucleosynthesis, 292
nudnik, 290–1
nullie, 199
nullify, nullification, 199
nut factory, 258
nylon stockings, 283

oak barren, 95
obflisticated, 201
obligate, 172
off: - base, 265; - his trolley,
     265; - the record, 261
O-Grab-me Acts, 200
Ohio, 113
Oh yeah, 279
oil: - belt, - derrick, - drill,
     - fever, - speculation, - strike,
     - well, 238
O.K., 265, 284–5, 284 *n.*
Okies, 279
Old Hickoryite, 199
Old Lights, 162
Old Tenor, 171
old wives, 158
Oldsmobile, 269
-ology, 297
one hundred percent American,
     262
on herd, 241
on the lam, 275
oodles, 240
ooze, 294
operator, 277
opium fiend, 263
opossum, 118, 120
Orangeade, 269

orbit, in, 302
ordinaries, 163
Oregon: - fever, 201; - jargon,
     224; - Trail, 218
organization, 287; - men, 289
organizer, 244
orthogenesis, 247
Oshkosh, 113
outer space, 302
out in left field, 265
output, 287
over: -drive, 282; -kill, 293;
     - the top, 271
ox-whip, 241
oy-oy, 251

packet ship, 173
packhorse men, pack men, 108
pack train, 108
Paddy, 233–4; dumb -, 233
padre, 223
Pagonchaumischaug, 114
pail, 139
paint, 218
painter, 97, 157
palace, 51, 169
paleface, 122
palm, 44, 95, 106
Palmolive, 269
pan, hardpan, 92
panhandle, 265; -r, 253, 265
panther, 97
pantyhose, 295
paper aristocracy, 199
papoose, 121
para-, 297
par for the course, 281
parking lot, 267
parking space, 254
parley voos, 274
parlor girl, 239
pass the buck, to, 248, 257

patio, 223, 289
patroon, 129; - lands, 152
patterns, 285
Patton, 149
pavement, 172, 177
pavilion, 53
pay, 172, 173; beaver -, 171;
    country -, 171; current
    country -, 110; - dirt, 205, 242;
    pork -, 110
payment, 110
pay off, 294
P.D.Q., 265
peacenik, 293
peart, 176
pecan, 158
pedageese, 293
pemmican, 122
Pennsylvania: - currency, 223;
    - Dutch, 147; - fireplace, 179,
    182; - German, 147
Pennsylvanian, 105
Pensacola, 145
peon, 222, 250; -age, 250
people sniffer, 293
pepperidge tree, 96
pernickety, 229
persimmon, 117; - beer, 160
pesky, 87
Petit, 148
petrochemist, 287
petting parties, 273
phase out, 296
phenomenology, 247
Philadelphia: butter, 173;
    - brick, 178; - paper money,
    222; - shilling, 171
phonetician, 247
phonograph, 246
photo, 260; -genic, 256
photophone, 246
photoplay, 261
pianola, 253

picayune, 171
pickaninny, 75
pig, 93
pigeon hunt, 240; - roost, 97
piggyback, 296
pile, making one's, 182
pill, fertility, 300
Pill, the, 300
pillowcase, 94
pilot, 214; -house, 213; river -,
    279
pin, 92
pine, 121; - bluff, 124; - barren,
    95
pinko, 280, 283
pink toothbrush, 282
pin-up girl, 286
pinxter, 127
piny woods, 95
pipe of peace, 122
pirogue, 135
pistareen, 166, 171
Pittsburgh, 205
plains, 186
plank, 200; - road, 205
planned obsolescence, 288
plant, to, 146
plantation, 74 and *n.*, 103;
    indigo -, rice -, 173
planter, 74 *n.*, 103
plastic, 302
platform, 200
play-by-play, 274
play the market, 278
plaza, 223
plea, 260
plow, 92
plumb crazy, 203
plunder, 85, 214, 216
Plymothean, 105
pocosson, 155
pointers, 241
pointing up, 285

poke, 139
pole, 155, 156
polecat weed, 158
political, politician, 72, 200
pond, 95
pone, 117, 122
poor, 281; - white trash, 164
poor joe, 192
Poplocracy, Poplocrat, 244
Populism, Populist, Populite,
    Populization, 244
porgy, 119
port, making, 221
portage, 131
posh, 304
Possum Trot, 240
post, 193
potato, 76, 115
potlatch, 224
poulet farci en cocotte, 284
pounedge, 93
powan, 120, 123
power, 216; - brakes, 282;
    - politics, 288; - press, 208
powwow, 120
pragmaticism, pragmatism, 247
prairie, 131, 219–21; - cart,
    205; - gumbo, 191; - schooner,
    221, 302
prairied, 221
prairillon, 221
praying mantis, 141 *n.*
preacher, 204, 216
pre-emption, 149, 155
Presbyterian, 79, 240
press, the, 169, 181
pretzel, 230
previously owned, 282
prewar, 260
probe, 260
processed, 281
program, to, 299
progress, 70, 75, 182, 207

promote, promotion, 277
Prosit!, 230
psychedelia, 292
psychedelic, 3
publisher, 181
puccoon, 119 and *n.*
puddings, 240
pulsar, 292
pumpernickel, 230
pumpkin beer, 163
pumpkin head, 166
punch-drunk, 265
punji stake, 293
punk, 265
pup tent, 286
push-over, 253
put, 173; - it all over, 277;
    - over, 277; - something over,
    251
put-up job, 258

quackle, 154
quadraphonic sound system, 303
quahog, 118
quake, 260
quartee, 171
quarter: - of ten, - till, - to,
    137; - path, - race, 184
questionize, 196
quicker than hell could scorch a
    feather, 202
quick-on, 296
quiddle, 198
quilt, 53, 140
quit, 260
q.t., on the, 266

raccoon, 117, 118
racing path, 184
racket, racketeer, 275
radiation sickness, 290

radic-lib, 296
radio, 256, 284
radio broadcasting, 274
radio music box, 268
radium, 256
raft, 158; -ing, 109
ragamuffin, 222
ragtime, 253, 264
rail: - lengths, timber, 107;
  - trees, 101
railroad, 213, 215, 238
railway, 213
raise, 167
rambunctious, 201
ramsquaddle, 196
ranch, -er, 222; -eria, -ito, 223
ranch-type, 289
range, 242
rapids, 131, 219
Rappahannock, 113
rationality, 183
rat race, 288
rattles, 157
rattlesnake, 97, 157
rayon, 276
razorback hog, 97
real estate business, 178
rebel spy, 238
rebuilt, 282
receptioning, 245
reckon, 105, 167, 197, 217
reconditioned, 282
Reconstruction, 289
record, on/off the, 261
Red-baiting, 280
red-bellied land snake, 158
redbud, 105
red ear kiss, 162
redemptioners, 143
red-eye, 202
Red Menace, 272
Red Scare, 274
redskin, 122

reflex circuits, 268
refuse tip, 259
release, 261
relevant, 301
reliable, 198
relief, 281
religion, 79; to get -, 216
religiosity, 183
religious, 241
rent parties, 280
Reo, 269
repossessed, 282
repressed, 273
resort: health, 244; summer,
  245
reticulated, 203, 204 n.
retiracy, 213
reverend, 216
reverse Newport, 245
review, 181
rhubarb, 281
ridingway, 110
riffle, 95, 216
rifle, 183
right, 106; - away, 197; - on!, 306
ring-tailed roarer, 202
Rio Grande, 145
rip-off, 292, 296
ripsnitious, 197
ripsnorter, 201
river: - pilot, 213; - town, 210;
  - trail, 155
road: chair -, stage -, wagon -,
  193; corduroy -, dirt -, plank,
  205; - hog, 267; macadam -,
  204
rock, 292; - 'n' roll, 288, 289
rockahominy, 122
rockaway, 204
rocking chair, 180
rockomastics, 303
rodeo, 223
roofscaping, 292

Roosevelt, 130
root hog or die, 201
rope ferry, 110
Rotary, 264
rotary sparks, 268
rotgut, 202
rotten rich, 280
rough and tumble, 202
rough rider, 262
round trip, 238
row house, 178
Royalists, 283
rubberneck, 83, 248
rub out, 275
ruffled-shirt gentry, 198
rumble, 298
rumpus room, 289
rum-running, 275
run, 95, 140
run, to, 172–3, 204; - across,
   -around, -in, -off, - up, 173
running boards, - gear, - ivy, 173
running with the machine, 208


Sabbath, 43; - Keepers, 162
sachem, 121
sack time, 286
saddlehorse, 152
safari, 301
safety, 252; - barge, 210; - bicycle,
   253
sag, to, 85
sagamore, 121
Saint, 303
St. Julian, 142
salami, 250
salat, 160
salesgirl, 249
Salisbury steak, 231
salt, 25; - lick, 295
Sambo, 190, 191
samp, 122

sandhiller, 164
sand lotter, 248
Sandy Hook, 125
Santa Claus, 126
Santa Fe, 145; - Trail, 218
sassafras, 76; - tea, 160
sauerkrauters, 250
sault, 131
savage as a meat ax, 203
savannah, 115
sawmill works, 106
scab, 208
scadoodles, 240
scads, 240
scalawag, 218, 238
scallyhoot, 241
scamper-down, 218
scary, 218
scathes, 93
scent spray, 259
sch-, 305
schepel, 127
schlimazel, 305
schlock, 305
schnorrologist, 305
schooner, 142
schout, 126
schussers, 304
Schuykill, 125
scientific, 66, 77
scoot, to, 218
Scotch, 146; -Irish, 146, 153
Scots-Irish, 153
Scottish, 189
scout, a good, 126
scow, 128, 218
scrannel, 85
scrawny, 85
scrimp, 87
scripture, 43, 79
scrub, 299; -bing, 304
scrumptious, 218
scuba, 399; -cide, 297

sculpfest, 296
sculpture, 53
scup, 120, 127
scuppaug, 119
scuppernong, 158
Seabees, 285
seafari, 301
Season, the, 169
secesher, 238
second-hand, 282
sedan, 276
seesaw, 137
selectman, 100, 295
selenodesy, 292
self, 79–80
self-made man, 207
sell, 277
servant, 106, 129, 143, 144, 185
service clubs, 264
setting pole, 109
settling accounts, 172
sewing: machine, 208; - girl, 248
sexism, 3
sexploitation, 300
sexplosion, 300
shadbush, 118
shade, 140
shadow-boxing, 265
shantytown, 248
shebang, 234
shedtowns, 280
sheep, 242
shell bark, 156
shell shock, 271
Shenandoah, 113
shenanigan, 234
Sherman's bummers, 238
shillelah, 235
shingle, 233; cedar -, cypress -, 173
Shining Mountains, 218
Shinola, 269
ship, to, 174

shipping charges, 174
shish kebab, 304
shivaree, 162
shoat, 94
shoe boots, 174
shoot, 216
shop, 107, 178–9
short bushel, 127
shotgun, 183
show, 252
show business, 252
shriek, 294
shruffe, 91
shtick, 305
shuck, 96
shunt, 214
shut-out, 261
sick, 85
side-paddle-wheelers, 210
sider, 241
sidetrack, 214, 290
sidewalk, 172, 177
Sierra Nevada, 145
siesta, 222, 223
sign, 159
silk grass, 158
silk-stocking gentry, 198
silver: beetle, 244; - spike, 242
Silver Land, 238
silvertip grizzly, 242
singing psalms to a dead horse, 201
sinker, 248
Sioux, 132
sissy, 248
sit-in, 294
sixpence, 171
skedaddle, 85, 241
skillet, 140
skipple, 127
skunk, 119; - bear, 157; -weed, 158
skydive, -diving, 295

skygodlin, 241
skylab, 304
skyscraper, 249
skytel, 301
slant, 261
slate, 260
slave quarter, 185
slawbank, 129
sledding, 102, 110
sleek, 148
sleeper, 248
Sleepy Hollow, 91
sleigh, 110
slide-out, 296
slip, 174
slippery elm, 156
slooney with the peedoodles, 10
slow bear, 240
slumism, 292
small potatoes, 218
smarty, 248
smash, 294
smearcase, 137, 139
smog, 3
smorgasbord, 284
smouch, 88
snafu, 286
snag, 212, 260
snake: - doctor, - feeder,
  - guarder, 140
snap beans, 140
snappish, 88
snicker, 87
snits, 153
snow, 21; -fari, 301; - job, 286;
  -mobile, 300; -shoe, 102
soap flakes, 282
soap opera, 281
sob: - sister, - story, - stuff, 261
Social Register, 245
society: - editor, - reporter, 244;
  key, 180
sociopath, 301

sockdolager, 201
soddy, 242
sofky, 160
soggy, 85
So I'll pay for it!, 305
solar plexus, 252
solid-state, 296
so long, 231, 257
sombrero, 222, 223
song-and-dance, 252
sophisticated, 299
soul, 35, 306
soul driver, 144
sounding, 307
sourwood, 295
southpaw, 265
Southward, 194
space, 77, 304
spaghetti, 250
span, 128
Spanish, 136; - beard, - Indian,
  - oak, - pistole, 136; - bits,
  - dollars, 110, 136, 171
spark plugs, 267
speakeasies, 278
Spearmint, 269
specie, 110, 240
species, 110
speck, 127
spectacle, 184
speed, 298, 303; - freak, 295
spellbinder, 248
spelling, 237
spell up/down, to, 237
spider, 140
spiel, 229; -er, -ing, 230
spindle, 140
spizerinctums, 240
splash, 294; -down, 295
splendiferous, 203
split ticket, 200
splurge, to, 218
spondulix, 218

spong, 92
spoon wood, 160
sporting columns, 275
sportscasters, 281
sportswriters, 260
spread-eagle, 301
spree, 142
spunk, 106; -y, 142
sputnik, 290–1
squall, 68, 78; -y, 108
square, 177, 178; - away, 248;
  - deal, 262, 280
squash, 118
squatter, 155
squaw, 121, 167
squiggle, 197; to -, 218
squirt, 218
stackpole, 101
stage road, 193
stake, 248
stampede, 223
stand, to, 204; - for, 257
standee, 211
star root, 158
star-spangled banner, 293
Staten, 125
stateroom passenger, 212
static, 281
station, 214; - break, 281
status symbol, 288
steam: - car, - carriage, 214;
  - ferry boat, - flat, - galley,
  - tow boat, 210
steamboat, 209–13
steamboat engineer, 210, 214
steamboat ferry, 218
Steamboat Gothic, 213
steamer, 210
stein, 230
step on the gas, 267
stereopticon, 246
sternwheeler, 210
stingray, 97

stirring one's stumps, 63
stivers, 110
stockholder, 247
stock ticker, 243
stoep bancke, 128
stone-toter, 104
stoop, 128
store, 107, 179; auction -,
  - clerk, dry-goods -, grocery -,
  -keeper, 170; - clothes, 163,
  174
storehouse, 170, 179
stover, 92
straight, 298
stray, 93
streamline, 190; -lining, 282
street-corner apple sellers, 280
strike, 242
string beans, 140
stump, to, 200, 218; -ed, 302
stymie, 281
suability, 88
suburban sprawl, 267
suburbia, 289
succotash, 122
suddent, 241
sugar tree, 95
suicidology, 297
sukiyaki, 284
summer resort, 245
Sunday Keepers, 162
surfari, 301
Susquehanna, 113
swamp, 91
swanga, 190
swap, 111
swastika, 283
sweat: - house, - tepee, 133;
  -shops, 244
sweet, 294
sweet shop, 257
swellhead, 218
swimming volcano, 210

swing, 280, 288
swing-by, 296
switch, 214
sycamore, 140
syn-, 291
syndicate, 275
System, the, 287

table hopper, 295
tackling, 109
tackroom, 109
tacky, 245
tail spin, 268
take it easy, 248
taken for a ride, 275
talented, 198
talkies, 258
tall timber, 156
tamale, 250
tank, 272
tarheel, 240
tarring and feathering, 161
tattle-tale gray, 282
T.B., 263
tea, 106; - party, 169; - pumps, 128
teach, 213 *n.*
tearcoat, 158
technetronic, 292
technic, 243
techy, 106
teen-agers, 288
teenybopper, 295
tee off, 281
teeter, 158
teeter-totter, 137
teeth powder, 170
teetotaciously, 201
teetotal, 232
tele-, 297
telegraph, 243
telephone, 246; - girl, 249;
　- pole, 293

telescope, to, 215
television: age, 289; - studio, 283
Telstar, 304
tempest, 139
tenderfoot, 242
tenement, 178
Tenor, 171
tenpins, 126
tent meeting, 216
tequila, 223, 250
-teria, 250
terrapin, 118
Texas: deck, 213; - fever, 201
thatch grass swamp, 95
theater, 53; - party, 252
thermos bottle, 269
thick milk, 153
think tank, 295
third party, 200
thistle bird, 158
threap, 88
tickled pink, 280
tightwad, 253
tillicum, 224
tilsom, 89, 192
tilt, 137
tilt-up, 158
timber, 106, 156
timothy grass, 182
tin-can show, 279, 280
tin Lizzie, 266
Tin Pan Alley, 264
tippety-bounce, 137
Toasterette, 269
tobacco, 76, 103, 115
tobacco boat, 103, 109
toboggan, 132
tomahawk, 118, 123, 167; - claim,
　- entry, - improvement, 155
Tommers, 252
tommy guns, 272
tom pung, 130, 132
toot, to go off on a, 278

toothache tree, 83, 156
tortilla, 223
total sensorium, 303
tote, 104, 105 *n.*, 166, 167, 190
totem, 16, 121
tourist court, 267
towhee, 158
town, 99, 177; -house, 178;
  - marshal, 100; - meeting, 99,
  167; -ship, 99
T.R., 262
trade, 31, 111
tradesman, 107
trading: - boats, 109; - post,
  144; - path, 108; - schooner,
  174
traffic engineer, 267
trail, 242
trailing through, 242
transatlantese, 293
transcendentalism, 247
transistor, 287
trash, to, 298
trashing, 292
treacle, 86
tree, to, 160
treeing, 168
tree primrose, 158
treff, 304
tribe, 25, 147
trigger man, 275
trip, 292
tripsit, 295–6
truck, 111, 254; - house, 167
trucking: house, 108; - master,
  111
true-blue, 203
trumpery room, 140
trust, 243, 244; - busting, 262
tuckahoe, 218
tulip tree, 95
tumble bug, 158
tune in, 303

tunesmith, 280
turn on, 303
turnpike, 148, 204; Dutch -, 130
turret, 272
TV, 290
tweeter, 303
two-car family, 267
two-level, 296.
tycoon, 287
typesetter, 247
typewriter, 248, 249

umbilical cord, 304
uncle, 186
Uncle Shylock, 274
underprivileged, 281
under the weather, 257
Uneeda, 269
union, 244
up, 77; - against, 257; -country,
  150; -land, 90; -lifter, 248;
  -stage, 265; -tight, 303
Upperco, 153
uppers, 303
urban blight, 293
urbanologist, 3
urban renewal, 288
urbicide, 297
used, 282
utility cores, 293
utilization of factors, 285

V-1, V-2, 286
vacuum cleaner, 270
vamoose, 223
Van Buren, 130
vandalize, to, 298
Van Kouwenhoven, 148
Vaporub, 269
vaquero, 192, 223
vendue, 126, 134

vibes, 299
vice crusaders, vice hounds, 263
vichysoisse, creme, 284
victrola, 270
Vieux Carré, 178
vigilante, 242
vigy, 242
Viking, 303
village virus, 278
Virginia, 103; - creeper, 104;
    - fence, 104; - gouger, 163;
    - honeycomb, 103; - tobacco,
    103, 173; - curency, 171;
    - iron, 173
Virginian, 105
Virginiasms, 167, 193
vlei, 127
vocational training, 264
voodoo, 191
voyageur, 131, 159, 216, 220
vrow, 128


Wabash, 132
wacko, 300
waffle, 128
wagon: - box, 218; family -, 205;
    - ford, 110; moving -, 205;
    - road, 193; - shop, 243
wagon, to, 174
wagonage, 174
walk-around, 253
walkie-talkie, 286
walking stick, 141 *n.*
walk-up, 265
Wall Streeters, 243
Wall Street plunger, 278
walnut, 95
wampumpeag, 121
ward club, 237
war paint, 122
war path, 122
wash bench, 239

waste, 100
water bed, 295
watershed, 95
Waves, 285
wayout, 295; -itude, 295
Wayunckeke, 114
weather, clerk of the, 259
weatherman, 259
weave room, weave shop, 208
weed, 205
weenie, 230
weequashing, 122
weirdie, 300
weirdo, 299–300
welfare, 262
western frontier, 154
wharf, 170
Wheatena, 269
wheel, 25; go for a -, 253
wheelbarrow boat, 210
whip-poor-will, 97
white-collar, 275
white slave traders, 263
white-tailed deer, 104
white tie, 300
whitewash, 198
whole-souled, 203
wiener, 230; -wurst, 230
wigwam, 121, 167
wild as a mustang, 241
wildcat, 200; - bank, 200
Wildcat, 303
wild lands, 194
Wild West show, 252
wire grass, 156
wireless, 256, 257
Wisconsin, 132
-wise, 297
witch hunts, 289
Wobblies, 262
wolf scalp, 158
wood: -corder, - field, 100;
    - lot, 196; - sawyer, - up, 212

woodchopper, 129
woodchuck, 97, 120
woodfish, 139
wooding place, 212
wood sawyer, independent as a, 212
woofer, 303
woolyneag, 158
wop, 250
workeyism, 208
workfare, 295
workmen's compensation, 262
worky, 208
worth shucks, 241
WPA, 280
wrathy, 218

yam, 190
Yank, 271
Yankee, 194, 217; - clipper, 173; -ism, 193; - peddler, 193; trickery, 193; - twang, 167
yankee, to, 167
yellow jacket, 104
yellow journalism, 259
Yes sirree, 232
Yid, 249
Yonkers, 125

ZIP, 300
zipper, 269, 270

# Index of Subjects

abbreviations, 261, 265–6, 280, 285, 287, 300

Academy, projects for an American, 7, 196; for a British, 15–16

Academy of Language and Belles Lettres, 196

Acadians, 187

Adams, Henry, 251

Adams, James Truslow, 4 *n.*, 90, 145 *n.*, 153 *n.*, 160 *n.*

Adams, John, 7, 15, 176

Adams, John Quincy, 170, 196, 198

Adams, Maude, 252

Addison, Joseph, 15, 115

Ade, George, 253

advertising, 269–70, 282

Aethelbert, 39, 42

Aetius, Flavius, 36

African languages, 189–92, 306–7

Agnew, Spiro, 200

Alcuin of York, 45

Aldhelm, 45

Alfred the Great, 45, 47

Algonquian, 116–17

Algonquian tribes, 116

Allen, Cecil, 244

Allen, Frederick Lewis, 273 *n.*, 274 *n.*, 277 *n.*

American Academy of Arts and Letters, 281

*American Dictionary of the English Language*, 196–7, 219

American English: abroad, 5, 197–8, 207, 256–8, 271, 279, 284, 304; controversy about, 4 ff., 84–6, 141, 197–8, 256–8; naming of, 194–5; sources of, 86–8, 177

American Indian, terms relating to, 122–3, 159, 167

American Indian languages, 16, 64, 113–15, 116–22, 154, 158–9, 160, 184, 222–4

*American Review of History and Politics*, 11

American Spanish, 221–2

*American Speech*, 138

*American Spelling Book*, 132, 237

*Ames Almanac*, 176

Amos and Andy, 283

Anatolian languages, 24

Anderson, Sherwood, 278

Anglo-Saxon, *see* Old English

*Anglo-Saxon Chronicle*, 47

Anglo-Saxons, 33–4, 36, 38;
    culture of, 40–2
Aquinas, Thomas, 77
Arabic, 54, 55, 58, 76, 191, 192
Arabs, 55, 56
Aramaic, 43
archaisms, 84–6, 88, 100, 156,
    215, 221–2
Aristotle, 14, 55, 59, 77, 78
Armada, 75
Ascham, Roger, 68
Astor, John Jacob, 236
*Athenaeum,* 85
Augustine, Saint, 42–3, 65
Australia, speech of, 156, 294
automobile terms, 254, 266–7,
    276, 282, 288
aviation terms, 267–8


*Babbitt,* 277, 278
Bacon, Francis, 70, 71, 74 *n.*, 77
Baldwin, Stanley, 257
Barfield, Owen, 53, 77 *n.*
Barnett, Lincoln, 34 *n.*, 45
Bartlett, John Russell, 86, 138,
    171, 228–9, 235, 241
Bartram, John, 182
*Basle Nomina Anatomica,* 259
Beard, Charles and Mary, 4 *n.*,
    74, 143
Beatles, the, 288
Beaumont and Fletcher, 97
Beaverbrook, Lord, William
    Maxwell Aitken, 284
Bede, The Venerable, 33, 36, 41,
    44, 45, 47
Benedictines, 47
Bentham, Jeremy, 198
*Beowulf,* 42
Bernhardt, Sarah, 252
Bertha, Queen of the Franks, 42
Bible, 44, 98

bicycling terms, 253–4
Birbeck, Morris, 204
*Birth of a Nation,* 267
Black Death, 59
Black English, 190, 309
Blackstone's *Commentaries,* 181
*Blackwood's Magazine,* 199
blends, 269, 300
Boethius, 47
Boone, Daniel, 201
borrowing, 18, 304
Boston *Evening Post,* 180
Boston *Herald,* 254, 255
Boston records, 99
Boston *Transcript,* 201
Boxhorn, Marcus, 14
Braddock, General Edward, 194
Bradford, William, 81, 136
Brahe, Tycho, 76
Brereton, W., 116
Brewster, William, 68
Bristed, Charles Astor, 233
British English in America, 105,
    168–9, 175, 181, 183, 258,
    271–2, 304
Brown, Claude, 306
Bruce, David, 154
Bryan, William Jennings, 278
Bryant, William Cullen, 11
Bunyan, John, 84, 93
bureaucracy, jargon of, 285
Burnaby, Andrew, 166, 193
Burns, Bob, 286
Byrd, William, 111
Byrd, William, II, 164
Byington, Steven T., 133


Caedmon, 44
Caesar, Julius, 28, 29, 30
Cahan, Abraham, 251
Canada, speech of, 294
canal terms, 209

Canby, Henry Seidel, 258
Canterbury, Archibishop of, 257
Capone, Al, 275
Cardell, William, 196
Carlisle, Lord, Frederick
 Howard, 129
Carnegie, Andrew, 236
Carrolls, the, 152; Charles -, 193
Carter, Robert, 163
Cartwright, Peter, 221
Castle, Irene and Vernon, 264
cattle calls, 139, 140
Cawdrey, Robert, 78
Caxton, William, 61
Celtic, 26, 40, 114
Celts, 22, 25, 28, 33, 41
*Century Magazine*, 104 *n.*, 246
Chaldean, 228
Charlemagne, 45
Chastelleux, Marquis de, 161 *n.*,
 177, 194, 198 *n.*
Chaucer, Geoffrey, 53, 67, 68,
 84, 85, 86, 94
*Chautauquan*, 247, 255
Chesterfield, Lord, *Letters* of, 181
Chinese language, 17, 274, 290
Chinese people in America, 250,
 308
Christianity: in Britain, 42–5;
 in England, 45, 79–81
Churchill, Winston, 62
Cicero, 65
Civil War terms, 238, 240
Clay, Henry, 202
club movement, 183
Cody, Buffalo Bill, 252
Ceolwulf, 36
Coeurdoushad, Gaston Laurent,
 17
Collinson, Peter, 227
Columbia *County Register,* 200
Columbus, Christopher, 76, 115
comic strips, 258, 261, 283

Commager, Henry S., 204 *n.*
commercial terms, 73–5, 107,
 111, 170, 175, 240, 243–4, 249
comparative linguistics, 17–20
*Congressional Globe*, 201
*Congressional Record*, 197, 246
Connecticut Historical Society
 Collections, 100
conservation terms, 262
consonant shift, 19
Conway, Jack, 253
Cooke, Alistair, 304
Coolidge, Calvin, 276
Cooper, James Fenimore, 10, 11,
 188, 197, 201, 207
Copernicus, 76
Corbett, Jim, 252
*Cosmopolitan*, 254
counter-culture terms, 292, 298,
 303
counterwords, 301–2
Cox, James, 274
Craigie, Sir William, 87, 257
Cresswell, Nicholas, 191
Crockett, David, 199, 201, 202,
 206, 234
Cromwell, Oliver, 142
Crusades, 56–7
Cunliffe, Marcus, 204 *n.*
currency terms, 110, 121, 170–3
Cynewulf, 44


*Daily Express* (London), 275
*Daily Telegraph* (London),
 172, 256
Danes in England, 45–9
Danish, 26, 47–9
*Dark Laughter*, 273
Darrow, Clarence, 278
Dartmouth, Earl of, 163
Darwinism, 247, 278
Davis, Richard Harding, 253

Defoe, Daniel, 15
Dekker, Thomas, 78
Dempsey, Jack, 275
Depression terms, 278 ff.
DeVere, M. Schele, 84, 86, 97,
    105, 108, 109, 119, 128, 133,
    135, 172, 188, 190, 206, 214,
    227
dialect in America, 105, 137–40,
    145, 167, 175, 176, 197,
    215–17, 228, 235–6, 282–3;
    sources of, 86–8, 105
dialect in Great Britain: middle
    English, 50, 59, 96; modern
    English, 93, 230; Old English,
    38
*Dialect Notes*, 138
Dickens, Charles, 198, 208
*Dictionary of American English*,
    138
*Dictionary of Americanisms*, 219
*Dictionary of the Vulgar
    Tongue*, 234
Didrikson, Babe, 281
Dillard, J. L., 190 and *n*., 192
*Discourse of Warre, The*, 65
*Dissertations on the English
    Language*, 7, 8
Donne, John, 85
Dooley, Mr., 253
Dorgan, T. A. (Tad), 265
Drake, Sir Francis, 75
Drant, Thomas, 64
Drew, John, 252
*Druid, The*, 6 *n*.
Dryden, John, 15
Dulanys, the, 152
Dunne, Finley Peter, 253
Duns Scotus, John, 80
Dutch, 14, 19, 26, 54, 55, 74,
    75, 76; in America, 125–9,
    142, 155, 156, 174, 178, 181,
    214, 230, 244

Dutch-related terms, 130, 146–7
Dyess, W. E., Lt. Col., 285

Eastman, George, 269
*Edinburgh Journal*, 209
*Edinburgh Review*, 11
Edison, Thomas, 243, 253, 270
Edward I, 54
Edward VIII, 256
electrical terms, 245–7, 270
Elwyn, Alfred L., 101
Elyot, John, 114, 117, 121
Elyot, Thomas, 65, 72, 78
Emerson, Ralph Waldo, 197, 247
*Encyclopaedia Britannica*, 36,
    305; Year Book, 292 *n*., 293 *n*.
*Engineering Magazine*, 269
Enlightenment, Age of, 15, 162
*English Dialect Dictionary*, 192
English language, ascendancy of,
    34, 52–3
Erie Canal, 209
ESD (English as a Second
    Dialect), 308
*European Magazine and London
    Review*, 9
Europeans, primitive, 24–6
Evans, Lew, 169
Everett, Edward, 203, 229

"Fibber McGee and Molly,"
    282
Fielding, Henry, 181
Finns, 142
Fiske, Minnie Maddern, 252
Fithian, Robert, 163
Fitzgerald, F. Scott, 273
Flemish language, 54, 55, 75
Flint, Timothy, 216, 243
folk etymology, 97, 132, 148–9
Ford, Henry, 266

foreigners, labels for, 249
*Fortune,* 287
Four Horsemen, 274
Fowler, H. W., 172
Franklin, Benjamin, 4, 8, 130,
    142, 145, 147, 165, 170, 179,
    181–2, 187, 227, 245, 277
Frémont, John, 220
French language, 14, 51, 53–4,
    58, 66–7; in America, 131–4,
    142, 144–5, 158–9, 219–20,
    235, 252, 304
French-related terms, 134
Freud, Sigmund, 80, 273
Frisian, 26, 38
Frobisher, Martin, 115
frontier speech, 154–60, 215–19
*Fundamentals, The,* 278

Galileo, 76
Garland, Hamlin, 234 *n.,* 248
Gehrig, Lou, 281
George III, 194
Germanic, 19, 26–9, 295, 306
German language, 14, 26, 29,
    55; in America, 139, 142, 148,
    152–3, 183, 228–32, 235, 241,
    250, 251, 286, 297, 304
Germans in America, 139, 142,
    144, 147, 148, 152, 155, 226,
    227, 231, 241, 283
Gerry, Governor Elbridge, 198
Gildas, Saint, 36
Goddard, Henry H., 263
*Gone with the Wind,* 283
*Good Housekeeping,* 270
Gothic, 26
Gower, John, 84, 86
*Grammatical Institute of the
    English Language,* 7, 237
Grateful Dead, 288
Great Awakening, 161–2

Greek language, 26, 28, 66–7, 298
Greek people, 22, 25
Gregory, Pope, 39, 42
Grimm, Jacob, 19, 293
Grose, 234
Guazzo, Stefano, 68
Guggenheim, Meyer, 236
Gullah, 187, 189, 190

Hakluyt, Richard, 76, 115
Hamann, Johann, 16
Hamilton, Alexander, 4
Hamilton, Governor James, 165
Hancock, Nathaniel, 111
Handy, W. C., 264
Hansen, Timothy, 182
Harding, Warren G., 272
Harnden, William F., 207
*Harper's Magazine,* 228, 238,
    242, 262, 267
*Harper's Weekly,* 264
Harriot, Thomas, 120
Harris, Joel Chandler, 187
Harrodsburg, Ky., *American,*
    206
Harte, Bret, 237, 250
Harvey, Gabriel, 69
Hawkins, John, 75, 76
Hawthorne, Nathaniel, 11
Hay, J., 81
Hearst, William Randolph, 259
Hebrew, 43, 228
"Helen Trent," 282
Hempstead records, 91, 92, 93 *n.,*
    127
Hennepin, Father, 133
Henry III, 52
Herder, Johann von, 16
Hindi, 292
Hindus, 22
historical perspective, 13–14
Hittite, 20, 24

Hobbes, Thomas, 74 *n.*
Hodge, Frederick W., 114
Holland, *see* Dutch
Holmes, Oliver Wendell, 243
Homans, George Casper, 102
Homer, 65
Hoover, Herbert, 278
Howe, Elias, 208
Howell, James, 109
Howells, William Dean, 243,
    248, 253
Hubbard, William, 123
Hudson Valley settlers, 147
Hume, David, 16, 181
Hume, John, 8
Humphreys, David, 100
Hundred Years' War, 59
Huntington records, 91
Hutchinson, Anne, 57
Hyacinth, Socrates, 239–41


Icelandic, 241
imagery, 25, 96–7, 108, 109,
    203, 302–4
India, languages of, 16, 22, 76;
    *see also* Sanskrit
individual, concept of the, 71
Indo-European languages, 19–24
Indo-Europeans, 21–4
Industrial Revolution in
    America, 207 ff.
internalization, 253
International Conference on
    English, 258
Irish-related terms, 234
Irish speech, 146, 226–7, 234–5
Irving, Washington, 10, 11, 113,
    205, 206, 243
Italian language, 10, 11, 113,
    205, 206, 243
Italic, 19
*It Happened One Night,* 283

Jackson, Andrew, 4, 199, 201,
    202
Jamaica, L.I., records, 101
James, Henry, 247
James, William, 247
James I, 120
Japanese loan words, 286, 304
jazz, jargon of, 288, 307
Jefferson, Thomas, 3, 4, 9, 83,
    89, 193, 196, 197, 199, 203,
    245
Jespersen, Otto, 293, 299
Jewett, Sarah Orne, 253
*Jewish Daily Journal,* 251
Jews in America, 146, 226,
    228, 249, 250–1, 305; influence
    on American speech, *see*
    Hebrew; Yiddish
John (King of England), 52
Johnson, Lyndon, administration
    of, 302
Johnson, Samuel, 5, 6, 16, 111,
    164, 169, 195, 197
Jones, Bobby, 281
Jones, Sir William, 17
Jonson, Ben, 62
Josselyn, John, 120, 124 *n.*,
    132
Joyce, P. W., 235
Jutes, 38


Kalem, T. E., 307
*Katzenjammer Kids,* 283
Kennedy, Edward, 301
Kennedy, John F., 298
Kepler, Johannes, 76
Kieran, James M., 280
Kilpatrick, James, 301
King William's War, 159
Knight, Sarah, 138, 187
Koch, Robert, 263
Korean War, influence of, 290

Krapp, George Philip, 84 *n.*, 87, 92, 100, 127, 188–9, 190, 192
Kurath, Hans, 87, 104 *n.*, 138, 139 *n.*, 154, 174, 189
Kurds, 22

labor terms, 208, 244
*Ladies' Home Journal*, 269
Landor, Walter Savage, 9
land-related terms, 89–92, 127, 149
Langland, William, 85, 86
Langley, Samuel, 267
Latin: in Britain, 43, 47, 54; in England, 54, 55, 58, 61, 66–7; on the Continent, 14, 26, 30–3
law (profession), 60, 149–50, 176
Law, John, 144
Lawson, John, 135, 158 *n.*
Leland, Charles G., 228
Lerner, Max, 289
Lewis and Clark Expedition, 219–20
*Life*, 287
Lincoln, Abraham, 237–8, 255
*Linguistic Atlas of the United States and Canada*, 87, 138, 140
Link, Robert H., 281
Lister, Lord, 269
*Literary Digest*, 264
literary terms, 78, 181
Lithuania, speech of, 21–2
Locke, John, 181
Lodge, Henry Cabot, 4, 8
Logan, James, 145
London newspapers, 172, 256, 275, 284
Longfellow, Henry Wadsworth, 11, 113

Longstreet, Augustus Baldwin, 197
Lonnsbury, J. F., 84, 88
Louis, Joe, 281
Lovell, Charles A., 224
Lowell, James Russell, 62, 84, 197, 198 *n.*, 219, 222, 237, 245
Lunenburg records, 98
Luther, Martin, 65, 79
Lydgate, John, 86

Madariaga, Salvador de, 294
Madison, James, 196
magazines, 258, 269, 270, 287
Magna Carta, 52
*Main Street*, 278
Major, Charles, 253
Malay, 76, 272
*Manchester Guardian*, 261
Manifest Destiny, 203
Mann Act, 263
Mansfield, Richard, 252
Marius, Gaius, 28
Marryat, Frederick, 177
Marshall, John, 170, 196
Martineau, Harriet, 208
Marx, Karl, 73
Maryland archives, 135
*Maryland Gazette*, 175
Mason, Julian, 192
Massachusetts Bay records, 100, 121 *n.*
Massachusetts Historical Society *Collections*, 100 *n.*, 146 *n.*
Massasoit, 119
Massinger, Philip, 62, 115
Mather, Cotton, 57, 98, 116, 122, 124, 145, 187
Mather, Increase, 144 *n.*
Mathews, Mitford M., 90 *n.*, 108, 127, 130, 131, 143, 162, 192, 214, 219, 230

Maverick, Hon. Maury, 285
McAllister, Ward, 244
McCallum, James Dow, 44
McCarthy, Senator Joseph, 289
McClellan, General George B., 255
McClure, S. H., 269
*McClure's*, 260
McCormick, Cyrus Hall, 208
McDavid, Raven J., Jr., 138 *n.*, 189
McGovern, George, 301
McGuffey's *Eclectic Reader*, 237
McKinley, William, 255
McKnight, George H., 154
McLuhan, Marshall, 303
McNamee, Graham, 275
medical terms, 57, 263
*Meet the Press*, 301
Melba, Nellie, 252
Mencken, Henry Louis, 63, 83, 113, 138, 186, 190, 192, 213, 218, 259, 277, 278, 282
mental atmosphere, 69–70, 206, 307
Mercator, Gerhardus, 76
Middle Ages, atmosphere of, 55–60
Middleton, Thomas, 85
*Middletown, U.S.A.*, 266
migration patterns (American), 141–5, 150, 152, 217–18, 227, 239, 249, 329
Milton, John, 85
Minuit, Peter, 125
Monk, Maria, 233
Moore, Francis, 5, 163 *n.*
More, Sir Thomas, 70, 74, 78
Morgan, John Pierpont, 229
movies, 253, 258, 261
Mulcaster, Richard, 78, 82
musical terms, 18, 68, 182, 191, 264, 280, 288

Nash, Thomas, 69
Nathan, George Jean, 278
*Nation, The*, 277
*Naughty Marietta*, 283
nautical terms, 21, 25, 75, 108–9, 214, 221
Negro: related terms, 185–6, 241; speech of, 167, 186, 187–90, 306; *see also* African languages
Nessler, Charles, 265
Nevins, Allen, 204 *n.*
New Deal terms, 280–1
*New England Magazine*, 208
*New England Palladium*, 8
New Jersey archives, 151 and *n.*, 177
New Orleans *Times-Picayune*, 207, 212, 301 *n.*, 302 *n.*, 308 *n.*
newspapers, 183, 193, 259 ff.
*New Statesman*, 258
*New Yorker, The*, 284
New York *Evening Post*, 261
New York *Herald-Tribune*, 276
New York *Journal*, 254, 259
New York *Mirror*, 205
New York *Sun*, 201, 244
*New York Times*, 280; *Magazine*, 285 *n.*
New York *Tribune*, 245
New York *Weekly Tribune*, 130
New York *World*, 259
New York World's Fair, 283
*Niles' Register*, 209
Normans, 49 ff.; effect on English speech, 50–3
Norse, 26
*North American Review*, 246, 255
Norwegian, 235
*Notes & Queries*, 246

occupational terms, 103, 106–9, 111, 170, 175, 238, 240–1, 249
Ogden, Dr. C. K., 293
Old English, 21, 35, 37 ff.; dialects of, 38
Old Frisian, 18
Old Gothic, 18
Old High German, 18
Oldmixon, John, 15, 184 *n*.
Old Norse, 18
Olds, R. E., 269
Old Saxon, 18
Old Spanish, 55
Olmsted, Frederick Law, 233, 251 *n*.
Orosius, 47
*Overland Monthly*, 239
*Oxford English Dictionary*, 27 *n*., 70 *n*., 93, 102, 109, 116, 192, 216

Paderewski, Ignace, 252
Pakenham, General Edward, 195
Panini, 17
Partridge, Eric, 273
patriotic terms, 81–2, 203
Peasants' Revolt, 59
Peck, Ellen, 300
Pei, Mario, 27 *n*., 39 *n*., 295
Penn, William, 113, 128, 145, 153
Pennsylvania Dutch, 147
*Pennsylvania Journal and Weekly Advertiser*, 6
*Pennsylvania Magazine*, 100
Pepperell, William, 111
Pepys, Samuel, 85
Perry, George S., 230
Persian: people, 22; speech, 55
Pétain, Marshal Henri, 284
*Peterborough Chronicle*, 50

Philipse, M., 129
Phillips, David Graham, 261
philosophical terms, 59, 60
Phipson, Evaçustes, 177 *n*.
phonemes, 23, 24 *n*.
Pickering, John, 154, 197
Peirce, C. S., 247
Pike, Zebulon, 220
Pitt, William, 198
place names, 37, 48, 88, 125, 145, 152, 240
pluralism, 308
Plutarch, 65
Plymouth records, 91 *n*., 93
Poe, Edgar Allen, 11, 197
Polish language, 291, 308
political terms: in America, 74, 198–200, 244, 255; in England, 72–3
Polo, Marco, 57
Pope, Alexander, 15
port cities, influence of, 173, 174–5
"Portia Faces Life," 282
Portland *Oregonian*, 230
Portuguese, 75, 115
Pory, John, 63
Powell, J. W., 116
prefixes, 67, 94, 232, 296, 305
*Principia, The*, 15
Procopius, 36
progress, concept of, 70–1
pronouns, 22, 48
Protestantism, 71, 79
provincialisms, 86
Provisions of Oxford, 52
public schools, 236–7, 308
Puerto Ricans, 308
Pulitzer, Joseph, 259
Puritans: in America, 98, 99; in England, 72, 80, 88
Puttenham, George, 86
Pytheas, 28

Quincy, Josiah, 167

radio: diction of, 281; influence
  of, 256, 268, 274, 281–3
railroad terms, 213–15, 238
Raleigh, Sir Walter, 75
ranching terms, 104, 222–3,
  240–1
*Reader's Digest*, 287
Reformation, 14, 70
reform terms, 262–4
*Reg'lar Fellers*, 283
religious terms, 23, 27, 32, 43–4,
  51, 53, 78–81, 161–2, 183,
  216, 277–8
Revere, Paul, 170
Rice, Grantland, 275
Richard I, 161
Richardson, Samuel, 181
Rivington, James, 175, 181
Roget's *Thesaurus*, 275
Rolfe, John, 103
Romans, 22, 25, 30, 31–3, 42–5
Roosevelt, Franklin Delano, 280
Roosevelt, Nicholas, 211
Roosevelt, Theodore, 255,
  261–2, 280
Rose, Billy, 283
Rotary Club, 264
Rowse, A. L., 62 n.
Rush, Benjamin, 9
Russian language, 290, 304
Russian Revolution, 272, 274
Ruth, Babe, 275


*Saginaw Evening News*, 246
salesmanship terms, 276–7
Saltonstall, 63
Samoset, 119
Sandburg, Carl, 238 n.
Sandys, George, 63
Sanskrit, 13, 14, 17, 24

Sapir, Edward, 117
Sarnoff, David, 268
Sassetti, Filippo, 14
*Saturday Evening Post*, 265 n.,
  269
*Saturday Review*, 295
Schlesinger, Arthur, 4 n.
Schumann-Heink, Madame, 252
scientific terms, 77, 276, 286–7,
  292
Scotch-Irish, 38, 142, 146, 149,
  153–4, 155, 162, 227
Scots, speech of, 142, 144, 164
Scott, Sir Walter, 198
Scythian, 14
Sears, Roebuck Catalogue, 140
Sewall, Samuel, 134
Shakespeare, 61, 62, 63, 70, 91–2
Shaw, George Bernard, 172
Shepard, Sam, 307
show business terms, 184, 252,
  264, 265, 306–7
Simon and Schuster, 275
simplification, 50–1
Skinner, Otis, 186
slang, contemporary, 298
Slavs, 22, 25
Smith, Alfred E., 261, 280
Smith, Captain John, 35, 96,
  103, 108, 115–21 *passim*,
  135, 160
Smith, Logan Pearsall, 13 n.,
  27 n., 56, 69, 71, 72
Smith, Seba, 197
Smith, Sydney, 11
Smollett, Tobias George, 181
society, 244–5
Sousa, John Philip, 252
South, speech of the, 102–5,
  163, 167, 186, 240, 288
South Carolina Historical
  Society *Collections*, 123 n.
Southey, Robert, 207

space terms, 208–9, 303–4
Spanish Civil War, 283
Spanish language, 14, 75, 76, 115; in America, 135–6, 145, 171, 221, 230, 238, 241, 242, 250, 288, 304
Spanish people in America, 135, 145
Spanish-related terms, 136
spelling, 7–8, 63, 113
Spenser, Edmund, 68
sports terms, 61, 126, 183–4, 238, 252, 261, 265, 275, 281
Spotswood, Governor Alexander, 152
Springfield records, 90
Squanto, 119
Stackhouse, Thomas, 15
steamboating terms, 209–13
Stearns, Harold, 278
Steffens, Lincoln, 259, 261
Steinway, Henry Engelhard, 229
Stevens, Harry Mozely, 265
Stewart, William A., 189, 309
Stowe, Harriet Beecher, 187
Stuart, Gilbert, 198
Stuyvesant, Peter, 126
Suckow, Ruth, 278
suffixes, 67, 94, 232, 296
*Sun Also Rises, The*, 273
surnames: in America, 147–9, 153; in England, 49, 147
Swedes in America, 134–5, 156
Swedish, 26
Swift, Jonathan, 15, 86, 183
Swinton, Colonel Sir Ernest, 272
Swiss in America, 142, 152
Sydney, Sir Philip, 78, 84
Syriac, 55

Tacitus, 29
tall talk, 203

Tarbell, Ida M., 259–60
Taylor, Deems, 278
teen-age speech, 288–9
television, 288–9
*Territorial Enterprise*, 229
Teutonic, *see* Germanic
Teutons, 22, 25, 26–34, 36
*This Week*, 287
Thucydides, 65
Tillson, Christiana Holmes, 216–17, 218 n.
*Time*, 283, 287, 295, 307 n.
Tindale, William, 72
Tocharian, 29
Tocqueville, Alexis de, 298
Tongan, 16
transportation terms, 109–10, 173–4, 193, 204–6; *see also* automobile terms; railroad terms; steamboating terms
Trollope, Frances, 211
*True Detective*, 275
Tuckerman, Henry T., 161 n., 166 n., 198 n.
Turkish, 304
Turner, Frederick Jackson, 151
Turner, Lorenzo, 189, 190, 192
Twain, Mark, 213, 225, 237, 239, 247, 249, 253, 262, 272, 295

underworld terms, 275
University of Missouri Studies, 219 n.
urban terms, 168–9, 177 ff., 205–6, 238–9, 292–3

Van Doren, Mark, 213 n., 234 n.
Vico, Giambattista, 16
Vietnam War, terms relating to, 293, 300

Vikings, *see* Danes
*Virginia Literary Museum*, 101,
   197
*Voice*, 264
Voltaire, 181


Waldo, John, 3 *n.*, 9
Walker, Felix, 199
Walsh, Robert, Jr., 11
War of 1812, effects of, 3–4, 10
Washington, George, 163, 180,
   193, 277
Watson, John B., 263
Weber and Fields, 252
Webster, Daniel, 196
Webster, Noah, 7–9, 12, 17, 86,
   99, 102, 126, 132, 138, 182,
   190, 194, 195, 219, 237,
   245; *Dictionary*, 196–7, 219;
   *Dissertations*, 7, 8;
   *Grammatical Institute*, 7,
   237; *Spelling Book*, 132, 237
*Webster's New International
   Dictionary*, 282, 295
welfare terms, 262
Welsh people in America, 142,
   227
Welsh speech, 14, 235, 241
West Aryan, *see* Europeans,
   primitive
Western speech, 202–3, 219–25,
   239–42
West Indian languages, 75, 96,
   115
*Westminster Gazette*, 262 *n.*, 268
Whatmough, Joshua, 301

*What Price Glory*, 273
White, Theodore, 301
Whitman, Walt, 113, 237
Whitney, Eli, 207
Wiener, Norbert, 298
Wilkins, Mary E., 253
William of Normandy, 50
Williams, Roger, 117, 122
Wills, Helen, 275
Wilson, H. L., 266
Wilson, Woodrow, 172, 266, 280
Winthrop, Governor John, 57,
   73, 106, 119, 129, 141
wireless, *see* radio
Wister, Owen, 248
Witherspoon, John, 6, 88, 100,
   138, 167
Wolfe, General James, 194
Wood, William, 97, 109, 117–18
Woodward, W. E., 277
*Word Study*, 277
World War I terms, 271–2
World War II terms, 284–6
Wright Brothers, 267–8
Wyatt, Thomas, 75
Wyclif, John, 59
Wyrtgoern, 33


*Yank*, 286
*Yankee*, 162
Yiddish, 228, 251, 290, 305
youth, vocabulary of, 288–9,
   299–300


Ziegfeld, Florenz, 252

A NOTE ABOUT THE AUTHOR

MARY HELEN DOHAN was born in Cincinnati, Ohio, and educated at Tulane University, where she received both B.A. and M.A. degrees in English and was awarded a Robert Sharp Fellowship. At various times she has been an instructor of English at Tulane, and her articles have appeared in women's magazines and educational journals. She lives in New Orleans with her husband, Robert D. Samsot, a retired Navy captain.

A NOTE ON THE TYPE

THIS BOOK was set on the Linotype in a type face
called Baskerville. The face is a facsimile reproduction
of types cast from molds made for John Baskerville
(1706–75) from his designs. The punches for the revived Linotype Baskerville were cut under the super-
vision of the English printer George W. Jones.

John Baskerville's original face was one of the fore-
runners of the type style known as "modern face" to
printers—a "modern" of the period A.D. 1800.

*Composed, printed, and bound
by The Haddon Craftsmen,
Scranton, Pennsylvania.
Typography and
binding design
by Clint
Anglin.*